Praise for *Innovative Corporate Performance Management*

"This book further expands the Strategy Focused Organization/Balanced Scorecard (SFO/BSC) methodologies of systematically operating and strategically growing an organization by utilizing a comprehensive Corporate Performance Management (CPM) process to continuously innovate any given business platform. The CPM process is "scientific" yet elevates strategy and results to a naturally evolving and innovative state.

Earlier in his career, I hired Bob as a consultant to help implement the SFO/BSC approach at Crown Castle International (NYSE:CCI) and have continued to utilize Bob's considerable skills in two other business platforms (M7 Aerospace and Intercomp Global Services) which are both multinational companies. His insight and direction have been invaluable."

—Ted B. Miller, Jr., President, 4M Investments, LLC

"Any executive looking for tangible strategies to improve their organizations results should read this book. Bob Paladino's experience and knowledge provide a practical process to help you succeed in today's challenging business environment."

—Tara Shuert, Executive Director, The American Strategic Management Institute

"Read this book if you want a practical guide—based on real experience—to take your organization to higher levels of performance. This is the best book out there on CPM."

—Carla O'Dell, President American Productivity & Quality Center (APQC)

"As the economy recovers from the Great Recession, the 'new normal' business environment requires that executive management rethink their organization's business model and how it will "Bob's follow-up book builds on the success from his previous best seller by providing excellent guidance on performance management based on extensive practical experience. Bob's writing style provides an easy read to a complicated subject."

—Todd Scaletta, Director Certified Management Accountants (CMA) Canada

"Bob Paladino has a wealth of experience and knowledge. He is very practical and his book reflects a practitioner who is a CPM expert. Read and apply the best practices and his insights to realize significant benefits at your company."

—Bob Howard, Vice President HR, Koppers Industries

"CPM has literally transformed M7 from a start-up organization that was operating in business unit silos with limited communication amongst the management team into an integrated company with a full understanding of cause of effect across the entire organization. Aiding the management team in fully understanding and reviewing the key aspects of its business on a continual basis is essential for any high performance organization."

—Kevin Brown, President and Chief Executive Officer, M7 Aerospace

"Paladino's books outline how others have achieved corporate performance excellence by creating the office of CPM. We've learned how to grow competence within our company for applying strategic planning, balanced scorecards, KPI's, innovation, Six sigma, benchmarking, Malcolm Baldrige, knowledge management and more by following the corporate performance management leadership process that company's in Bob's examples have perfected. Bob lays it all out in easy to read fascinating examples of company after company that created the office of CPM."

—Jon Yarbrough, CEO, Video Gaming Technologies, Inc.; 2005 Ernst & Young National Entrepreneur of the year

"Bob's teachings on CPM have become the cornerstones of how we communicate strategy and run the day-to-day business. His real world examples born from his relationships with top performing companies offer unique insight and guidance. This book brings Bob's expertise directly to the reader in a way that should benefit any business leader today."

—Michael Ramke, CEO of Intercomp Global Services

"When we recently launched an intensive CPM process throughout all of our global distribution centers, CPM (and Bob Paladino) was a tremendous reference for our leaders. Our biggest win after reading the book was addressing cross-functional cooperation. The book's tips, methods and examples put our team on the same page for implementing what was a "new" process for many of our employees. Using the Five Key Principles of Corporate Performance Management, we were able to simplify our operations while delivering even greater value to our valued customers."

—Greg Nickele, President and Chief Executive Officer, The Martin-Brower Company

"Our strategy management efforts in Lockheed Martin IS&GS-Civil are based on the simple yet powerful notion that when leaders engage employees in the organization's strategy - performance will improve."

—Josh Stalker, Sr. Manager, Lockheed Martin, IS&GS-Civil, Strategy Management

"The corporate performance review has encouraged the senior management team to take a long view. As an electric utility we have always been very adept in addressing immediate operational issues. By having performance measures that inform longer-term objectives, such as culture change, we are able to keep our focus on a sustained change initiative."

—Gary Gates, President and CEO, Omaha Public Power District

"In the current business climate, the challenges presented to leaders are immense. Add in Health Care Reform dictating change, and the standard way of doing business is immediately obsolete. The need not only for change, but for rapid change is staggering. Bob's approach to CPM and his ability to tailor it to an ever changing environment, along with navigating multiple industries, is what leads executives through the challenging times. Having worked with him in a variety of industries, he continually proves his ability to bring the required change and the associated success to businesses of all shapes and sizes, often where others have failed. Any executive who stared into the mirror this morning wondering how to steer their company through the financial, political and people changes that are more prevalent than ever, will benefit from *"Innovative Corporate Performance Management."*

—Dev Warren, Director of Process Improvement, Blue Cross and Blue Shield of Montana

"Being accelerated change a constant for most organizations, Bob keeps bringing innovative approaches with plenty of examples on how top organizations have moved to make change work for them. This book will definitely be a help for those executives that have a good insight of the implications of change for their organization, but are seeking for solid approaches to manage innovation and change successfully."

—Imelda Borunda Carrillo, Director, Tecnológico de Monterrey, ITESM

"Bob Paladino is in a special category of individuals who can explain the issues and benefits associated with corporate performance management. He not only draws on his deep experiences as an implementer, but he combines this with research of organizations that have been successful with deploying and integrating the suite of performance management methodologies. This book takes real-life experiences of organizations and synthesizes them into the key lessons and principles that others can follow."

—Gary Cokins, author, *Performance Management: Integrating Strategy Execution, Methodologies, Risk, and Analytics* (Wiley)

"Corporate Performance Management has provided the City of Coral springs with a mechanism to improve our processes and thereby the results that we provide to our residents and business community."

—Susan Grant, Director of Human Resources, City of Coral Springs

Innovative Corporate Performance Management

Five Key Principles to Accelerate Results

BOB PALADINO

WILEY

John Wiley & Sons, Inc.

Published by John Wiley & Sons, Inc., Hoboken, New Jersey.
Published simultaneously in Canada.

For general information on our other products and services or for technical support,
please contact our Customer Care Department within the United States at
(800) 762-2974, outside the United States at (317) 572-3993 or fax (317) 572-4002.

Wiley also publishes its books in a variety of electronic formats. Some content that
appears in print may not be available in electronic books. For more information about
Wiley products, visit our web site at www.wiley.com.

Library of Congress Cataloging-in-Publication Data:

Paladino, Bob, 1959–
    Innovative corporate performance management: five key principles to accelerate
results/Bob Paladino.
       p. cm.
    Includes index.
    ISBN 978-0-470-62773-0 (hardback); 978-0-470-91259-1 (ebk);
        978-0-470-91260-7 (ebk); 978-0-470-91261-4 (ebk)
  1.   Organizational effectiveness. 2.   Management. 3.   Performance–Case studies.
4.   Executives. I. Title.
    HD58.9.P353 2010
    658.4–dc22
                                                                        2010021351

Printed in the United States of America
10 9 8 7 6 5 4 3 2 1

My Family

I dedicate this to my wife, Ellen, for her positive attitude, and to my children, for keeping me inspired.

Our Freedom

I am grateful for my freedom of speech
and have enormous respect for those who have preserved it.
"Be on your guard; stand firm in the faith;
be men of courage; be strong." 1 Corinthians 16:13

Consistent with my first book, I will continue to donate royalties to fund injured soldiers returning home and the United Flight 93 Tower of Voices Memorial near my home. It contains 40 wind chimes; sounds in the wind are a living memory of the 40 persons honored, many of whom's last contact was through their voices. To express your appreciation, please go to www.honorflight93.org and www.saluteheroes.org, both IRS Section 501(c)(3) nonprofit organizations.

Principled Living

I believe in "Principled Living," giving back to the community, and his firm tithes donations to numerous nonprofit organizations dedicated to educating, honoring, defending, and helping fellow Americans. "We live by faith, not by sight."
2 Corinthians 5:7

Waste no more time talking about great souls and how they should be. Become one yourself!

—Marcus Aurelius Antoninus

Contents

Preface   xi

Acknowledgments   xv

CHAPTER 1   Introduction   1

CHAPTER 2   Research and New Case Company Results   9

CHAPTER 3   Five Key Principles of CPM: Best Practices Model   35

CHAPTER 4   Principle 1: Establish and Deploy a CPM Office
                and Officer   47

CHAPTER 5   Principle 2: Refresh and Communicate Strategy   91

CHAPTER 6   Principle 3: Cascade and Manage Strategy   183

CHAPTER 7   Principle 4: Improve Performance   259

CHAPTER 8   Principle 5: Manage and Leverage Knowledge   345

CHAPTER 9   Five Key Principles: Self-Diagnostic and Corporate
                Performance Management Roadmap   395

Index   *401*

Preface

What do award-winning companies know that eludes most of today's executives? How do they organize and innovate to achieve outstanding results in their fields of endeavor? What core and innovative processes and best practices do they have in common to leverage in challenging times to succeed? How have they overcome what a recent CEO study calls the "Change Gap," or the ability to innovate and change in a challenging market?

In good times, strengths and weaknesses of a business model are often overlooked. In bad times, as with the global recession, weaknesses often come to the forefront. Market forces and prolonged recession have caused organizations to rethink their business models and innovate through best practices. I was intrigued how several companies have thrived and innovated.

Since my first book, *Five Key Principles of Corporate Performance Management*, I have researched a new class of winning organizations.

The case companies in this book have amassed over 175 noteworthy awards. Research with brand-new award winners over the past two years revealed over 130 new, innovative corporate performance management (CPM) best practices for this book; hence I selected the title *Innovative Corporate Performance Management: Five Key Principles to Accelerate Results.*

As for the roadmap, Chapter 1 reveals survey results from over 1,000 global CEOs on their expectations for continued change and moreover their ability to manage change, the "Change Gap." Chapter 2 includes case companies' over 175 awards, honors, and notable performance results, essentially how they have thrived in the most challenging economic climate since the 1930s.

Chapter 3 contains the proven set of CPM processes we call the CPM process blueprint that captures how award-winning organizations earned their coveted awards and to help you establish your CPM capabilities. This chapter discusses CPM roles for each process and explores the 30-plus common core best practices exhibited by all 25 companies in both books. The over 130 new, innovative best practices are shared in Chapters 4 through 8, in each case for appropriate context and for better understanding.

Five Key Principles of Corporate Performance Management	Core Common Best CPM Practices	New Innovative, Company Specific Best Practices	Total CPM Best Practices
Principle 1: Establish and deploy a CPM office and officer	8	8	16
Principle 2: Refresh and communicate strategy	6	39	45
Principle 3: Cascade and manage strategy	9	31	40
Principle 4: Improve performance	5	30	35
Principle 5: Manage and leverage knowledge	6	24	30
Totals	34	132	166

Chapters 4 through 8 are each dedicated to one of the Five Key Principles of CPM. This approach will enable you to review a principle and actively learn how 11 award winners apply best practices to optimize it. For instance, if you consult Chapter 5, Principle 2: Refresh and Communicate Strategy, to learn about strategic planning, you would read 11 cases on how they deployed strategic planning including their unique best practices. Throughout the book you will also see key strategic frameworks, managerial models, strategy maps, balanced scorecards, process models, communications plans, quality improvement tools, screenshots, charts, graphs, and more. My hope is to accelerate your organization's results.

Chapter 9 reviews CPM research resources to continue your journey and expand your knowledge base, and conduct a self-scoring diagnostic to conduct monthly, to trace your journey toward excellence.

This book encapsulates comparisons among and between numerous organizations that are thriving in spite of the most challenging economic conditions by almost every measure since the Great Depression. Award recipients therefore provide guidance to enable you to rapidly implement your strategy through integrated CPM efforts. In short, they have unselfishly shared their "Coca-Cola" formulas with you.

My Continuing Promise

This book provides practical executive and practitioner best practice examples on how to establish the new CPM office to manage strategy using integrated CPM processes. I am fortunate to have experienced hundreds of improvement programs and projects at Fortune 500 companies, government agencies, and nonprofit organizations over the past 20-plus years. I am glad to report that most were successful. In this book, I am not evangelizing theory but rather providing proven, real-world implementation insights from award-winning organizations.

Acknowledgments

This book could not have been possible without the special contributions from a number of organizations, clients, executives, and practitioners. More important than contributions to this book is the recognition they deserve for efforts to advance the field of corporate performance management, the results they helped achieve for their organizations, and their value-centric approach to performance.

APQC: Carla O'Dell, President; Cindy Hubert, Executive Director; the APQC team; and numerous member company research project participants.

ASMI: Tara Shuert, Executive Director, Amanda Ward, Brynn Bradbury, and the ASMI team.

Cargill Corn Milling (CCM): Nicole Reichert for co-authoring this case. Materials and content adapted from company documents.

City of Coral Springs: Susan Grant for her substantial contributions to this case; without her it would not have been possible.

Delta Dental of Kansas, Inc: Linda Brantner, President and CEO; and Amy Ellison, VP Human Resources for their substantial contributions to this case; without them it would not have been possible.

John Wiley & Sons: Sheck Cho, Executive Editor, and the Wiley publishing team.

Lockheed Martin, IS&GS: Ken Asbury, President, Lockheed Martin (LM) Information Systems & Global Services (IS&GS)-Civil, Ken Carlsen, Director, LM IS&GS-Civil, Strategy Management, Josh Stalker, Senior Manager, LM IS&GS-Civil, Strategy Management for their substantial contributions to this case; without them it would not have been possible. Josh Stalker deserves special mention for having provided the majority of the information for this case.

M7 Aerospace: Ted Miller (Chairman of the Board), Kevin Brown (President and Chief Executive Officer), Philip O'Connor (Vice President Human Resources & Organizational Development), Rebekkah Gurkin Marketing/Sales/Communications Graphics Design Specialist), Andy Plyler (Vice President Business Development), Todd Lazar (Vice President Quality Assurance), Emory (Buck) Kilgore (Vice President Manufacturing), Joseph F. Furnish (Vice President Engineering), Brian Dannewitz (Vice President Supply Chain Management & Spare Sales), Charles Miller (Vice President

Government Business Development), Steven Leland (Vice President Government Programs), Mark Provost (Director, Engineering), Mark Weiler (Controller), and Peter Kastis (Manager Financial Planning and Corporate Development)

Mueller, Inc.: Mark Lack, Planning & Financial Analysis Manager, for his substantial contributions to this case; without him it would not have been possible.

NSTAR: Susan Johnson, Director Corporate Performance Management, and Kathryn Leonard, Communications Specialist, for her substantial contributions to this case; without her it would not have been possible.

OPPD: Deeno Boosalis, Manager Business Strategy, and Cherie Carlson, Manager Corporate Performance Management for their substantial contributions to this case, without which it would not have been possible. Tad Leeper, Manager Talent & Performance, provided knowledge and guidance on how corporate performance management ultimately motivates its employees on a personal level. He provided invaluable insights into the role of talent development and corporate culture in implementing corporate performance management.

Poudre Valley Health System: Pam Brock, Vice President, Marketing and Strategic Planning, for her substantial contributions to this case; without her it would not have been possible. Selected content adapted from company documents.

Public Service Electric and Gas (PSE&G): I acknowledge Joe Martucci, Performance Leader, for his co-authoring of the PSE&G case.

Sharp HealthCare (SHC): Nancy G. Pratt, RN, MS; Senior Vice President Clinical Effectiveness, for her substantial contributions to this case; without her it would not have been possible.

CHAPTER 1

Introduction

What do award-winning companies know that eludes many of today's executives? How do they organize and innovate to achieve outstanding results in their fields of endeavor? What core and innovative processes and best practices do they have in common that they can leverage in challenging times to achieve success? How have they overcome what a recent CEO study calls the "change gap," or the ability to innovate and change in a challenging market?

In good times, strengths and weaknesses of a business model are often overlooked. In bad times, as with the global recession, weaknesses often come to the forefront. Market forces and prolonged recession have caused organizations to rethink their business models and innovate through best practices. I was intrigued by how several companies have thrived and innovated, particularly in one of the worst recessions since the Great Depression. Leaders were kind enough to share their stories with me. Research in this book focuses on core best practices from my first book[1] and on how award-winning organizations have developed dozens of new, innovative best practices not only to survive but also to lead their sectors.

That some should be rich shows that others may become rich, and, hence, is just encouragement to industry and enterprise.

—Abraham Lincoln

What about the First Book?

My first book, *Five Key Principles of Corporate Performance Management*, was published in January 2007 and to my surprise was the number 1 release on the largest global Web channels, Amazon and Barnes & Noble. For three years it has continued to be the number 1 corporate performance management (CPM) title (from over 2,500 titles globally). All royalties are donated to www.honorflight93.org to honor the families of Flight 93 and www.saluteamerica.org to assist wounded soldiers to rebuild their lives. Since this book builds on the first, I will share some of the strategic backdrop and research highlights from the first book that motivated its publication.

In 2001, I was fortunate to be invited by the CEO of Crown Castle International (a telecommunications company) to be the senior vice president of global performance (CPM office) and to form and deploy a new CPM office. Crown shortly thereafter experienced what is now referred to as the telecom meltdown. The economic backdrop and research showed conditions were very challenging, as demonstrated by the following:

- *Kaplan and Norton*, co-inventors of the Strategy Focused Organization and Balanced Scorecard, and my former employers and mentors, discovered that "9 out of 10 companies fail to implement their strategies" and that four barriers (vision, people, management, and resources) were responsible for these shortcomings.[2]
- *Fortune* magazine reported, "If making the Fortune 100 best lists is an enormous accomplishment, consider how tough it is to repeat the feat every single year. Just 22 companies have appeared on our list every year since its 1998 inception." Between 1998 and 2004, the turnover of Fortune 500 companies has been staggering.[3]
- *Booz Allen Hamilton's* study, "Why CEOs Fall: The Causes and Consequences of Turnover at the Top," showed turnover among chief executives soared 53 percent between 1995 and 2001. The number of CEOs who left their jobs under pressure more than doubled during that period, and average CEO tenure plunged more than 23 percent, according to the study of 2,500 publicly traded companies.[4]
- *Drake Beam Morn's (DBM)* study, "CEO Turnover and Job Security," revealed that two-thirds of the world's companies have changed CEOs at least once in the last five years.[5]

In response, my team and I relentlessly searched for methods and best practices from award-winning companies to share with the Crown organization to assist in improving our performance.

We researched, visited, and collaborated with over 40 award-winning organizations that encompassed all types of business models including government, quasi-government, publicly traded, privately owned, and nonprofit; and that participated in numerous sectors including aerospace, financial services, telecommunications, consumer products, utility, pharmaceutical, entertainment, communications, and high technology hardware and software.

This research revealed a common DNA consisting of 30+ CPM best practices that were grouped by the Five Key Principles:

Principle 1: Establish and deploy a CPM office and officer.
Principle 2: Refresh and communicate strategy.
Principle 3: Cascade and manage strategy.
Principle 4: Improve performance.
Principle 5: Manage and leverage knowledge.

The companies of the executives who generously shared their methods with us have earned an impressive roster of awards and honors, including the following:

- U.S. President's Malcolm Baldrige National Quality Award (MBNQA)
- Kaplan and Norton Global Balanced Scorecard Hall of Fame Award
- Deming Quality Award
- American Productivity & Quality Center Best Practice Partner Award
- State Quality Awards (based on MBNQA criteria)
- *Fortune*'s "100 Best Companies to Work For"
- Several other honors and awards in each case

In truth, I was thrilled to direct Crown's global improvement efforts with a very supportive and collegial executive team and employee base. The CPM best practices started to take hold, and Crown earned several notable, globally recognized awards and honors, including the following:

- The *Wall Street Journal* ranked Crown in the Top 20 Most Improved Companies in Shareholder Value (out of 4,000).
- The company's share price appreciated from $1 to over $30 during my tenure.
- The company won the Balanced Scorecard Hall of Fame Award from Kaplan and Norton.
- The company won the American Productivity & Quality Center Best Practice Partner Award.

This was the beginning of the Five Key Principles model (shown in Exhibit 1.1) that has since been used by dozens of organizations to emulate the winners, with striking results. This model has been updated based on the results of new research.

Innovation and Accumulated Knowledge

Since the Crown experience and the publication of my first book, I was often asked if I would follow up on the initial book and continue the research. I became intrigued by how several companies led their sectors prior to and

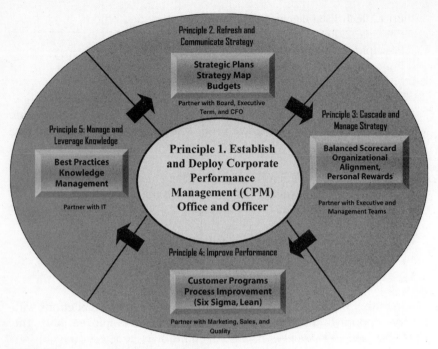

EXHIBIT 1.1 Five Key Principles of CPM

© Copyright 2007 Bob Paladino & Associates, LLC.

during one of the worst recessions since the Great Depression, and I decided to pursue further research on them for this sequel. The case companies have amassed over 175 distinguished awards and honors.

Innovation has been at the heart of our existence and advancement for centuries. Alchemists would argue that innovation is really our natural state. Exhibit 1.2 chronicles some innovations spanning 5,000 years for us to ponder and appreciate.[6]

To put a sharper point on our need to embrace and adapt to an increasingly innovative society, consider the following trends.

The U.S. Congress invented the U.S. patent system in 1790. In 1883, the U.S. Patent and Trademark Office processed only a few hundred patents. However, between 1977 and 2008, a deluge of 2,096,055 patents were filed.[7] This is not a uniquely American experience, for every society has its way of expressing innovation or creativity.

Globally, the World Intellectual Property Organization reports the explosion of patents and ideas in its annual report. Consider that it took almost

EXHIBIT 1.2 Innovation Highlights

BC	Inventions/Innovations
3000	Abacus invented by the Chinese
2800	The 12-month, 365-day calendar devised in Egypt
1550	Earliest surviving medical textbook written in Egypt
700	First purpose-made sundials appear
650	Standardized coins used by Greece
400	The catapult, the first artillery weapon, is invented by Greece
312	Work begins on the Appian Way, the first great Roman road
210	Archimedes, the Greek scientist, invents the Archimedean screw

AD	Inventions/Innovations (Inventor)
1440	Printing Press (Johannes Gutenberg)
1494	Double Entry Accounting (Friar Luca Pacioli)
1642	Adding Machine (Blaise Pascal)
1668	Reflecting Telescope (Isaac Newton)
1673	Microbiology (Anton van Leeuwenhoek)
1742	Franklin Stove (Benjamin Franklin)
1760	Bifocal Glasses (Benjamin Franklin)
1793	Cotton Gin (Eli Whitney)
1800	Electric Battery (Alessandro Volta), Volts, Voltage so named
1824	Braille (Louis Braille)
1836	Colt Revolver (Samuel Colt)
1867	Baby Formula (Henri Nestle')
1869	Air Brake (George Westinghouse)
1889	Automobile (Karl Benz) later Mercedes Benz
1895	Wireless Telegraph (Guglielmo Marconi)
1903	Airplane (Wright Brothers)
1942	Nuclear Reaction (Enrico Fermi)
1947	Instant Photography (Edwin Land), the Polaroid Land Camera
1976	Personal Computer (Steve Jobs and Steve Wozniak)
1998	Google (Sergey Brin and Larry Page)

100 years for Japan to reach a level of 150,000 patent filings per year, but only 20 more years to reach almost 450,000 patent filings per year. The rate of innovation is clearly accelerating. The United States, China, and Europe have all attained 150,000 or more filings per year.[8]

Failing to understand and embrace change and innovation can be costly. Did you know the following companies were removed from the S&P 500 index during this past decade?[9] What happened? They failed to innovate on one level or another.

Anheuser Busch
AT&T Corp.
Bear Stearns Cos.
Seagram Co.
Alcan, Inc.
BellSouth Corp.
Circuit City
Countrywide Financial
COMPAQ
Dow Jones & Co.
Enron Corp.
Global Crossing
Lehman Brothers
Lucent Technologies
Merrill Lynch
Maytag
Nortel Networks
Bank One
Reebok International
Adolph Coors Co.
Rohm & Haas Co.
Schering-Plough Corp.
Times Mirror
Unicol Corp.
Wachovia Corp.
WorldCom Inc.
Wyeth

CEO Study Reveals the "Change Gap"

One of the most comprehensive CEO global surveys by IBM[10] in late 2009, which studied over 1,000 leaders of the largest global enterprises in Europe (403), North and South America (358), and Asia (359), revealed the following astounding insights:

- Organizations are bombarded by change, and many are struggling to keep up.
- Eight out of ten CEOs see significant change ahead, and yet the gap between expected change and the ability to manage it has almost tripled since the prior year's CEO study.
- CEOs view more demanding customers not as a threat, but as an opportunity to differentiate. CEOs are spending more to attract and retain increasingly prosperous, informed, and socially aware customers.

- Nearly all CEOs are adapting their business models; two-thirds are implementing extensive innovations.
- More than 40 percent are changing their enterprise models to be more collaborative.

In the 2006 CEO survey, 57 percent of CEOs felt their companies changed successfully, yet 65 percent of CEOs felt change would continue, a change gap of 8 percent.

In the 2009 CEO survey, 61 percent of CEOs felt their companies changed successfully, yet 83 percent of CEOs felt change would continue, a change gap of 22 percent.

More astonishingly, the change gap expanded from 8 percent to 22 percent, an increase of 275 percent in just three years.

Also, while the number of companies that successfully manage change has increased slightly, the number reporting limited or no success has risen by 60 percent. So what is causing this growing gap? Constant change is certainly not new. But companies are struggling with its accelerating pace. Everything around them seems to be changing faster than they can.

I thank the 11 leadership teams for generously sharing the innovative CPM journeys of their award-winning companies, which have defied the odds and thrived in these challenging times. My hope is that you as a reader will gain key insights, leverage these CPM best practices to accelerate results, and realize your full potential.

Notes

1. Bob Paladino, *Five Key Principles of Corporate Performance Management* (Hoboken, NJ: John Wiley & Sons, 2007).
2. Paladino, *Five Key Principles*, 11.
3. "Blue Ribbon Companies 2004," www.fortune.com (accessed November 4, 2005).
4. Paladino, *Five Key Principles*, 12.
5. Robert Grossman, "Forging a Partnership Executive Turnover," *HR Magazine*, April 2003, 16.
6. "Great Idea Finder Innovation Timeline," www.ideafinder.com (accessed December 28, 2009).
7. U.S. Patent and Trademark Office, March 2009, 7.
8. World Intellectual Property Organization, *World Patent Report: A Statistical Review*, 2008.
9. Andrew Garcia Phillips and Carolyn Cui, "Companies Removed from the S&P 500 This Decade," *Wall Street Journal*, R4.
10. IBM Institute for Business Value, *CEO Enterprise of the Future*, IBM Global Services, 2008.

CHAPTER 2

Research and New Case Company Results

In this chapter we review in-depth cases and best practices of CPM from companies that have received awards and honors and achieved notable performance results. These companies have earned over 175 awards. Chapter 3 contains Principles 1–5, the proven set of CPM processes leveraged by award-winning organizations to earn their coveted awards that will help you establish your CPM capabilities. Chapters 4 through 8 contain the comprehensive cases and all core and innovative best practices.

Research for my first book identified the following award-winning organizations, spanning government, commercial, and nonprofit models across multiple sectors, that were kind enough to share their stories and best practices. Their awards include:

- U.S. President's Malcolm Baldrige National Quality Award (MBNQA)
- Kaplan and Norton Global Balanced Scorecard Hall of Fame Award
- Deming Quality Award
- American Productivity & Quality Center (APQC) Best Practice Partner Award
- State Quality Awards (based on MBNQA criteria)
- *Wall Street Journal*'s "Top 20 Most Improved Companies in Shareholder Value"
- *Fortune*'s "100 Best Companies to Work For"
- Several other honors and awards in each case

This book's Winners' Circle includes:

- Cargill Corn Milling (CCM)
- City of Coral Springs[1]
- Delta Dental of Kansas, Inc.

- Lockheed Martin IS&GS
- M7 Aerospace
- Mueller, Inc.
- NSTAR
- Omaha Public Power District
- Poudre Valley Health System
- Public Service Electric and Gas (PSE&G)
- Sharp HealthCare

These organizations and their business units are leaders in their sectors and have many recognized areas of expertise:

- Aerospace (design, engineering, manufacturing, maintenance, repair, and overhaul)
- Agricultural (food, feed, and fermentation)
- Aviation (fixed and rotary wing, unmanned and manned aerial vehicles)
- City management (fire, police, public education, parks, public safety)
- Consumer products
- Customer service
- Defense and national security (U.S. Army, Navy, and Air Force; Department of Homeland Security, FBI, CIA)
- Education
- Energy production (fossil, wind, solar, gas, nuclear), transmission, and distribution
- Engineering (electrical, chemical, bio, mechanical, nuclear, aviation, civil)
- Government
- Green products and services
- Health care (providers, professional medical disciplines, insurers, services)
- Hospital and health networks
- Industrial products
- Insurance products and services
- Information technology (software, systems integration, hardware)
- Maintenance and reliability
- Manufacturing (discrete and continuous process)
- Municipal corporation (fire, police, public education, parks, public safety)
- Professional services
- Retail stores
- Steel, alloy, and composite design, fabrication, and construction
- Supply chain management and distribution
- Wholesale and distribution

Awards, Honors, and Notable Performance Results

The following sections describe case companies' awards and honors and their notable performance results in what was again the most trying of economic times since the 1930s. The case companies have amassed over 175 awards and honors (or medals). They are multiple award winners, serial success stories. Any one of the following awards would be notable, but these organizations have won scores of awards and honors. This research reinforces the saying, "Winners win."

Cargill Corn Milling (CCM)

AWARDS AND HONORS

- Malcolm Baldrige National Quality Award (MBNQA).
- CCM received Cargill's highest recognition, the Chairman's Award for Business Excellence (three times).
- CCM's Wahpeton, North Dakota plant was selected as an *Industry-Week* Best Plant in 2007 based on comprehensive excellence in all metrics.
- Coors Brewing Company Supplier of the Year.
- Frito-Lay Supplier of the Year.
- H.J. Heinz Supplier of the Year.

HIGHLIGHTS, NOTABLE PERFORMANCE RESULTS

- CCM has an *innovative culture* focused on both incremental improvement and creating distinctive customer value. Two metrics, the Idea Ratio (ideas per employee) and dollar savings from innovative ideas, support the CCM value of "Be Innovative." Over the last three years CCM has saved over $15 million from innovative ideas generated from its Ideas to Innovation (i2i) system. Discussions with Cargill's flour milling business led to the goal of 0.5 idea per employee.
- CCM monitors an *Innovation Index* on its Employee Engagement Survey, a measure used to examine its innovation culture and environment and look at levels of creativity and risk taking. The Innovation Index is calculated using the responses to the following statements:
  - My unique talents and views are maximized at work.
  - I am encouraged to share ideas and carry out solutions.
  - My business has a process to move ideas into action.
  - We provide solutions that add unique value to Cargill and customers.
- CCM provides customers with over two dozen "implemented *innovative* solutions" every quarter.

- CCM Food, Feed, and Fermentation (3F) Teams work on product innovation.
- Food safety results are superior ratings of over 900 points, the highest level, for all five categories evaluated during audits for six consecutive years. Customers rely on and use the results of these audits in lieu of performing their own quality audits.
- Error-free deliveries by Food, Feed, and Fermentation market segments exceeded performance by a MBNQA recipient for the past four years.
- Complaints per shipment are better than four-sigma, at 0.2 percent for the past four years.
- Rejections per million shipments are comparable to *IndustryWeek*'s index of top ten best plants for four consecutive years.
- Employee engagement score has been in the Hewitt *Best Employers* 60 to 100 percent engagement score range for three consecutive years.
- Employee satisfaction score (employees that "Agree" or "Strongly Agree") have been trending up for critical key engagement factors such as quality of work/life, work activities, advancement opportunities, effective communication, and development and growth activities.
- CCM achieved the Society of Maintenance and Reliability Professionals' world-class level of Operational Reliability Effectiveness Rate, the ratio between actual production and commercial demand.

City of Coral Springs

AWARDS AND HONORS

2008–2009

- Malcolm Baldrige National Quality Award.
- Governor's Sterling Award; a distinction that made Coral Springs the first municipality in the nation to win a state-sanctioned Malcolm Baldrige–based award.
- The city became the first organization to be a repeat winner of the Florida Governor's Sterling Award.
- Long history of awards as shown next.

2007

- Tree City USA (12 consecutive years)
- GFOA Distinguished Budget Award (16 consecutive years)
- GFOA Achievement in Financial Reporting (27 consecutive years)

2006

- 100 Best Communities for Young People (2nd)
- Safest City Awards (10th in nation)
- Advanced Life Support Team (1st place)
- APQC Best Practice
- *Money* Magazine Best Places to Live

2005

- 100 Best Communities for Young People
- Safest City Awards (23rd in Nation)
- 50 Fabulous Places to Raise Your Family
- ICMA CPM Award
- FWCPOA Safety Award
- Sterling Team Showcase Award
- SFMA Team Showcase Award
- South Florida Chapter, American Society for Quality, Quality Practitioner of the Year—Chris Hefl in NATOA/Discovery Networks Excellence in Government Programming Awards—Best Overall Television Station

2004

- IACP Community Policing Award
- Florida City of Excellence
- ICMA CPM Certificate of Distinction
- FGCA Crystal Award (1st place) for Best Annual Report
- Florida Print Awards—Award of Excellence, "2003 State of the City Report"

2003

- Florida Governor's Sterling Award (2nd)
- Legal Aid Services of Broward County "For the Public Good" Diversity Award
- Latin Chamber Estrellas Award—Leadership in the Hispanic Community
- NATOA/Discovery Networks Excellence in Government Programming Awards—Best Overall Television Station
- FGCA Crystal Award (1st place) for "Pediatric Drowning Prevention PSAs"
- National Recreation & Parks Association—Best Overall Communicator
- Digital Cities "Top 10" Best Website in the Nation (#2)
- National Private Industry Awards—Telly Award for Best Sports Video, Telly Classic Award for Best PSA, "Drowning Prevention," and Telly Classic Award for Best Social Issues Programming, "Sex, Drugs & Alcohol"

2002

- Digital Cities "Top 10" Best Website in the Nation (#9)
- FRPA Media Excellence Award for Best Recreation Catalog (1st place)

2001

- Digital Cities "Top 10" Best Website in the Nation (#9)
- American Society of Landscape Architects' Award of Excellence—Sandy Ridge Sanctuary

2000

- FGCA Crystal Award (1st Place) for Best External Publication (*Citizen* magazine)
- 3CMA/NLC Savvy Award (1st place) for Best Employee Training Publication for "Employee Guide to Benefits"
- AAA Bond Rating

1999

- National Performance Review "Best Practice" NUSA Neighborhood of the Year—Forest Hills
- National Safety Council Safe City of the Year
- #1 "Kid Friendly" city in Florida

1998

- Sterling Team Showcase Award
- 4th place National Quality Team Showcase
- SFMA Team Showcase Award
- Multi-Cultural Advisory Committee named "Promising Practice" by One America in the 21st Century—The President's Initiative on Race

1997

- Florida Governor's Sterling Award

HIGHLIGHTS, NOTABLE PERFORMANCE RESULTS

- On Residents' Overall Quality Rating Key Intended Outcome (KIO), Coral Springs sustained its position as the benchmark in comparison to other peer group cities for overall quality for a decade. The city compared favorably with ICMA benchmark cities.
- Businesses' Satisfaction with Overall Quality of Services rating was at or above peer group city ratings.

- Fractal response in eight minutes or less by the fire department for fire calls, which is at or above ICMA benchmark cities.
- Fractal response in eight minutes or less by the fire department for EMS calls. Coral Springs is performing better than other ICMA benchmark cities.
- In crime rate incidents per 100,000, Coral Springs' crime rate is lowest in the state and the fourth lowest in the nation for cities with populations of 100,000–499,999. The city had the 10th lowest crime rate in the United States overall, in all categories.
- Eighty-nine percent of schools earned an A grade in comparison to 68 percent of schools in Broward County, Florida. A letter grade, A through F, is assigned to each school based on student performance on the Florida Comprehensive Assessment Test in reading, math, and writing.
- The Residents' Value Rating (residents rate whether they feel their taxes are appropriate relative to the service level they receive from the city) held steady at over 70 percent for five years.
- The majority of residents (93 percent) are satisfied with the range of recreation programs offered by the city.
- Communicating effectively with customers is essential for building relationships and is a key driver of resident satisfaction.
- The majority (over 90 percent) of business representatives would recommend the city to others, indicating business loyalty and the potential for long-term relationships.
- Residents who have used Emergency Medical Services are satisfied with the service they received. Coral Springs is on par with ICMA benchmark cities that ask their residents the same question.
- Ninety-three percent of residents who have used the Fire Department are satisfied with the service they received.
- Over 90 percent of residents express satisfaction with park maintenance and appearance.
- For police response time, total average time from receipt of top-priority police telephone call to arrival on scene (in seconds), Coral Springs compares well to other ICMA benchmark cities.
- The city's goal is to provide high service levels while maintaining a low millage rate. Coral Springs has the lowest millage rate in Broward County as compared to local cities of 70,000 population or more.
- On employee productivity (employees per 1,000 residents), as compared to other large cities within Broward County, as population has grown, this number has remained constant—reflecting sustained high productivity from continuous improvement efforts.
- Coral Springs has a very low employee turnover rate and it has been getting lower since 1996. City emphasis on employee satisfaction and well-being has influenced this result.

- A very high level of employee satisfaction has been sustained for over ten years. The majority of city employees "would recommend working for the city to a friend."
- For sick leave per 1,000 hours worked, the low number is attributable to the city's Wellness Program and incentives such as sick leave buy-back.
- For positions that do not require testing, Coral Springs' recruitment cycle time is lower than for ICMA benchmark cities, at 15 days.
- Ninety-seven percent of residents' feel safe in city parks during the day. A safe community is a key customer requirement.
- The number of residents who feel safe in their neighborhood after dark has risen in recent years, to 86 percent.
- On water accountability, the average amount of water lost per year is less than 5 percent—the difference between the quantity of water supplied to the city's network and the metered quantity of water used by the customers has dropped steadily.
- On employees' ratings of ethics and integrity, the majority of employees agreed with the statements: "Overall, I think my organization is highly ethical" and "The city's commitment to integrity has been clearly communicated to all employees."

Delta Dental of Kansas, Inc.

AWARDS AND HONORS

- Kansas Center for Performance Excellence presented the distinguished Kansas Excellence Award, the state's top honor, awarded to organizations that have demonstrated the highest level of quality and organizational performance excellence
- Balanced Scorecard Hall of Fame Award, Kaplan and Norton
- Harvard Business School Hall of Fame Case
- Corporate Friend of Children Hall of Fame Award
- *Wichita Business Journal*, "Best in Business" for the company's financial results, community involvement, and innovation
- Finalist in "Best Places to Work," *Wichita Business Journal*

HIGHLIGHTS, NOTABLE PERFORMANCE RESULTS

- During the period 2001 through 2009 gross revenues increased 266.5 percent from $63,055,700 in annual revenues to $231,100,000 in annual revenues.
- Market share increased to 31 percent of the statewide market.

- During the period 2001 to 2009, its customer base, based on the total number of covered lives, grew by 184.6 percent from 299,972 enrollees to 853,774 enrollees.
- Overhead expenses as a percentage of annual revenues were reduced from 10.3 percent in 2001 to 7.8 percent as of December 31, 2009.
- Network growth: The percentage of Kansas dentists who participate in Delta Dental of Kansas grew from 79 percent in 2001 to 90 percent in 2009.
- Number of total employees rose from 59 in 2001 to 110 in 2009.
- Average speed to answer customer service calls was 6 seconds.
  - Ninety-nine percent of telephone inquiries were resolved on the first call.
  - Call abandonment rate was 1 percent.
  - Call center survey cards showed 99 percent of callers were "satisfied" or "very satisfied."
- More than 1,500,000 claims were processed during 2009.
  - Auto adjudication rate of 70 percent was achieved.
  - 99.95 percent of claims were processed within 15 days.

Lockheed Martin IS&GS

AWARDS AND HONORS

- Two Nunn-Perry Awards for the corporation's participation on two teams in the Department of Defense (DoD) Mentor-Protégé Program (2009)
- James S. Cogswell Outstanding Industrial Security Achievement Award (2008 and 2009); Department of Defense Security Service
- Acterra Business Environmental Award for transportation and commuting (2009)
- Waste Reduction Awards Program (WRAP) award for outstanding waste reduction efforts (2009)
- Secretary of Labor's New Freedom Initiative Award (2008)
- Large Business Prime Contractor of the Year (2008), NASA Johnson Space Center
- Balanced Scorecard Hall of Fame Award (2007), Kaplan and Norton
- *IndustryWeek's* Best Plants in America Award (2007)
- *Aviation Week* & Space Technology Program Excellence Award (2006)
- Excellence Award for Best Use of Technology in a Shared Services Organization from the International Quality & Productivity Center (2006)
- Recipient of the First Beacon Award (2005) for celebrating diversity in the workforce, presented by the National Association of Women Business Owners

EXHIBIT 2.1 IS&GS Financial Results

($ millions)	2009	2008	2007	2006
Net sales	12,130	11,611	10,213	8,990
Operating profit	1,011	1,076	949	804
Backlog at year end	*	13,300	11,800	10,500
Assets	*	7,593	7,477	7,054

*Data not available at time of preparation.

- Ranked #1 in *Minority Engineer* magazine's "Top 10 Defense Contractors" (2005)

HIGHLIGHTS, NOTABLE PERFORMANCE RESULTS Through the efforts of the Lockheed Martin Information Systems & Global Services (IS&GS) Mission Services organization emerged the new IS&GS-Civil product line, including a series of notable performance results from its use of CPM methods. From a financial perspective, Lockheed Martin reports several financial indicators at the business-area level (i.e., IS&GS) as shown in Exhibit 2.1. Additionally, several leading indicators made notable improvements that bode well for sustained and continued performance.

- Customer
  - Winning key customer programs in a highly competitive market, especially in adjacent markets
  - High award fee scores
- Process
  - Improved leverage of lean and six sigma processes (e.g., LM21 Operating Excellence), 100 percent on plan
  - Increasing focus on customer relationship management processes
  - Improvement in staffing agility
  - More than 50 percent of strategic actions, per Balanced Scorecard process, accomplished within six months
- Workforce
  - More than 250 percent improvement in mentoring participation (i.e., mentors)
  - Full spectrum leadership development and engagement; more than 85 percent of leaders with a formal plan
  - More than 90 percent of employees and their leaders actively engaged in career development planning efforts

M7 Aerospace

AWARDS AND HONORS

2009

- **Northrop Grumman World Class Team Supplier Award.** For the third consecutive year M7 Aerospace won a supplier award from Northrop Grumman Corporation. M7 Aerospace was selected to receive a 2009 World Class Team Supplier award for its consistently demonstrated outstanding achievements and support of Northrop Grumman programs.

2008

- **Excellence in Innovative Supply Management (EISM) Award.** For the third year in a row M7 was one of just six companies to win this award, which is given annually to recognize and reward organizational excellence in the purchasing and supply management field. Awarded by the Southwest Forum and the Institute of Supply Management (ISM).

2007

- **Northrop Grumman World Class Team Supplier Award.**
- **Excellence in Innovative Supply Management (EISM) Award.**

2006

- **Northrop Grumman Platinum Source Supplier Award.** M7 Aerospace received a Platinum Source Supplier Award from Northrop Grumman Corporation in recognition of "sustained excellence as a supplier of quality products and on-time delivery to Northrop Grumman Integrated Systems."
- **Excellence in Innovative Supply Management (EISM) Award.** yes
- **The Boeing Company Supplier Quality Award.** The Boeing Company honored M7 Aerospace for its manufacturing support of Boeing's C-130 Avionics Modernization Program (AMP). Work performed by M7 includes fabricating sheet metal parts, building hydroform parts; painting and priming; and building cable assemblies and bending tubes for precise applications.

HIGHLIGHTS, NOTABLE PERFORMANCE RESULTS The following results, organized by Balanced Scorecard (BSC) financial, customer, process, and
people perspectives, were sourced from the company's set of BSCs for
the most recent year. Since M7 Aerospace is privately held, several
financial results are confidential and have been expressed as percentage
results.

Financial and Customer (lagging indicators)

- Financial: M7 Aerospace has increased consolidated revenue by over
  500 percent during the past five years.
- Financial: M7 Aerospace has increased consolidated EBITDA by over
  1,000 percent in the past two years.
- Financial: C23 Business Unit maximized cash flow by reducing accounts
  receivable over 60 days past due from $140,000 to zero.
- Financial: Engineering Services Business Unit maximized cash flow by
  reducing accounts receivable over 60 days past due from $160,000 to
  zero.
- Customer: C23 Business Unit achieved customer-provided "Customer
  Performance Assessment Report" (CPAR) ratings of "very good" for most
  of the year.
- Customer: Engineering Services Business Unit achieved Boeing customer Best Rating for Quality for most of the year.
- Customer: Engineering Services Business Unit achieved Boeing customer Best on Schedule Rating for Quality for most of the year.

Process and People (leading indicators)

- Process/Productivity: Supply Chain Management BU response time to
  provide parts to C23 BU program was green, under 30 minutes for the
  entire year.
- Process/Productivity: Nonreimbursable overtime was under budget for
  the entire year.
- Process/Productivity: Government Business Development BU increased
  the number of new Programs Identified for Evaluation from four to 32
  in one year, an increase of 800 percent.
- Process/Productivity: C26 Peru program inventory accuracy exceeded
  agreed target of 98 percent, a key customer requirement, for most of
  the year.
- Process/Productivity: Maintenance Repair and Overhaul (MRO) BU
  amount of backlog booked exceeded target for six consecutive
  months.

- Process/Productivity: MRO BU on-time delivery of services to internal customers or other M7 BUs was at or above target of 97 percent for the year.
- Process/Productivity: MRO BU on-time delivery of services to external (outside M7 family of BUs) customers was at or above target of 97 percent for the year.
- Process/Productivity: Parts/Spares BU secured more new customers than target for most of the year.
- Process/Productivity: Quality BU increased percentage of in-bound parts cleared in 24 hours from 78 percent to 90 percent.
- Process/Productivity: Finance Support Unit (SU) provided necessary business analytics within 12 days after month end consistently throughout the year.
- Process/Productivity: Contracts SU maintained all contract terms as current over 90 percent of the time for the entire year.
- Process/Productivity: Corporate Development SU provided timely quotes and modeling services over 95 percent of the time for the whole year.
- Process/Productivity: Corporate Development SU provided delivered Consolidated Scorecards on time 100 percent of the time all year.
- People: HR SU improved the selection and hiring process, and the percentage of employees successfully completing the hiring probationary period (30/60/90–day appraisals) increased to 90 percent.
- Information Technology: IT SU completed 100 percent of targeted training and certifications for the entire year.
- Representative lean six sigma team results: "Dock to Stock Span Time Reduction" project team successfully reduced work-in-progress from 206.1 jobs to 38.3 jobs, an 81 percent decrease, and reduced process lead time from 30 hours to 5.2 hours, an 82 percent decrease!

Mueller, Inc.

AWARDS AND HONORS

- Balanced Scorecard Hall of Fame Award, Kaplan and Norton
- Best Business Intelligence Solution, IBM Information on Demand

HIGHLIGHTS, NOTABLE PERFORMANCE RESULTS Gross revenue and return on assets (ROA) have always been the main outcome measures of Mueller's president. It is President Davenport's company, so the bottom line ends with him. These are the outcome measures that allow Mueller to grow as fast as the company can use retained earnings and without destroying its culture of small town values.

- Revenue grew 40 percent from 2003 to 2006.
- Return on assets grew 80 percent from 2003 to 2006.
- Financially the company has prospered, reaching annual revenue of approximately $250 million in 2008, a compound annual growth rate of 12.5 percent over the previous year.

NSTAR

AWARDS AND HONORS

- Ranked by the *Boston Globe* as a "Globe 100" Company.
- Named as one of the "100 Most Trustworthy Companies" by Forbes.com.
- Consistently named a "Tree Line USA Utility."
- Gold-level LEED-certified headquarters.
- Listed in the Top 40 Charitable Contributors by the *Boston Business Journal*.
- Lead sponsor of the NSTAR Walk for Children's Hospital Boston.

HIGHLIGHTS, NOTABLE PERFORMANCE RESULTS

- Met Wall Street expectations of earnings and dividend rate growth.
- Achieved total positive shareholder return of 5.6 percent for 2009. This marks NSTAR's 13th consecutive year of positive total shareholder return, a record unmatched by any company in the S&P 500 and Fortune 1000.
- Worked effectively and in a leadership role in an evolving regulatory and energy environment.
- Improved customer satisfaction scores for the fourth consecutive year.
- Maintained top quartile operating performance.
- Significantly increased performance on key metrics over the past five years.
- NSTAR achieved many of the highest levels of performance in the industry as shown in Exhibit 2.2.

Omaha Public Power District (OPPD)

AWARDS AND HONORS

- "Highest in Customer Satisfaction among Midsize Utilities in the Midwest" in the J.D. Power and Associates Electric Utility Residential Customer Satisfaction Study, nine years in a row.

EXHIBIT 2.2 NSTAR Results

Performance Measure	Actual Performance	Description of Measure	Industry Achievement
Electric Service Reliability	15.6 months	Average frequency of customer service interruptions.	First quartile and best-ever performance
Electric Service Restoration	58.7 minutes	Average time to restore customer service interruptions.	First quartile
Response to Gas Emergencies	99.7 percent	Percentage of gas customer emergency calls responded to within one hour.	First quartile
Call Center Performance	85.3 percent	Percentage of customer calls answered in less than 30 seconds.	First quartile
Meter Reading	98.9 percent	Percentage of meters read on schedule.	Second quartile
Billing Timeliness	99.7 percent	Percentage of customer bills issued on schedule.	First quartile
Safety	2.8	The rate of days out of work or restrictions or prevention of performing normal work due to work related injury or illness.	Second quartile
Total Shareholder Return	+5.6 percent	Combination of share price appreciation and dividends paid to shareholders.	Outperformed industry and stock market for the last 2, 3, 5 and 10 year periods.
Credit Rating	A+	An assessment by rating agencies of the credit-worthiness of the corporation.	Highest among EEI's Utility Peer Group.
Customer Satisfaction	84.2 percent	Average satisfaction score for customers interviewed after contacting NSTAR's call centers with a request or inquiry.	Overall customer satisfaction as measured by JD Power & Associates is above average for utilities in the eastern U.S.
Employee Satisfaction	77 percent favorable	Surveys progress toward creating a favorable workplace as perceived by NSTAR employees.	These results considered "High Performing" per national norms.

- Power Engineering Penn Well Corp. named OPPD's 600-megawatt Nebraska City Station Unit 2 one of three finalists for the best coal-fired project of 2009 award.
- OPPD has been named the winner of the annual Young Professionals Choice Award, which recognizes an organization in the Greater Omaha community that excels in efforts to attract, retain, and develop young professionals.
- Employees of OPPD's Fort Calhoun Station (FCS) have received the nuclear energy industry's B. Ralph Sylvia Best of the Best Award, winning a competition with over 200 other nominees for the Top Industry Practice honor.
- Fort Calhoun achieved Top Quartile Institute Nuclear Power Operators Performance Index.
- Nuclear Energy Institute (NEI) reelected W. Gary Gates, president and CEO of the Omaha Public Power District, as vice chairman of the board.
- OPPD was named Tree Line USA Utility in 2009 (each year for the last five from APPA, National Arbor Day Foundation, and National Association of State Foresters).
- OPPD (FCS) won Best of Best Award from NEI in May 2009.
- Energy Star Leadership in House Award from U.S. EPA (2009).
- Gary Gates, chairman of the board (NEI) in 2009, Mutual of Omaha Board 2007, and president of the Omaha Chamber of Commerce (2010).
- Corporate Communications won Public Relations Society of America Award (2009).
- Named one of Greater Omaha's Safest Companies by the National Safety Council, Greater Omaha Chapter (2008).
- OPPD (FCS) won Top Industry Practice Award from NEI in 2008.
- Top Ten of nation's Top Alternative Fuel Vehicle Fleets 2007 (named by *Automotive Fleet* magazine, sponsored by Ford Motor Company).

HIGHLIGHTS, NOTABLE PERFORMANCE RESULTS The following results, organized by Performance Scorecard (PSC) financial, customer, process, and people perspectives, were sourced from the company's set of PSCs for 2009; J.D. Power ratings span multiple years as noted.

Customer

- OPPD Overall Customer Satisfaction Index score of 694
  - Components of OPPD Overall
    - Corporate Citizenship score (627)
    - Communications score (638)
    - Billing and Payment score (759)

- Power, Quality, & Reliability score (760)
- Price (611)
- Customer Service (744)
- 95 percent Customer Satisfaction—Annual Large Customer Survey
- 91 percent Customer Satisfaction—After Call Surveys, Residential Segment

Financial

- AA Bond Rating—Standard & Poors.
- AA+ Bond Rating—Moody.
- Green Power Revenue exceeded target by 20 percent.
- Field Collection of delinquent accounts exceeded target by 56 percent.
- No monetary fines.

Process

- Number of retail customers with interruptions lasting more than four hours performed 33 percent under target.
- Reduction in number of circuits having momentaries greater than 14 exceeded the target by 27 percent.
- As a result of OPPD energy efficiency programs, Peak MW's Reduced exceeded the targeted amount by 70.6 percent.
- Employees volunteered an average of 10.4 hours per person.
- Fort Calhoun Nuclear Power Station Institute Nuclear Power Operators (INPO) Fuel Reliability Indicator (quarter average) 8 points, green performance.
- Fort Calhoun Nuclear Power Station INPO Fuel Defects (quarter average) 2 points, green performance.
- Fort Calhoun Nuclear Power Station INPO Fuel Reliability.

Indicator, 12-Month Top Quartile

- Process Innovation Highlight: The OPPD research team devised a method to accurately assess the susceptibility of stainless steel and other alloys to stress corrosion cracking. Their research will make it possible to find tiny flaws in metal that take 20 years to develop.
  - Avoidance of unnecessary replacement of expensive components, saving $7 million since 1999
  - Reduction in radiation exposure, cutting 10 to 50 person-rem of combined exposure to workers
  - Improved safety and efficiency across the entire nuclear energy industry, if adopted by other utilities

People

- On the rate for employee days away from work, restricted time, or transfers (DART rate), performed 37.6 percent below the established target.
- Employee participation in Wellness Programs exceeded the target by 10.5 percent.
- Retention rate for the past three years for key groups (combined minority, female, young professionals, and graduates of the employee education plan) within the company was over 93 percent.
- Retention rate over the past three years for diverse hires within the company was 95 percent.

Poudre Valley Health System (PVHS)

AWARDS AND HONORS

- **Malcolm Baldrige National Quality Award (2008).** Poudre Valley Health System was the only health care organization to receive the nation's top presidential award for organizational innovation and performance excellence in 2008. The award is recognition that the health system offers the nation's highest level of performance excellence and patient care that is among the best in the world. Established by Congress, the award honored PVHS for achieving excellence in every aspect of its health care business, including clinical quality, customer service, and staff, physician, and volunteer service.
- **Colorado Performance Excellence Peak Award (2004 and 2008).** The Colorado Performance Excellence program (CPEx) presented Poudre Valley Health System with the state's highest award for performance excellence. The health system is the first to receive the award since CPEx began reviewing the performance of Colorado organizations in 2001. The award recognizes excellence in the way PVHS approaches its business of health care and uses information, results, and customer feedback for making improvements.
- **American Nurses Association Award for Outstanding Nursing Quality.** In 2008, Poudre Valley Hospital was the first and only hospital in the nation to receive this American Nurses Association award. The ANA, which represents 2.9 million registered nurses, presented PVH with the award to recognize the hospital's sustained excellence in nursing quality, as determined by the ANA's National Database of Nursing Quality Indicators. PVH received the award again in 2009.
- **Best Place to Work (2008 and 2009).** *Modern Healthcare* named Poudre Valley Health System as one of America's 100 Best Places to

Work in health care. The award recognized that PVHS has successfully built workplace excellence and enabled employees to perform at their optimal level.

- **Magnet Prize (2009).** Poudre Valley Hospital's Community Case Management Program received this national award from the American Nurses Credentialing Center and Cerner Corporation. The award recognizes innovative nursing programs and practices in hospitals that are designated as Magnet Hospitals for Nursing Excellence by the American Nurses Credentialing Center.
- **100 Top Hospitals Award (2001, 2004, 2005, 2007, and 2008).** Thomson Healthcare, the nation's leading independent company that tracks hospital performance, named Poudre Valley Hospital as one of the nation's 100 top hospitals for superior clinical outcomes, patient safety, and operational and financial performance. PVH was the only hospital in the Rocky Mountain region to be named to the list for five consecutive years and the only hospital designated as a Magnet Hospital for Nursing Excellence during each year from 2004 to 2008. (Thomson Healthcare was known as Solucient prior to 2007.)
- **HealthGrades.** HealthGrades has recognized Poudre Valley Hospital with multiple awards for its clinical excellence. The awards, which represent the highest scoring of the nation's full-service hospitals, include:
  - Distinguished Hospital Award for Clinical Excellence (2006–2009)
  - Distinguished Hospital Award for Patient Safety (2005–2009)
  - Award for Outstanding Patient Experience (Poudre Valley Hospital and Medical Center of the Rockies for 2009/2010 and Poudre Valley Hospital for 2009)
  - Women's Health Excellence Award (Poudre Valley Hospital for 2009/2010)
  - Specialty Excellence Award in Cardiac Care (Poudre Valley Hospital in 2009)
  - Special Excellence Award in Coronary Intervention (Poudre Valley Hospital in 2009)
  - Gastrointestinal Care Excellence Award (2007 and 2008)
  - Joint Replacement Excellence Award (2007 and 2008)
  - Orthopedic Surgery Excellence Award (2006–2009)
  - Pulmonary Care Excellence Award (2007 and 2008)
  - Stroke Care Excellence Award (2006–2009)
- **Beacon Award for Critical Care Excellence (2008 and 2009).** The American Association of Critical Care Nurses honored the Medical Center of the Rockies' two intensive care units for following the best evidence-based practices used in the health care industry.
- **100 Most Wired and 25 Most Wireless Awards (2004–2008 for both awards; 2009 for the 100 Most Wired Award).** *Hospital & Health*

Networks, the national journal of the American Hospital Association, named Poudre Valley Health System as one of the nation's 100 Most Wired and 25 Most Wireless organizations for use of information technology. PVHS is one of 15 health care organizations in the nation to be recognized annually four times in a row as a Most Wired and Most Wireless organization. Recognition is based on the magazine's annual study of how hospitals use information technology to address key areas involving safety and quality, customer service, business processes, workforce issues, and public health and safety.

- **Avatar International Awards.** Avatar is an independent firm that conducts ongoing patient satisfaction surveys for PVHS and more than 300 other hospitals and health systems in the United States. Avatar awards to PVHS include Innovation Award to Poudre Valley Hospital and Innovation Awards to the Medical Center of the Rockies Emergency Department, Radiology Department, and Mother/Family Care Unit (2008) for developing programs that resulted in significant improvements in patient satisfaction scores; Most Improved Patient Care Award and two Innovation Awards programs that enhance patient care (2007); Award for Most Improved Inpatient Care Patient Satisfaction Scores (2006); Most Improved in Inpatient Care Award and Most Improved in Outpatient Care Award for improved patient satisfaction scores (2005); and Five Star National Award for exceeding patient expectations (2004).
- **Innovative Users of Information Technology Awards (2004–2006 and 2008).** PVHS was named to *InformationWeek's* prestigious list of the 500 companies that are the most innovative users of information technology in the United States. Membership on the annual list shows that a company is among the nation's best in using information technology in its business practices.
- **America's 50 Best Hospitals Award for Orthopedic Care (2003–2005 and 2009).** *U.S. News & World Report* named Poudre Valley Hospital as one of America's 50 best hospitals for orthopedic care.
- **National Research Corporation's Consumer Choice Awards (2004–2008).** National Research Corporation, an industry leader in measuring the performance of health care organizations, recognized Poudre Valley Hospital with a Consumer Choice Award as one of the nation's top hospitals. PVH was one of only 200 hospitals in the nation to receive a Consumer Choice Award each year. The annual award was based on an NRC survey that asked local consumers to name the hospital in their region with the highest quality and image.
- ***The Bond Buyer's* Deal of the Year Award (2005).** Poudre Valley Health System received national recognition for the financing of its new

regional hospital, Medical Center of the Rockies. PVHS was among ten of the 14,000 eligible organizations to receive *The Bond Buyer's* 2005 Deal of the Year Award, which honors the most innovative municipal deals conducted across the country. *The Bond Buyer* is a national daily newspaper of public finance. The award recognizes PVHS' success in crafting a deal that will save the locally owned, not-for-profit health system $6 million a year in interest expenses.

- **VHA Awards (2004 and 2005).** In 2005, VHA Veterans Health Association recognized Poudre Valley Hospital with the Leadership Award for the operational excellence that is required for a hospital to be redesignated as a Magnet Hospital for Nursing Excellence by the American Nurses Credentialing Association. In 2004, VHA Mountain States named PVH's Lifestyle Challenge Program as the best community health program in the six-state Rocky Mountain region.
- **Awards for Best in Larimer County, Colorado (2003 and 2004).** In 2003, the *Fort Collins Coloradoan* named Poudre Valley Health System as the Best Company in the county in its annual judging of the Best in Business in Larimer County. In 2004, the *Coloradoan* presented PVHS with the newspaper's Best in Healthcare Award. Larimer County, where PVHS is headquartered in Fort Collins, is an urban and rural area with a population of a quarter of a million people.
- **Emergency Services Award (2004).** The *Northern Colorado Business Report*, which reports on business issues in northern Colorado and Wyoming, honored the Poudre Valley Hospital Emergency Services Department with the Emergency Services Award as part of the newspaper's annual presentation of six local Health Care Heroes Awards.
- **Achievement, Commitment and Excellence Award (2004).** Occupational Health Services of Poudre Valley Hospital received the national Achievement, Commitment and Excellence (ACE) Award for performing a high number of complex evaluations for people who sustained occupational injuries. The evaluations are critical in measuring a person's injury and developing treatment for recovery. The award was presented by WorkSTEPS, an organization that tracks national occupational health data.

HIGHLIGHTS, NOTABLE PERFORMANCE RESULTS

Patient/Medical Care Measures

- PVH (Poudre Valley Hospital) and MCR (Medical Center of the Rockies) Percent of Patients Receiving Evidence-Based Care was consistent with National Quality Improvement Goals both at or above competitor rates for three disease categories: acute myocardial infarction (heart attack), heart failure, and pneumonia.

- MCR RN Hours per Patient Day approached National Database of Nursing Quality Indicators (NDNQI) best quartile rates.
- PVH inpatient mortality rates declined every quarter in 2007 from 10 percent to zero percent.
- Neonatal intensive care unit outcomes are in the top 25 percent outcome rates for five categories.
- PVH's Average Length of Stay by Injury by all four Severity Scores (minor, moderate, major, and severe) were reduced for four consecutive years.
- Critical Medication Errors, errors per 100 doses, declined over a four-year period.
- Mortality Rate within 30 days of the Primary Operation declined each year from 0.79 percent to 0.00 percent over five years.
- PVH medical and surgical rates of patient falls per 1,000 patient days were in NDNQI's top 25 percent quartile.

Patient Satisfaction Measure Ratings

- The percentage of survey respondents who selected the top response (strongly agree) out of five possible responses is approaching 80 percent.
- PVH patient retention and loyalty scores ("I would recommend PVH/MCR without hesitation to others") have been above 80 percent for five consecutive years.
- PVH, at over 70 percent, outscored competitive hospitals on service levels in 9 and 10 ratings: "Using any number from 0 to 10 where 0 is the worst hospital possible, what number would you use to rate this hospital during your stay?"

Financial Measures

- PVH Profit per Discharge rate was in the top 10 percent in the United States in 2006.
- PVHS ranked above the U.S. top 10 percent in liquidity based on Moody's definition that health care organizations in solid financial position should have 90 to 100 days' cash on hand.

Employee Measures

- PVHS Employee Survey results meet or exceed the national top 10 or 20 percent in 14 of the 16 categories in the Management Science

Association (MSA) survey. MSA is an independent national firm that conducts employee opinion surveys.

Public Service Electric and Gas (PSE&G)

AWARDS AND HONORS

- Balanced Scorecard Hall of Fame Award, Kaplan and Norton
- Dow Jones Sustainability Index Company
- *Fortune* magazine, Most Admired Companies
- *New Jersey Business* magazine, Best Corporation of the Year
- New Jersey, Top 12 Places to Work
- White House Council on Environmental Quality Coastal Award
- Platt's Global Energy Award Finalist in four categories:
  - Energy Company of the Year
  - CEO of the Year
  - Sustainable Technology of the Year
  - Green Energy Initiatives of the Year
- National Electric Reliability One Award four of the last five years for the best electric reliability in the nation
- Best Utility Company in Implementing Best Practices
- American Gas Association (AGA) National Employee Safety award for the best employee safety record in the nation

HIGHLIGHTS, NOTABLE PERFORMANCE RESULTS

- $3.5 billion available liquidity.
- 102 consecutive years of dividend payouts.
- PSE&G performance reflects strong operations in difficult markets, reaffirming 2009 operating earnings guidance (*Wall Street Journal*).
- PSE&G stock was approximately 50 percent higher at year end 2006 than it was for the same period in 2004.
- PSE&G total shareholder return for the past ten years has substantially outpaced two major market indices, Standard & Poor's 500 and the Dow Jones Utilities.
- The electric outage duration rate, which measures the length of time a customer is out of service, decreased to 66 minutes in 2006 from 101 minutes in 2002.
- The OSHA accident severity rate, which measures the amount of time an employee is out ill due to an OSHA injury, decreased to 8.48 percent in 2006 from 36.21 percent in 2002.

Sharp HealthCare (SHC)

AWARDS AND HONORS

- Malcolm Baldrige National Quality Award (MBNQA)
- California Performance Excellence (CAPE) Eureka Gold Sharp Health-Care (SHC)
- California CAPE Eureka Silver SHC
- California CAPE Eureka Bronze SHC
- ANCC Magnet Designation Sharp Grossmont Hospital (SGH) and Sharp Memorial Hospital (SMH)
- Excellence in Patient Safety and Health Care Quality based on Leapfrog Survey (SMH, SGH)
- 50 Exceptional U.S. Hospitals based on Leapfrog Survey (SMH)
- Press Ganey Summit Award Sharp Coronado Hospital and Healthcare Center (SCHHC) for Top 5 percentile in Patient Satisfaction (three years)
- San Diego Better Business Bureau Torch Award for Marketplace Ethics (SHC)
- Verispan/*Modern Healthcare* Top 100 Integrated Healthcare Networks (three years)
- San Diego Society for Human Resources Management, Workplace Excellence Grand Prize
- American Heart Association (AHA) Get with the Guidelines Sustained Performance Achievement (SMH)
- American Heart Association Get with the Guidelines Performance Achievement (SGH)
- 100 Best Places to Work in Information Technology (two years)
- 100 Most Wired awards for nine consecutive years

HIGHLIGHTS, NOTABLE PERFORMANCE RESULTS

- San Diego consumers rated Sharp the highest on quality measures and preference for health care services across all of the major service lines.
- Consumer satisfaction rates place Sharp Health Plan (SHP) in the top quartile across the nation for six years in a row.
- Inpatient Diabetes Mean Blood Glucose Level reduced for four years in a row.
- Glycemic Control Percentage in Joint Replacement Patients improved for five quarters in a row.
- Acute Myocardial Infarction (heart attack) Beta Blockers at Discharge, most Sharp entities in top decile nationally.
- Acute Myocardial Infarction Mortality lower than national benchmark, all locations for three years.

- Harris Hip Functional Status Improvement (Pre-Op to One Year Post-Op) outperforms national benchmark three years in a row.
- Sharp Home Care Improvement of Patient Transfer Ability outperforms national benchmark three years in a row.
- Sharp Bariatric Program Results beat national benchmarks in all four complication types five years in a row.
- System Ventilator Associated Pneumonia Rates outperformed national quartile four years in a row.
- For Agency for Healthcare Research and Quality Patient Safety Indicators, outperformed national benchmarks in 11 safety indicators.

Note

1. The City of Coral Springs was also featured in Bob Paladino, *Five Key Principles of Corporate Performance Management* (Hoboken, NJ: John Wiley & Sons, 2007). Since the publication of that book, the city has earned the Malcolm Baldrige National Quality Award and has some exciting new best practices to share.

CHAPTER 3

Five Key Principles of CPM: Best Practices Model

This chapter provides the Five Key Principles core CPM process blueprint, definition, and discussion of key process roles and core best practices. It also contains selected innovative best practices from each of the case companies. Since over 130 new innovative best practices were identified, it will be more instructive to include all of them in their respective cases. This positioning provides not only strategic context but also a clear link to the comprehensive case discussion. Cases contain best practices, key strategic frameworks, managerial models, strategy maps, balanced scorecards, process models, communications plans, quality improvement tools, testimonials, screenshots, charts, graphs, and more. My hope is that these examples will help to accelerate your results.

CPM Core Process Blueprint and Key Roles

Careful research of the 25 cases reveals they follow a discernable set of core CPM processes organized within the Five Key Principles. These processes are arrayed in Exhibit 3.1 to provide strategic context and a working framework to assist you in your organization.

The CPM office members will play one of three key roles in executing the CPM core processes with participants. We will use the strategic planning process in parallel to illustrate the following four roles:

1. **Process Sponsor.** The sponsor is typically the most senior executive accountable for the process outcomes and for overseeing the process owner. The process sponsor for the Strategic Planning process at Crown was the CEO and the board strategy subcommittee for governance.

EXHIBIT 3.1 CPM Core Processes

CPM Principles 1-5 Roadmap Key Supporting Processes	Year 1				Year 2				Year 3	
	Q1	Q2	Q3	Q4	Q1	Q2	Q3	Q4	Q1	Q2
Principle 1: Establish & Deploy CPM Office										
■ Executive Sponsorship & Trusted Advisor process										
■ Recruit, Train and Manage Enterprise CPM Expert process										
■ CPM Principles 2-5 Management process										
■ Manage CPM Centers of Excellence process										
Principle 2: Refresh & Communicate Strategy										
■ Strategic Planning process										
■ Enterprise Risk Management process										
■ Budgeting and Strategic Initiative process										
■ Strategic Communications and Change Management processes										
Principle 3: Cascade & Manage Strategy										
■ Corporate Balanced Scorecard process										
■ Business and Support Unit Balanced Scorecard processes										
■ Team and Personal Scorecard and Goal processes										
■ BSC Automation and Meeting Management processes										
Principle 4: Improve Performance										
■ Customer and Competitor Survey and Innovation processes										
■ Quality Improvement and Innovation processes										
■ Benchmarking process										
Principle 5: Manage & Leverage Knowledge										
■ Best Practice and Innovation Sharing process										
■ Mentor and Development process										

2. **Process Owner.** The owner is typically the senior leader accountable to the sponsor for managing the process and is usually a process subject matter expert (SME). The process owner for the Strategic Planning process at Crown was the CPM officer (me).

3. **Process Facilitator.** The facilitator is typically the individual who interacts day to day directly with process participants to drive the process and integrate the process with other key processes. The process facilitator of the Crown Strategic Planning process varied at each stage. At the beginning it was me, then I partnered with Bain Consulting to facilitate a multitrack strategic planning offsite, thereafter facilitation reverted to me. This process was then integrated with the risk management process and the budgeting process for capital and operational financial planning.

4. **Process Participant.** The process participants are typically subject matter experts, those who will be accountable for the process outcomes and/or are the recipients of the process outcomes. The process participants in the Crown Strategic Planning process were a broad senior team including the board of directors, the executive management team, the senior leadership team, outside industry SMEs, and a few selected high-potential employees for grooming purposes.

As we turn our attention toward the CPM process blueprint, let us continue by reviewing a few examples prior to a deeper reading of the cases.

In Principle 1 it is vital for the CPM officer to have and maintain CEO or executive sponsorship and "earn" the trusted advisor role with the CEO direct reports team. If you establish a CPM office in a business unit or function, then simply translate "CEO" to be the highest level executive in your organization. Also, your CPM officer may report to a CEO direct report, so you will have to translate this discussion accordingly.

In Principle 2 the CPM office leader, for example, would ensure the integration of strategic planning and enterprise risk management (ERM) so that strategic planning informs the company risk profile and vice versa. If the strategy calls for market expansion in Brazil, then the ERM function would inform the executive team of inherent risks, whether they be currency, product liability, labor, political, and so on, that would have to be mitigated for a successful deployment of the new strategy.

As a final example, in Principle 3, the CPM office leader, for instance, would deploy the measurement and management program throughout the enterprise. You may determine that a pilot is warranted prior to full rollout. In some instance business conditions may warrant broad-based deployment, as we experienced at Crown Castle.

Instead of reviewing all of the CPM processes, I suggest that you review these at your own pace as you review the cases in Chapters 4 through 8 and

EXHIBIT 3.2 CPM Executive Education Implementation Plan

New Co.–Integrated CPM Executive Education Plan by Month

Principle, Course No., Name	1	2	3	4	5	6	7	8	9	10	11	12	13	14	15	16	17	18
1.1 Establish CPM Office	■																	
2.1 Formulate Strategy		■																
2.2 Prepare Strategic Plan			■															
3.1 Build Strategy Map and BSC				■														
3.2 Align and Motive with BSC						■			■		■				■		■	■
3.3 Manage Using BSC								■		■		■				■		■
4.2 Improve Using Six Sigma #1													■		■			■
4.2 Improve Using Six Sigma #2												■			■	■		■
4.3 Improve Using 10 Step #1										■			■					
4.4 Improve Using 10 Step #2												■			■		■	■
4.5 Improve Customer Focus											■				■		■	■
5.1 Leverage Knowledge												■			■			■

permit the award-winning companies to describe how their CPM processes function to drive outstanding results.

Notice the timeline or forward calendar for the CPM officer's planning horizon is two to three years in scope for deployment and ongoing management of the CPM core processes. Here we borrow the metaphor of a quarterback facilitating the design and rollout of the plays from a playbook, in effect integrating and choreographing the CPM processes.

CPM Core Process Learning Model

Exhibit 3.2 provides a roadmap of how we deployed the Five Keys at Crown Castle International sequentially over the period of the first year. The Five Keys research and best practices have been converted into 12 two-day management courses modeled after the award winners. This model has since been adopted by numerous companies to systematically adopt the best practices to accelerate results. However, not all companies have adopted these principles, processes, and best practices in sequential order. Some have pursued them concurrently, and others have built them based on business needs and to enable the strategic plan.

Principle 1: Establish and Deploy a CPM Office and Officer

The optimal first step to becoming a high-performing CPM enterprise is deploying *Principle 1: Establish and deploy a CPM office and officer* for your enterprise. The CPM office and officer are at the center of the five CPM principles and facilitate deploying the remaining four principles. Not all winners have started here; however, they all, at some point, came to the realization that this is a dedicated role. Principle 1 consists of several best practice elements, shown next.

Core Best Practices (recognized and used by all case companies)

- **Executive sponsorship.** CEO actively sponsors the CPM office and CPM projects for a sustained period and with the right visibility to enable maturity.
- **Organizational level and reporting relationship.** CPM office executive reports to the CEO.
- **CPM office staff.** Small senior team experienced in change programs.

(Continued)

- **Leadership, influence factors.** Able to organize cross-organizational, virtual teams to drive results in all CPM methods.
- **Ownership of CPM processes and methods.** The office owns or substantially influences the portfolio and methods of CPM processes enterprisewide.
- **CPM, industry, and company knowledge.** CPM team possesses deep expertise in strategic planning, initiative management, BSC, and knowledge management. One or more team members have deep industry- and company-specific knowledge to help guide resolution of project issues.
- **Collaborative maturity.** Experienced in working horizontally and vertically through the organization.
- **Ability to learn.** Open to new ideas, methods, and approaches; able to streamline, integrate, and adapt methods; able to think concurrently.

Innovative Best Practices: Selected Examples

- CCM's CPM office works effectively across a complex, multiple-entity enterprise including Cargill Corporate, Cargill's segment operations, and multiple geographies in a complex matrix organization.
- PSE&G has demonstrated its CPM industry leadership with top decile results in several utility benchmarks and hosted numerous visits from other companies to showcase the CPM office organization and its processes.
- Lockheed Martin IS&GS optimizes the ROI of its CPM office by minimizing the number of full-time personnel.
- Sharp HealthCare has formalized an expanded, formalized performance improvement infrastructure consisting of Champions, Change Agents, Executive Steering Committee, and CEO council.

Principle 2: Refresh and Communicate Strategy

Principle 2, Refresh and Communicate Strategy, links back to the four barriers and ability to close the change gap. Most enterprises fail to effectively translate their strategies to operations and communicate their strategies to employees. We learned earlier that most employees are neither conversant with nor comprehend their role in driving the organization's strategy. Principle 2 consists of several best practice elements shown next.

Core Best Practices (recognized and used by all case companies)

- **Strategic planning.** Leverage the strategic planning process as either owner or partner to understand changing market conditions including competitor, supplier, rival, and potential entrants and substitutes in the marketplace.
- **Core and adjacent products and services.** Define and determine core and adjacent products and services to focus on highest probabilities for success.
- **Strategic plan.** Produce a comprehensive strategic plan.
- **Strategy mapping.** Develop corporate- and department-level strategy maps containing objectives along four perspectives including financial, customer/constituent, process, and people. Observe strategy map design parameters of 20 to 25 objectives.
- **Link strategic planning and budgeting processes.** Link strategic planning to the budgeting process, partner, and budgeting with finance to provide for a seamless continuum.
- **Communications plan.** Communicate strategy throughout the organization using a comprehensive communications plan.

Innovative Best Practices: Selected Examples

- CCM strategic planning process sources innovative ideas from employees, referred to as Ideas to Innovation (i2i), customers, expert panels, suppliers, and other stakeholders. Innovative product ideas, service ideas, operation ideas, or business model ideas must survive each step of Strategic Review (SR) analysis.
- City of Coral Springs strategic planning process involves customers enabling key requirements, secured from over 15 customer input sources, to be included in strategic goals, KIOs, and cascaded down through the organization. This strategic planning process has been recognized as a best practice by numerous third-party organizations such as National Performance Review, American Productivity and Quality Center, Government Finance Officers Association publications, the Florida Institute of Government programs, and Fitch.
- Delta Dental of Kansas has developed and managed the strategic S-curve or profile for the rollout of innovative ancillary products.
- PSE&G, in a strategic business innovation, has pioneered innovation strategy with placement of solar panels on over 200,000 utility poles, an industry first on this scale.

(Continued)

- PSE&G, in a second strategic business innovation, has pioneered strategy of a deepwater wind farm consisting of 96 turbines located 20 miles offshore to reduce visual signature.
- M7 Aerospace uses several separate but integrated analytics (core and adjacency, five forces, and SWOT) to innovate and formulate strategy; this is far more comprehensive and inventive than most companies.

Principle 3: Cascade and Manage Strategy

Principle 3, Cascade and Manage Strategy focuses on translating the outputs from Principle 2 into strategic objectives and measures that are actionable by employees. A key influence on development of these best practices and credit goes to Kaplan and Norton and experiences from leading one of their largest consulting divisions. Principle 3 consists of several best practices shown next.

Core Best Practices (recognized and used by all case companies)

- **Partner with business owners.** Partner with line and staff leadership team members to gain support and influence as partners to help them achieve results.
- **Develop level 1 BSC.** Translate strategy into level 1 BSC measures and measure targets at the highest organizational level.
- **Leverage proven BSC or comparable method.** Observe BSC or comparable design parameters, assigning one to two measures to each strategy map objective.
- **Cascade BSC to lower levels.** Cascade and align level 1 BSC to levels 2, 3, 4, and so on, depending on organizational and accountability structures.
- **Align support services.** Identify and define measures for all support services that align with levels 1 and below.
- **Align teams and individual employees.** Define personal BSCs for teams and/or individuals that align with higher-level and support services Balanced Scorecards.
- **Link compensation.** Align rewards, recognition, and compensation programs to the Balanced Scorecard.

- **Manage using measures.** Manage BSC meetings to address the appropriate mix of strategic and operational issues; link these issues with Principle 4: Business Improvement.
- **Automate measurement.** Implement CPM software to manage BSC program with links to other principles.

Innovative Best Practices: Selected Examples

- CCM Senior Leadership Team introduced the Performance Measure Alignment Matrix to identify measures that must appear on business plans produced during the annual business planning process. For example, to promote the *Be Innovative Value*, the team decided that every business plan must include the metric, implemented idea savings.
- The City of Coral Springs has incentive programs to encourage initiative and innovation; these include the Instant Employee Recognition Program, the Project and Performance Bonus Program, and the Gain Sharing Program.
- The City of Coral Springs has established process owners and process measure metrics (cycle time, cost, customer satisfaction) to identify variation and to *initiate innovation*. In process measures, for instance, EMS response times are tracked daily to determine if there is unacceptable variation, and to take corrective action.
- Delta Dental of Kansas draws from numerous external and inventive data sources to secure benchmark and competitive information to inform its BSC results.
- Lockheed Martin IS&GS has embedded innovation into its BSC objectives and measures: P9 is Champion solutions for citizen-to-government interaction, which is measured by P9.1, the number of customer solution awards.
- M7 Aerospace utilizes an innovative shared or virtual BSC to link and align multiple business units and supporting departments to deliver on customer requirements.

Principle 4: Improve Performance

Principle 4, Improve Performance, focuses on improving customer and competitor intelligence and business improvement processes. Key influences on this section were my training and facilitation of GE Six Sigma Black Belt teams; collaboration with Motorola University, the pioneers of six sigma;

and exposure and use of quality methods such as CI 10 Step, 5S, Priority Action Matrices, and PDCA. In concert with Principle 3, if your BSC indicates underperformance, then it would be incumbent upon you to launch an initiative to improve performance. Principle 4 consists of several best practices shown next.

Core Best Practices (recognized and used by all case companies)

- **Prioritize improvement projects.** Identify and prioritize strategic and operational initiatives projects to improve organization's performance along financial, customer or constituent, process, and people dimensions.
- **Leverage customer facing processes.** Develop and exercise customer and constituent facing processes to understand and recalibrate processes around changing customer needs. Gather customer and competitor intelligence using regular customer surveys, focus groups, call centers, and related methods and approaches. Leverage process improvement methods.
- **Leverage process improvement methods.** Design and maintain ongoing process improvement methods and problem solving to identify and eliminate root causes of issues.
- **Realize value from benchmarking.** Leverage benchmarking and comparative methods to identify and regularly improve core and support processes.
- **Create a performance culture.** Create a virtual community of practitioners to coordinate initiative completion.

Innovative Best Practices: Selected Examples

- Be Innovative is a CCM Value. CCM utilizes a formal approach, Ideas to Innovation (i2i), to systematically capture and track innovative ideas relating to new discoveries, cost efficiencies, process improvements, and creative ways to meet business goals and objectives. In addition, CCM supports a culture of innovation through quarterly and annual recognition, monthly BSC communications, innovation website, sponsoring location innovation champions, and a business unit innovation team.
- CCM has formalized innovation in its key work process, "Manage Idea & Concept Generation," where CCM utilized an external

resource to help create the innovation process and to provide it with a database for tracking innovative ideas before bringing this capability in-house. The i2i process supports CCM's Values of Be Innovative and Promote Collaboration.

- The City of Coral Springs goes beyond traditional training on performance improvement methods to encourage innovation. Its work system design is based on four principles that support city values and encourage innovation. They are customer focus, empowerment, continuous improvement, and team-based operations.
- Poudre Valley Health System starts building relationships with patients and other customers long before they come to the organization seeking services and continues throughout their care and after their discharge.
- PSE&G has innovated performance management in the utility and gas industries and is the ongoing benchmarking and best practices clearinghouse for multiple participating companies.

Principle 5: Manage and Leverage Knowledge

Principle 5, Manage and Leverage Knowledge, focuses on capturing and reusing enterprisewide intellectual property to leverage the organization's best minds, best practices, and innovations. As enterprises increasingly rely on knowledge workers, it is essential to have core knowledge management (KM) processes embedded in the organization to capture and propagate best-in-class and world-class results. Key influences for development of this section were my Crown KM program, but particularly the KM expertise shared selflessly by Carla O'Dell, president of APQC, and her talented KM team. In concert with Principle 3, if your BSC informs you of a location that performs in the top quartile or decile, then it is advantageous to understand, document, and share this location's winning formula with all locations. Principle 5 best practices are shown next.

Core Best Practices (recognized and used by all case companies)

- **Develop KM processes.** Establish and leverage best practice identification, gathering, and sharing processes and technology solutions.
- **Leverage technology.** Partner with the information technology function to launch and maintain KMS.

(Continued)

- **Develop expert locater systems.** Design and use expert locater systems to capture systems employee skills inventory within the enterprise to accelerate problem solving in Principle 4 and to optimize human capital.
- **Link KM with improved process performance.** Link best practice or knowledge management processes with Principle 4 processes to capture solutions and innovations.
- **Share best practices.** Share best practices with strategic planning processes to better understand core competencies and possible strategic advantages.
- **Maintain a virtual KM Network.** Establish and maintain virtual network of KM experts throughout the enterprise to optimize results.

Innovative Best Practices: Selected Examples

- CCM, in a more sophisticated, expanded model than most award-winning companies, transfers relevant knowledge and best practices from and to not only customers but also suppliers and partners.
- CCM leverages numerous forum and approaches to best practice sharing including Centers of Expertise (COEs), PDGs, cross-functional improvement teams *for innovation*. For instance, Mill-Feed PDG team works with Cargill Sweeteners Europe to collect, transfer, and share best practices for mill and feed operations for 31 worldwide mills. Examples of COEs include Cargill IT, CFIS IT, Energy Risk Management, Maintenance and Reliability, and Corporate Procurement.
- City of Coral Springs Process Improvement teams not only drive organizational innovation, but also share nationally (and win awards). The emergency medical response process improvement team was the state's team showcase winner and placed fourth overall in the nation in 1998. The Citation System Improvement Team was the state's team showcase winner in 2005 and competed in the nationals in May 2006.
- DDKS' employee I.D.E.A. program fosters innovation by providing an avenue for employees to share ideas, suggestions, and feedback regarding the organization, tied to the company's strategy map.
- Poudre Valley Health System links its knowledge, *innovation* best practice sharing to its competency, leadership, and development models.
- PSE&G pioneered best practice sharing among over 20 gas and 20 electric companies.

Principle 1: Establish and Deploy a CPM Office and Officer

The world is full of willing people, some willing to work, the rest willing to let them.

—Robert Frost

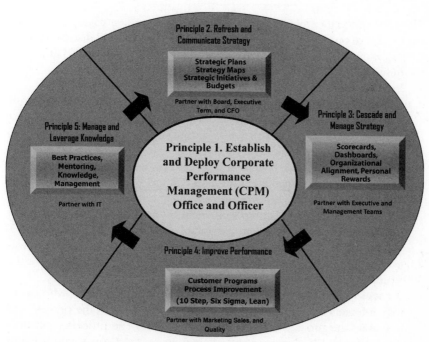

© Copyright 2010, Bob Paladino Associates LLC.

The first step to becoming a high-performing CPM enterprise is *Principle 1: Establish and deploy a CPM office and officer* for your enterprise. The CPM office and officer are at the center of the five CPM principles and facilitate deploying the remaining four principles. Not all award winners have started here; however, they all, at some point, came to the realization that this is a dedicated role. In a few cases we have seen a distributed but integrated adaptation of this role where executive team collaboration has been very successful. Your company may adopt a different title, so look beyond your title to the substance of the role. Principle 1 consists of several best practice elements.

Careful research of the cases in this book reveals they follow a discernible set of core CPM processes organized within the Five Key Principles. These CPM processes were arrayed in Exhibit 3.1 to provide strategic context and a working framework to assist you in your organization. Note that *Principle 1, Establish and Deploy CPM Office and Officer*, consists of four CPM processes, though some organizations have expanded beyond these core processes.

Manage CPM Centers of Excellence Process Example

The CPM office members play one or more of three key roles in executing the CPM core processes with the fourth, participants. We will discuss *Manage CPM Centers of Excellence Process* roles my CPM office deployed at award-winning Crown Castle International to illustrate:

- **Process Sponsor.** The sponsor is typically the most senior executive accountable for the process outcomes and for overseeing the process owner. As the CPM officer, I was the process sponsor for the Manage CPM Centers of Excellence Process.
- **Process Owner.** The owner is typically the senior leader accountable to the sponsor for managing the process and is usually a process subject matter expert. The process owners for Manage CPM Centers of Excellence Process at Crown were each of my direct reports, who were respective experts at CPM competencies. For instance, the VP for global performance maintained the six sigma program; one small aspect was to maintain his center of expertise (COE) in SharePoint Services for the company globally.
- **Process Facilitator.** The facilitator is typically the individual who day to day interacts directly with process participants to drive the process and integrate the process with other key processes. The process facilitators for Manage CPM Centers of Excellence Process at Crown were each of my direct reports, who facilitated the design, training, and rollout of their

functional competencies. For instance, the VP for global performance maintained the six sigma COE in SharePoint Services for the company globally.

■ **Process Participant.** The process participants are typically subject matter experts, those who will be accountable for the process outcomes and/or are the recipients of the process outcomes. The process participants for Manage CPM Centers of Excellence Process were the entire employee base at large. At one point or another all employees interacted with CPM office personnel.

Prior to turning our attention toward the in-depth cases, let us review the core best practices practiced by the award-winning companies in this book. See each case that follows for their innovative new best practice, so you can appreciate the context and relevance of them to their organizations.

Principle 1: Establish and Deploy a CPM Office and Officer Core Best Practices

■ **Executive sponsorship.** CEO actively sponsors CPM office and CPM projects for a sustained period and with the right visibility to enable maturity.

■ **Organizational level and reporting relationship.** CPM office executive reports to the CEO.

■ **CPM office staff.** Small senior team experienced in change programs.

■ **Leadership, influence factors.** Able to organize cross-organizational, virtual teams to drive results in all CPM methods.

■ **Ownership of CPM processes and methods.** The office owns or substantially influences the portfolio and methods of CPM processes enterprisewide.

■ **CPM, industry, and company knowledge.** CPM team possesses deep expertise in strategic planning, initiative management, BSC, and knowledge management. One or more team members have deep industry- and company-specific knowledge to help guide resolution of project issues.

■ **Collaborative maturity.** Experienced in working horizontally and vertically through the organization.

■ **Ability to learn.** Open to new ideas, methods, and approaches; able to streamline, integrate, and adapt methods; able to think concurrently.

Award-Winning Case Organizations: Meet the Innovators

Cargill Corn Milling North America: Best Practice Case

Cargill Corn Milling North America (CCM), headquartered in Minneapolis, Minnesota, is a manufacturer of value-added corn- and sugar-based products serving the food, feed, and fermentation market segments. CCM is a business unit of Cargill, Incorporated, a privately held international provider of agricultural, food, and risk management products and services. Cargill entered the corn milling business in 1967 with the acquisition of a small plant located in Cedar Rapids, Iowa. Over the past four decades, CCM has grown by focusing on its customers, developing its employees, and expanding its product portfolio into more value-added products. Plants were built in Dayton, Ohio; Memphis, Tennessee; Eddyville, Iowa; Blair, Nebraska; and Dalhart, Texas. CCM later leased the Wahpeton, North Dakota plant. Cargill's Dry Corn Ingredient business unit joined CCM as a product line, adding plants in Indianapolis, Indiana, and Paris, Illinois. This growth has increased CCM complexity and diversity while enhancing its ability to provide distinctive value and become the partner of choice for its customers.

CCM delivers over 60 products to over 3,000 customers. Product delivery mechanisms include pipeline connections with co-located customers, and bulk truck, rail, and barge shipments. CCM production locations and terminals load over one thousand product shipments each day. Services provided to customers include technical service, utilities and administration service, and third-party marketing and sales services. Technical service includes problem solving and application development. Utilities and administration support are provided for co-located customers. Marketing and sales services are provided for sugar producers and ethanol producers, referred to as marketing alliances. These services are marketed separately to leverage production capacity and the distribution network to help these producers find the best markets.

The corn milling process is primarily a continuous process consisting of:

- **Dry Corn Grinding:** Preparing dry corn for sizing.
- **Wet Corn Separation:** Separating corn into four basic components: germ, feed, meal, and starch.
- **Conversion:** Continuous and batch processes used to convert starch slurry into dextrose and fructose.
- **Refining:** Processes used to clean and purify product prior to shipping.
- **Fermentation:** Enzymatic transformation of organic compounds by microorganisms.

Technologically advanced distributed control systems are used to operate and troubleshoot the equipment and processes at all CCM facilities.

CCM's corporate functions, plants, and terminals are networked together. CCM employees interface daily with computer hardware and software systems to control the production and distribution processes or to access data and information required to perform their work. Significant equipment used in production facilities includes processing and storage tanks, screening and sizing equipment, grind mills, high-pressure steam boilers, centrifuges, rotary vacuum filters, steam tube dryers, flash dryers, enzyme reactors, isomerization columns, demineralization columns, carbon columns, check filters, pumps, evaporators, weigh scales, lab and process instrumentation, fermenters, and sterilizers. Equipment used in terminals includes storage tanks, product load and unload pumps, weigh scales, and lab equipment.

EXECUTIVE VIEWS ON PERFORMANCE MANAGEMENT AND IMPROVEMENT

At Cargill, we challenge ourselves every day to be leaders in our industries and provide the highest quality service and products to our customers. We challenge ourselves to maintain safe, process-oriented workplaces, and to continuously measure our success and to never stop learning.

These are some of the same principles that the examiners for the Malcolm Baldrige National Quality Award look for each year as they select the organizations that will receive the highest presidential honor for innovation and performance excellence.

Alan Willits, Cargill Corn Milling President

Receiving the Malcolm Baldrige National Quality Award is the culmination of over 40 years of continuous improvement. This was achieved through the hard work of thousands of current and former Corn Milling employees.

Ron Fiala, Process Improvement Manager,
Cargill Corn Milling North America

ORGANIZATION CCM is part of the Cargill Food Ingredients and Systems (FIS) platform. The FIS platform produces a broad spectrum of ingredients, from core ingredients to specialty ingredients to ingredient systems to finished food systems. The CCM president leads the Corn Milling Senior Leadership Team (SLT) and the Senior Management Team (SMT). The SLT is a group of senior CCM leaders responsible for setting CCM strategic direction and policy. The SMT is a larger group, which includes the SLT, product line leaders, functional area leaders, commercial managers, and facility managers. The SMT is responsible for business unit communication, resource allocation, and engagement. CCM utilizes a product line structure and matrix management approach to leverage knowledge within common functions.

CCM leadership teams in coordination with the Cargill Enterprise Development Team (EDT) use several integrated CPM processes to improve business performance including the following:

- SLT uses the CCM Leadership System to establish the vision and values, communicate organizational performance and governance, define direction, and deploy strategy and plans.
- Systematic Strategic Review (SR) and Annual Business Planning (ABP) processes are used to set the strategic direction and identify tactical actions. These processes, in turn, result in formation of collaborative strategic teams. For instance, Design New Strategy may have up to five subteams: Steering, Food, Feed, Fermentation, and Operation Excellence teams.
- Monthly business performance review meetings analyze CCM BSC results and identify opportunities for improvement.
- Business Excellence, Cargill's organizational framework for continuous improvement, is used to create and sustain competitive advantage based on the Malcolm Baldrige National Quality Award model.

CCM SLT owns the SR process and utilizes the Enterprise Development Team (EDT) to lead the process. The EDT is a separate department of the Cargill Food Ingredient and Systems platform consisting of employees with diverse backgrounds and experiences.

CCM does not have one specific person or a specific department in charge of CPM. Instead this responsibility is shared across the SLT. CCM has adopted what is being referred to as a distributed model, or virtual CPM model. In particular, as a business unit within Cargill, corporate provides them with additional CPM resources such as EDT and COEs. They can utilize these functions to enhance their strategy development processes, their ability to identify and share best practices, and their ability to obtain comparable data. CCM's key CPM processes are more fully described in subsequent chapters.

CORE AND INNOVATIVE BEST PRACTICES   CCM exercises the core best practices and has advanced knowledge in this area with a new, innovative best practice.

Principle 1: Establish and Deploy a CPM Office and Officer

(Note: These are normative titles to simplify the discussion, yours may vary.)

- **Executive sponsorship.** President actively sponsors CPM function; however, distributes ownership of key CPM processes across the senior leadership team.
- **Organizational level and reporting relationship.** CPM SLT members report to the CCM president.
- **CPM office staff.** Small senior team experienced in change programs.
- **Leadership, influence factors.** Able to organize cross-organizational, virtual teams to drive results in all CPM methods.
- **Ownership of CPM processes and methods.** The office owns or substantially influences the portfolio and methods of CPM processes enterprisewide.
- **CPM, industry, and company knowledge.** CPM team possesses deep expertise in strategic planning; initiative management; BSCs; best practices; and knowledge management. One or more team members have deep industry- and company-specific knowledge to help guide resolution of project issues.
- **Collaborative maturity.** Experienced in working horizontally and vertically through the organization.
- **Ability to learn.** Open to new ideas, methods, and approaches; able to streamline, integrate, and adapt methods; able to think concurrently.
- **Innovative Best Practice.** CCM's CPM function works effectively across a complex, multiple entity enterprise including Cargill Corporate (EDT), Cargill's segment operations, and multiple geographies in a complex matrix organization.

City of Coral Springs: Best Practice Case

Coral Springs, Florida, is a centrally planned community incorporated in July 1963. The city is 23.93 square miles with 54 percent of the land designated as residential land use. Approximately 131,257 residents call Coral Springs home, making it the fourth largest city in Broward County and the 13th largest in the state of Florida. There are a wide range of housing types, as well as retail and commercial properties, and one square mile designated as industrial. Unlike most South Florida cities, Coral Springs, whose population has a median age of 36.2 years, is a city of young families; 29 percent of the population is under 18 years old.

The city delivers a broad array of products and services through seven operating departments, seven support departments, and four "wholly-owned" subsidiaries. Products and services are delivered primarily through City of Coral Springs employees, or alternatively, through carefully selected suppliers or partners. Products and services delivered by city employees have two distinguishing characteristics. First, departments are very flat; there is a short chain of command. This promotes short cycle-times and employee empowerment. Second, the focus is on the customer, which means accessible services provided by pleasant, helpful staff. Products and services delivered through suppliers and partners are managed through contracts with specific performance standards.

EXECUTIVE VIEWS ON CORPORATE PERFORMANCE MANAGEMENT

Corporate performance management has provided the City of Coral Springs with a mechanism to improve our processes and thereby the results that we provide to our residents and business community.

Susan Grant

The Budget and Strategic Planning manager leads the Corporate Performance Management division of the Department of Financial Services, which is responsible for the following core processes:

- **CPM processes (e.g., strategic planning, performance improvement/measurement system, major initiatives, six step quality).** The Budget and Strategic Planning division is charged with developing the bi-annual strategic plan and the annual business plan and budget. In addition, the division oversees performance measurement as well as benchmarking projects. Major initiatives are implemented by relevant departments, and process improvement initiatives are coordinated by Human Resources.
- **Staffing (number, skills).** Budget and Strategic Planning manager, two senior financial analysts; one financial analyst. In addition to analytical skills, must be able to understand department operations and be able to communicate and relate to department personnel.
- **How it operates.** This function may collaborate with other functions to ensure the foregoing processes are integrated. Collaboration and cooperation with other departments is essential in the preparation of the strategic plan, business plan, and budget as well as progress reporting on measures and initiatives.

EXECUTIVE TEAM The CPM function serves internal business leaders with the foregoing services. The primary internal customers include the following members of the executive and leadership team:

- Michael S. Levinson, City Manager
- Ellen Liston, Deputy City Manager
- Erdal Donmez, Deputy City Manager

CORE AND INNOVATIVE BEST PRACTICES City of Coral Springs exercises the core best practices shown next.

Principle 1: Establish and Deploy a CPM Office and Officer

- **Executive sponsorship.** CEO actively sponsors the CPM office and CPM projects for a sustained period and with the right visibility to enable maturity.
- **Organizational level and reporting relationship.** CPM office executive reports to the CEO. Budget and Strategic Planning manager reports to a deputy city manager.
- **CPM office staff.** Small senior team experienced in change programs.
- **Leadership, influence factors.** Able to organize cross-organizational, virtual teams to drive results in all CPM methods.
- **Ownership of CPM processes and methods.** The office owns or substantially influences the portfolio and methods of CPM processes enterprisewide.
- **CPM, industry, and company knowledge.** CPM team possesses deep expertise in strategic planning, initiative management, BSC, and knowledge management. One or more team members have deep industry- and company-specific knowledge to help guide resolution of project issues.
- **Collaborative maturity.** Experienced in working horizontally and vertically through the organization.
- **Ability to learn.** Open to new ideas, methods, and approaches; able to streamline, integrate, and adapt methods; able to think concurrently.

Delta Dental of Kansas: Best Practice Case

Delta Dental of Kansas, Inc. (DDKS) is a not-for-profit dental service corporation that provides underwriting and administration of dental benefits to employer groups, associations, and unions whose headquarters are in

Kansas. Founded in 1972, Delta Dental of Kansas is the largest dental benefits provider in the state, serving more than 850,000 enrollees. Delta Dental of Kansas' corporate headquarters is in Wichita, Kansas, and the company maintains sales offices in Overland Park and Topeka. Presently, the company employs 110 people. DDKS is a member of Delta Dental Plans Association, a system of nationwide dental service plans that serve more than 54 million Americans and represent more than $14 billion in revenue. Currently, Delta Dental Member Companies (MCs) hold about 31 percent of the nation's dental benefits market share.

EXECUTIVE VIEWS ON CPM

Best practice-sharing has been instrumental in exchanging ideas and furthering our organizational development.

The Balanced Scorecard has helped to foster a culture of customer service excellence, which is the hallmark of our reputation in the group dental benefits market. Through implementation of the BSC system, our company has been able to align its strategy and develop a culture where all employees are pulling in the same direction.

We found that rapid implementation and tying scorecard performance to compensation in the early stages helped accelerate acceptance and buy-in at all levels of the organization.

       Linda Brantner, President and CEO (and former COO)

With the balanced scorecard, our employees know what is expected of them and how success will be rewarded if they meet their goals and the company does as well.

The balanced scorecard has become a common language of communication across the organization. Because we also tie our core values into our performance management system, it sends a clear message of the importance of culture along with numeric results.

          Amy Ellison, VP Human Resources

CPM ORGANIZATION Amy Ellison, vice president, Human Resources, leads CPM efforts at DDKS. She reports directly to the president and CEO.

Ms. Ellison operates a virtual CPM office. As department head for Human Resources, she has direct line supervision for the HR team with master's level and bachelor's level HR educational backgrounds, as well as the front desk "first impressions" specialist. The virtual CPM office also encompasses the LT members who lead their own team's performance and share roles in the strategy development and performance management component for the organization. Due to the company's small size, performance management responsibilities are collectively performed.

Ms. Ellison serves a variety of roles in support of the CPM function, including planner and participant in the strategic planning and succession planning processes, executive sponsor for corporate strategic initiatives, as well as champion and facilitator of the balanced scorecard and knowledge management processes throughout DDKS. These key CPM processes are more fully described in subsequent chapters.

CORE AND INNOVATIVE BEST PRACTICES   DDKS exercises the core best practices shown next.

Principle 1: Establish and Deploy a CPM Office and Officer

- **Executive sponsorship.** CEO actively sponsors the CPM office and CPM projects for a sustained period and with the right visibility to enable maturity.
- **Organizational level and reporting relationship.** CPM office executive reports to the CEO.
- **CPM office staff.** Small senior team experienced in change programs.
- **Leadership, influence factors.** Able to organize cross-organizational, virtual teams to drive results in all CPM methods.
- **Ownership of CPM processes and methods.** The office owns or substantially influences the portfolio and methods of CPM processes enterprisewide.
- **CPM, industry, and company knowledge.** CPM team possesses deep expertise in strategic planning, initiative management, BSC, and knowledge management. One or more team members have deep industry- and company-specific knowledge to help guide resolution of project issues.
- **Collaborative maturity.** Experienced in working horizontally and vertically through the organization.
- **Ability to learn.** Open to new ideas, methods, and approaches; able to streamline, integrate, and adapt methods; able to think concurrently.

Lockheed Martin, Information Systems & Global Services: Best Practice Case

Lockheed Martin (LM), headquartered in Bethesda, Maryland, is a global security company led by Robert J. Stevens, chairman, president and chief executive officer, that employs about 146,000 people worldwide and is principally engaged in the research, design, development, manufacture, integration, and sustainment of advanced technology systems, products, and services. The majority of LM's business is with the U.S. Department of Defense (DoD) and federal government agencies, with additional customers including international governments and some commercial sales. LM's operating units are organized into four broad business areas: (1) Aeronautics, includes tactical aircraft, airlift, and aeronautical research and development; (2) Electronic Systems, includes missiles and fire control, naval systems, platform integration, simulation and training and energy programs; (3) Information Systems & Global Services (IS&GS), includes C4I, federal services, government and commercial IT solutions; and (4) Space Systems, includes space launch, commercial satellites, government satellites, and strategic missiles lines of business.

This case study covers efforts within the IS&GS business area, specifically the Mission Services business unit that, due to a significant reorganization, evolved into the IS&GS-Civil product line (i.e., business unit) between 2008 and 2009. IS&GS-Civil employs approximately 14,000 of the men and women of LM with annual sales projected to exceed $4 billion in 2010. Led by president Ken Asbury, IS&GS-Civil's strategy is "Complete Citizen Services" reflecting a focus on customers serving citizens in areas such as energy, health care, space exploration, transportation, and national security.

Some of the products and services of IS&GS-Civil include:

- Air Traffic Management Systems
- Albania National Airspace Modernization Program
- Automated Flight Service Stations
- Bioastronautics
- Biometrics
- Census Systems
- Contact Center Solutions
- Cyber Security and Enterprise Architecture
- Customer Support Centers
- e-Customs Partnership
- Electronic Records Archive
- Electronic Suspense Tracking and Routing System
- Energy Business Services
- Energy Efficiency Services
- Enterprise IT Solutions
- Environmental Services
- Financial Solutions
- Flight Services
- Host Sustainment Information and Knowledge Solutions

- Human Capital
- Human Spaceflight and Life-Sciences Solutions
- Information Asset Management
- Integrated Space Command and Control
- Integrated Submission and Remittance Processing System
- IRS Solutions
- Managed Services
- Next Generation Identification (NGI)
- Public Health Informatics
- Training Solutions
- Transportation Worker Identification Credential
- Wireless and Mobile Computing

It is important to note that as of December 2009 LM as a corporation had not adopted the BSC framework as its primary mechanism to describe and communicate strategy. IS&GS-Civil is the only business unit that has adopted it in this fashion, though the use of the BSC model is promoted and leveraged in many ways across the corporation, for example, the Information Technology strategy and alignment in the Space Systems business area of LM.

EXECUTIVE VIEWS ON CORPORATE PERFORMANCE MANAGEMENT

It is very important that our strategy is clearly articulated, our leadership team commits to it enthusiastically, and our employees have a solid understanding of both its concepts and their roles in making it a reality. Our experience has shown us that through an effective use of tools like the BSC and strategy management practices we can make that happen.
Ken Asbury, IS&GS-Civil, President

As we rolled out the Balanced Scorecard we began to see a remarkable improvement in "team first" behavior among our LMMS president's executive leadership team.
Ken Carlsen, IS&GS-Civil, Director,
Strategy Management, U.S. Navy Admiral (ret.)

In describing the key characteristics of full spectrum leaders at LM, president and CEO Bob Stevens stated that ". . .great leaders deliver results." They turn strategy into reality. They keep their focus on the goal, and don't quit when the going gets tough. Because when we say "We never forget who we're working for" at LM, we mean it. Helping customers meet their most challenging goals is the core of our corporate vision.
Robert J. Stevens, LM Chairman,
President and Chief Executive Officer, Director

Our strategy management efforts in LM IS&GS-Civil are based on the simple yet powerful notion that when leaders engage employees in the organization's strategy—performance will improve.

Josh Stalker, Sr. Manager, LM IS&GS-Civil, Strategy Management

CPM ORGANIZATION The IS&GS-Civil Strategy Management organization, equivalent in nature to the concept of a Corporate Performance Management office, is responsible for the performance management processes associated with advancing the organization's strategy and reports directly to the business unit president, Ken Asbury. The leadership of the Strategy Management organization consists of Ken Carlsen, director, a retired U.S. Navy rear admiral, who leads the organization, and Joshua Stalker, senior manager, the subject matter expert and manager of the strategy management processes. Both Ken and Josh are full-time employees and have one additional full-time strategic planner, Tanya Price, as part of their team. At the part-time level, some key team members that helped shape the overall efforts included representatives from Finance (e.g., Brenda Hollingsworth), Communications (Abbie Anderson, Beth Matthews, Liz Morse, Lisa Tucker), and Lean Six Sigma (e.g., Keith Earle). Additionally, each line of business (e.g., Transportation, Energy, etc.) and functional organization (e.g., Human Resources) generally provides one point of contact that acts as the primary interface for strategy management for their organization. These lines of business and functional representatives comprise the "Core Team" and their annual part-time support is approximately a 10 percent commitment. This structure illustrates the company's focus on being lean and minimizes the time commitment of the lines of business and functions.

The CPM philosophy is to minimize the number of full-time personnel (three to five) in the CPM office and use a part-time matrix approach, similar to collateral duty, for additional support throughout the organization. The Strategy Management organization believes this is important to demonstrate to the business that the organization is focused on delivering value versus growing its size. These connections, via the matrix support relationships, are important because they help keep costs down, ROI high, and maintain a closer connection to front-line challenges and opportunities; that is, it helps minimize the silo effect. These matrix personnel are referred to as the "Core Team" and generally pursue one representative per department/line of business who is funded by that organization. The organization manages its processes and engagement so that the core team can plan on their role requiring approximately 10 percent of their time. This approach reflects a focus on the high-value elements of strategy management processes (i.e., the 80/20 rule).

The strategy management processes utilized in IS&GS-Civil are based on the use of the tools and concepts such as the Balanced Scorecard and strategy-focused organization (e.g., Robert S. Kaplan and David P. Norton), corporate performance management (e.g., Bob Paladino), change management (e.g., John Kotter), and others key to motivating and influencing people to act upon organizational priorities. Several of the processes managed include strategy development (e.g., creation of strategy maps and Balanced Scorecards), organizational alignment (e.g., cascading aligned Balanced Scorecards), communications planning (e.g., messaging campaigns and materials), quarterly strategy reviews, leadership coaching on strategy practices, initiative management and portfolio alignment (e.g., IT investments, Lean Six Sigma events), and employee engagement.

EXECUTIVE TEAM CPM direct and virtual members provide their service to all IS&GS Civil lines of business including energy, health care, space exploration, transportation, and national security, consisting of 14,000 employees.

CORE AND INNOVATIVE BEST PRACTICES IS&GS exercises the core best practices and has advanced knowledge in this area with a new, innovative best practice.

Principle 1: Establish and Deploy a CPM Office and Officer

- **Executive sponsorship.** CEO actively sponsors the CPM office and CPM projects for a sustained period and with the right visibility to enable maturity.
- **Organizational level and reporting relationship.** CPM office executive reports to the CEO.
- **CPM office staff.** Small senior team experienced in change programs.
- **Leadership, influence factors.** Able to organize cross-organizational, virtual teams to drive results in all CPM methods.
- **Ownership of CPM processes and methods.** The office owns or substantially influences the portfolio and methods of CPM processes enterprisewide.
- **CPM, industry, and company knowledge.** CPM team possesses deep expertise in strategic planning, initiative management, BSC, and knowledge management. One or more team members have deep industry- and company-specific knowledge to help guide resolution of project issues.

- **Collaborative maturity.** Experienced in working horizontally and vertically through the organization.
- **Ability to learn.** Open to new ideas, methods, and approaches; able to streamline, integrate, and adapt methods; able to think concurrently.
- **Innovative Best Practice.** LM IS&GS philosophy is to realize high ROI on its CPM function by keeping it small with both centralized and virtual team members to serve its 14,000-employee organization.

M7 Aerospace: Best Practice Case

Ted B. Miller, founder and chairman of M7 Aerospace, has a long history of corporate successes. As a visionary, he invented the cell tower industry in the mid-1990s and founded and brought to market the global leader Crown Castle International, a case in *Five Key Principles of Corporate Performance Management*.[1] Crown went on to win three very prestigious recognitions: the global Balanced Scorecard (BSC) Hall of Fame Award, the American Productivity and Quality Center (APQC) Best Practice Partner Award, and the *Wall Street Journal's* "Top 20 Most Improved in Shareholder Value Ranking" from over 4,000 publicly traded companies. The stock price went from $1 to over $30. Crown is the number one case study as ranked by Harvard Business School Publishing. Major milestones in M7 Aerospace's evolution and emergence as an award-winning player in the multiple dimensions of the aerospace and defense industries are shown next. As chief performance officer (CPM officer) of Crown Castle International, it was my honor to work for Mr. Miller and to collaborate with the Crown leadership team to collectively earn the prestigious awards noted. That experience inspired my first book and kindled the passion to try to advance the knowledge in this field of study to this day.

- April 2003: M7 Aerospace begins business. Employment totals 175.
- October 2003: Aero Structures Manufacturing fabricates first Metro parts.
- November 2003: M7 becomes certified supplier to Lockheed Martin.
- January 2004: M7 team is awarded $400 million C-20 contract.
- July 2004: M7 becomes a certified supplier to Northrop Grumman.
- July 2004: M7 contracts with FedEx for 30 ATR Aircraft cargo conversions.
- February 2005: M7 awarded $300 million army contract.
- April 2005: M7 named a certified supplier to Boeing.

- June 2005: M7 teams with Augusta Westland to build doors for US101 helicopter.
- May 2006: Delivered 40th ATR cargo conversion.
- July 2006: M7 receives first Erickson Air Crane airframe section for over-haul.
- March 2007: M7 receives first manufacturing order from Spirit Aerosystems.
- April 2007: M7 receives first Sikorsky helicopter manufacturing order.
- March 2008: KC-135 Stratotanker Spoilers contract.
- April 2008: Army CMWS program.
- July 2008: Army Pro-Line Glass Cockpit Avionics program.
- November 2008: M7 wins EISM award for third year in a row.
- October 2009: M7 wins new Army CLS contract.
- June 2009: M7 wins Northrop Grumman Supplier of the Year Award.
- July 2009: M7 wins first contract with Bell Helicopter.
- November 2009: M7 wins Northrop Grumman World Class Team Supplier Award.

EXECUTIVE VIEWS ON CORPORATE PERFORMANCE MANAGEMENT

CPM has literally transformed M7 from a start-up organization that was operating in business unit silos with limited communication among the management team into an integrated company with a full under-standing of cause and effect across the entire organization. Aiding the management team in fully understanding and reviewing the key aspects of its business on a continual basis is essential for any high-performance organization.

Kevin Brown, President and Chief Executive Officer

The whole strategic evaluation process has been a great opportunity to get some of our new personnel's ideas and strategies on the table as well as rekindle our legacy employees' thoughts and perspectives. The BSC has given us a consistent perspective of how other departments are doing and how their capabilities could potentially assist upcoming ventures.

Steve Leland, Vice President, General Manager, Government Programs

The BSC has allowed us to do the analysis necessary to put the proper resources in place to improve our business.

Mark Provost, Director, Engineering

The Balanced Scorecard has been instrumental in driving M7 Aerospace toward best in class processes and procedures.

Brian Dannewitz, VP Supply
Chain Management and Spares Sales

CPM ORGANIZATION   M7 established a CPM function in January 2005 with Kevin Brown, then CFO, focused on facilitating the development of BSCs for corporate, 10 level 2 business units, and support units. Since then, Mr. Brown has been steadily promoted through the executive ranks to CEO and has expanded the performance function with additional competencies focused on strategic planning, budgeting, quality, customer surveying, rewards and recognition, and knowledge management, which are described more completely in the following chapters. He also has formed a virtual team consisting of several key functional experts throughout the organization:

- Andy Plyler, VP Business Development (BD), responsible for strategic planning and client relationship management.
- Todd Lazar, VP Quality Assurance, in charge of all quality programs and customer certifications.
- Phil O'Connor, VP Human Resources and Organizational Development for recruiting, compensation, and recognition.
- Mark Weiler, Controller, focused on Planning and Budgeting, and a BSC Champion.
- Pete Kastis, Manager Financial Planning and Corporate Development, contributes as a BSC Champion.
- Donna Sanchez, Director of Finance/Government Programs, also contributing as a BSC Champion.
- Brian Dannewitz, VP Supply Chain Management and Spare Sales.

Brown has assigned each of his senior leaders to one of three executive committees to facilitate corporate initiatives in the areas of strategy, internal processes, and human development.

Brown states, "The committees were organized to ensure that key corporate initiatives were getting the proper amount of attention and that they were managed by a cross-functional team versus being dictated from a separate department. This is essential to get buy-in from the team and support for the initiatives taking place."

EXECUTIVE TEAM   The CPM office serves internal business leaders with the foregoing services. The primary internal customers include the following members of the executive and leadership team:

- Tom Boyle, Director, Information Technology
- Kevin Brown, President and Chief Executive Officer, M7 Aerospace
- Brian Dannewitz, Vice President, Supply Chain Management & Spare Sales
- Joseph F. Furnish, Vice President, Engineering
- Emory (Buck) Kilgore, Vice President, Manufacturing

- Jim Kirk, Director, Legal and Contracts
- Todd Lazar, Vice President, Quality Assurance
- Steven Leland, Vice President, Government Programs
- Charles Miller, Vice President, Government Business Development
- Philip O'Connor, Vice President, Human Resources and Organizational Development
- Andy Plyler, Vice President, Business Development
- Donna Sanchez, Director of Finance
- Mark Weiler, Controller

CORE AND INNOVATIVE BEST PRACTICES M7 exercises the core best practices and has advanced knowledge in this area with a new, innovative best practice.

Principle 1: Establish and Deploy a CPM Office and Officer

- **Executive sponsorship.** CEO actively sponsors the CPM office (M7 Aerospace does refer to this CPM function with this title) and CPM projects for a sustained period and with the right visibility to enable maturity.
- **Organizational level and reporting relationship.** CPM office executive reports to the CEO.
- **CPM office staff.** Small senior team experienced in change programs.
- **Leadership, influence factors.** Able to organize cross-organizational, virtual teams to drive results in all CPM methods.
- **Ownership of CPM processes and methods.** The office owns or substantially influences the portfolio and methods of CPM processes (e.g., strategic planning, quality, BSC, etc.) enterprisewide.
- **CPM, industry, and company knowledge.** CPM team possesses deep expertise in strategic planning, initiative management, BSC, and knowledge management. One or more team members have deep industry- and company-specific knowledge to help guide resolution of project issues.
- **Collaborative maturity.** Experienced in working horizontally and vertically through the organization.
- **Ability to learn.** Open to new ideas, methods, and approaches; able to streamline, integrate, and adapt methods; able to think concurrently.

> ■ **Innovative Best Practice.** M7 executive team routinely invites their direct reports to CPM meetings that include strategic planning, BSC design and review, and quality project updates to build company CPM bench strength and future leadership team members.

Mueller, Inc.: Best Practice Case

The business began three quarters of a century ago when Walter Mueller opened the Mueller Sheet Metal Company in Ballinger, Texas. Walter built the family business by providing quality water cisterns crafted from sheet metal to local farmers and ranchers. Over the years, his sons, Harold and James, expanded the business to include other sheet metal products related to building construction. In 1984 the Burly Corp., a privately held Texas company owned by the Davenport family, acquired Mueller Supply Company from the Mueller brothers. Since that time Mueller, Inc. has undergone rapid expansion, becoming a leading manufacturer of preengineered metal building and residential metal roofing products. Today, Mueller, Inc. serves the central and southwest U.S. markets from 28 distribution and three manufacturing locations, employing 600 people, while continuing in its heritage of directly serving the end user with quality metal building products. Mueller is a customer-focused company that values growth and the opportunities for advancement it generates. While maintaining a strong financial base, Mueller is committed to continuing its long-term growth rate through satisfied customers.

Mueller's annual revenue was $250 million in 2008.

EXECUTIVE VIEWS ON PERFORMANCE IMPROVEMENT

Mueller is part of a changing landscape in the steel buildings and components marketplace. At the same time, the company is also faced with the task of continued growth and continued success. As part of this challenge Mueller needed to not only dig its heels in more, in terms of staking its ground in the market, but also in terms of hammering out the details of what its strategic plan and goals were going to be. With the Balanced Scorecard (BSC) as our main vehicle of communication, and a strategic plan which outlined what I wanted for my company's future, Mueller set to work at gathering all employees on board. We wanted everything across the entire organization to tie into strategy—from our products, to our customers, to our employees and to our drive. Mueller has been successful to ends we could not have imagined attainable without the guidance and support the BSC has provided throughout our organization. It shows us the direction we are headed, and when we begin to veer off that path. It lets us know of upcoming obstacles, and how best to navigate through them. It lets us know when others are coming close to us on our path so we can best decide how to outmaneuver them. It also lets us know when that path should change direction so as best to reach our end destination. The BSC has been, and continues to be, an incredible journey for all involved. Because of its guidance and direction, Mueller has been, and will continue to be, successful as a leader in its marketplace through use of the BSC.

Bryan Davenport, President, Mueller, Inc.

Everything comes up through my department, and then we configure and set it up the way the user needs it. The standard, for the most part, is set in my department. And we have periodic reviews to assess what's working and what's not. Management buy-in for the project is also critical. In the case of Mueller, the top executive was sold on the idea from the outset, which helped pave the way for its success. The CEO has been a champion of the Balanced Scorecard and management reporting system right from the beginning. The scorecard is really the reflection of his vision. When you have your CEO's approval, it makes it much easier to get things done.

Mark Lack, Planning & Financial Analysis Manager

PERFORMANCE ORGANIZATION Mark Lack, planning and financial analysis manager, leads key CPM efforts and reports to the highest level executive, president and owner Bryan Davenport. He provides services to his colleagues, members of the management team, as follows:

- Bryan Davenport, President
- Phillip Arp, Chief Financial Officer
- Jeff Benton, Corporate HR Manager
- Mike Fry, Marketing Manager
- Greg Efferson, Corporate Purchasing Manager
- Rayome' Soupiset, Corporate Operations Manager
- Evanet Gallant, Corporate IT Manager
- Joel Davenport, General Counsel
- Tommy Hollis, Western Region Sales Manager
- Lynn Becker, Central Region Sales Manager
- Rho Winder, Eastern Region Sales Manager

Mark Lack serves as the head of the CPM office and coordinates and facilitates strategic planning, strategy mapping, planning and budgeting, initiative prioritization, customer satisfaction, BSCs, BSC reporting, alignment, communications, and best practice processes. These CPM processes are more fully described in subsequent chapters.

Mark, along with CEO Bryan Davenport and CFO Phillip Arp, created the first BSC, implemented it, and now manage by using it throughout the company. All company metrics that relate to the strategy (and budget) are evaluated by Mark's office to ensure that they fall within the prescribed strategy and that there is no disconnect between the strategy and its execution. The organizational alignment, strategy development, reviews, and communication are all handled by Mark's office. His office also manages the progress updates of strategic initiatives and integrates strategic priorities with other support functions.

While strategy is discussed at some level every day, Mark arranges executive meetings to discuss strategy formally every quarter. This practice includes updates on strategic advances and a review of initiatives and market comparisons. These quarterly reviews ensure the BSC strategy and performance are top of mind.

Mark manages the CPM processes at Mueller with support of virtual teams from other corporate departments.

CORE AND INNOVATIVE BEST PRACTICES   Mueller exercises the core best practices and has advanced knowledge in this area with a new, innovative best practice.

Principle 1: Establish and Deploy a CPM Office and Officer

- **Executive sponsorship.** President actively sponsors CPM office called Planning & Financial Analysis and CPM projects for a sustained period and with the right visibility to enable maturity.
- **Organizational level and reporting relationship.** CPM office works closely with the president. CPM office experienced in change programs.
- **Leadership, influence factors.** Able to organize cross-organizational, virtual teams to drive results in all CPM methods.
- **Ownership of CPM processes and methods.** The office owns or substantially influences the portfolio and methods of CPM processes enterprisewide.

- **CPM, industry, and company knowledge.** CPM team possesses deep expertise in strategic planning, initiative management, scorecards, and best practice sharing. One or more team members have deep industry- and company-specific knowledge to help guide resolution of project issues.
- **Collaborative maturity.** Experienced in working horizontally and vertically through the organization, with over 30 branch locations, for instance.
- **Ability to learn.** Open to new ideas, methods, and approaches; able to streamline, integrate, and adapt methods; able to think concurrently.
- **Innovative Best Practice.** Mueller's CPM office works effectively across a complex, multiple-entity enterprise as part of a larger system.

NSTAR: Best Practice Case

NSTAR is the largest Massachusetts-based, investor-owned electric and gas utility. The company transmits and delivers electricity and natural gas to 1.4 million customers in eastern and central Massachusetts, including more than one million electric customers in 81 communities and 300,000 gas customers in 51 communities.

KEY EVENTS NSTAR has undergone significant positive change over the past 12 years, beginning with the creation of the company itself. In 1999, Boston Edison, Commonwealth Energy, and Cambridge Electric merged to become NSTAR, streamlining service delivery to customers in the region. The merger came on the heels of a shift in Massachusetts to a deregulated energy market, which required utilities to divest their energy generation business. NSTAR sold all of its power generation facilities, including the first U.S. sale of a nuclear plant, located in Plymouth, Massachusetts.

In 2005, NSTAR worked with state leaders and customer advocates to design an innovative electric rate agreement, freezing delivery rates for seven years. This agreement has provided stable customer prices without sacrificing key investments in NSTAR's systems to ensure improved safety and reliability. One of those critical investments was the construction of a new 345kV transmission line to Boston. Completed in 2008, this line enables NSTAR to bring cheaper power into the region, enhancing capacity and further reducing customer costs.

NSTAR has also stayed ahead of the shifting energy climate, greatly expanding its residential and business energy efficiency programs, as well as offering NSTAR Green, a wind-generated electricity option for customers. In addition, NSTAR received close to $20 million in federal stimulus dollars to support smart grid, smart metering, and renewable energy projects. NSTAR also began efforts in 2009 to make the company greener through a strategic multiyear plan aimed at reducing its carbon footprint.

NSTAR'S BUSINESS MODEL   NSTAR's mission has a simple, yet critical focus: deliver great service to customers. To accomplish that goal, NSTAR has remained committed to the safe, reliable delivery of electricity and gas, obtaining the best rates for customers, and providing them with an array of options to be more energy efficient.

NSTAR's revenues are specifically derived from transmission and distribution rates per kilowatt hour for electricity, or per therm for natural gas. Because of the deregulated energy environment in Massachusetts, NSTAR makes no profit on the actual cost of energy: that cost of power is simply a pass-through to customers under the Massachusetts regulatory model.

NSTAR sees increased profits through load growth from new and existing customers, as well as mining efficiencies in its day to day operations. NSTAR also frequently works to achieve regulatory incentives relative to customer service and operational performance levels.

FOCUSING ON THE FUTURE   NSTAR continues to look at ways to enhance investments in its electric and gas delivery systems, as well as promote renewable options and efficiency programs. NSTAR is currently working with other utilities to construct a transmission line from Canada to Massachusetts, which would bring hydroelectric power to eastern Massachusetts. NSTAR is also moving ahead with its Smart Grid pilot project and plans to triple the dollars spent on energy efficiency programs. All of this work remains part of the company's mission to deliver great service to customers.

EXECUTIVE VIEWS ON CORPORATE PERFORMANCE MANAGEMENT

NSTAR's success in creating a performance-based culture is a result of strong executive vision and support, solid foundation of tools and processes, and a talented performance management team. In my opinion, the key to NSTAR's successful performance-based culture is its talented core team, who crafted the tools and processes needed to support the culture, and guided the leadership team to effectively adopt and use these tools on a daily basis. The core team wisely started with the CEO and senior team to achieve buy-in. With the aid of an online performance management dashboard, the senior team promptly implemented rigorous operational reviews of performance. These reviews are grounded in well-defined and easily presented metrics on a monthly basis, or more frequently if needed. This review process was quickly adopted by all of the organizations and has become just the way we do things at NSTAR.

Penni McLean-Conner, Vice President, Customer Care

Corporate performance management at NSTAR has been the impetus for developing a culture focused on delivering results for customers and shareholders that improves year over year. Having a clear corporate strategy, set of operating objectives, and scorecard with the appropriately aligned key performance measures in place enables employees at every level to understand how their work contributes to company goals and results. Our executive process of developing, tracking, and reviewing our scorecard on a monthly basis allows for open dialogue and cross-functional action planning to address issues or trends affecting our performance. It also drives regular communication throughout the organization about our progress and what needs to be done to improve. Our corporate performance management system also ties to our individual goal setting and reward programs so that accountability is clear and compensation is aligned. Since 2002, when we established our corporate performance management process and group, we have experienced year-over-year increases in organizational performance along every dimension—shareholder, customer, regulator, employee—and are therefore living proof that what gets measured gets managed!

Christine M. Carmody, Senior Vice President, Human Resources

CPM ORGANIZATION: THE BEGINNING OF CPM AT NSTAR NSTAR created its Corporate Performance Management department in late 2001 after a difficult summer. A series of system failures during warm weather left many customers with long power outages. This sent customer satisfaction ratings plummeting and placed NSTAR in a challenging position to change its approach to system maintenance, as well as customer service. After instituting changes to the executive team, organizational structure, key processes, and leadership capabilities, Chairman, President, and Chief Executive Officer Tom May led the company on a new journey to establish a performance-based culture. In order to bring senior-level attention and focus to a shift to a performance-based culture, NSTAR's CPM department reported to NSTAR's senior vice president and chief financial officer.

CPM has a staff of seven and is led by Susan Johnson, the director of corporate performance management. CPM is responsible for developing and measuring the key corporatewide and business unit–specific performance goals; working with the executive team to highlight and ensure continual attention to performance; measuring and communicating NSTAR's performance results against benchmarks and best practices; and supporting the executive team in determining and executing business improvement initiatives for continuous improvement.

CPM supports the corporation as a whole, as well as each individual business unit. Therefore, CPM staff members are aligned to one or more NSTAR business units. This enables them to become experts in specific business units within the company, creating line of sight performance metrics in each area that support the corporate strategic plan.

EXECUTIVE TEAM CPM direct and virtual members provide their service to NSTAR executive and leadership team members including:

- Thomas May, Chairman, President and Chief Executive Officer
- James Judge, Senior Vice President and Chief Financial Officer
- Douglas Horan, Senior Vice President, Strategy, Law and Policy
- Joseph Nolan, Senior Vice President, Corporate Relations and Customer Care
- Christine Carmody, Senior Vice President, Human Resources
- Werner Schweiger, Senior Vice President, Operations
- Geoffrey Lubbock, Vice President Strategy and Financial Planning
- Penelope Conner, Vice President, Customer Care
- Philip Lembo, Vice President, Treasurer
- Ellen Angley, Vice President, Supply and Procurement
- Robert Weafer, Vice President and Controller
- Craig Hallstrom, Vice President, Electric Operations
- Philip Andreas, Vice President, Gas Operations
- Paul Vaitkus, Vice President, Electric Transmission and Distribution System Operations
- Larry Gelbein, Vice President, Engineering
- Katherine Kountze-Tatum, Vice President and CIO

CORE AND INNOVATIVE BEST PRACTICES NSTAR exercises the core best practices shown next.

Principle 1: Establish and Deploy a CPM Office and Officer

- **Executive sponsorship.** CEO actively sponsors the CPM office and CPM projects for a sustained period and with the right visibility to enable maturity.
- **Organizational level and reporting relationship.** CPM office executive reports to the chief financial officer.

- **CPM office staff.** Small team experienced in change programs.
- **Leadership, influence factors.** Able to organize cross-organizational, virtual teams to drive results in all CPM methods.
- **Ownership of CPM processes and methods.** The office owns or substantially influences the portfolio and methods of CPM processes enterprisewide.
- **CPM, industry, and company knowledge.** CPM team possesses deep expertise in strategic planning, initiative management, BSC, and knowledge management. One or more team members have deep industry- and company-specific knowledge to help guide resolution of project issues.
- **Collaborative maturity.** Experienced in working horizontally and vertically through the organization.
- **Ability to learn.** Open to new ideas, methods, and approaches; able to streamline, integrate, and adapt methods; able to think concurrently.

Omaha Public Power District: Best Practice Case

Omaha Public Power District (OPPD) is a public electric utility in the state of Nebraska. It is one of the largest publicly owned electric utilities in the United States, serving more than 340,000 customers in 13 southeast Nebraska counties. OPPD was formed in 1946 as a political subdivision of the state of Nebraska. A publicly elected eight-member board of directors sets rates and policies.

EXECUTIVE VIEWS ON PERFORMANCE MANAGEMENT AND IMPROVEMENT

The corporate performance review has encouraged the senior management team to take a long view. As an electric utility we have always been very adept in addressing immediate operational issues. By having performance measures that inform longer-term objectives, such as culture change, we are able to keep our focus on a sustained change initiative.

Gary Gates, President and CEO

By cascading corporate objectives and measures to business units and division levels we have aligned the entire organization around OPPD's top priorities. Consistent measures across horizontal tiers of the company allow us to direct our attention to the appropriate areas.

Adrian Minks, Vice President, Essential Services Business Unit

Continuous process improvement is the key priority at OPPD. We have identified key business processes that transcend many divisions. Developing overall process improvement measures that are shared by those divisions, we have created a unity of purpose around this effort.

Konstantine (Deeno) Boosalis, Manager, Business Strategy

The corporate performance measures have provided the basis for our company incentive plan. The plan uses key outcome measures and process measures as the funding mechanism. This has served to focus our employees on current results as well as the leading drivers of future results.

Cherie Carlson, Manager, Corporate Performance Management

CPM ORGANIZATION AND KEY PROCESSES The virtual CPM function is sponsored by Adrian Minks, the vice president of essential services. The CPM has wide latitude to interact directly with the CEO and senior management team in developing and implementing the CPM function.

OPPD does not use the CPM title to name this organization; it is used in this case study as a normative title. OPPD leverages a virtual CPM function consisting of the following functions and participants.

Deeno Boosalis, manager of business planning and strategy, and his team, consisting of Cherie Carlson, manager of corporate performance, are responsible for primarily leading the core CPM processes:

- **Strategic Issues Assessment.** Design and direct broad-based process for identification and analysis of key strategic issues with the potential of significantly impacting OPPD. Develop possible future scenarios for the electric utility industry based on the trends. Gain consensus from the senior management team as to which future scenario will be the basis for planning.
- **Strategic Direction.** Develop models and tools for building consensus on OPPD strategic direction and manage process for senior management development of vision, critical success factors, and corporate objectives.
- **Strategy Development Process.** Design and direct a decision process for developing corporate strategies. Analyze potential corporate strategies by establishing, coordinating, and advising cross-organizational teams.
- **Corporate Measures and Targets.** Identify corporate measures that support the goals and critical success factors and direct target setting process with senior management.
- **Cascade Strategic Plan to Business Units.** Oversee development of business unit and division plans. Conduct approval and review of plans with senior management for alignment with strategic plan and other

business units. The manager of corporate performance reports to this position.

- **Strategic Review Sessions.** Facilitate senior management review of corporate measures and strategic initiatives.
- **Communicate Strategy.** Develop strategic plan and strategy map, and communicate corporate strategy to the company.
- **Corporate Opinion Research.** Manage all opinion research including internal and external customer research to satisfy the primary research needs of the individual business units and to support corporate measures and strategic assessment.
- **Business Continuity Planning.** Develop/implement a corporate plan for minimizing danger to life, health, and property and continuing operations in the face of emergency events. Ensure all single contingency emergency plans (T&D, nuclear) coordinate with corporate plan in large-scale emergency.

Tad Leeper, manager, human resources, together with his HR colleagues, is responsible for:

- Spearheading the High Performance Organization (HPO) program
- Facilitating success factors for performance management
- Linking Performance Scorecard (PSC) goals with team and individual goals
- Facilitating documentation of HR processes

Joe Waszak, manager, operations, and his team are responsible for:

- Conducting process mapping and ensuring process standardization
- Deploying process improvement methods linked to PSC results
- Facilitating other business improvements and special projects using Project management methodology (PMM) framework

Matthew Pohl, manager, nuclear cost management and planning, and his team are responsible for:

- Championing the use of strategy maps and PSCs down through the field nuclear business unit divisions and departments
- Integrating PSCs and core nuclear processes and process level measures
- Facilitating PSC meetings with division and department heads
- Interfacing with nuclear industry groups, WANO and Institute Nuclear Power Operators (INPO) to share best practices
- Benchmarking OPPD performance against industry performance along several standard system parameters

Verlyn Kroon, manager, information technology, and his IT division of professionals are responsible for:

- Championing the use of strategy maps and PSCs down through the IT division and departments
- Providing IT support for deploying the PSCs throughout the enterprise
- Providing benchmarking and best practice sharing opportunities and forums as board member with AIM Institute, a consortia of IT professionals in Nebraska

Tim Burke, vice president, employee and customer relations, has:

- Pioneered use of business unit performance measures before the CPM office established Performance Scorecards throughout OPPD.
- Established performance measures as the basis for evaluating work performance and determining compensation.
- Modified and expanded the business unit's existing process to correspond with the CPM standard.

The foregoing CPM processes are described in more depth in later chapters. In summary, OPPD deploys a mixed centralized and decentralized integrated CPM network to optimize performance enterprisewide.

EXECUTIVE TEAM The virtual CPM team collaborates with executive and senior leadership team members and provides services to the following key internal customers:

- President and CEO W. Gary Gates manages the entire company (level 1).
- Five vice presidents manage portfolios of functions (level 2):

   1. Vice President and Chief Financial Officer Edward E. Easterlin
   2. Vice President Nuclear Chief Nuclear Officer David J. Bannister
   3. Vice President Employee and Customer Relations Timothy J. Burke
   4. Vice President Essential Services Adrian J. Minks
   5. Vice President Operations Dale F. Widoe

- Division directors and managers lead functional divisions (level 3) consisting of multiple departments.
- Department managers and supervisors lead departments (level 4).

CORE AND INNOVATIVE BEST PRACTICES OPPD exercises the core best practices and has advanced knowledge in this area with a new, innovative best practice.

Principle 1: Establish and Deploy a CPM Office and Officer

- **Executive sponsorship.** President and CEO, with the vice president of essential services, sponsor virtual CPM office and CPM projects for sustained period and with the right visibility to enable maturity.
- **Organizational level and reporting relationship.** CPM office executive reports to the CEO direct reports.
- **CPM office staff.** Small senior team experienced in change programs and integrated with other functions as noted.
- **Leadership, influence factors.** Able to organize cross-organizational, virtual teams to drive results in all CPM methods.
- **Ownership of CPM processes and methods.** The office owns or substantially influences the portfolio and methods of CPM processes enterprisewide.
- **CPM, industry, and company knowledge.** CPM team possesses deep expertise in strategic planning, initiative management, PSC, performance management, and knowledge management. One or more team members have deep industry- and company-specific knowledge to help guide resolution of project issues.
- **Collaborative maturity.** Experienced in working horizontally and vertically through the organization.
- **Ability to learn.** Open to new ideas, methods, and approaches; able to streamline, integrate, and adapt methods; able to think concurrently.
- **Innovative Best Practice.** OPPD has effectively leveraged deep, functional competencies and expertise from across the organization to form an integrated corporate and field-based CPM network and function.

Poudre Valley Health System: Best Practice Case

Poudre Valley Health System (PVHS) is a locally owned, private, not-for-profit organization that provides care to residents of northern Colorado, Nebraska, and Wyoming. Headquartered 60 miles north of Denver in Fort Collins, Colorado (service area population 500,000), PVHS dates back to 1925, when Poudre Valley Hospital (PVH) opened its doors as a 40-bed hospital on the outskirts of Fort Collins. Recognizing in 1999 that the health care landscape was rapidly changing, and the focus on high-quality, low-cost care would become ever more important, PVHS chose to employ the Malcolm Baldrige National Quality Program criteria and began participating in the Colorado Performance Excellence (CPEx) program in 2001. PVHS remains one of only two recipients, and the only health care recipient, of the CPEx Peak Award, Colorado's top Baldrige-based recognition (it has received the award twice) and has received consecutive Baldrige site visits since 2005. On this Baldrige journey, PVH has expanded and diversified into PVHS—a regional medical hub with a service area covering 50,000 square miles (roughly the size of Florida).The organization's vision is to provide world-class health care, with a mission of providing innovative, comprehensive care of the highest quality, exceeding customer expectations.

PVHS offers a full spectrum of health care services, including emergency/urgent care, intensive care, medical/surgical care, maternal/child care, oncology care, and orthopedic care. PVHS' unique focus areas include:

- One of Colorado's largest cardiac centers
- The only Level IIIa Neonatal Intensive Care Unit between Denver and Billings, Montana
- Level II and III trauma centers
- National Top 50 Orthopedic Center
- Bariatric Surgery Center of Excellence

PVHS also offers role model community health programs that prevent injury or illness and help the medically underserved. The PVHS model of patient- and family-centered care drives delivery of health care services. The process for involving patients in their care begins with facility and service design and continues throughout key health care processes. PVHS uses two primary care delivery mechanisms—partnerships and interdisciplinary teams.

EXECUTIVE VIEWS ON PERFORMANCE IMPROVEMENT

It is my job to make this the best place you have ever worked. If I'm not doing my job, tell me.
                    Rulon F. Stacey, Ph.D., FACHE President/CEO Executive

PVHS provides each employee, including employed physicians, a thorough orientation before they ever set foot in their department. Senior leadership is there to let them know they have a voice in the future of PVHS and they—no matter their role—will provide world-class health care. Likewise, volunteers experience a thorough orientation session prior to beginning their volunteer duties. Reaching each workforce member is key to gaining their trust and inviting them to be an integral part of driving innovation and excellence.

Pam Brock, Vice President, Marketing and Strategic Planning

MARKETING AND STRATEGIC PLANNING FUNCTION　　Pam Brock, vice president, marketing and strategic planning (MSP), and her department oversee the business marketing, outreach, and the strategy development and deployment process. Ms. Brock, a member of the PVHS senior leadership team, reports to the highest level executive and provides services to her colleagues, the Senior Management Group (SMG) shown next. Brock coordinates and facilitates strategic planning, including the annual process for setting and deploying the vision, mission, and values described in Chapter 5.

The Senior Management Group consists of the PVHS CEO and the following leaders:

- Rulon F. Stacey, Ph.D., FACHE President/CEO
- Pam Brock, Vice President, MSP
- Stephanie Doughty, Chief Financial Officer
- Diane Gross, Corporate Counsel
- William Neff, MD, Chief Medical Officer
- Russ Branzell, Chief Information Officer
- Patti Oakes, VP, Human Resources
- Kevin Unger, CEO, Poudre Valley Hospital
- Dan Robinson, COO, Poudre Valley Hospital
- Craig Luzinski, Chief Nursing Officer, PVH
- George Hayes, CEO, Medical Center of the Rockies
- Doug Faus, COO, Medical Center of the Rockies
- Kay Miller, Chief Nursing Officer, MCR
- Barb Yosses, VP, Ambulatory Services

The organization's director of process improvement, Priscilla Nuwash, coordinates a range of key contributors in the organization to drive performance improvement. PVHS has seven multidisciplinary performance excellence teams focused on the Baldrige categories to function as systemwide oversight committees. These performance excellence teams have defined roles in: (1) the annual performance excellence cycle, and (2) monthly monitoring of key performance measures. Performance excellence teams may recommend PDCA initiatives, and the Process Improvement department evaluates, approves, and oversees all system PDCA initiatives. Process Improvement staff participate in each performance excellence team and coordinate improvement efforts between the seven teams, as well as quarterly learning opportunities for all team members. The seven performance excellence teams are the following:

1. Leadership Committee provides feedback to SMG on vision, mission, and values deployment, communication processes, governance, legal/ethical environment, and community support.
2. Strategy Team develops methodologies to deploy the strategic plan and provide understanding about how strategy drives the organization.
3. Customer Service Steering Committee provides leadership and oversight of service excellence initiatives.
4. Knowledge Management develops processes for selecting, team gathering, analyzing, managing, and improving data, information, and knowledge, including definition, analysis, and review of cascading BSC measures.
5. Workforce Focus Team evaluates and improves workforce processes that impact turnover, vacancy, culture, and safety.
6. Process Improvement identifies, evaluates, and monitors key processes, including those that have gone through the rigorous PDCA process.
7. Key Measures Team coordinates stringent reviews of key measures by Performance Excellence teams.

Each Performance Excellence Team is led by a PVHS senior leader and is comprised of additional leadership and multidisciplinary front-line staff. The goal is to utilize a broad range of opinions and ideas to drive change and innovation throughout the organization.

CORE AND INNOVATIVE BEST PRACTICES   PVHS exercises the core best practices and has advanced knowledge in this area with a new, innovative best practice.

Principle 1: Establish and Deploy a CPM Office and Officer

(CPM is a reference title. PVHS refers to its performance organization as MSP.)

- **Executive sponsorship.** CEO actively sponsors MSP and CPM projects for a sustained period and with the right visibility to enable maturity.
- **Organizational level and reporting relationship.** MSP office executive reports to the CEO.

- **CPM office staff.** Small senior team experienced in change programs.
- **Leadership, influence factors.** Able to organize cross-organizational, virtual teams to drive results in all CPM methods. For instance, MSP partners with the CFO to conduct key analytics to share with the executive team during strategic planning process.
- **Ownership of CPM processes and methods.** The office owns or substantially influences the portfolio and methods of CPM processes enterprisewide.
- **CPM, industry, and company knowledge.** CPM team possesses deep expertise in strategic planning; initiative management; scorecards; quality tools; and knowledge management. One or more team members have deep industry- and company-specific knowledge to help guide resolution of project issues.
- **Collaborative maturity.** Experienced in working horizontally and vertically through the organization.
- **Ability to learn.** Open to new ideas, methods, and approaches; able to streamline, integrate, and adapt methods; able to think concurrently.
- **Innovative PVHS Best Practice.** PVHS's MSP function works effectively across a complex, multiple-entity enterprise as part of a larger health care system. The goal of PVHS's MSP function, through its strategy development and deployment process, is to include multiple stakeholders in the decision making toward forward-thinking and innovative strategy. Stakeholders include board members, physicians, staff, volunteers, community, patients, patient families, business leaders, and so on.

Public Service Electric and Gas: Best Practice Case

Public Service Electric and Gas Company (PSE&G), is a more than 100 year-old company headquartered in Newark, New Jersey. It is one of the largest investor-owned utilities in the nation, with revenues of $7.6 billion in 2008 and with total assets of $14.6 billion. In 2008, PSE&G delivered 48,148 GWhs of electricity and 3,440 million therms of natural gas to approximately 5.5 million New Jersey residents, about 70 percent of the state's population. The company franchise territory is just less than 2,600 square miles and is heavily populated, commercialized, and industrialized. It encompasses most of New Jersey's largest municipalities, including its six largest cities—Newark, Jersey City, Paterson, Elizabeth, Trenton, and Camden—in addition to approximately 300 suburban and rural communities. This service territory contains a diversified mix of residential, commerce, and industry areas, including major facilities of many nationally prominent corporations along with some of the wealthiest, by per capita income, communities in the nation. PSE&G has a little over 6,450 employees of which about 80 percent are represented by four major unions.

PSE&G distributes electricity and gas to end-use customers within its designated service territory. All electric and gas customers in New Jersey have the ability to choose an electric energy and/or gas supplier. PSE&G earns no margin on the commodity portion of its electric and gas sales. PSE&G earns margins through the transmission and distribution of electricity and gas.

The electric and gas transmission and distribution business has minimal risks from competitors. PSE&G's transmission and distribution business is minimally impacted when customers choose alternative electric or gas supplies. The demand for electricity and gas by PSE&G customers is affected by customer conservation, economic conditions, weather, and other factors not within PSE&G's control. In addition, PSE&G also offers appliance service and repairs to customers throughout its service territory.

PSE&G is a subsidiary of its parent company, Public Service Enterprise Group (PEG), a Fortune 500 company traded on the NYSE.

EXECUTIVE VIEWS ON CORPORATE PERFORMANCE MANAGEMENT

PSE&G is committed to sustainability and the key ingredients that drive long-term financial growth: operational excellence, disciplined investment, and environmental leadership, as well as the health and safety of our employees, customers, and the communities in which we operate. Our membership in this prestigious index (Dow Jones Sustainability Index) is noteworthy.

The implementation of the BSC has not only introduced a consistent and structured methodology to articulate our strategy and measure performance, it has been one of the primary catalysts that have transformed our culture within PSE&G. The focus on achieving a clearly defined strategy unified the company and our breakthrough performance improvements have been recognized on a national basis. All our employees now understand what they do and how well they do it, on a day by day basis, which contributes to the overall success of the company.

Ralph Izzo, Chairman, President, and CEO PSEG

We've expanded our credibility with customers as a result of the awards we've won; with regulators because they see the outcomes and the numbers; and internally with our board, which has given us additional resources. As for employees, they see added jobs and activities that are going to result in their benefiting from shared savings. People are seeing the bigger picture. The BSC is not an end-all, but it's a means to move the business forward.

Ralph LaRossa, President and COO PSE&G

Success comes to those that are passionate about what they do and how they go about doing it. Being able to demonstrate how everyone contributes to success has been one of the key factors in driving excellent performance at PSE&G.

Joe Martucci, Performance Leader PSE&G

CPM ORGANIZATION PSE&G uses a variation of CPM terminology, the Performance Measurement Group (PMG). Joe Martucci, performance leader, directs this performance group, and his direct report team consists of himself and three business analysts.

Mr. Martucci also has an indirect report team consisting of a champion network embedded in each of the four major business organizations:

1. Customer Operations
2. Electric Delivery
3. Gas Delivery
4. Renewable and Energy Solutions

The PMG is organizationally a part of the Utility Finance (UF). UF has responsibility for managing the company strategy and for all aspects of performance measurement. This includes financial budgeting and adherence, Balanced Scorecard (BSC) reporting, benchmarking, targeting setting, strategy and metrics reevaluation, and other aspects of the business planning process. PSE&G believes that having the four processes managed by a single group has been very effective in the success of its efforts, and PSE&G has shared this approach with many companies who have visited them in an attempt to duplicate it within their companies. The other operating companies within the PSE&G family have adopted this approach and structure.

EXECUTIVE TEAM UF serves internal business leaders with the foregoing services. The primary internal customers include the following members of the executive and the senior leadership teams:

- Ralph Izzo, Chairman, President and CEO PSE&G
- Ralph La Rossa, President and COO PSE&G

- Jorge Cardenas, Vice President, Gas Delivery
- John Latka, Vice President, Electric Operations
- Dave Daly, Vice President, Asset Management
- Joe Forline, Vice President, Customer Operations
- Al Matos, Vice President, Renewable Energy Solutions
- Mark Kahrer, Vice President, Finance, PSE&G

CORE AND INNOVATIVE BEST PRACTICES   PSE&G exercises the core best practices and has advanced knowledge in this area with a new, innovative best practice.

Principle 1: Establish and Deploy a CPM Office and Officer

- **Executive sponsorship.** CEO actively sponsors PMG (CPM office) and CPM projects for a sustained period and with the right visibility to enable maturity.
- **Organizational level and reporting relationship.** PMG (CPM office) executive reports to the CEO.
- **CPM office staff.** Small senior team experienced in delivering change programs.
- **Leadership, influence factors.** Able to organize cross-organizational, virtual teams to drive results in all CPM methods.
- **Ownership of CPM processes and methods.** The office owns or substantially influences the portfolio and methods of CPM processes enterprisewide.
- **CPM, industry, and company knowledge.** CPM team possesses deep expertise in strategic planning, initiative management, BSC, and knowledge management. One or more team members have deep industry- and company-specific knowledge to help guide resolution of project issues.
- **Collaborative maturity.** Experienced in working horizontally and vertically through the organization.
- **Ability to learn.** Open to new ideas, methods, and approaches; able to streamline, integrate, and adapt methods; able to think concurrently.
- **Innovative best practices.** PSE&G has demonstrated its industry leadership and hosted numerous visits from other companies to emulate its PMG organization and its processes.

Sharp HealthCare: Best Practice Case

Sharp is the largest Integrated Health Care Delivery System (IDS). Note this is an industry term in San Diego County and the parent company of all Sharp entities. In 1953, with a donation of land from the Philip L. Gildred family and $500,000 from rancher Thomas E. Sharp, ground was broken for Donald N. Sharp Memorial Community Hospital, which opened in 1955 to provide general hospital care for San Diego residents. In response to the changing landscape of health care delivery in the early 1980s, Sharp embarked on a strategy to develop a vertically integrated network of health care facilities and providers. Today, the Sharp system consists of four acute-care hospitals, three specialty hospitals, two affiliated medical groups, a health plan, three long-term care facilities, a liability insurance company, and two philanthropic foundations. Sharp offers a full continuum of care, including:

- Emergency care
- Outpatient care
- Inpatient care
- Mental health care
- Hospice care
- Rehabilitation
- Home care
- Primary and specialty care
- Long-term care
- Urgent care

Sharp, with over 23 subspecialties of medicine and surgery, also offers state-of-the-art treatment for multiorgan transplantation, hyperbaric medicine, and a level-two trauma center. Licensed to operate 1,870 beds, Sharp provides care to approximately 785,000 individuals annually, including more than 350,000 health maintenance organization enrollees. At the end of the 2006 fiscal year, Sharp reported $1.3 billion in assets and $1.8 billion in net revenues. Approximately 35.7 percent of Sharp's revenue is derived from senior and commercial capitated managed care contracts (premium revenues). Fee-for-service and managed care government-sponsored reimbursement (Medicare and Medi-Cal) account for approximately 41.8 percent of Sharp's gross patient charges.

More than 2,000 volunteers, primarily retirees, contribute throughout Sharp. They provide "meet and greet" services and assist in fundraising and the gift shops. Approximately 2,600 physicians have privileges at Sharp hospitals, with more than 1,500 of these physicians providing ambulatory care through Sharp's two affiliated medical practices.

September 2001, Sharp launched The Sharp Experience, a performance-improvement initiative designed to transform the health care experience and make Sharp the best place to work, the best place to practice medicine, and the best place to receive care. Today, everything at Sharp, from strategic planning to performance evaluations to meeting agendas, is aligned with Six Pillars of Excellence: Quality, Service, People, Finance, Growth, and Community.

MALCOLM BALDRIGE QUALITY AWARD CRITERIA A key milestone in Sharp HealthCare's journey to transform the health care experience was the selection of the Malcolm Baldrige National Quality Award criteria as the quality standard. Sharp leaders wanted to continue to stretch the organization with the transformation structure already established called The Sharp Experience. The Baldrige program offered the means to set goals high with lofty targets that would raise performance a notch every year.

The Baldrige standard provided Sharp HealthCare with accountability and aspiration to improve processes and results. It established process improvements through welcome feedback and specific measurements. It asked leaders to think differently and front-line staff to take ownership of the importance of what they do every day to make the organization better. Baldrige principles offered rigor and structure that allow a good organization to become an excellent one.

EXECUTIVE VIEWS ON PERFORMANCE IMPROVEMENT

Sharp has been on a six-year journey to transform the health care experience for employees, physicians, and patients. The Baldrige criteria and our unwavering commitment to quality satisfaction and continuous improvement have helped us toward our vision to be the best place to work, practice medicine, and receive care and ultimately to be the best health care system in the universe.

Mike Murphy, President and CEO

We will continue to set higher annual goals, higher targets. It is the right thing to do for our patients, staff, physicians, and volunteers. We will raise our performance a notch every year.

Nancy G. Pratt, RN, MS; Senior Vice President, Clinical Effectiveness

CLINICAL EFFECTIVENESS ORGANIZATION Sharp's executive leaders have been committed as a cohesive and collaborative force toward excellence from the onset of The Sharp Experience. This teamwork is evident with the Executive Steering Committee consisting of 17 senior leaders including the system CEO/president, the executive vice president, the CEOs of all entities, all senior vice presidents, and the system medical director. These leaders share a unified dedication to challenge the conventional and stretch the organization to be the best. It was no surprise when the Executive Steering Committee embraced the Baldrige program and unanimously agreed to pursue the Baldrige standard of excellence.

A noteworthy role on Executive Steering is that of the champion for performance improvement. At Sharp, this role is the Clinical Effectiveness department, where its leader, Nancy G. Pratt, RN, MS, Senior Vice President, facilitates transparency, quality, patient safety, and organizational performance improvement.

Other vital areas under her direction are clinical service lines and clinical decision support. She leads key CPM efforts and reports to executive Daniel L. Gross, Executive Vice President, Hospital Operations, Sharp HealthCare.

SHARP HEALTHCARE'S EXECUTIVE LEADERSHIP Clinical Effectiveness coordinates or facilitates quality and safety strategic planning; dashboard report card measurement; six sigma tools including CAP (change acceleration program), DMAIC (define, measure, analyze, improve, and control), Lean Six Sigma, and workout; and knowledge management best practices.

Additionally, the Clinical Effectiveness team coordinates with a range of other key contributors in the organization to drive performance improvement. The team's participation and inputs contribute to the following:

- CEO Council, a weekly meeting of Sharp's hospital CEOs and executive vice president to facilitate integration and to problem-solve.
- Executive Steering consists of 17 senior leaders including the system CEO/president, the executive vice president, the CEOs of all entities, all senior vice presidents, and the system medical director.
- Leadership Development Session, an educational session held four times a year (the fourth is in conjunction with the All-Staff Assembly) for Sharp leadership, providing career development opportunities to gain depth of experience and insight from peers, outside experts, improvement projects, and action teams across multiple assignments and entities.
- Change Agents, those leaders who facilitate CAP and Work-Out™ by instilling new tools and techniques across the system and coaching other leaders on change facilitation.
- Pillar of Excellence Awards, annual system awards to outstanding individuals, action teams, and departments that demonstrate superior performance under one of Sharp's Six Pillars of Excellence. Pillar Award winners are selected from each entity's Center of Recognized Excellence (C.O.R.E.) Award given annually to outstanding individuals, action teams, and departments at each Sharp entity that demonstrate superior performance under one of Sharp's Six Pillars of Excellence.

- Champions, key individuals assigned to strategic initiatives to ensure accountability.
- Employee Forums, quarterly employee meetings held at Sharp entities to provide Report Card updates, communicate Sharp's business results, and educate staff on specific Sharp Experience learnings. Communication Expos are a form of Employee Forums.
- Trailblazers of Excellence, best-practice units, departments, or functional areas within Sharp HealthCare.

Sharp's key CPM processes are more fully described in subsequent chapters.

CORE AND INNOVATIVE BEST PRACTICES Sharp exercises the core best practices and has advanced knowledge in this area with new, innovative best practices.

Principle 1: Establish and Deploy a CPM Office and Officer

- **Executive sponsorship.** CEO actively sponsors CPM office called Clinical Effectiveness and CPM projects for sustained period and with the right visibility to enable maturity.
- **Organizational level and reporting relationship.** CPM office executive reports to the EVP.
- **CPM office staff.** Small senior team experienced in change programs.
- **Leadership, influence factors.** Able to organize cross-organizational, virtual teams to drive results in all CPM methods.
- **Ownership of CPM processes and methods.** The office owns or substantially influences the portfolio and methods of CPM processes enterprisewide.
- **CPM, industry, and company knowledge.** CPM team possesses deep expertise in strategic planning; initiative management; scorecards; six sigma tools including CAP (change acceleration program), DMAIC, lean, and workout; and knowledge management. One or more team members have deep industry- and company-specific knowledge to help guide resolution of project issues.
- **Collaborative maturity.** Experienced in working horizontally and vertically through the organization.

- **Ability to learn.** Open to new ideas, methods, and approaches; able to streamline, integrate, and adapt methods; able to think concurrently.
- **Innovative Best Practice.** Sharp's CPM office works effectively across a complex, multiple entity enterprise, each with either a CEO or president, as part of a larger health care system.
- **Innovative Best Practice.** Sharp has formalized an expanded performance improvement infrastructure consisting of Champions, Change Agents, Executive Steering Committee, and CEO council.

Note

1. Bob Paladino, *Five Key Principles of Corporate Performance Management* (Hoboken, NJ: John Wiley & Sons, 2007).

CHAPTER 5

Principle 2: Refresh and Communicate Strategy

Planning is an unnatural process; it is much more fun to do something. And the nicest thing about not planning is that failure comes as a complete surprise.

—Sir John Henry-Jones

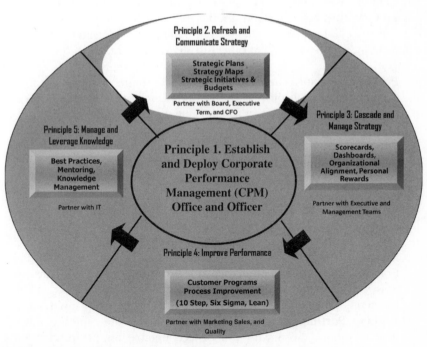

© Copyright 2010 Bob Paladino and Associates, LLC.

The CPM Office will often play multiple roles related to *Principle 2, Refresh and Communicate Strategy.* Most enterprises I studied realize the value of a comprehensive strategic planning process using multiple methods and tools to understand and decipher strategic opportunities, or what some call the game changers.

CPM Core Process Blueprint and Key Process Roles

Careful research of the cases in this book reveals they follow a discernable set of core CPM processes organized within the Five Key Principles. These processes were arrayed in Exhibit 3.1 to provide strategic context and a working framework to assist you in your organization. Note: *Principle 2 Refresh and Communicate Strategy* consists of four integrated CPM processes. Some case organizations have expanded beyond these core processes.

Strategic Planning Process Example

The CPM office members will play one or more of three key roles in executing the CPM core processes with the fourth, participants. We will focus on the strategic planning process at award-winning Crown Castle International where I functioned as the CPM officer to share an example:

1. **Process Sponsor.** The sponsor is typically the most senior executive accountable for the process outcomes and for overseeing the process owner. The process sponsor for the Strategic Planning process at Crown was the CEO and the board strategy subcommittee for governance.
2. **Process Owner.** The owner is typically the senior leader accountable to the sponsor for managing the process and is usually a process subject matter expert (SME). As the CPM officer, I was the process owner for the Strategic Planning process at Crown.
3. **Process Facilitator.** The facilitator is typically the individual who day-to-day interacts directly with process participants to drive the process and integrate the process with other key processes. The process facilitator of Crown's Strategic Planning was me in collaboration with Bain Consulting to facilitate multitrack offsite strategic planning. This process was then integrated with the risk management process and the budgeting process for capital and operational financial planning.
4. **Process Participant.** The process participants are typically subject matter experts, those who will be accountable for the process outcomes and/or are the recipients of the process outcomes. The process

participants in the Crown Strategic Planning process were a broad senior team including the board of directors, the executive management team, the senior leadership team, outside industry SMEs, and a few selected high potential employees for development and grooming purposes.

Prior to turning our attention toward the in-depth cases, let us review the core best practices recognized by all companies in this book. See each case that follows for their innovative best practice, so you can appreciate the context and relevance of the practices to their organizations.

Principle 2: Refresh and Communicate Strategy Best Practices

- **Strategic planning.** Leverage the strategic planning process as either owner or partner to understand changing market conditions including competitor, supplier, rival, and potential entrants and substitutes in the marketplace.
- **Core and adjacent products and services.** Define and determine core and adjacent products and services to focus on highest probabilities for success.
- **Strategic plan.** Produce a comprehensive strategic plan.
- **Strategy mapping.** Develop corporate- and department-level strategy maps containing objectives along four perspectives including financial, customer/constituent, process, and people. Observe strategy map design parameters of 20 to 25 objectives.
- **Link strategic planning and budgeting processes.** Link strategic planning to the budgeting process, partner and budgeting with finance to provide for a seamless continuum.
- **Communications plan.** Communicate strategy throughout the organization using a comprehensive communications plan.

Award-Winning Case Organizations: Meet the Innovators

Cargill Corn Milling North America: Best Practice Case

Cargill Corn Milling (CCM) supports parent Cargill's vision *to become the global leader in nourishing people.* CCM's vision, which includes the purpose, mission, and values along with core competencies shown previously, defines its culture and provides guidance, alignment, and integration for all stakeholders and their activities. The CCM purpose reflects Cargill's long-term strategy. The mission was first established in 2000 and has been modified to reflect additional product line opportunities and customer and market needs. The values reflect the characteristics and behaviors needed to accomplish the purpose, mission, and long-term strategies. Values are guiding principles for all stakeholders and are integrated throughout the business. Core competencies are key areas of expertise providing sustainable advantage. CCM's vision includes:

- **Purpose.** To be partner of choice of the customers we serve.
- **Mission.** CCM delivers distinctive value to customers in:
  - Food, including high-fructose corn syrup (HFCS), corn syrup, sugar, corn oil, and dry corn ingredients (DCI).
  - Feed, including gluten feed and gluten meal.
  - Fermentation, including ethanol, acidulants, and industrial starch.
- **Values.** Demonstrate integrity, injury free, expand customer focus, be innovative, develop talent, promote collaboration, demand accountability, strengthen communities.
- **Core Competencies.** Risk management and origination; technical support; supply chain management; corporate social responsibility.

The CCM leadership team in coordination with the Cargill Enterprise Development Team (EDT) exercises several integrated CPM processes to improve business performance including the following:

- The SLT uses the CCM Leadership System (see Exhibit 5.1) to establish the vision and values, communicate organizational performance and governance, define direction, and deploy strategy and plans.
  Systematic strategic review (SR) and annual business planning (ABP) processes are used to set the strategic direction and identify tactical actions.
- Monthly business performance review meetings analyze CCM's BSC results and identify opportunities for improvement.
- Business excellence (BE), Cargill's organizational framework for continuous improvement, is used to create and sustain competitive advantage based on the Malcolm Baldrige National Quality Award model.

STRATEGIC CONTEXT   CCM operates in extremely competitive markets offering unique challenges for each of its product lines. Since 1999, the corn sweetener industry has been impacted by a decline in demand, a restricted Mexican border for imports, and rising energy, transportation, and processing ingredient costs. The challenging market situation has resulted in industry consolidation. More recently, because of the rising fuel costs and substantial government subsidies, ethanol as a fuel additive has become

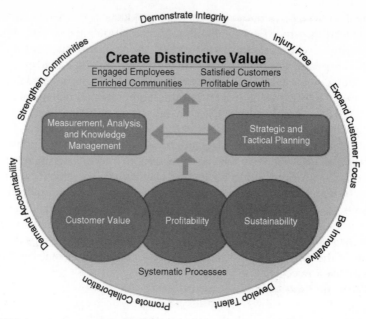

EXHIBIT 5.1 CCM Leadership System
Courtesy of Cargill Corn Milling.

much more attractive. Corn is now being valued for its capacity to create fuel rather than food or feed, putting more pressure on food manufacturers.

STRATEGIC PLANNING/FORMULATION   CCM's approach to business strategy formulation consists of two distinct processes: the longer-term strategy review (SR) process and the short-term annual business planning (ABP) process. Both processes are essential to the development of the overall business strategies and tactical plans.

Strategy Review (SR) Process   The SLT performs the SR annually to determine how CCM will approach strategic planning each year. Although the SR process is an annual process it can be executed at any point during the year based on key changes to the business environment. This process uses inputs such as the current CCM strategy, CCM core competencies, product line knowledge, and current and future market trends to determine how CCM will proceed with the strategy process. The SLT anticipates public concerns with its products and operations during Strategy Review. During the environmental scan, information and new insights are reviewed. CCM utilizes expert panels to gather information and develop insight into potential future concerns related to CCM products and operations. Product line leaders gather information about potential public concerns through their contacts with customers, trade associations, academia, and through Cargill's corporate affairs business. The CCM environmental manager develops strategic plans to address environmental issues. Environmental business plans are developed using input from the environmental managers at each location. These employees work with other companies as well as local, state, and national regulatory agencies to understand the direction of future policy changes. All production facilities have representation, including facility managers involved with relevant government and private organizations. For example, manufacturing facility environmental managers belong to a variety of nongovernmental organizations that monitor environmental quality issues. All managers also participate in their respective local emergency planning commissions. Membership in such organizations allows facilities to discover community opinions and concerns before major issues develop. As part of the SR, the SLT will review current core competencies and make adjustments if needed.

There are three possible outcomes of this SR process:

Option 1: Continue with the current strategy.
Option 2: Update the current strategy (UCS).
Option 3: Design a new strategy (DNS) to fundamentally change the
    direction of the business.

The outcome of each option is the CCM strategic plan. This process gives CCM maximum flexibility and agility while creating the strategy. For example, the 2004 CCM strategy utilized the DNS process to create a new CCM strategic plan because of significant predicted changes in the business environment. In 2007, CCM determined the business was fundamentally headed in the right direction and therefore utilized the UCS process to make slight course corrections. The final step of the SR process is integrated with the Key Sustainability work process, Manage Human Capital Strategy. The human capital strategy is based on the strategic plans and outlines the initiatives and actions required to support core competencies, strategic challenges, and the capability inventory assessment plans.

Annual Business Planning (ABP) Process   ABP is a formal systematic process used to create the short-term, one-year tactical business plans for CCM overall, product lines, functional areas, Process Development Group PDG, and facilities. The result of this annual process is 39 integrated one-year business plans. The process begins in March, after the completion of the annual budget process, with final business plans completed in May. The process owner is the SLT, and the process steps are the following:

Step 1. The SLT prepares a CCM overall plan based on the current strategic plan, annual budget, corporate initiatives, and SLT initiatives. The CCM overall plan includes next year's initiatives and target measures.

Step 2. The SLT selects a Tiger Team to manage the remainder of the process. This team works with the product lines, functional areas, PDG, and facilities to ensure alignment of all business plans; communicates completion deadlines; and ensures consistent content and format.

Step 3. The CCM business plan is used as a starting point for development of all product line, functional area, and PDG business plans. Leaders of these groups are responsible for the completion of their individual draft plans and work with their respective teams reviewing all proposed initiatives for likelihood of success, resources required, and fit with overall CCM direction.

Step 4. The Tiger Team reviews the draft business plans of all product lines, functional areas, and PDGs, making recommendations to ensure consistency and alignment. Product line, functional area, and PDG plans are finalized from these recommendations.

Step 5. The next step is the integration of CCM, product line, functional area, and PDG business plans with facility business plans. Facility leadership teams are responsible for creating the facility business plans.

Step 6. The Tiger Team reviews the draft facility business plans and makes recommendations to ensure consistency and alignment. From these recommendations, facility plans are finalized.

Step 7. The SLT updates the CCM BSC, discussed in Chapter 6, based on annual and strategic plans.

Step 8. The ABS process is integrated with the Performance Management process because business plans are drivers for the employee individual key result areas completed in July.

Every year CCM evaluates and improves short-term planning processes in response to the shifting business environment including factors of supply and demand, customer consolidation, competitor alliances, and development of value-added products. In 2003, the SLT created the Tiger Team to drive the process. In 2006, a formal system to capture feedback from the business plan owners on how to improve the ABP process was implemented. In 2007, all business plans were converted to a Web-based system and a scoring mechanism was added to measure progress and achieve the demand accountability company value.

During the UCS and DNS processes, CCM utilizes a variety of people, both internal to CCM and external, to give feedback and opinions, and analyze data. By pulling in these individuals with their different professional backgrounds and knowledge bases, it captures a picture of the industry, customers, and competition. In addition, a number of data sources are utilized to provide fact-based decision making.

Strategic Plan SWOT Analysis/Environmental Scans   As part of the UCS and DNS processes, EDT leads CCM teams in SWOT analyses and environmental scans. The key factors considered during the SWOT analysis/environmental scans include customer expectations, market conditions, technological innovations, global challenges, pressure on the industry, political climate changes, health concerns, capacity utilization and capabilities, potential new products, energy costs, competitive environment, human resource capacity, regulatory environment, industry and competitor consolidation, supplier and partner needs. Any changes in these key factors will be detected during the analysis.

Early Indicators of Major Shifts   CCM utilizes many sources, both internal and external to CCM, and processes within the SR process to collect relevant data and information in order to detect shifts in technology, markets, customer preferences, competition, and to address these key drivers when developing the strategic plan. To substantiate and enhance the data-based analysis for the SR, the EDT gathers additional information from sources including the following:

- **Technology.** CCM maintains memberships in professional organizations, has close ties with vendors, and utilizes the process development groups to detect best practices in their area of expertise.
- **Markets.** To ensure direct customer input into the SR, CCM utilizes information from various listening and learning mechanisms. As illustrated, the primary methods of obtaining strategic customer information and preferences are from direct sales contact and expert panels. CCM uses direct sales contacts such as corporate account leaders (CAL) and national account managers (NAM) as single points of contact to obtain relevant plans and directions from key strategic customers. Other sources include information from organizations such as the Corn Refiners Association (CRA) and trade journals.
- **Customer Preferences.** Information is accessed based on relationships formed with customers through CAL and NAM along with technical service, customer service, and R&D personnel. Complaints recorded within the customer relationship tracking system are used to gain insight into customer requirements and preferences.
- **Competition.** CRA data, public records (i.e., environmental permits), and annual reports are used to gather information.

- **Regulatory Environment.** Legal teams, lobby firms, CRA, and other organizational memberships provide information.

Expert Panel Process (EPP)   The EPP is used to identify or validate industry drivers defined as established and emerging trends and potential shocks with regard to customers, consumers, technology, government regulations, suppliers, and industry players. This process is owned by the EDT and was added as a cycle of improvement to enhance the data-driven analysis with subjective insights. An expert panel consists of industry experts, key customers, retired employees of key customers, and others knowledgeable in the industry being studied.

Evaluate the Ability to Execute Strategic Plan   As part of the strategy review, strategy teams perform several formal analytical evaluations of initiatives to determine whether an initiative should be included in the final strategy. Some of the comparative analyses for initiatives include: strategic fit within CCM versus attractiveness; risk profile versus net present value; and value for customer versus feasibility of deployment. All initiatives included in the final CCM strategic plan will be implemented within the three- to four-year time frame. A formal Cargill capital planning process supports the initiatives. Ongoing monitoring of performance, including execution of the capital plan, and environmental scans may trigger a UCS and changes in the CCM strategic plan. Product line, process development group, and facility leaders are responsible for executing the initiatives within the strategic plan. Ultimately the SLT is accountable to the platform for the performance of the strategic and capital plan.

Addressing Strategic Challenges and Advantages   Strategic challenges and advantages along with core competencies are used as drivers for the strategy review process to ensure the company is gaining appropriate leverage from CCM strengths. The SR balances short- and longer-term challenges and opportunities with multiple teams working on different strategic time horizons during the planning process. For example, the UCS or DNS will look at objectives anywhere from one to ten years out depending on the scope of the strategic analysis. The varied background and perspectives of SR participants on these teams is by design and intended to help ensure that the strategic objectives provide a balance for all stakeholders by soliciting wide input during the analysis of key drivers. Innovative ideas are sourced from employees, referred to as Ideas to Innovation (i2i), customers, expert panels, suppliers, and other stakeholders. Innovative product ideas, service ideas, operation ideas, or business model ideas must survive each step of SR analysis (net present value, internal rate of return, etc.) like any other objective in order to become part of the strategic plan.

Development of Action Plans   The strategy review is used to create CCM's strategic plan and define the scope, including resources required, of each key strategic objective. The CCM Strategic Plan is used as a driver for the ABP process. Therefore, tactical plans for all CCM functional areas, product lines, process development groups, and facilities are directly linked and aligned with the CCM Strategic Plan. This linkage ensures the creation and deployment of action plans throughout the business unit to achieve the strategic objectives. For strategic objectives that are longer-term. the objectives are assigned to an SMT member as the sponsor.

Prioritization and Ensuring Adequate Resources   CCM uses a formal, annual Cargill capital planning process and the human capital strategy to ensure financial and people resources are available to support accomplishment of action plans. The SMT is responsible for allocation of resources to support accomplishment of projects, objectives, and action plans. Needs are funneled to the SMT including specific capabilities, length of time required, and starting date. The SMT will then make requests to facilities, PDGs, or functional areas for assistance. For example, the start-up of the Blair, Nebraska expansion project required specialized resources including chemists, operations technicians, and supervisors for a two-month period. CCM assessed financial risk using tools such as net present value and internal rate of return. All projects are subjected to this scrutiny and only the biggest payback projects are implemented.

Capital Planning Process (CPP)   The CPP is a formal Cargill process with CCM's portion owned by the CCM senior engineer. The outcome of this process, the capital plan steps, include the following:

1. The senior engineer and the SMT use the strategic plan to drive nonbase capital needs (i.e., strategic investments, expanded capacity, and new product lines).
2. Plant engineers develop base capital needs (i.e., money used to improve a facility, such as major equipment replacement and energy recovery).
3. Senior engineer reviews all nonbase and base capital needs for the entire business unit. All projects must have an internal rate of return calculated in order to prioritize.
4. CCM's funding request is forwarded to the platform and eventually to the corporate level.
5. Cargill decides how much capital to allocate to each platform and business unit based on overall profitability, capital availability, and the overall direction of the company.
6. Capital allocated to CCM is controlled by the senior engineer and decisions on where to spend base and nonbase capital are driven by

strategies, facility improvements, high-priority projects, and changing business needs throughout the year.

Modifications of Action Plans The annual business planning process is used to develop annual tactical goals and plans. The CCM BSC is reviewed monthly at SMT meetings along with indicators reflecting progress on implementation of strategic objectives. If there are shifts in the environment or in performance of the business plan requiring a change or rapid execution of new plans, the SMT will lead the review and determine if modified action plans are necessary. The enterprise development team leads the analysis of strategic objectives. Models or information used to study any objective are kept for future reference, allowing an objective to be reevaluated if basic assumptions or circumstances change. If a rapid change is required, the product line, process development group, or facility leaders responsible will lead meetings to define the circumstances, analyze the information, and deploy modified action plans including modified individual key result areas, if necessary. For example, in January 2008, a corn syrup summit was held to review every issue around production, customer feedback, initiatives, and projects for the corn syrup product line. A cross-functional group, including operations, QA, finance, HR, and product line leaders, was used to ensure diversity of ideas in developing action plans. Plans developed at the summit are being implemented.

Key Action Plans   CCM has responded to its competitive challenges through two strategic thrusts: diversification and rationalization. Strategically, CCM has diversified its business with the addition of a new product line, brand extension, alliances/agreements, go-to-market strategies, and rationaliziation of production capabilities. The following is an example of short- and longer-term action plans to support a strategic objective of "Build the systems and culture that sustain high employee engagement."

- **Key Action Plan Example (Short-Term).** Define a structure for performing employee focus groups, action plan development, and accountability.
  - Approach: SMT defines accountabilities for focus group sessions and develops a key result area for all managers and supervisors. HR trains focus group facilitators on how to conduct effective listening sessions including communication of results, discussion of results, and development of action plans. Managers and supervisors hold focus group listening session for all natural teams and compile data from listening sessions. Each natural work team creates action plans.
  - Deployment: All sites and personnel.

- Learning: Engagement survey score and employee comments from focus groups analyzed for trends and patterns.
- Integration: Link to performance management process, CCM BSC analysis, career development, training, and compensation.
- **Key Action Plan Example (Longer-Term).** Create a strategic approach to improve overall CCM employee engagement.
  - Approach: SLT defines members of strategy committee, including SMT members. Engagement strategy committee maps a strategic approach for CCM engagement including fact-finding, discussions, and decision making with managers.
  - Deployment: Communicate and execute the strategy with 100 percent understanding of the personal implications of the plan.
  - Learning: Engagement survey score and improved business results (safety, customer satisfaction, community enrichment, and earnings).
  - Integration: Link to performance management process, CCM BSC analysis, career development, training, and compensation.

Key Performance Measures and Indicators   The key CCM BSC performance measures, described in Chapter 6, include high-level metrics used to provide indicators of progress on strategic objectives, initiatives, and business results and are developed during the ABP process. All business plans have specific metrics linked to the CCM BSC and are aligned to achieve balance for key deployment areas and stakeholders. Alignment of CCM employees with strategy occurs with the linkage of the strategy review process, the ABP process, and the performance management process, which leads to creation of employee key result areas (KRAs).

INTEGRATING RISK INTO STRATEGIC PLANNING AND MANAGEMENT   CCM purchases millions of bushels of corn each year, which represents its largest raw material cost. Risk position limits are governed by the Cargill commodity risk committee (CRC), which sets specific limits for each of Cargill's business units. Position limits are monitored daily to ensure compliance to established position limits. Exceptions to preauthorized limits must be granted by the CRC. Members of the CRC are Cargill senior executives.

COMMUNICATING STRATEGY   Effective information flow and two-way communication are achieved using several systematic processes including SLT tours, conference calls, town hall/quarterly meetings, and department/functional area meetings. Annual SLT tours are conducted at each plant and in Minneapolis. These meetings allow the plants to share their successes and opportunities and learn how CCM is performing. During the tour, the SLT members spend time with various groups allowing time for two-way communication. Conference calls are held regularly (monthly, bimonthly, or weekly) based on the subject matter and utilize agendas to ensure effective communication. For example, a weekly production planning call is utilized to optimize production and a monthly employee engagement call is used to share practices and focus this group on improving overall engagement. Town hall/quarterly meetings are held at every plant and in Minneapolis to review results and initiatives, and provide formal opportunities to generate two-way discussion of pertinent business unit topics. Department and functional area meetings are used to review progress, generate action plans, and provide two-way discussion of concerns.

CORE AND INNOVATIVE BEST PRACTICES CCM exercises the core best practices discussed earlier; plus it has advanced knowledge in this area with new, innovative best practices.

Principle 2: Refresh and Communicate Strategy

- **Strategic planning.** Leverage the strategic planning process as either owner or partner to understand changing market conditions including competitor, supplier, rival, and potential entrants and substitutes in the marketplace.
- **Core and adjacent products and services.** Define and determine core and adjacent products and services to focus on highest probabilities for success.
- **Strategic plan.** Produce a comprehensive strategic plan.
- **Strategy mapping.** CCM does not use.
- **Link strategic planning and budgeting processes.** Link strategic planning to the budgeting process, partner and budgeting with finance to provide for a seamless continuum. Weighting point system used for capital expenditures.
- **Communications plan.** Communicate strategy throughout the organization using a comprehensive communications plan.
- **Innovative Best Practice.** CCM integrates risk into strategic planning and management to optimize strategic outcomes; most companies treat these key elements as separate events or work streams.
- **Innovative Best Practice.** CCM strategic planning process integrates experts from within CCM, parent Cargill, and outside Cargill to formulate its strategic plan.

(Continued)

- **Innovative Best Practice.** CCM strategic planning process sources innovative ideas from employees, referred to as Ideas to Innovation, customers, expert panels, suppliers, and other stakeholders. Innovative product ideas, service ideas, operation ideas, or business model ideas must survive each step of SR analysis.
- **Innovative Best Practice.** CCM focuses and balances its strategy review consisting of three subprocesses: (1) continue with current strategy, (2) update current strategy, or (3) design a new strategy to change direction of business, all on the longer term; and its annual review process on the short-term upcoming year.
- **Innovative Best Practice.** CCM uses a formal, annual Cargill capital planning process and the human capital strategy to ensure financial and people resources are available to support accomplishment of action plans.
- **Innovative Best Practice.** CCM has developed one of the most comprehensive, integrated bidirectional communications plans on strategy to its employees among dozens of companies reviewed, consisting of annual, quarterly, monthly, bimonthly, weekly, and daily formalized frequencies among multiple channels.

City of Coral Springs: Best Practice Case

The city's mission and purpose, vision, and core values guide the formulation of its strategic plan.

- **Mission and Purpose.** The city's mission is "to be the nation's premier community in which to live, work, and raise a family."
- **Vision.** Community visioning retreats are held to reach consensus on the direction for the city. The city's strategic priorities, developed in commission workshops, are an outline of that direction
- **Core Values.** The city's organizational culture is best expressed in five core values underlying this vision:

  1. *Customer Focus.* Demonstrate a passion for customer service.
  2. *Leadership.* Establish an inspiring vision that creates a government that works better and costs less.
  3. *Empowered Employees.* Empower the people closest to the customer to continuously improve the organization's quality and services.

4. *Continuous Improvement.* Commit "every day, in every way, to getting better and better."

5. *Sustainability.* Work toward efficient and cost-effective solutions to protect and conserve natural resources, maintain economic viability, and ensure a healthy and safe quality of life for current and future generations.

The senior management team directs staff in the implementation of commission policies and manages city operations. Twenty-seven citizen advisory committees and boards linking directly to the city's seven strategic priorities are highly involved in city government, providing input on customer priorities and requirements.

VISIONING SUMMIT   The environmental scan and the visioning process are designed to focus the organization on creating and balancing value for customers and other stakeholders. The scan includes input from and data on the satisfaction and needs of customer segments. This is accomplished primarily through cross tabulation of data in the resident and business surveys and the SWOT survey completed by members of advisory groups and employees.

CITY STRATEGIC PLANNING PROCESS   At the highest level, the city's strategy development and deployment model uses information and analysis as the basis for strategic and business plans that set priorities, objectives, and programs for the year. The annual budget quantifies these plans, defining programs and services that provide direct output to citizens. Those outputs are measured and analyzed in a "feedback loop."

The city has an extremely well-defined strategic planning process. Exhibit 5.2 shows the city's performance improvement system.

At the strategic level, an environmental scan supplies data and information for the planning process and forms the basis for the strategic plan and business plan. The business plan lists specific new services and service improvements that will be affected by teams in the fiscal year. Key intended outcomes (KIOs) are established to measure citywide progress against the strategic plan. Negative variation in these measures initiates an assessment of whether a process improvement or change in tactics is needed. At the operational level, in-process measures, complaint tracking data, ideas from empowered employees, information on innovations in other communities, and new developments in a field trigger department-level improvement initiatives. Other processes that focus operations on performance improvement are training, reward and recognition, and leadership communications. The process of developing the business plan establishes

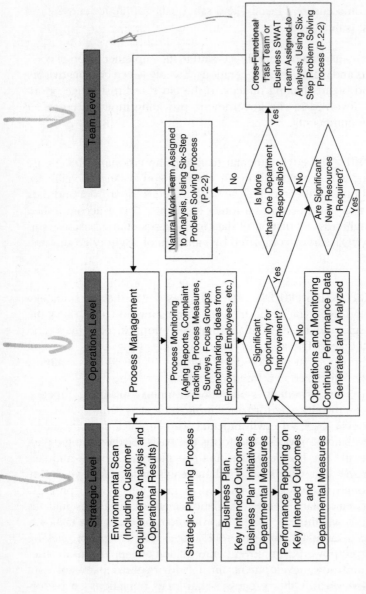

EXHIBIT 5.2 City of Coral Springs' Performance Improvement System Courtesy of City of Coral Springs.

priorities for major process improvement projects. The strategic priorities and consistency with city values are the basis for the decision to implement a process improvement project. Unit and department improvement initiatives are selected based on how they impact objectives. These projects support business and strategic objectives because objectives at all levels are aligned.

TIME-PHASED STRATEGY DEVELOPMENT The commission began a process of strategic planning designed to identify the issues that must be addressed to achieve the city's mission and that will persist over the lifetime of the strategic plan.

Reviewed and updated annually, the strategic plan creates a shared vision for the future of the community. These long-range policy issues, or seven strategic priorities, developed by the city commission and reaffirmed during the fiscal years 2007–2009 strategic planning process, emphasize the values of the community:

1. Customer-involved government
2. Neighborhood and environmental vitality
3. Financial health and economic development
4. Excellence in education
5. Youth development and family values
6. Strength in diversity
7. Traffic, mobility, and connectivity

For each priority, a set of directional statements are developed, which define broad objectives that help focus activities on desirable outcomes. Then two to ten KIOs are set for each priority to determine if a priority has been successfully addressed. KIOs are measurable outcomes at the strategic level. City staff then respond to the strategic plan (longer-term planning) with a business plan (short-term planning) for implementing the policy direction through specific programs and initiatives. With the strategic priorities and indicators set, the operations of the city are reviewed and redirected to bring the strategic vision to life. Specific actions, programs, capital purchases, staffing requirements, and funding levels are developed in response to the needs identified in the strategic plan. Through this process, policy formation and deployment cascades throughout the organization; key terms are defined as follows:

- *Strategic Priority*—The commission identifies the vital issues.
- *Directional Statement*—The commission sets broad goals.
- *Key Intended Outcomes*—The commission identifies desired results.

- *Initiatives*—Staff allocate activities, resources, personnel, financial investment, and time planned for the year to achieve each key intended outcome.
- *Performance Measures*—Staff set specific and measurable data points indicating the effectiveness of processes designed to support the key intended outcomes.

The business plan document is a direct outgrowth of the strategic priorities, capturing the city's vision in a quantifiable form, improving decision making and resource allocation. This model is used to monitor performance through variance analysis of goal to actual; linking budget line items to measurable activities; and identifying value-added and non-value-added activities.

The business plan is an organic document in that it is continually revisited throughout the year and may be amended by a majority vote of the commission. Changes in the environment may require realignment of resources to continue to keep city staff on target to meet the KIOs and strategic priorities.

Departments set goals to meet strategic needs. To meet these goals, programs within the departments have specific objectives that are measured through performance measures. Individual staff members' objectives and performance measures are then linked to the program objectives. Each employee knows what the end result should be and how it contributes to the strategic plan. The performance measure tables included with each department's summary in the annual budget document are designed to show how the program objectives support the strategic priorities. Performance measures are explicitly related to the KIO that they support and the strategic priorities that they fulfill.

STRATEGIC PLANNING AND CUSTOMER INPUTS   The strategic planning process begins in January of even-numbered years based on election cycles when staff begin collecting data for the environmental scan, which includes input from over 15 customer feedback sources ranging from surveys and town halls to focus groups and the city blog, as well as management and policy analysis of emerging issues, demographic trends, and financial conditions.

A strategic planning workshop is convened in the spring, where staff and the commission discuss strategic challenges and advantages, using a workbook that consists of the following sections:

- **Financial Health.** A description of the current financial condition of the city with information on the financial trend monitoring system (analysis of current data) and five-year forecast (a long-term financial planning tool).

- **Environmental Scan.** Demographic trends, an economic analysis, land development trends, service demand generators, technology changes and issues, legislative challenges, and emerging issues are presented that will have an impact on the city during the next three to five years.
- **Customer Requirements Analysis.** Summaries of customer feedback from the resident survey, business survey, neighborhood meetings, SWOT (Strengths-Weaknesses-Opportunities-Threats) results, and public visioning exercises are included to identify trends and affinities.
- **Performance Analysis.** A summary of the quarterly performance review, the status of KIOs, and a projection of the composite index are included to describe the current performance of the organization.
- **Mission, Core Values, and Strategic Priorities.** Current versions are included to provide a basis for discussing future needs.
- **Benchmarking.** Comparative data on key areas with discussions of possible improvement projects.
- **Current Initiative Update.** A review of the current year business plan initiatives. In-depth presentations are made on some of the emerging issues, important initiatives, or cross-functional process improvement team results, as warranted.

Typically, research on key issues uncovered in the environmental scan such as shifts in technology or the regulatory environment are highlighted. Challenges to the organization's continuity of operations plan (COOP), the emergency response plan, are also addressed when necessary. Time is also spent reviewing customer feedback and the strengths, weaknesses, opportunities, and threats identified by key stakeholders. Potential blind spots are identified by ensuring the comprehensiveness of data from many sources and through the forward-looking analysis of emerging issues facing the city.

BUSINESS PLAN AND FUNDING INITIATIVES AND DEPARTMENT BUDGETS A senior management team staff retreat is held in May to discuss proposed business plan initiatives. Each initiative is discussed, analyzed, and weighed against the others until a slate of initiatives is reached through consensus. A business planning workshop is held in June with the City Commission to present the proposed slate of business plan initiatives, including major capital projects and new programs, and to solicit feedback and input. A second workshop is held in July to present the refined plan with associated budget projections to the commission. Both workshops are televised and open to the public. Once the business plan is approved, departments use it as their action plan for the next year. Supervisors link program milestones, individual work plans, and each employee's incentive pay system review objectives to the business plan during the October review period.

The city manager and the senior management team meet weekly to discuss progress relative to the plan, and any concerns are addressed through the business planning process. In addition, the city manager meets quarterly with each department director to ensure the plan is progressing as expected by revisiting the KIOs. The bulk of the strategy-level deployment is addressed by this point, so staff spend the rest of July and August preparing the proposed budget for public hearings in September. Resolutions and ordinances are voted into place and the new fiscal year begins October 1. Budget staff prepare the adopted budget and planning documents by December and the cycle starts again in January.

To ensure continuous improvement and test the soundness of the system, an annual review of the system is made in January. Management and budget office staff gather feedback from departments, the commission, and other end-users on the ease of use and outcomes of the system. A standing business SWOT team for business planning analysis meets to discuss recommendations and results of the process review, as well as feedback from senior management team retreats and individual staff efforts in evaluating the strategic planning process.

The strategic objectives (priorities) are supported by directional statements and specific objectives called KIOs, with the annual goal for each. Due to the nature of the planning process, the practice is always to set goals for each measure for both years, although many of the KIOs will be used over many years, with appropriate adjustments to the goals made on an annual basis. By creating the strategic plan through analysis of customer feedback, environmental conditions, and organizational performance, the city ensures that the challenges identified in the organizational profile are addressed through strategic priorities. *Opportunities for innovation are identified the same way.* Once challenges and opportunities are identified, the organization can deploy responsibility for achieving policy goals through the business plan, departmental work plans, and individual incentive pay system objectives.

COMMUNICATING STRATEGY   The city makes data and information available to employees, suppliers, partners, collaborators, and customers using a variety of methods. Information dissemination to customers includes publications, public events, Slice of the Springs neighborhood meetings, public hearings, public postings, personal contacts, CityTV, CityRadio, *City Page* ads, city blog, podcasts, CCR, direct e-mail and eNews broadcast e-mails, and the city's Web site. Customers also receive data and information when they interact with the city in the delivery of city services. The traditional venues for these interactions are at the customer's home or business, or at a city facility. However, the Internet continues to grow as a communications tool that allows customers to interact with the city at their convenience via the city's

Web site. Currently, a customer can use the Internet to submit various types of forms, place and track citizen complaints, inquire about or pay a water bill, check the status of a building plan review, request or check the status of a building inspection, renew occupational licenses, apply for a job, register for recreation programs, watch CityTV streaming video or video-on-demand, and participate in weblog conversations.

CORE AND INNOVATIVE BEST PRACTICES   The city exercises the core best practices identified earlier and has advanced knowledge in this area with new, innovative best practices.

Principle 2: Refresh and Communicate Strategy

- **Strategic planning.** Leverage the strategic planning process as either owner or partner to understand changing market conditions including competitor, supplier, rival, and potential entrants and substitutes in the marketplace.
- **Core and adjacent products and services.** Define and determine core and adjacent products and services to focus on highest probabilities for success.
- **Strategic plan.** Produce a comprehensive strategic plan.
- **Strategy mapping.** In lieu of a strict Kaplan and Norton strategy map, the city develops its major strategic priorities, each with two to ten KIOs, linked initiatives, and related measures across financial, customer, process, and employee parameters.
- **Link strategic planning and budgeting processes.** Link strategic planning to the budgeting process, partner and budgeting with finance to provide for a seamless continuum.
- **Communications plan.** Communicate strategy throughout the organization using a comprehensive communications plan.
- **Innovative Best Practice.** City of Coral Springs' business plan is recognized as an organic document that will adjust and be used dynamically in response to changing market conditions; this contrasts with a static approach to business planning. Changes in the environment may require realignment of resources to continue to keep city staff on target to meet the KIOs and strategic priorities.
- **Innovative Best Practice.** City of Coral Springs' strategic planning process or system has been recognized as a best practice by numerous third-party organizations, National Performance Review,

(Continued)

American Productivity and Quality Center, Government Finance Officers Association publications, the Florida Institute of Government programs, and Fitch.

- **Innovative Best Practice.** City of Coral Springs' strategic planning process involves customers enabling key requirements, secured from over 15 customer input sources, to be included in strategic goals, KIOs, and cascaded down through the organization.
- **Innovative Best Practice.** City of Coral Springs' approach to communicating strategy is far more comprehensive in scope, extending outside the City. The city makes data and information available not only to employees but also suppliers, partners, collaborators, and customers using a variety of methods.

Delta Dental of Kansas: Best Practice Case

Delta Dental of Kansas (DDKS) leadership plays an important role in the development and deployment of company strategy, and in setting and reaffirming organizational vision and values. With a strategy map in place and the Balanced Scorecard (BSC) system to establish targets and track progress, the mission, vision, and values of the organization provide a framework for leadership. To set and endorse organizational vision, values, and strategy, DDKS leaders engage in the long-range planning (LRP) process annually. In assessing the corporation's direction and strategy, competitive and market data are reviewed, as well as an analysis of the company's strengths, weaknesses, opportunities, and threats (SWOT), best business practices, and other relevant planning information. More recently, an analysis of the potential impacts of the political, economic, social, and technological (PEST) environment on the organization and its constituents has become part of the LRP discussions. Combining LRP elements from DDKS leaders with input from the board of directors allows the company to confirm, change, and/or redirect organizational vision and values annually. The company strategy map is reviewed during the LRP process. Core values and visual elements are reinforced through employee communications, including such publications as the annual report and long-range plan documents. Quarterly assessments of employee performance relating to the core values are combined with Balanced Scorecard progress to determine performance results for each individual, thus deploying the company's vision and values across all levels of the organization. Goals are established for the company, department, and individual based on company strategy, with accountability for results. Merit and incentive decisions are based on performance metrics in addition to values assessments. With the mission, vision, and values being key foundations for company strategy, there is expectation and responsibility for leadership to cascade the mission, vision, and values throughout the workforce and through all employees to key suppliers, partners, customers, and other stakeholders.

- **Mission and Purpose:** To become the first choice of Kansans for quality dental benefit programs
- **Vision:**
  - To improve oral health for all Kansans
  - To be a household name
  - To increase access by constituents
  - To retain employees who know they make a difference
  - To set the standard in service
  - To never be satisfied
- **Core Values:**
  - Excellence in reputation—being part of the best
  - Continuously setting the service standard
  - Taking pride in what they do through hard work and integrity
  - Fiscal responsibility
  - Commitment to and respect for all constituents

Leadership oversight of BSC initiatives and metrics ensures that commitments to all constituent groups are a point of focus and that results are monitored. All constituents have targeted actions designated by the strategy map to ensure communication and obtain input through client satisfaction surveys and other forums. Key suppliers are required to meet service-level commitments.

There is a high level of personal commitment by leaders to engage in community involvement; to serve on community, civic, professional, and charity boards and committees; and to be heavily involved with special events in support of those organizations. Leadership team (LT) commitment is demonstrated by supporting community events in the workplace for programs that are in direct support of the company's visional elements.

LEADERSHIP TEAM Strategic objectives are established for each plan year in support of the mission, with the primary accountability tool being the Level I BSC. Timelines are initially established during the LRP stages with input/review of the board of directors, with milestones and BSC results reported to the board of directors' compensation committee quarterly and to the full board.

As a component of the organization's assessment of agility, a SWOT analysis is completed during the LRP process by the LT and is reviewed with the board of directors. The company has experienced significant growth during the past five years. Organizational agility has been required to meet additional staffing and training needs in order to serve large clients while continuing to deliver excellent service as evidenced by constituent survey results. Through investigation, constituent input, and application of business concepts such as the S-curve, the rollout of ancillary products through a new start-up company resulted from the LRP process and strategic initiatives.

As health care costs rise and companies' benefit dollars shrink, DDKS must educate employers that unbundling dental benefits is worthwhile. DDKS has to compete in the cost arena against companies who can spread their costs over multiple product lines. This impacts DDKS's ability to compete in a market where price becomes increasingly more important.

Notwithstanding its strong market position, continued new growth and retention will become increasingly challenging because of significant market saturation. Accordingly, DDKS is exploring additional ancillary lines of business.

STRATEGIC PLANNING PROCESS   Strategic planning and execution are central to the success of DDKS as an organization. The framework for reviewing strategy has evolved over time with the implementation of the BSC format providing a means to take a fresh look at the organization, its markets and services, and to target growth and the processes, enhance customer feedback mechanisms, and delineate the learning and growth environment essential to long-term success. During the rollout of the new strategy map and BSC tool, increased attention was placed on strategy within DDKS and the tie to corporate strategy of all departments and individuals in the organization. It was during this stage of the company's history when core values were clearly identified with visional elements and the mission statement was simplified and reemphasized in employee communications.

Strategic planning is now a year-round process at DDKS, with set parameters regarding the formalization of outcomes constructed on an annual basis. Exhibit 5.3 identifies the steps in the LRP process, encompassing data research and analysis from a variety of resources, including constituent surveys and economic development conferences.

The purpose of the LRP is to develop and confirm strategic and visionary direction for the company and arrive at corporate objectives for the following plan year, with targets and measurement criteria. Focus is placed on defining effective growth options and alignment of strategy in order to successfully grow the company's operations. The board of directors engages in proprietary SWOT and political, economic, social, and technological (PEST)

EXHIBIT 5.3 Long-Range Planning Process

Steps	Participants	Inputs	Outputs
1: Market Analysis	LT, Sales and Marketing, Finance, BOD, selected employees as needed	PIC's, constituent surveys and meetings, economic industry data, regulatory environment, targeted research	Analysis for LT pre-planning, BOD enrichment sessions, one-on-one CEO/BOD discussions
2: LRP Pre-planning Sessions	Strategic Planning Team	Facilitators meeting issue identification, status on current year corporate initiatives, LT and BOD discussions	Business strategy theme, directions and goals for LRP LT session, pre-work/materials
3: LT 2-day Planning Session	LT, Facilitator	Market analysis, session pre-work, planning theme, facilitator input	Proposed Mission, visional elements, core values, hedgehog, SWOT, S-curve 5-yr projection for product development, current/future org profiles, draft of 3-yr LRP and 1-yr corporate initiatives
4: Board/LT Planning Retreat	LT, BOD, Facilitator	Business theme concepts, step 3 outputs, preliminary budget implications	Concept approval for LRP and Level 1 BSC targets
5: Approval and Action Planning	LT, BOD	Proposed 3-yr LRP, including strategy map, level 1 BSC, hedgehog, corporate initiatives, SWOT, executive summary	Approved LRP document with supporting budget and Level 1 BSC targets/measures
6: Communication and Deployment	LT, BOD, all employees	LRP document, Level 1, II, III BSCs, business plans for corporate initiatives, milestones and timelines, initiative tracking tool	Dashboard tracking, all employee quarterly updates, LT review of corporate initiatives with tracking tool, performance management system based on results of Level 1, II, III BSC, BOD oversight

Courtesy of Delta Dental of Kansas.

analyses with the leadership team keep LT since you use it shortly to exchange ideas on the other draft segments of the LRP and preliminary budget to support the plan. Market analysis is a key element. Sources for competitive data, including use of an outside facilitator and consideration of DDPA analysis, help preclude being blindsided by critical considerations overlooked by the planning team. Timing of the planning process is designed to coincide with the budget development and approval process, allocating resources for key corporate initiatives resulting from the LRP. The LRP discussions include relevant business themes and identification of any hot-topic or market/product–sensitive issues to be included, in the context of strategy. A three- to five-year time period is reviewed from the standpoint of a future organizational profile to provide a forward focus for the planning. The organizational profile includes market, distribution, growth, and other key perspectives.

A five-year cycle has been used historically for planning to center discussion on the long-term vision and goals of the company. While a five-year time frame is used for the future profile and product development/market analysis, the outcome of the LRP process is a three-year document prepared with input from the board of directors. For financial targets and growth projections, the three-year profile has provided a more realistic time frame for intermediate planning purposes. An important output of the planning cycle is the determination of the following year's BSC objectives at the corporate level, including one-year action plans for corporate initiatives identified during the LRP discussions, thus setting the stage for deployment and accountability for results, concurrently with the budget planning cycle.

Specific action plans with accompanying budgets are generated to reach desired outcomes. Corporate initiatives are supported by detailed business plans and milestone timelines. Specific progress regarding corporate initiatives and BSC goals are reported to the compensation committee of the board of directors and the full board quarterly.

In addition to constituent perspectives obtained through surveys and formal and informal interactions with staff, customer preferences are channeled through the LT. Industry trends, technology, and constituent preferences are evident in sales calls, professional impact councils (PICs) with the dental community, as well as request for proposal (RFP) requirements. Competition is assessed through formal data analysis as well as firsthand through the bid process, finalist presentations to prospective customers, and feedback from the RFP process. LT and BOD enrichment sessions provide updates with market analysis prior to LRP sessions and year-round. Technology discussion is prevalent during LRP sessions. Information technology is a component of competition that is considered through existing operations and the RFP process for group administration. DDPAfocuses on technology as an association, and member companies keep MC it is reused provide expertise in assessing common challenges.

From review of the current and organizational profiles, as well as the competitive market analysis, hedgehog, BSC results, and projections, factors are considered to ensure long-term organizational sustainability. The S-curve analysis and market predictions provide important data for directing strategy. The S-curve represents the growth cycle of a business or product, usually illustrated as a horizontal figure S. At the lower point of the S a business/product is in the beginning stages, with the upward slope of the letter illustrating major growth. With maturity or market penetration, the slope of the S-curve flattens and then bends downward, representing decline of the business or product cycle. DDKS has used this concept to illustrate potential growth through ancillary benefit products and strategic opportunities.

Once corporate initiatives are established through the LRP process, detailed business plans are written for each and supported by timelines and milestone goals. An initiative tracking tool is used to chart and review progress for LT meetings each month and readily reflects the on-time status of projects.

Key long-term strategic objectives are included on the strategy map. Strategic objectives are reflected in each of the perspectives: financial, customer, process, and learning and growth. The Level I BSC identifies the strategic objectives for the annual plan year as the most important goals for the year. These are solidified with metrics and target goals for each calendar quarter. The BSC approach provides a means to set goals and track progress for each perspective of the organization, with inputs in the learning and growth and process sections, and customer and financial results being outputs. Department strategy maps also serve to align functional areas with company strategy and serve as another reference point for implementation purposes.

Strategic objectives are designed to address strategic challenges, advantages, and opportunities identified through the LRP process, considering market analysis, the hedgehog concept, product development cycles, and other important LRP components. As a result of the SWOT analysis, strategic objectives are identified as corporate initiatives to address *opportunities for innovation* in products and services, operations, and the business model. Innovation is a strategic theme under internal processes and organizational resources are allocated to projects in support of that theme. An example of incorporation of innovation and organization sustainability strategy is the initiative surrounding the new for-profit, wholly owned subsidiary currently being launched. This strategy was identified through the SWOT analysis over a period of years, and corporate initiatives were put in place over a two-year time frame to further delineate the action plans required to research and launch this vehicle for strategic market and product expansion.

By design, the customer perspective of the DDKS strategy map identifies universal as well as group-specific expectations and positions a balance between them. The Level I BSC identifies satisfaction level targets and outcomes by constituent group, with constituent surveys also serving as a resource for identifying future initiatives or refining scorecard targets and measures. Organization objectives reflect a customer focus in all other perspectives of the BSC as well, taking into account different constituent group expectations. Objectives are cascaded to the department and individual levels from standpoints of delivery and accountability.

STRATEGIC INITIATIVES AND BUDGETING   With organizational objectives established for the plan year, action plans are developed and deployed throughout the organization to achieve these key strategic objectives. Corporate initiatives are assigned to an LT member for implementation responsibility.

Corporate initiatives are identified through the LRP process and are reflected on the Level I company BSC for the year in which research or implementation occurs. Corporate initiatives have potential impact for the organization as a whole and progress versus plan on each of these initiatives, which have leadership team member(s) as an executive sponsor, is tracked and reviewed monthly by the LT. Departmental initiatives, while still tied to company strategy, are reflected in department business plans and shared with the LT.

A separate initiative budget item is included to review corporate initiative costs as a portfolio apart from regular budget items. This provides for better tracking of expenses associated with new strategy initiatives. For departmental initiatives in support of company strategy, department heads are responsible for the financial and other resources accompanying them, with accountability on the Level II and Level III BSC again tied to compensation.

COMPETITIVE ADVANTAGE   DDKS differentiates itself from its competitors in three key areas. First, customer service is its number one priority. With the implementation of the voice over Internet protocol (VOIP), customer service representatives, with prior dental office experience and/or training on dental procedures, can answer calls in a matter of seconds.

Second, although DDKS provides dental benefits to employees across the country, it is located in Kansas and concentrates on its local presence. It stresses personalized customer service, easy access to sales, management, and operational teams, and its commitment to the Kansas community. In addition, DDKS offers a Guarantee of Service Excellence (GOSE) program to its customers. GOSE promises exceptional service in five key areas and is backed by financial refunds should DDKS fail to deliver on any aspect of the promise.

Third, DDKS continuously sets the service standard by surveying constituents and implementing plan changes that will provide the most benefit.

STRATEGY MAP   DDKS adopted the Kaplan and Norton Strategy Map and BSC approach. The DDKS strategy map consists of strategic objectives across the four financial, customer, process, and learning and growth perspectives.

The DDKS strategy map is reviewed annually during the LRP process, with any changes made accordingly. As an organizational communication tool, it is used to illustrate the strategic inputs important for the organization in the learning and growth and process perspectives, as well as the desired outcomes in the customer and financial perspectives, in support of the mission featured at the top of the map. The core values of the organization are shown in the learning and growth perspective, stressing the importance of these values for the organization. Processes are defined according to four different themes, with some initiatives supporting more than one of the following themes: solutions innovation, customer loyalty, efficiency and effectiveness, and external influences. The customer perspective includes four external constituent groups, with some basic expectations consistent across group purchasers, enrollees, dentists, and insurance professionals.

COMMUNICATING STRATEGY   The three-year LRP is presented to all employees at the first quarterly all-employee meeting along with the BSC targets for the year and corporate initiatives. In fact, a strategy logo was designed to reinforce the strategy concept with color-coded steps representing the four perspectives of the strategy map as components of "Knowledge, Commitment, Success." This tool is instrumental in helping to support strategic objectives, deliver training for skill enhancement, and document results.

CORE AND INNOVATIVE BEST PRACTICES   DDKS exercises the core best practices discussed earlier and has advanced knowledge in this area with new, innovative best practices.

Principle 2: Refresh and Communicate Strategy

- **Strategic planning.** Leverage the strategic planning process to understand changing market conditions including competitor, supplier, rival, and potential entrants and substitutes in the marketplace. Complete a comprehensive SWOT and PEST analysis.

(Continued)

- **Core and adjacent products and services.** Define and determine core and potential adjacent products and products and services to focus on highest probabilities for success.
- **Strategic plan.** Produce a comprehensive strategic plan.
- **Strategy mapping.** Develop corporate and department level strategy maps containing objectives along four perspectives including financial, customer/constituent, process, and people. Observe strategy map design best practices of 20 to 25 objectives.
- **Link strategic planning and budgeting processes.** Link strategic planning to the budgeting process to provide for a seamless strategy to financial continuum.
- **Communications plan.** Communicate strategy throughout the organization using a comprehensive communications plan.
- **Innovative Best Practice.** Develop and manage the S-curve or profile for the rollout of ancillary products.
- **Innovative Best Practice.** Strategic planning is now a year-round process, demonstrating flexibility and dynamism at DDKS, recognizing and addressing changing market conditions, and leveraging both SWOT and PEST methods.
- **Innovative Best Practice.** Separate initiative budget item is included to review costs as a portfolio apart from regular budget items. This provides for better tracking of expenses associated with new strategy initiatives.

Lockheed Martin, Information Systems & Global Services: Best Practice Case

The strategy of the Lockheed Martin (LM) Information Systems & Global Services (IS&GS)-Civil organization is clearly and demonstrably owned by the business unit's president, Ken Asbury. The full executive leadership team (i.e., the business unit president's direct reports) assumes collective ownership of the strategy. Since IS&GS describes its strategy using a strategy map and BSC, it leverages the framework's ability to foster alignment and accountability. The executive leadership team members volunteer to be an advocate for one or two of the strategic objectives in a role called the Performance Advocate (PA). In addition to the collective ownership of the organization's strategy, each PA is responsible for advancing the objective. This includes initial efforts such as defining the objective more thoroughly, then establishing what the organization must focus on and bringing to bear measures and targets aligned with that focus (i.e., what gets measured gets done). Additional leadership responsibilities of the PA include the fostering of significant initiatives or investments to advance the objective as well as modest actions to maintain incremental momentum. It is through this combination of executive ownership at the business unit president level and the collaborative ownership by the full executive team, enabled by the PA role, that establishes the leadership foundation for the success of the strategy and its management processes. Strategy is shared through IS&GS-Civil Strategy Communications:

- **Mission and Purpose:** The purpose of LM IS&GS-Civil is to support customers across the civil government, helping them transform how the government provides service to the citizen.
- IS&GS strategy is simply stated as "Complete Citizen Services."
- **Vision:** Across LM, employees share a common vision. "Powered by Innovation, Guided by Integrity, We Help Our Customers Achieve Their Most Challenging Goals."
- **Core Values:** Across LM, employees share a common set of core values. "Perform with Excellence—Respect Others—Do What's Right."

STRATEGIC PLANNING PROCESS   The strategic planning processes across LM IS&GS-Civil are aligned and formulated so that each organization envisions and formulates a strategy deemed effective for its unique customer and market (i.e., which customers, solutions, and services to target and develop). In formulating these elements of strategy, the teams use three primary methods or approaches including (1) assessing their strengths, weaknesses, opportunities, and threats (SWOT), (2) Michael Porter's Five Forces, and (3) PESTEL and to a lesser extent custom approaches. Since SWOT and the Five Forces have been defined in other cases, let us turn our attention to exploring PESTEL.

PESTEL stands for political, economic, social, technological, environmental, and legal analysis and describes a framework of macro-environmental factors used in the environmental scanning component of strategic management:

- **Political.** Factors are how and to what degree a government intervenes in the economy. Specifically, political factors include areas such as tax policy, labor law, environmental law, trade restrictions, tariffs, and political stability.
- **Economic.** Factors include economic growth, interest rates, exchange rates, and the inflation rate.
- **Social.** Factors include the cultural aspects and include health consciousness, population growth rate, age distribution, career attitudes, and emphasis on safety. Trends in social factors affect the demand for a company's products and how that company operates.

- **Technological.** Factors include ecological and environmental aspects, such as R&D activity, automation, technology incentives, and the rate of technological change. Furthermore, technological shifts can affect costs, quality, and lead to *innovation*.
- **Environmental.** Factors include weather, climate, and climate change, which may especially affect industries such as tourism, farming, and insurance.
- **Legal.** Factors include discrimination law, consumer law, antitrust law, employment law, and health and safety law.

These strategies are aligned to the overall market focus of IS&GS-Civil (i.e., citizen services) and contribute to the overall financial commitments of LM detailed in the long-range plan (LRP) (i.e., orders, sales, EBIT, ROS, cash, ROIC, etc.). Further, these strategies are in alignment as a corporation, that is, LM integrates the IS&GS leadership framework called full spectrum leadership (FSL) into the BSC structure in a thematic manner.

The FSL framework is comprised of five key elements of effective leadership called Imperatives:

1. Deliver Results.
2. Build Effective Relationships.
3. Shape the Future.
4. Energize the Team.
5. Model Personal Excellence, Integrity, and Accountability.

The five FSL imperatives are the integrating framework of annual performance objectives and incentives throughout LM. On an annual basis, employees submit their annual performance objectives using the FSL imperatives in line-of-sight to their respective leader. Since these imperatives are also integrated into the IS&GS-Civil BSC, they foster vertical alignment to corporate objectives and a logical linkage to the annual performance objective-setting process.

STRATEGIC INITIATIVES AND BUDGETING   IS&GS-Civil strategic initiatives come in two varieties. One is a focus on initiatives pursued via research and development (R&D) processes that lead to capabilities for customers. Generally, R&D funding is pursued through business cases and leadership sponsorship. Budgets are allocated based on availability and value. The other type of initiative is internally focused, for example, an enterprise resource planning investment. Similar to internally funded R&D investments, these investments are considered through a business case and leadership sponsorship and budgets are allocated on an annual basis for these investments. The execution of these initiatives vary from informal prototyping and development to rigorous application of program and development methods, for example, levels of Software Engineering Institute (SEI) Capability Maturity Model (CMM) processes are applied.

CMM is a service mark owned by Carnegie Mellon University and refers to a development model elicited from actual data.

When it is applied to an existing organization's software development processes, it allows an effective approach toward improving them. The Capability Maturity Model involves the following aspects:

- **Maturity Levels.** A five-level process maturity continuum where the uppermost (fifth) level is an ideal state where processes would be systematically managed by a combination of process optimization and continuous process improvement.
- **Key Process Areas.** A key process area (KPA) identifies a cluster of related activities that, when performed collectively, achieve a set of goals considered important.
- **Goals.** The goals of a key process area summarize the states that must exist for that key process area to have been implemented in an effective and lasting way. The extent to which the goals have been accomplished is an indicator of how much capability the organization has established at that maturity level. The goals signify the scope, boundaries, and intent of each key process area.
- **Common Features.** Common features include practices that implement and institutionalize a key process area. There are five types of common features: commitment to perform, ability to perform, activities performed, measurement and analysis, and verifying implementation.
- **Key Practices.** The key practices describe the elements of infrastructure and practice that contribute most effectively to the implementation and institutionalization of the KPAs.

Five levels are defined along the continuum of the CMM, according to the SEI: "Predictability, effectiveness, and control of an organization's software processes are believed to improve as the organization moves up these five levels. While not rigorous, the empirical evidence to date supports this belief."

The CMM provides a continuum along which process maturity can be developed incrementally from one level to the next. Skipping levels is not allowed or feasible.

- **Level 1 Initial (Chaotic).** It is characteristic of processes at this level that they are (typically) undocumented and in a state of dynamic change, tending to be driven in an ad hoc, uncontrolled, and reactive manner by users or events. This provides a chaotic or unstable environment for the processes.

- **Level 2 Repeatable.** It is characteristic of processes at this level that some processes are repeatable, possibly with consistent results. Process discipline is unlikely to be rigorous, but where it exists it may help to ensure that existing processes are maintained during times of stress.
- **Level 3 Defined.** It is characteristic of processes at this level that there are sets of defined and documented standard processes established and subject to some degree of improvement over time. These standard processes are in place (i.e., they are the AS-IS processes) and used to establish consistency of process performance across the organization.
- **Level 4 Managed.** It is characteristic of processes at this level that, using process metrics, management can effectively control the AS-IS process (e.g., for software development). In particular, management can identify ways to adjust and adapt the process to particular projects without measurable losses of quality or deviations from specifications. Process capability is established from this level.
- **Level 5 Optimized.** It is characteristic of processes at this level that the focus is on continually improving process performance through both incremental and innovative technological changes/improvements.

Within each of these maturity levels are key process areas that characterize that level, and for each KPA there are five definitions: (1) goals, (2) commitment, (3) ability, (4) measurement, and (4) verification.

COMPETITIVE ADVANTAGE The competitive advantage of LM IS&GS-Civil is multifaceted and enhanced by the breadth of the LM corporation's ability to solve large problems. An example of this is the upgrading of the world's air traffic management infrastructure to state-of-the-art systems and processes. Another important competitive advantage is that IS&GS-Civil's technical capabilities are broad, deep, and cutting edge. An example of this is its leadership in biometrics as well as information security. Both of these advantages are enhanced its ability to leverage the breadth of capabilities and expertise across LM, which is referred to internally as horizontal integration. IS&GS has had many experiences when its customers are engaged in a challenging problem or opportunity that requires LM's highly specialized skills or technology.

STRATEGY MAP
Four Perspectives The LM IS&GS-Civil strategy map (see Exhibit 5.4) has strategic objectives placed among four perspectives: financial, customer, process, and workforce. The objectives in IS&GS-Civil's strategy describe

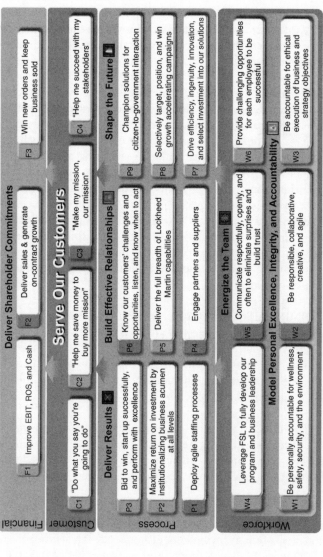

EXHIBIT 5.4 LM IS&GS-Civil Strategy Map

Courtesy of Lockheed Martin.

125

where it must excel in order to ensure long-term success and deliver on its complete citizen services strategy. Additionally, the map reinforces LM's corporate values and vision. The strategy map is a communication tool that describes an organization's strategy, and the leadership team is selective on both what is communicated and how it is communicated. One of the underlying goals with the use of the strategy map is to articulate it, balancing the need to be reasonably thorough, succinct enough to manage its complexity, and at a level where nothing proprietary is communicated so that it can be shared openly in any forum.

Three Strategic Themes   Leadership also believes it is important to reinforce the integrated nature of strategy in terms of cause and effect. Using three vertical themes illustrated by various colors, they are generally aligned to the FSL imperatives, (1) deliver results, (2) build effective relationships, and (3) shape the future, each with vertical theme spanning all four perspectives. These indicate some of the important relationships between objectives in the strategy. This is important in terms of understanding the strategy each objective is a piece of an integrated puzzle. Additionally, since one of the tenets of the strategy is thinking long term, the concepts reflect areas that will require a multiyear focus, coupled with the explicit requirement that the strategy map must remain fixed for a minimum of two years before any revisions can be made to the map, barring any major changes to the organization or markets.

COMMUNICATING STRATEGY   IS&GS recognizes that communicating strategy is one of the most important aspects of an organization's ability to execute its strategy, second only to leadership accountability. A key component of this is a solid partnership between the strategy management team and the communications organization. Strategic communications depicts the numerous channels leveraged by the CPM team.

Audiences   The IS&GS-Civil CPM office primarily focuses on three discrete audiences: executive leadership (e.g., unit president, vice presidents), mid-level leadership (e.g., directors, managers, team leads), and all employees. Each of these groups has different responsibilities and information needs in the effort:

1. The executive leadership team is provided several hours of training on the BSC and strategy management concepts. This group also spends notable time in the development and management of the strategy from creation of the strategy map to a complete BSC (i.e., measures, targets, and initiatives). Additionally, they play a key role in shaping messages that they flow into their organizations regarding what the strategy is,

how it is progressing, and where their line of business or function needs to apply some focus.

2. The mid-level leaders are the most critical link in the communications path because they hold more influence over the day-to-day activities of employees than any other person in the organization. Their role is to translate the strategy to actionable tasks for their employees, and this makes them critical to strategy execution.

3. The next audience of focus is employees as a group. The CPM team shares succinct overviews of the BSC and strategy management concepts, summaries of strategic performance, and reinforces the actions needed by all employees the mid-level leaders are driving.

Communication Channels The CPM team utilizes every communication channel available in a coordinated manner to press messages into the organization. The communication philosophy is summed up in the mantra "7 times 7 ways." It means that for every critical message it needs to deliver, it will communicate the message seven times using seven different channels. This does not translate into 49 messages, but puts the message out in seven slightly different but similar ways using seven different channels.

The communication channels include:

- *Leaderlink*: a weekly newsletter for leaders (e-mail)
- *Inside IS&GS-Civil*: a weekly newsletter for all employees (e-mail)
- Memos from leadership (usually e-mail)
- Webcasts/multicasts: live streaming video on their intranet
- *IS&GS Connect*: a quarterly print newsletter (print)
- Presentations: preparing and distributing presentations for leaders to share with their teams
- Posters: printed posters placed in high-traffic areas across multiple sites
- Promotional items: for example, the now famous strategy pens, a pen with a retractable picture of a strategy map
- Face-to-face sessions: this may include Lunch & Learn sessions
- Annual leadership meetings: generally an annual or biannual gathering of executive and mid-level leaders for a face-to-face conference
- Strategy website: placing key information on the intranet website
- President's blog: an intranet blog where the IS&GS-Civil president shares regular information about efforts, success, and challenges across the business.

It is clear from this list of communication channels that most organizations have these and likely others as well. The challenge is inevitably making the time to communicate messages effectively using them. Additionally, major campaigns such as the launch of the strategy map are managed separately and replace annual messaging events when they overlap.

CORE AND INNOVATIVE BEST PRACTICES   IS&GS-Civil exercises the core best practices identified earlier and has advanced knowledge in this area with new, innovative best practices.

Principle 2: Refresh and Communicate Strategy

- **Strategic planning.** Leverage the strategic planning process as either owner or partner to understand changing market conditions including competitor, supplier, rival, and potential entrants and substitutes in the marketplace.
- **Core and adjacent products and services.** Define and determine core and adjacent products and services to focus on highest probabilities for success.
- **Strategic plan.** Produce a comprehensive strategic plan.
- **Strategy mapping.** Develop corporate- and department-level strategy maps containing objectives along four perspectives including financial, customer/constituent, process, and people. Observe strategy map design parameters of 20 to 25 objectives.
- **Link strategic planning and budgeting processes.** Link strategic planning to the budgeting process, partner and budgeting with finance to provide for a seamless continuum.
- **Communications plan.** Communicate strategy throughout the organization using a comprehensive communications plan.
- **Innovative Best Practice.** LM IS&GS-Civil leverages the "7 times 7 ways" approach, a far more comprehensive plan than most companies have, to communicate key messages, a select few in a given year, in a coordinated manner to three audiences using 12 communications channels.
- **Innovative Best Practice.** LM IS&GS-Civil integrated three major, complementary, strategic themes or frameworks across all four perspectives of its strategy map and BSC structure.
- **Innovative Best Practice.** LM IS&GS-Civil leverages and integrates multiple strategic planning methods (SWOT, Five Forces, and PESTEL) in a complementary manner to realize their benefits and overcome possible shortcomings relying on one method.

M7 Aerospace: Best Practice Case

M7 Aerospace's vision, mission, and management philosophy guide its strategic planning process.

- **Vision:** To become the premier global supplier of best-in-class, high-quality services on time and at competitive prices to the aerospace industry.
- **Mission:** To achieve substantial growth through offering premium integrated services and products to exceed the expectations of our commercial and defense aerospace customers.
- **Management Philosophy:** M7 has implemented the Balanced Scorecard and Strategy Focused Organization methodologies throughout the organization to drive performance and assign accountability.

STRATEGIC PLANNING PROCESS M7 Aerospace initiates a comprehensive strategy formulation process that leads to development of an integrated corporate, business unit, and support unit strategic plan. Once the integrated plans are defined, the CPM team updates and refreshes strategic and operational budgets, strategy maps, and BSC targets for the next year. Exhibit 5.5 depicts the strategic planning process.

The strategy formulation process is initiated with strategic input documents (SIDs) containing essential data sets from which numerous analyses can be performed, company annual reports and industry reports including customer, competitor, supplier, regulatory, key process, technology, and other information sets. The SIDs includes key information on strategic planning elements with primary and secondary accountability for each.

SIDs provide clear focus on industry, competitive, and other required data sets for analyses. For example, it is essential to collect "market/sizing" information that could provide insights into the addressable market for multiple M7 business units such as manufacturing, government services, supply chain management, and staffing services. The following sections provide an example of the strategic planning process and methods applied to one business unit.

With fully populated SIDs the strategy team is now well positioned to conduct four key analytics: (1) core and adjacency analysis, (2) Five Forces analysis, (3) SWOT analysis, and (4) benchmarking analysis. Since each analytic is intended for a specific purpose, they are used in combination to optimize strategy formulation. For instance, a SWOT does not necessarily contemplate the core and future adjacent businesses. Similarly, the Five Forces does not have visibility into threats (outside the Five Forces elements) such as government intervention, employee talent shortages, and so on.

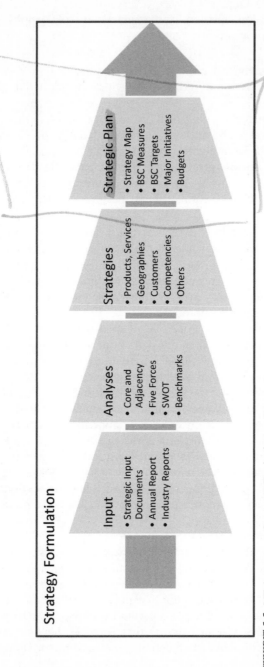

EXHIBIT 5.5 M7 Aerospace Strategic Formulation Process

Courtesy of M7 Aerospace.

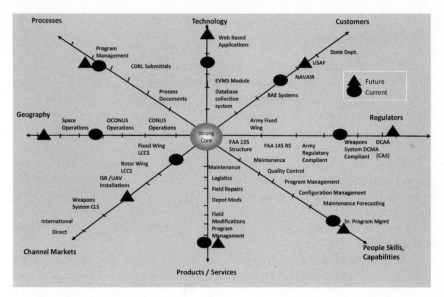

EXHIBIT 5.6 Core and Adjacency Analyses

Courtesy of M7 Aerospace.

Core and Adjacency Analysis   Core and adjacency analysis (see Exhibit 5.6) consists of the team identifying core competencies along eight strategic vectors (e.g., markets, customers, services) and evaluating options to expand business outward into relevant adjacent services one or two steps removed from the current offerings. Notice the "Channel Markets" growth vector (at 7 o'clock) where the company is currently engaged in the fixed wing market (dark circle). The strategy team has explored several adjacent market segments that offer opportunities for expansion including rotor wing/helicopters and ISR/AUV installations (dark diamond), a market estimated at $6 billion, and possibly further out to the weapons system CLS. The strategic planning team similarly explored core and adjacent opportunities along the technology; customer; regulator; people, skills, and capabilities; products and services; geographic; and processes vectors.

Porter Five Forces Analysis   The strategy team conducted a thorough Porter Five Forces model to identify the power indices among and between this BU and its rivals, suppliers, new entrants, substitutes, and customers. The Five Forces analytic identified key market dynamics among value chain players that could offer strategic advantage, or conversely offer strategic threats and risks. It is important to understand the power ratings, where a strong supplier rating would imply suppliers have leverage over your business in pricing, delivery, and so on, and a weak rating would imply the opposite. This logic is consistent with the other rating scales.

1. Supplier power ratings: low, moderate, strong
2. Rivalry power ratings: weak, strong, intense
3. New entrants power ratings: easy, medium, difficult
4. Substitute service power ratings: few, several, many
5. Buyer power ratings: low, moderate, strong

The strategy team's analysis reveals that the customer (DoD) buying power rating is strong based on the following factors: The government will competitively bid, invoke contract cancellation and penalties, exercise discretion, and intervene at various points, to name a few. This analysis relates back to our core and adjacency analysis of the ISR/UAV market, which is 100 percent DoD driven.

All five market forces (supplier, customer, substitutes, new entrants, and rivalry/competitors) have power ratings based on key factors or innate characteristics. At a high level this market has strong customer/government power and strong competitive rivalries. These factors may necessitate a new strategy of forming joint ventures or partnerships with other players to reduce the rivalry, as an example. Power ratings for new entrants and substitutes are low, so risk is low of new players or services supplanting M7's capabilities. Suppliers have moderate power, so there is little threat of margin erosion or supply chain disruptions.

SWOT Analysis The strategy team conducts a SWOT analysis where the strengths and weaknesses internal analysis of capabilities revealed 12 strengths or what this BU does exceptionally well, and four weaknesses or what they could do better. As we link the SWOT and Five Forces analytics, note one strength, "#1, strong program management for government programs," and another strength, "#5, relatively low-cost wage scale for program office personnel," both of which could mitigate the risks identified in our Five Forces analysis around competitive bidding and government intervention.

Opportunities and threats reflect an outward or external view of the marketplace. The team identified six opportunities the company could capitalize on, and four threats or external roadblocks that could impede its progress. As we link the SWOT with the core and adjacency analytics, please note the opportunity "#4, ISR or ASE" (airplane service extension), an adjacent market also identified in our core and adjacency analysis.

Linking analytics provides cross validation, or in some cases reveals a flaw in the logic that needs to be remediated.

FORMULATE AND EVALUATE STRATEGIES   Based on the three foregoing analytics, the strategy team identified five potential strategies that warrant an initial review using a risk and reward matrix. The strategies included:

1. Win additional ASE design/installation fixed wing program.
2. Win initial rotor wing modification program.
3. Win upcoming CLS contract.
4. Team, purchase, or merge with technology company for new ISR or ASE product line.
5. Win Pro-line 21 avionics installation on additional aircraft type.

This risk reward matrix has four quadrants to help facilitate discussion about the tradeoffs of pursuing a "portfolio" of strategies. The four quadrants include:

1. High Risk and High Reward: These strategies could be "game changers" and offer the greatest upside with commensurate risks.
2. Low Risk and High Reward: These strategies are referred to as "plums," since you have the upside value potential with lower risk factors.
3. High Risk and Low Reward: These strategies are "dogs" and should be avoided.
4. Low Risk and Low Reward: These strategies are "easy wins" and present an easier opportunity to capitalize on financial results with low risk.

The five strategies were analyzed using the risk and reward matrix, which revealed there were no dogs or easy wins. Focusing on two strategies and their placement on the matrix:

- *Strategy #1, win additional fixed wing programs:* This strategy is a "plum" that leverages the current core competency (see core and adjacency analysis) and company strengths in project management (see S in SWOT).
- *Strategy #4, team, purchase, or merge with a technology company:* for new ISR or ASE product line. This strategy is a possible "game changer" but also recognizes this is not a current core competency (see core and adjacency analysis), and manages the risk of the strong customer power rating (see Five Forces customer).

STRATEGIC INITIATIVES AND BUDGETING   The two strategies just discussed will be further evaluated using a more comprehensive business case. M7 Aerospace formulates its strategic plan for all business units and at the corporate level consisting of numerous strategies. The compilation and review of all strategies and related business cases will result in a portfolio of strategic initiatives in the company budget including those requiring integration and alignment among and between business units. The portfolio of strategies will in turn inform changes to the capital structure, such as the mix between current and new debt and equity for strategy execution.

INTEGRATION OF STRATEGIC PLANNING WITH PLANNING AND BUDGETING   The results of the strategic planning process guide formulation of the company financial budgets. There is an iterative analysis to synchronize strategies with operating budgets. For instance, let us assume Strategy #4, new markets and related action plans, indicates that the UAV/ISR market will require partnering with a larger player to bid on government programs, which will take six months to launch and submit the first proposal. How does this relate to the BU financial model? The BU financial model target calls for increasing revenue by 50 percent in the next operating cycle, so the UAV/ISR strategy will not possibly contribute for at least six months, perhaps nine months. Therefore the team will evaluate expanding and or accelerating Strategy #1 organic growth to complement the #4 strategy. The tradeoffs are evaluated among all strategies until a final version is established to proactively manage the BU for the following year.

Forecast of projected revenues and historical margins are used to provide a baseline financial forecast and budget. Integrated services require each BU to match up intercompany transactions and staffing requirements accordingly (i.e., quality headcount is a direct relationship with increase in manufacturing forecast).

STRATEGY MAP: THE CAUSE AND EFFECT DIAGRAM   M7 Aerospace adopted the Kaplan and Norton Strategy Map and BSC methodology five years ago. The strategic plan therefore is considered input into revisions to the corporate and BU portfolio of strategy maps and BSCs. Strategy maps are often referred to as cause and effect or linkage diagrams for they reveal the leading and lagging objectives across the four perspectives, reading from bottom to top: people (learning and capabilities), process, customer, and financial. Continuing our example, the strategy map in Exhibit 5.7 contains the new strategies for the government business unit.

Reading from bottom to top causally, strategic people (P) objective "P2, maintain regulatory EPA, safety, and government security requirements" represents being qualified to engage in government DoD contracts. P2 will drive internal process (I) objectives, most notably "I3, sell integrated services and solutions," which will focus on penetrating the new AUV/ISR market. Both strategic objectives P2 and I3 will in turn deliver on customer objective "C0, award term points (ATP) ratings." Strategy objective C0 represents the

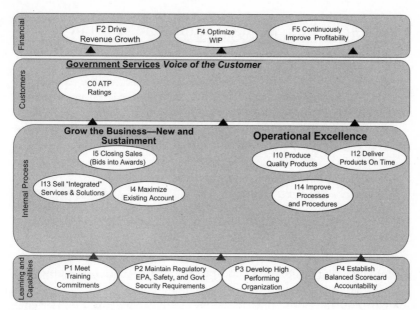

EXHIBIT 5.7 Strategy Map
Courtesy of M7 Aerospace.

integration of M7 Aerospace and the government procurement ratings, a key aspect of delivering on the new ISR contracts. Ratings or points are awarded by the DoD for on-time delivery and project management, for instance. Finally, the success of the C0 objective will deliver strategic finance (F) objective "F2, drive revenue growth."

COMMUNICATIONS STRATEGY M7's communications strategy is wide ranging, leveraging over a dozen channels to reach its employee base. The communications plan is defined with communications channel/forum, frequency, information content, audiences, and owners clearly identified. Through this plan the corporate and BU strategies, BSCs, BSC results, major initiatives, and the key enablers such as compensation, evaluation programs, rewards and recognition plans are communicated and understood by employees. The communications plan also provides for developmental opportunities for both leaders and managers to participate by engaging employees.

CORE AND INNOVATIVE BEST PRACTICES M7 Aerospace exercises the core best practices identified earlier and has advanced knowledge in this area with new, innovative best practices.

Principle 2: Refresh and Communicate Strategy

- **Strategic planning.** Leverage the strategic planning process as either owner or partner to understand changing market conditions including competitor, supplier, rival, and potential entrants and substitutes in the marketplace.
- **Core and adjacent products and services.** Define and determine core and adjacent products and services to focus on highest probabilities for success.
- **Strategic plan.** Produce a comprehensive strategic plan.
- **Strategy mapping.** Develop corporate- and department-level strategy maps containing objectives along four perspectives including financial, customer/constituent, process, and people. Observe strategy map design parameters of 20 to 25 objectives.
- **Link strategic planning and budgeting processes.** Link strategic planning to the budgeting process, partner and budgeting with finance to provide for a seamless continuum.
- **Communications plan.** Communicate strategy throughout the organization using a comprehensive communications plan.
- **Innovative Best Practice.** M7 uses several separate but integrated analytics (core and adjacency, Five Forces, and SWOT) to innovate and formulate strategy; this is far more comprehensive and inventive than what is done by most companies.
- **Innovative Best Practice.** M7 concurrently develops corporate strategies based on "common" BU strategies, as well as "unique" BU strategies. This is a multifaceted and sophisticated conglomerate- or portfolio-based strategic planning process.
- **Innovative Best Practice.** M7 fully integrates its strategic planning and planning and budgeting processes providing for the funding of strategic initiatives. This is referred to as strategic budgeting.
- **Innovative Best Practice.** M7's communications plan and strategy is far more innovative and wide-ranging than those of most award-winning organizations.

Mueller, Inc.: Best Practice Case

This case offers interesting insights into a four-stage performance-driven culture (PDC) maturity model that parallels Mueller's growth and increasing level of business and CPM sophistication through the years. While it is clear that today Mueller has a PDC, its path has been evolutionary over 25 years rather than revolutionary. And while the company has made its greatest

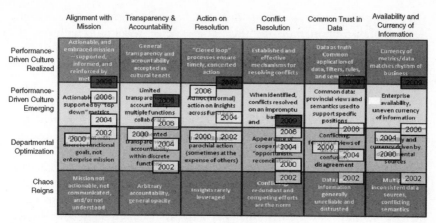

EXHIBIT 5.8 Performance-Driven Culture Maturity Model

Courtesy of Mueller, Inc.

progress in its journey over the last ten years in particular, it is during that time that the company experienced its greatest setbacks. This emerges by mapping several defining events that represent stages at Mueller on its PDC maturity model (see Exhibit 5.8). The following paragraphs start post "Chaos Reigns" stage with the "Departmental Optimization" stage and bring us to the present-day "Performance Driven Culture Realized" stage.

STAGE 1: CHAOS REIGNS At this point a new management structure had been defined and staffed, in anticipation of the CFO's retirement. According to leader Phillip Arp, "The entire organizational structure was fairly rigid with respect to all the processes feeding up to the owners. So you had a rigid structure with rigid processes—planning processes and everything else. That is the way a small company generally is. You have to build those processes in order to do that. So they realized they needed to build a corporate staff to prepare for a larger company, so they started hiring."

They established a distinct IT function, a human resources department, a strategic planning function, a new CFO, and regional sales managers, all reporting to Davenport. To reinforce the new management structure, prepare for growth, and continue to improve efficiency and return on assets, Mueller had earlier decided to implement a far-reaching ERP system—commencing Mueller's very difficult ERP odyssey. Mueller has taken on the impossible task of implementing all modules of a new ERP system in what employees refer to as the "big bang." A very painful implementation ensued as Mueller attempted to simultaneously implement sales order entry, manufacturing, distribution, and accounting. The extreme amount of disruption, time, resource, and expense was unforeseen and, for a period, Mueller was thrown back into near-chaos (the bottom stage). This distracted almost everyone, especially management, and turned 2002 and part of 2003 into the "lost year."

STAGE 2: DEPARTMENTAL OPTIMIZATION   At this point the ERP system had become stable enough to be used and significant amounts of varied business data were now being collected. During this period, the traditional revenue planning and forecasting process was modified in favor of the BSC branch target system that employed a predetermined expense and resource model for each range of anticipated revenues. This branch target system helps management achieve greater efficiency and predictability in its sales model through standardization.

Says Davenport, "We came up with the idea of buckets. If we are operating at this level, here is what we should look like. If we are operating at this level, here is what we should look like. So managers who are responsible for headcount, hours of production, and so on can see what the volumes are. Their objective is just to get it to that level. What do you need to know where you are against your target? Your target is predetermined once a year, sometimes twice, but we have tried to move to a system that affords us a lot of flexibility. This is contrary to the American idea of management, which is, 'By golly, you set a target and you make it happen.' But it works for us."

Mueller also implemented its BSC solution in this stage, managed by finance. According to Lack, "Alignment with the mission really became much stronger in 2004."

The BSC further articulated the mission, made accountability more plausible, and helped improve Mueller's performance in virtually every category. This was especially true for alignment with mission and action on insights, which climbed into the "performance-driven culture—emerging" stage. However, key areas of transparency and accountability, conflict resolution, common trust in data, and availability and currency of information saw only modest improvements in this stage and remained stuck in "departmental optimization."

STAGE 3: PERFORMANCE-DRIVEN CULTURE—EMERGING   Building on these wins, this marked the turning point to a performance-driven culture. In Davenport's words, "Today I feel like we're a mature management team. People understand and accept their responsibilities and roles, and we work together as a team. There is no one person that has unnecessary exposure or is going to make critical decisions, but everybody is going to be impacted by somebody else or dependent on somebody else so we try. It's more of a team attitude toward solutions and addressing issues and addressing opportunities than certainly there was 10 years ago and 20 years ago."

By 2006, the ERP system was functioning well, and its reliability and credibility were well established. All of management relied on the BSC, although it had not yet been cascaded to manufacturing. Added to this was operational reporting to complement the aggregated views of metrics provided by the BSC. This was especially helpful to the sales organization, which had become more sophisticated in its use of information and was asking for more complex reports.

Its newfound ability to behave as a performance-driven culture and as a single "organism" was tested during this year as Mueller acquired four new branches from a competitor. To its credit, Mueller was able to absorb these new branches and employees—completely automating them with all of its systems—in less than two months. Says Lack, "The moment when I was awed with the processes we now have in this company was when we did the acquisition. In literally less than 30 days and we were up and running as the Mueller organization with the signs, employees, computers, and systems in place. And we did all four locations in one day."

Says Davenport, "We worked out what had to be done and everybody took their part. HR was off interviewing and setting up the processes we were going to have to go through to incorporate the employees we wanted to bring on. Accounting was setting up doing all the preparatory work to get ready. We had a ton of work. And it really wasn't a major disruption because again all of these processes were so standardized that it's just a matter of executing it."

STAGE 4: PERFORMANCE-DRIVEN CULTURE—REALIZATION During this stage, Mueller continued to refine its systems, expand the number of branches, and become more disciplined in its use of performance management and BI.

According to Lack, "We saw an improvement in our management schedule and processes. People now are concerned and ask things like, 'Why is this order sitting here?' and 'What do we need to do to get these orders invoiced?' When we have scrap, they ask, 'What's going on with the scrap? Why is our scrap so high?' People started asking the questions that they couldn't before because they didn't have the information and the understanding of why it was important."

Mueller also continued to improve its rankings on the Maturity Model. Through consistency and determination, Mueller rose to the level of "performance culture realized" for alignment with mission, action on insights and common trust in data, and availability and currency of information.

In many cases, companies engage in performance management initiatives after a "wake-up call" of some sort, either externally or internally driven.

Mueller is an exception to this rule. Under Bryan Davenport's leadership, Mueller has patiently and deliberately moved forward, investing heavily, enduring setbacks, but never wavering in its commitment to its core values, its mission, and the fervent ownership of performance improvement initiatives.

Mueller reviews the four-stage maturity model to actively understand its current position and desired future state. This model aids in its strategic planning process discussed next.

STRATEGY DEVELOPMENT   Mueller has a well-defined strategic planning process; key elements include business purpose, strategic analytics, strategic vision, and strategy map; deployment tools are discussed in Chapter 6. Mueller's purpose is to deliver the *best total value* to end users of metal building and residential metal roofing products in the Central and Southwestern United States. Mueller's strategy is to directly manage the customer relationship by providing convenient access, reliable products, dependable services, and total solutions at the lowest total cost funded through operating efficiency improvements.

To execute Mueller's purpose, the organization embraces cultural values:

- Seek continuous improvement.
- Demonstrate integrity and professionalism.
- Manage relationships on the basis of what's right, rather than who's right.
- Maintain a high awareness of the total market environment.
- Make decisions by selecting the best of all available alternatives.
- Measure performance by results and the methods used.

The accomplishment of Mueller's business purpose will produce sustainable growth and superior investment returns.

STRATEGIC INNOVATIONS   The strategic planning process revealed significant internal and external challenges. The president and executives agreed that the issues facing Mueller were crucial turning points in the company's history. The competitive landscape was changing at this time and Mueller needed a way to manage the organization if it was to continue to grow. Muller conducts a regular assessment of the market and realized it was faced with several significant external and internal challenges. A few changes in strategies are described next.

First, Mueller *strategically innovated* by shifting from selling steel products to value-added selling. Many companies sell steel products, so Mueller needed to differentiate itself. The focus for sales shifted from selling steel sheets to selling entire projects, a complete solution. Mueller can do all of this more efficiently and at a lower total cost of ownership for the customer than if the customer went to multiple vendors. Thus, the entire focus of sales and the company's business model shifted from selling components of a project to selling the complete project end to end. This shift in business models meant a total retraining for sales on how to sell; this included professional sales skills, customer service skills, and a reengineering of the entire sales force.

Second, Mueller strategically innovated by shifting its sales focus from primarily contractors to the end user. At the beginning of its BSC implementation Mueller examined its sales process and discovered that the middle person in most sales was a contractor who controlled the customer relationship. Mueller wanted to own this customer relationship and interact directly with end-use customers to improve customer service. Mueller took an innovative approach here, however, as a salesperson makes the same commission from a direct sale as from a sale to a contractor. A sale to a contractor is easier to make and often results in repeat sales—so there was no incentive to improve direct customer relationships. Mueller chose to communicate that the focus of the organization was to provide higher added value service. Mueller added technology, resources, and training to aid salespeople in better servicing the customer set as productively as possible. Mueller made sure to communicate that it wanted to reduce its dependency on contractor sales and build direct relationships with end users.

"If we manage the customer relationship correctly, it will reflect on our business performance," Lack explains. "By gaining more control over our information, we've created some strategic shifts in the way we view customers."

CORPORATE STRATEGY MAP Mueller has translated its strategic plan into a strategy map, a leading-edge framework co-invented by Kaplan and Norton. Briefly, the strategy map contains strategic objectives across four perspectives; reading from bottom to top in a causal manner these include people (learning and capabilities), internal process, customers, and financial. Mueller translates the strategic plan into a strategy map and has realized success because tangible goals have been set up for clear identification of executables, Mueller's strategy map, and accompanying BSC.

Mueller has two overarching themes: growth and efficiency. Everything the organization does is managed along those themes, either by helping to grow through customer service and sales or by making a process better for more efficient operations.

STRATEGIC OBJECTIVES In our first strategic innovation example, one of Mueller's strategic process objectives is "Manage Construction Services." The new lighter buildings Mueller began constructing were part of the growth strategy. To enable manufacturing the buildings, Mueller funded an initiative to secure new machinery.

In our second example, one of Mueller's strategic process objectives is to "Provide Financing Services." To meet customer demands, Mueller began taking credit cards as a form of payment as well as offering financing options (see preceding objective) for its customers. These undertakings meant partnering with Wells Fargo and coordinating with the credit department. Every credit card purchase costs Mueller a discount fee for the purchase, so Mueller identified how this would affect the organization in meeting its strategic goals. In the end, the added customer value outweighed the other costs, especially from the increased revenue gained from the convenience to the customer.

In our final example, one of Mueller's financial objectives is to "Maximize Return on Assets (ROA)" shown at the top of the strategy map. If Mueller borrowed money it could grow five times as fast as its current rate. However, the business purpose and the values intersect to where the company believes *growing organically* is the best way the organization can continually add value to best serve the company and its customers without outstripping its culture.

ALIGNING MAJOR INITIATIVES   Mueller ensures initiatives are aligned, defined, and prioritized with the strategy. At Mueller, initiatives are tested against the BSC and are added as part of the process if they are in alignment with the overall goals and strategy. Mueller's strategy map has been in place for nearly seven years, and the strategy has maintained itself. Mueller will not change the strategy to fit an idea, unless it is a major business foundation–changing idea. Initiatives that do not provide a level of increased value to the end user of Mueller's products are not considered.

One such initiative that Mueller measured and chose to pursue was the manufacturing and selling of custom rollup doors. It began producing its own rollup doors to match the various colors of the other products it sells.

The BSC and the strategic initiatives are reviewed every quarter in a formal meeting, and performance, existing initiatives, and any challenges are discussed and worked on.

INTEGRATION OF STRATEGIC PLANNING AND BUDGETING   Mueller reengineered its budgeting process to align more closely with the strategic planning process and the company strategy. The newly reengineered budgeting process was characterized by the following attributes:

- Centralized guidance (through CPM office).
- Corporate objective driven.
- Objective development integrated and highly correlated.
- Sales forecast based on honest assessment of customers and markets.

- Budget development leveraged to communicate targets or expectations of performance.
- Individual performance contracts based on strategic and operational objectives.

The key benefits of the new budgeting process include:

- Strategic requirements define the budget.
- Clear communication of expectations.
- Peer group results among locations sets the expectations.
- Focus is on solutions and execution.

FUNDING STRATEGIC INITIATIVES: THE STRATEGIC BUDGET Every part of Mueller's budget is driven by the strategy. Initiatives and spending are not undertaken without the strategy in mind. Managers are allowed to manage within their department as long as it does not go against the values and principles of Mueller. Each manager has a specific limit for discretionary spending. Executive meetings are used to discuss bigger expenditures, such as new purchases and research into initiatives.

For example, Mueller was constructing its buildings at the higher end of the ranges of engineered specifications. This ensured better quality, but used more steel and consequently cost more weight. However, Mueller found that price-sensitive customers were comparing its product against lighter buildings (fabricated steel prices are determined mostly by weight), so it needed to start making its buildings fall within the lower end of the specification ranges without sacrificing quality. Mueller needed new machinery to do this, and so it held meetings to determine budgeting for such an initiative. Because building lighter buildings would help satisfy end user needs, a budget for new machinery for this initiative was approved.

STRATEGIC SCENARIO PLANNING During the strategic planning process and during the year Mueller prepares several alternative scenarios or forecasts of its performance to guide decision making. The idea allows Mueller to view potential outcomes based on varying economic conditions. If the trends point towards one scenario, expectations can be communicated to achieve needed financial and operational results.

COMMUNICATING STRATEGY Mueller's vision, values, and goals are formally documented and conveyed to all employees. The president's active role in participating in driving strategy execution has been critical to the successful implementation and execution of the BSC at Mueller. Mueller believes active participation and ownership by executives is fundamental to a successful BSC. This executive drive helps to promote the importance of the BSC and company alignment with strategy execution, in addition to giving Mueller president Bryan Davenport more visibility over the direction of his company.

Mueller reports the company's performance to its board and stakeholders as it uses the BSC as a primary method of communicating performance and stressing importance across the organization through various communication channels.

CORE AND INNOVATIVE BEST PRACTICES   Mueller exercises the core best practices identified earlier; plus it has advanced knowledge in this area with new, innovative best practices.

Principle 2: Refresh and Communicate Strategy

- **Strategic planning.** Leverage the strategic planning process as either owner or partner to understand changing market conditions including competitor, supplier, rival, and potential entrants and substitutes in the marketplace.
- **Core and adjacent products and services.** Define and determine core and adjacent products and services to focus on highest probabilities for success.
- **Strategic plan.** Produce a comprehensive strategic plan.
- **Strategy mapping.** Mueller leverages a corporate strategy map using the Kaplan and Norton methodology.
- **Link strategic planning and budgeting processes.** Link strategic planning to the budgeting process, partner and budgeting with finance to provide for a seamless continuum. Mueller reengineered its budgeting process to more closely synchronize with the strategic planning process.
- **Communications plan.** Communicate strategy throughout the organization using a comprehensive communications plan.
- **Innovative Best Practice.** Mueller has developed insights into a four-stage performance-driven culture maturity model that parallels Mueller's growth, increasing level of business, and CPM sophistication through the years.
- **Innovative Best Practice.** Mueller has successfully integrated its strategies to thrive in a more challenging environment, selling solutions and repositioning itself with end customers.
- **Innovative Best Practice.** Mueller provides for a strategic budget, thus formalizing funding for strategic initiatives.
- **Innovative Best Practice.** Mueller models its performance under different strategic scenarios, testing hypotheses and modifying its strategies to optimize results.

NSTAR: Best Practice Case

NSTAR reinvigorated its company mission statement, "We're committed to delivering great service," as part of its shift to a performance-based culture, reflecting employees' ongoing commitment to delivering great service.

CPM ORGANIZATION AND COLLABORATION WITH NSTAR DEPARTMENTS: THE STRATEGIC PLANNING PROCESS In addition to CPM, the overall performance management function can be characterized as an organizational hybrid of three departments, which collaborate with the executive team to develop a strategic plan, associated long-term financial plan, annual operating plan, and performance measurement plan. These groups include:

- Strategic planning—develop the strategic plan
- Budgeting and forecasting—create the operating plan
- Corporate performance management—establish performance goals and initiatives

The strategic plan is the umbrella for all financial, operational, and performance actions at NSTAR. This plan's development is managed by the Strategic Planning department, which includes two full-time employees and is headed by the director of strategic planning and business development. This small team leads the development of NSTAR's long-term (five-year) strategic plan. Strategies are augmented when appropriate, enabling the company to react to any issues on the horizon, as well as address emerging challenges or opportunities.

Strategic planning organizes an annual executive retreat where company leaders discuss and develop strategies. The meeting involves all company officers, as well as key department directors. Outcomes from this event translate into action items included in NSTAR's annual business plan. Over the past several years, the executive meetings have kicked off major initiatives, including electric system infrastructure enhancements, customer experience improvements, development of a corporate safety culture, and more.

NSTAR also holds a separate retreat of the board of trustees, where key strategic items are reviewed and discussed among the board and executive management. For example, NSTAR's 2009 meeting included topics concerning Smart Grid technologies, electric vehicles, energy storage and batteries, expansion of energy efficiency programs, and transmission infrastructure.

Next, strategic planning collaborates with forecasting and financial experts to establish the financial plan associated with NSTAR's strategy. Models are developed to create scenarios illustrating levels of earnings and profits based on numerous inputs such as assumptions of risk, breakdowns of customer energy demand, regulatory outcomes, weather, reliability trends, and growth. NSTAR's senior team is fully engaged in the development and approval of the combined strategic/financial corporate plan.

The entire executive team broadly reviews the corporate plan via the business planning process. This cross-organizational executive process ensures communication and understanding of the long-term plan and seeks to obtain feedback on operational, customer, or employee impacts or changes needed to meet the plan.

STRATEGIC INITIATIVES AND BUDGETING The business planning process is orchestrated by the Budgeting and Forecasting department and includes the senior team, executive team, and CPM. The business planning process schedule of events occurs throughout the year, so executive leaders can present next year's business plan to the senior team. These meetings culminate in the final development of the corporate spending plan, corporate operational and improvement plan, and annual targets for key performance measurements.

The Budgeting and Forecasting department has a staff of eight, reporting to the director of budget and controls. This team creates a two-year look-ahead corporate budget in line with NSTAR's long-term strategic and financial plan. During the business planning cycle, they lead executive review meetings to explain the progress on the development of the plan and its assumptions and risks. They also collaborate with each business unit to develop more detailed organizational and department budgets, as well as allocate funding based on strategic and operating priorities.

As a part of the business planning process, CPM coordinates with the NSTAR senior team to develop a set of "Priority Initiatives." These priority initiatives further drive NSTAR's efforts to deliver great service to customers, improve performance, reduce costs, and meet the strategic and operational plans. Each month, progress toward each of these priority initiatives is reported and discussed among the executive team using the monthly scorecard package called the Executive Performance Review.

In 2009, NSTAR embarked on an initiative to further reduce costs and improve performance. This new process augments the business planning process in three major ways: leveraging benchmarking and best practices to learn about how better performers approach their business; cross-organizational planning and prioritization with vice presidents to establish key improvement initiatives; and using a common methodology and approach to project management and process improvement.

STRATEGIC CORPORATE GOALS NSTAR maintains a set of seven "corporate goals" as part of its strategic and operating plans. When NSTAR identifies its business improvement initiatives, all must be mapped to these seven areas, which serve as the foundational elements of what the company aims to achieve each year. These goals are:

1. Maintain strong financial performance.
2. Drive operational efficiency.
3. Promote a positive company image.
4. Make safety a priority.
5. Build workplace engagement.
6. Improve the customer experience.
7. Maintain secure and reliable power delivery systems.

COMMUNICATING STRATEGY A key component of NSTAR's performance culture journey has been to ensure that employees remain aware of the company's customer service, operational, and employee-centered performance goals and progress. Early on, CPM teamed up with human resources and corporate communications to execute a comprehensive communications campaign aimed at the following:

- Promoting the importance of improving NSTAR's performance
- Educating employees on the relationship between the work they do every day and overall company performance
- Regularly relaying NSTAR's progress toward meeting desired performance levels

Since this early campaign, NSTAR has implemented several other methods to increase employee engagement and awareness around performance. Each month, CPM creates the executive performance review and assembles other scorecard materials and analytics for key operating areas. Much of this performance information is made available corporatewide via NSTAR's company intranet, as well as through regular updates in NSTAR's daily newsletter.

Managers throughout the company also devote time at staff meetings to review performance, where leaders share information about local and company performance using the scorecards and other related information. Innovations and ideas surface at scorecard meetings, leading to further performance improvements at every level.

CORE BEST PRACTICES NSTAR exercises the core best practices identified earlier.

Principle 2: Refresh and Communicate Strategy

- **Strategic planning.** Leverage the strategic planning process as either owner or partner to understand changing market conditions including competitor, supplier, rival, and potential entrants and substitutes in the marketplace.

(Continued)

- **Core and adjacent products and services.** Define and determine core and adjacent products and services to focus on highest probabilities for success.
- **Strategic plan.** Produce a comprehensive strategic plan.
- **Strategy mapping.** NSTAR leverages seven corporate strategic goals that directly address financial, customer, process, and people perspectives.
- **Link strategic planning and budgeting processes.** Link strategic planning to the budgeting process, partner and budgeting with finance to provide for a seamless continuum.
- **Communications plan.** Communicate strategy throughout the organization using a comprehensive communications plan.

Omaha Public Power District: Best Practice Case

Omaha Public Power District's (OPPD's) main thing (focus), mission, and vision provide direction to the strategic planning process.

OPPD Strategic Plan

- **OPPD Main Thing: To exceed customer expectations.** As a public power organization, OPPD has the highest commitment to serving our customer-owners. We recognize that our product is essential to the health and well-being of our customers and the community. Fulfilling these profound obligations requires exceeding customer expectations for reliability, cost, service, and citizenship.
- **OPPD Mission: Deliver high-value electricity and other essential services to our customers.** Electricity is our core business. We will strive to increase the value of our product by surrounding it with supporting services, information, and customer conveniences. OPPD is more than a commodity provider of electricity; we create value by partnering with our customers to satisfy their needs.
- **OPPD Vision: To be nationally recognized as a leader in public power.** OPPD will continue to be a vertically integrated public power utility. OPPD has always been recognized as exemplary in operations, customer service, and financial standing. We will strive to be nationally recognized for excellence in all aspects of our operations. We will be an example of how public power can effectively adapt to a rapidly changing business environment through leadership and *innovation*.
- OPPD Core Values

- Our success is built on a foundation of core values—safety, accountability, commitment to customers, excellence, teamwork, and family orientation.

STRATEGIC PLANNING PROCESS The OPPD manager of strategy and business planning (CPM office) facilitates the strategic planning process; participants in this process include the CEO, VP BU leaders, and directors and managers of divisions and departments. Strategic planning process participants focus first on the internal assessment of OPPD internal strengths and weaknesses.

Strategic Planning Internal Analysis The internal analysis is conducted to identify and evaluate strengths and weaknesses. The senior management team began this effort by brainstorming a list of characteristics (e.g., effective risk management, effective cost management, electric reliability, in no particular order) that define an "Ideal Utility." Following the brainstorming session, the senior management team independently rated each characteristic on two criteria:

1. Priority: The importance of each characteristic in defining an ideal utility
2. Gap: The difference between an ideal utility and OPPD's current state of each characteristic

The results were compiled including the mean score and the degree of consensus (based on average deviation) for each characteristic. This exercise encouraged focused discussion regarding OPPD's internal performance resulting in a consensus as to the priority and gap for each characteristic. The outcome of the workshop was a determination of top ten characteristics for:

- Strengths: Characteristics with high priority and very low gap ratings
- Weaknesses: Characteristics with high priority and high gap ratings

This was followed by a discussion on how strengths could be leveraged and weaknesses mitigated. For example, the senior team felt that cost management could be improved by adopting a culture of continuous process improvement.

Strategic Planning External Analysis The external analysis starts by compiling a list of key trends and issues in the energy sector that have the potential of significantly impacting OPPD. OPPD senior and division managers submitted their candidate issues. Other trends and issues identified by industry groups (Large Public Power Council) and the industry press were included.

The trends and issues were categorized using the PEST (political, economic, social, and technology) structure.

Using OPPD's risk management process, key trends and issues were rated by probability of occurrence and potential impact on OPPD by all senior and division management. Those issues that represented high probability and impact were used in the scenario planning process.

By examining the relationships among industry trends, clusters of mutually inclusive and self-reinforcing trends emerge. These clusters become key drivers of various scenarios. Generally three or four different scenarios are developed. The electric utility has traditionally been staid and predictable, but is now in a time of great uncertainty. A working scenario allows OPPD to "put some stakes in the ground so that our planning can go forward." Signposts are key future events that describe how the scenario will unfold. They are identified for all scenarios. Signposts are regularly reviewed to assess the continuing validity of the working scenario and other scenarios.

OPPD's ten-year working scenario chosen by OPPD is described next.

A highly centralized energy policy is the key driver of this scenario. This follows a trend of diminished local autonomy for electric utilities over the last two decades. Starting with the Clean Air Act, followed by Federal Energy Regulatory Commission–mandated Regional Transmission Organizations (RTO) and the North American Electric Reliability Corporation (NERC) standards, fewer decisions are being made at the local level. This trend accelerates as portrayed in the following signposts (partial list):

- Nuclear and other carbon-free generation emerge as incentives, research is increased, and two waves of nuclear construction occur.
- The Midwest becomes a wind generation exporter as it is the only mature renewable able to initially meet the renewable energy standard driven by the desire to be energy independent.
- Hybrid electric vehicles become common due to increasing gas mileage standards. Plug-in hybrids and all-electric cars begin to take a greater market share in the second half of the decade. Vehicle-to-grid (V2G) infrastructure develops allowing these vehicles to be both a source and sink for electricity. Plug-in fuel cell cars emerge.
- Net books replace PCs as Internet saturation and cloud computing increases. 4G networks spur phone-based computers that people use to manage their lives. Internet-ready home appliances become the standard, resulting in home automation becoming the standard building design.
- After a few years, customer-owned generation takes hold, especially small-scale wind and solar. This is driven by higher electricity rates. The "green chic" of having the first solar shingles on your block becomes a driver of social status. Micro-grids soon follow as "green" neighborhoods

and commercial parks sprout up and want to take advantage of load diversity and shared back-up generation.

- The surge of nonutility generation (wind, customer generation, small gas) entering the market brings a new deregulation effort.

This scenario is described by time-phased changes (signposts) to the utility market. There are numerous utility market forces and external variables ranging from smart grids to nuclear power, and from solar and battery breakthroughs to be considered and many near- and long-term assumptions necessary to support a capital-intensive, long lead time construction- and maintenance-based company.

Strategic Planning Gaps and External Threats The working scenario identifies the threats and the opportunities in the external environment as well as projecting when and how they will evolve. The gaps identified in the internal assessment inform needed changes to OPPD's internal processes.

Using this information, the senior management team participated in another workshop to brainstorm the "Grand Strategy." The team assumed it was the year 2020 and the working scenario was a reality. The Grand Strategy is a one-page document that answers the following questions:

- What will OPPD look like in 2020, if we are to achieve our customer outcomes, our stakeholder outcomes, and our financial outcomes?
- How will we mitigate the threats and take advantage of the opportunities presented in the scenario?
- What weaknesses will be magnified in the scenario and how will we address them?
- What current strengths can be leveraged in the scenario?

This exercise identifies how OPPD will have to change to be successful. Change is managed by identifying strategic initiatives. In scenario planning some strategic initiatives are selected because they are robust (i.e., are relevant in all of the scenarios). Continuous process improvement is a strategic initiative that meets this definition. Other strategies are chosen because they are optimal in the most likely scenario. A renewable energy strategy and Smart Grid initiatives exemplify these strategies.

The Grand Strategy is further clarified by creating goals, measures, targets, and strategic initiatives.

Strategic Planning: Goals, Measures, Targets, and Strategic Initiatives Based on the strategic planning process outputs the leadership team will form strategic goals (what they want to accomplish), PSC measures, and targets (rates of performance). If there is gap between current PSC measure performance and

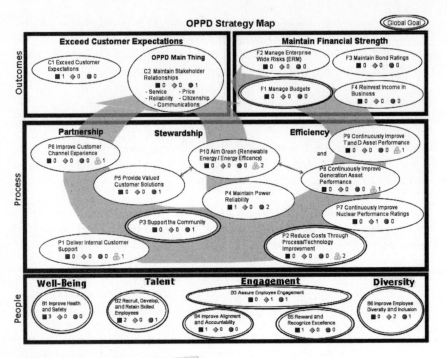

EXHIBIT 5.9 OPPD Strategy Map
Courtesy of Omaha Public Power District.

a new strategic target, the team will formulate a strategic initiative to close the gap. Closing a gap will require a change in processes at OPPD and is usually reflected in the process section of the strategy map shown in Exhibit 5.9. Strategic initiatives may include a change or update to the OPPD assets such as plant expansion, transmission, and/or distribution network modifications based on the long-term system plan, or investment in renewable energy such as wind, thermal, or solar.

STRATEGIC INITIATIVES CAPITAL AND O&M PLANNING PROCESS OPPD uses a strategy development process whereby the broad concepts for change are shaped into defined strategic initiatives with enough detail to enter the capital and O&M Operations and Maintenance planning process as a project. This stage-gate process starts with the broad, loosely defined ideas and concepts that represent the grand strategy. Decision points (stage-gates) are added so the concepts can be reviewed by senior management as they are developed. This ensures that concepts can be culled if they do not merit further development and the attendant expense of market or technology tests.

The culmination of this process is the funding of the strategic initiative as a project or a portfolio of capital and O&M projects.

STRATEGY MAP OPPD leverages the Kaplan and Norton strategy map toolset to translate its new strategy into a one-page pictorial representation for deployment throughout the company (see Exhibit 5.9). We will describe representative strategic goals in each of the four perspectives: people, process, customer, and financial. Global goals represented with a double circle represent strategic goals that are required throughout the entire organization on all strategy maps. For example, F1, Manage Budgets, is required of all business units, divisions, departments, and teams to ensure focus on financial stewardship of ratepayer funds.

In the *people perspective* the team identified five strategic goals that provide enabling or foundation behaviors (B) for improving process perspective execution; a few include:

- "B1 Improve Health and Safety" is concerned with the safety, health, and wellness of OPPD's employee base.
- "B2 Recruit, Develop, and Retain Skilled Employees" is focused on filling open positions with skilled employees, building employee skills, and retaining those in key positions.

In the *process perspective* the team identified three themes, partnership, stewardship, and efficiency, to group strategic goals that focus on customer facing processes; one includes:

- "P2 Reduce Costs Through Process and Technology Improvements" formalizes the company's commitments to innovation and productivity enhancements to the business.

In the *customer perspective* the team aligned customer requirements with the J.D. Power criteria for customer surveys that include:

- "C2 OPPD Main Thing" consisting of five categories: service, price, reliability, citizenship, and communications.

In the *financial perspective* the team aligned financial goals with the company business model and its fiduciary responsible to ratepayers:

- "F1 Manage Budgets" focuses on the stewardship of company funds and adherence to company budgets.
- "F2 Manage Enterprise Wide Risks" incorporates strategic, operational, financial, audit, and other risks into the strategy.

STRATEGIC COMMUNICATIONS   The CPM team partnered with the corporate communications team to prepare and deploy a comprehensive strategic communications plan for the company. This plan identified three major employee audiences, three messages, and numerous channels and message time frames phased by calendar quarters.

The three audiences include level 1 senior management, level 2 business unit leaders and their teams, and level 3 division leaders and their teams.

The three messages included: (1) project status and update, (2) sharing of strategy maps, PSCs and major initiatives, and (3) PSC results from operations. Notice the frequency of each message type with (1) and (2) eventually being replaced with message (3) on a monthly basis to reflect the PSC becoming a regular, repeatable process for managing the business.

The channels were primarily existing meeting structures that were transformed by using new content derived from the strategy maps and PSCs.

The strategic communications plan shown in Exhibit 5.10 also provided for a focused release of new PSCs through the company intranet along with the use of iconic themes and related metaphors. Images were selected for the nine themes OPPD used to categorize the goals in their strategy map. Along with the images, movie clips were selected that further exemplified the theme. The images were shared in posters and screensavers. The use of images and movie clips helped employees better understand how the strategic theme tied to the work they were accountable for. These strategic themes were communicated in multiple channels as well. A strategic plan booklet used the themes to launch the descriptions on what the corporate goals were to achieve; notepads with the themes on each of the pages were given to every employee; and leadership and division meetings used the movie clip segments to further communicate and drive home the intent of the themes in the strategic plan.

OPPD's intranet site CPM page also centralized information on the strategic plan in an effort to ensure employees had access to the components of the plan and to encourage transparency of information. To ensure employees could view the monthly updates of the measures on the corporate PSC, a copy was added to the intranet for those who did not have access to the Performance Scorecard software tool. OPPD also communicated using a strategy map demonstrating how the themes fit into the strategic perspectives. This image was tied together with an overall theme of "AIM HIGH." Users could move their mouse over the words and the image would pop up for each theme.

CORE AND INNOVATIVE BEST PRACTICES   OPPD exercises the core best practices identified earlier; plus it has advanced knowledge in this area with new, innovative best practices.

Legend:
- **A** Project Update
- **B** Share Strategy Maps, PSCs, Initiatives
- **C** Review PSC performance

Timeline: This Year (3Q: J A S; 4Q: O N D) — Next Year (1Q: J F M A M; 2Q: J J A S; 3Q)

Audience	Message	Channel	Messenger	Timeline markers
Level 1 Senior Management (weekly)	A	Monthly Meeting	Deeno	A A (4Q); C C C C C (Next Year)
	B	Monthly Meeting	Adrian/Deeno	B B B (4Q)
	C	Monthly Meeting	Deeno/SMT Owners	C (3Q Next Year)
Level 2 BU Leaders and Their Teams	A	BU Monthly Meeting	Deeno	A A A (4Q); C C C C C (Next Year)
	B	BU Monthly Meeting	BU Leaders and Direct Reports	B B B (4Q)
	C	BU Monthly Meeting	BU Leaders and Direct Reports	C (3Q Next Year)
Level 3 Division Leaders and Their teams	A	e-mail/Newsletter/Intranet	Gary - All employee communication	A (4Q); A (2Q Next Year)
	B	BU and Division Town Hall Meetings all employees	BU & Division Leaders	B B B (4Q)
	C	Monthly Meetings	Division Leaders/Deeno/Cherie	C C C C C C (Next Year); C (3Q)

EXHIBIT 5.10 Strategic Communications Plan

Courtesy of Omaha Public Power District.

Principle 2: Refresh and Communicate Strategy

- **Strategic planning.** Leverage the strategic planning process as either owner or partner to understand changing market conditions including competitor, supplier, rival, and potential entrants and substitutes in the marketplace.
- **Core and adjacent products and services.** Define and determine core and adjacent products and services to focus on highest probabilities for success.
- **Strategic plan.** Produce a comprehensive strategic plan.
- **Strategy mapping.** Develop corporate- and department-level strategy maps containing objectives along four perspectives including financial, customer/constituent, process, and people. Observe strategy map design parameters of 20 to 25 objectives.
- **Link strategic planning and budgeting processes.** Link strategic planning to the budgeting process, partner and budgeting with finance to provide for a seamless continuum.
- **Communications plan.** Communicate strategy throughout the organization using a comprehensive communications plan.
- **Innovative Best Practice.** OPPD has developed a very sophisticated and robust scenario planning process that incorporates numerous industry, political, econometric, customer, technological, and behavioral elements and variables.
- **Innovative Best Practice.** OPPD integrates risk into strategic planning and management to optimize strategic outcomes; most companies treat these key elements as separate events or work streams.
- **Innovative Best Practice.** OPPD has designed and deployed a comprehensive communications plan that incorporates clear audiences, messages, channels, messengers, and frequencies to ensure employee understanding and participation in company strategy.
- **Innovative Best Practice.** OPPD has formalized its CPM programs through two strategic goals on its strategy map: (1) process goal "P2 Reduce Costs Through Process and Technology Improvements" formalizes the company's commitments to innovation and productivity enhancements to the business; and (2) people behavior goal "B4 Improve Alignment and Accountability" focuses on aligning individuals with their scorecards linked to company strategy.

Poudre Valley Health System: Best Practice Case

Poudre Valley Health System (PVHS) is the market leader in its primary market, which includes Fort Collins, Loveland, the I-25 corridor, and surrounding Larimer County. In this primary market, which accounts for 75 percent of PVHS' revenue, PVHS is approaching a 65 percent market share—up nearly 10 percent over the past five years. Competitor market shares have dropped. Demographers expect the region's population to almost double over the next two decades. To keep pace with this population growth in a way that supports the organization's vision and mission, PVHS opened its second hospital, Medical Center of the Rockies (MCR), as a joint venture with Regional West Medical Center (RWMC) in early 2007. PVHS' secondary market reaches south to the Northern Denver Metro Area, north to Central Wyoming, east across western Nebraska, and west to the Colorado/Utah border.

STRATEGIC CONTEXT PVHS' key strategic advantages and challenges associated with organizational sustainability present information about relationships between strategic advantages and challenges, core competencies, strategic objectives (SOs), and the strategic plan.

Strategic Advantages

- Low workforce vacancy and turnover
- Strong market/financial position in economic downturn
- Minimal duplication of core health care services
- Innovative technology, programs, and methodologies
- Focus on the future
- Community health involvement
- High-quality care, competitive charges to consumer
- Performance excellence

Strategic Challenges

- Managing labor, financial, and other internal resources in response to market demand, health care reform, and other external factors
- Maintaining and expanding market share
- Maintaining and expanding partnerships
- Maintaining world-class clinical outcomes

The PVHS strategy development and deployment process employs the Global Path to Success (GPS) (see Exhibit 5.11), which serves as the PVHS leadership system for setting and deploying the vision, mission, values, and strategic objectives throughout the organization:

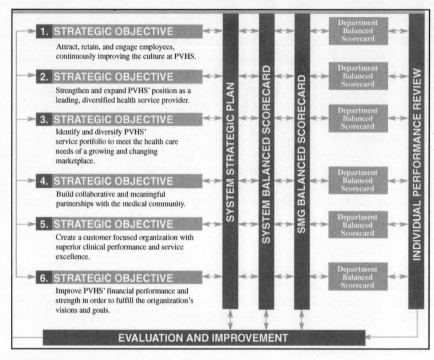

EXHIBIT 5.11 Global Path to Success

Courtesy of Poudre Valley Health System.

- Vision: To provide world-class health care
- Mission: To be an independent, nonprofit organization providing innovative, comprehensive care of the highest quality and exceeding
  customer expectations
- Values: quality, compassion, confidentiality, dignity/respect, equality,
  integrity

STRATEGY DEVELOPMENT PROCESS The PVHS strategy development and
deployment process (SDD) is a continuous seven-step cycle described next
that ensures active involvement of multiple stakeholders.

Key players in the SDD process are the board of directors, senior management group (SMG), and leadership team (more than 70 department
directors), which collectively gather extensive data from staff, physicians,
volunteers, patients, the community, partners, collaborators, and suppliers.
The goal of SDD is to provide a process where fact-based SO selection drives
a strategic plan, and then systemwide deployment optimizes resources to

operationalize the plan. With that goal in mind, PVHS has a five-year, longer-range strategic plan that supports a ten- to 15-year strategy. PVHS' short-term plan covers a one-year time frame, with built-in agility to rapidly respond to opportunistic projects or sudden threats that come up within the one-year planning horizon. Monitoring plan progress and making just-in-time, results-based adjustments give PVHS a distinct competitive advantage within its expanding northern Colorado marketplace.

Step One: Review Process   The SDD process begins at the annual winter SMG retreat, when SMG assesses progress on the previous year's strategic plan and evaluates the SDD process. Each year, SMG identifies improvement opportunities in the SDD process and makes appropriate adjustments to the process.

Step Two: Gather and Analyze Data   Quarterly, the MSP gathers and analyzes zip code- and procedure-based market-share, financial, and demographic data to identify trends for out- and in-migration, population growth, physician admissions, and utilization. Examples of analyses include: (1) correlations between market share and out-migration data; (2) trends for volume and market share by product line and service area; (3) physician admission trends; and (4) service line and market forecasts. The CFO and (CPM office) Marketing and Strategic Planning (MSP) department SP VP are the owners of this organizational knowledge, with data from numerous sources including (1) key stakeholder interviews (partners, physicians, volunteers, board chair); (2) SWOT analyses and environmental assessments technology analysis; and (3) other key data from physicians, staff, patients, partners, suppliers, collaborators and volunteers.

SMG uses these data for information: (1) quarterly to monitor progress toward SOs, detect shifts in technology or markets, and identify potential blind spots; and (2) annually to support SDD. The CFO and VP of MSP prioritize the results of their data analysis and present them at the annual winter SMG retreat—attended by medical staff leaders—to provide data for SWOT analysis. Through the SWOT analysis, SMG identifies strategic advantages and challenges and reviews proposals for new services, evaluating them based on whether they (1) support achievement of the VMV and SOs; (2) meet key customer requirements; (3) enhance strategic advantages or address strategic challenges; and/or (4) meet community needs.

SMG also identifies (1) opportunities for innovation, such as lab automation and the planned cancer center; and (2) strategies, such as MCR's hospital within a hospital, that would be best deployed in partnership with another organization. At the conclusion of the retreat, SMG agrees on strategy recommendations to present to the board of directors and proposals that warrant further analysis, including financial and other risk assessment, by the Decision Support department. In parallel and in support of the strategy recommendations, the CIO prepares a five-year information technology (IT) plan, SMG members update facility master plans, and the CFO finalizes the five-year financial and capital plans.

Step Three: Develop and Prioritize Strategies   At the board retreat in April, the CFO and MSP VP present the results of their extensive data aggregation and analysis activities (Step 2), and the board of directors and SMG engage in a rigorous discussion about the future of the organization, including a SWOT analysis. The board of directors and SMG then evaluate and approve major new directions in the strategic plan and yearly goals for each SO. If necessary, they adjust the VMV and SOs every three years, to ensure early detection of major shifts in technology, markets, customer preferences, and competitive and regulatory environments. SMG and the board of directors hire an external consultant to conduct a ten- to 15-year strategy analysis. Based on this information, the VP of MSP prepares the strategic plan, including SO-specific goals, for review by the Board Strategic Planning committee and final approval by the board of directors in late September.

Step Four: Set Action Items and Goals   Based on the strategic plan, SMG, in coordination with the director of process improvement, uses a systematic process to determine measures for the system Balanced Scorecard (BSC), the key mechanism for measuring and tracking organizational performance relative to SOs. From the system BSC, individual SMG members create the aligned SMG BSCs and set appropriate goals and benchmarks. SMG then presents these BSCs to the leadership team, which works with SMG to coordinate goals between facilities and set goals for individual departments.

Step Five: Review and Allocate Resources   Based on the financial plan and in support of the strategic plan, the CFO, with input and approval from SMG, determines budget parameters for capital, revenue, expenses, and FTEs (full time equivalents). The CFO communicates these parameters to SMG, with historical data from the past two years and forecasted expenditures for the remaining current year. Using these parameters, SMG and directors work with staff and physicians to develop budgets and staffing plans for the coming year. At this time, the CIO queries managers for their projected resource needs and balances those needs with the IT plan. The Board Finance committee completes the budget in November. In support of organizational agility, SMG establishes a contingency fund for smaller urgent/emergent capital projects that fall outside the regular budget process.

Step Six: Communicate and Align In December, the board reviews and approves the proposed budget, strategic goals, and system BSC, matching the resources required to carry out the SOs with available resources and adjusting strategic goals to accommodate action items that are not funded.

Step Seven: Review Progress and Develop Action Plans SMG and directors review system and department BSCs monthly relative to goals specific for each SO. If a system BSC result falls short of the goal, the point person for that metric develops an action plan, which is approved and monitored by SMG. The CEOs and CFO meet monthly to ensure systemwide deployment. PVHS senior leaders rely on the systematic, fact-based SDD process to facilitate rigorous and timely discussions about the future of the organization. Prior to the winter SMG retreat, the MSP leads the leadership team in a SWOT analysis. SMG completes another SWOT with the board at the April board of directors meeting, aggregates and correlates the results of these SWOT analyses, and reviews the short- and long-term strategy analysis (SDD Step 3). This exhaustive environmental assessment, in conjunction with the five-year IT, financial, and capital plans, provides early indications of major shifts in technology, markets, the competitive collaborative environment, and regulatory requirements and can be used in assessing the strategic plan. With the visionary leadership of SMG and the board of directors, PVHS has a unique ability to drive changes in health care industry structures and ensure long-term sustainability. PVHS' SOs are listed in Exhibit 5.12.

The SOs address opportunities for innovation by identifying six critical areas for success: workforce, partnering with the medical community, market expansion, service diversification, quality, and finance. For each SO, the organization sets goals that *drive innovation*. For instance, for almost a decade, PVHS has continued to set stretch goals for voluntary staff turnover so that now the organization is a national role model. Achievement of the SOs, as measured by the PVHS BSC, strengthens the organization and creates a foundation for long-term sustainability. To balance short- and longer-term challenges and opportunities, SDD identifies SO-based action items and goals for one- and five-year planning horizons and allocates resources for both. By collecting and analyzing data from all stakeholders, SDD is able to balance stakeholder needs.

INTEGRATION OF STRATEGIC PLANNING WITH COMMUNITY INVOLVEMENT In the primary service area, PVHS is an active member of the role model Joint Community Health Strategic Planning Committee (JCHSPC), a regional, interagency collaboration to improve community health by developing a

EXHIBIT 5.12 Strategic Objectives

SO Figure R1-1	KEY GOALS 2.1(b)1	KEY SHORT-TERM PLANS 2.2a(4)	KEY LONGER-TERM PLANS 2.2a(4)	KEY PERFORMANCE INDICATORS 2.2a(6)	PERFORMANCE PROJECTIONS 2008/2012	
					PVHS	COMPETITOR
1	Reduce voluntary turnover	Implement retention and exit interviews	Achieve regions lowest rates and U.S. top 10%	Voluntary turnover	67-10%/5%	14%/10% 8%*
	Maintain strength in employee satisfaction	Develop action plans for lowest dimension of culture survey	Raise lowest dimension	Lowest dimension score on culture survey	4.5/>4.5	n/a
	Achieve vacancy rate in U.S. top 10%	Implement recruitment plans	Achieve rates that are lowest in region and within national top 10%	Vacancy rate	2.3%/<2.3%	1.7%*
2	Strengthen overall service are market share	Establish marketing strategies specific to service area/product line needs	Align marketing strategies with strategic plan	Primary service area market share	61%/65%	7%/5%
				Total service are market share	29.1%/31.8%	21.7%,19.7%
3	Support facility development	Develop Cancer Center	Open Cancer Center	Cancer Center fundraising	$7.5M/$30M	n/a
				Oncology market share	27.5%/31%	n/a
4	Enhance physician relations	Initiate physician engagement survey tool	Achieve top box physician engagement goals	Physician engagement survey	80%/>80%	80%*
5	Establish PVHS as leader in patient safety, patient satisfaction, quality improvement, and outcomes	Implement Thomson database/software	Achieve top 10% for all service lines	CMS core measures	Top 10% for PVHS/for service lines	See Figures 7.5-9-11*
		Continue to hardware "We're Here for You"	Become national benchmark for top box (patient satisfaction)	Overall top box	80%/>80%	n/a
				HCAHPS referral	80%/>80%	80%*
				HCAHPS loyalty	80%/>80%	75%*

#	Objective	Action	Target	Measure		
	Achieve Joint Commission national patient safety goals	Initiate and deploy PDCA terms for goals below 90% compliance	Achieve 100% compliance	National patient safety goals compliance	90%/100%	90%/100%
6	Monitor, compare, and strengthen PVHS financial position	Compute and trend financial flexibility components quarterly	Achieve financial flexibility index of 11	Financial flexibility index	85/11	7.6/7.6 11*
		Achieve budget	Achieve 5-year financial plan	Net income actual to budget		
				Operating cost per unit of service (percent variance)	±25%/±25%	n/a
				Operating revenue per unit of service (percent variance)		

Courtesy of Poudre Valley Health System.

community health plan and creating a central data repository. JCHSPC uses a systematic four-step process to determine community health needs:

1. Compile and analyze data. JCHSPC members meet quarterly to analyze data and allocate resources. Data come from a variety of external and internal sources.
2. Identify and prioritize needs. JCHSPC works with an epidemiologist to identify needs, determine the relative health burden of each need, and evaluate how successful interventions have been in other communities. The group then prioritizes response efforts relative to available resources.
3. Determine response. JCHSPC matches programs/initiatives with the most appropriate response organization(s), based on alignment with each organization's SOs. The PVHS community health director works through PVHS SDD to secure resources needed for programs or initiatives assigned to PVHS.
4. Evaluate and improve. Data analysis is ongoing so that community health leaders can gauge the effectiveness of response efforts and make adjustments or shift resources as appropriate. The committee also evaluates the process for determining community health involvement/support and adjusts the process as appropriate.

COMMUNICATING STRATEGY Senior leaders devote significant time and resources to communicating with and engaging the workforce. Staff engagement and frank, two-way communication between senior leaders and staff begins on an employee's first day on the job, when the PVHS CEO addresses attendees in new employee orientation (NEO): "It is my job to make this the best place you have ever worked. If I'm not doing my job, tell me." In addition to formal communication mechanisms, senior leaders engage the workforce through informal settings, such as focus luncheons, leadership rounding, and system or department celebrations and social events.

CORE AND INNOVATIVE BEST PRACTICES PVHS exercises the core best practices identified earlier and has advanced knowledge in this area with a new, innovative best practice.

Principle 2: Refresh and Communicate Strategy

- **Strategic planning.** Leverage the strategic planning process as either owner or partner to understand changing market conditions including competitor, supplier, rival, and potential entrants and substitutes in the marketplace.

- **Core and adjacent products and services.** Define and determine core and adjacent products and services to focus on highest probabilities for success.
- **Strategic plan.** Produce and deploy a comprehensive strategic plan.
- **Strategy mapping.** PVHS does not use.
- **Link strategic planning and budgeting processes.** Link strategic planning to the budgeting process, partner and budgeting with finance to provide for a seamless continuum.
- **Communications plan.** Communicate strategy throughout the organization using a comprehensive communications plan.
- **Innovative Best Practice.** PVHS has developed one of the most comprehensive, integrated bidirectional communications plans among dozens of companies reviewed, consisting of annual, quarterly, monthly, bimonthly, weekly, and daily formalized frequencies among multiple channels.
- **Innovative Best Practice.** PVHS integrates strategy planning with community involvement. PVHS is an active member of the role model Joint Community Health Strategic Planning Committee (JCHSPC), a regional, interagency collaboration to improve community health by (1) developing a community health plan and (2) creating a central data repository. JCHSPC uses a systematic process to determine community health needs.

Public Service Electric & Gas Best Practice Case

The vision, strategy, and values of Public Service Electric & Gas (PSE&G) include the following:

- **PSE&G Vision: P**eople providing **S**afe and reliable, **E**conomic and **G**reen energy
- **PSE&G Strategy:** Top national decile performance in safety and top national quartile performance in reliability, cost, and environmental metrics within the first year of the five-year plan.
- **PSE&G Values:** Leadership in people, safety, reliability, economic and green includes many key elements.

As one example, Leadership in People means:

- Holding ourselves to the highest ethical standards
- Appreciating diversity ... and treating each other with respect and dignity

- Living up to our commitments
- Working together to set and achieve stretch goals
- Communicating openly and honestly

STRATEGIC PLANNING PROCESS   PSE&G begins its strategic and business planning in June each year and it is completed by December with chairman and board's approval of the five-year plan, financials, and targets.

Beginning in January PSE&G begins to collect benchmarking data results for its BSC metrics from a panel of peer companies to set the national benchmark performance. These updated benchmarks are the basis of the upcoming target-setting process. In early May PSE&G sponsors best practices conferences with leading companies focused on key operating processes. The best practices are identified and either begin to be implemented or are included in the following year's business plan. By June benchmark data results are available and reviewed by the business leaders. This begins the business planning cycle. PSE&G reviews any gaps in achieving strategy (top decile or quartile) and completes SWOT, customer, and systems analyses and the current business operating environment analysis, which provides input into any change in company strategy and budgeting processes described in the next sections.

The analysis is completed by September with a two-day offsite meeting attended by the utility senior leadership team (SLT). The competitor analysis typically includes benchmarking for PSE&G to verify top decile and quartile performance. This involves a review of all available benchmarking data. Some metrics have data sets representing over 70 U.S. utilities. Included in the offsite is an annual review of the current BSC metrics, and a determination is made whether there will be any changes or amendments to the coming year's BSC. Major strategic initiatives are discussed regarding the impact to customers, natural gas or electric infrastructure and reliability, shareholder value, or revenue enhancement and projections. Based on the foregoing, PSE&G prepares the financial and nonfinancial measures and targets, which are approved by the chairman in December.

STRATEGIC PLANNING AND ENTERPRISE RISK MANAGEMENT   PSE&G has an asset management group whose primary function is focused on enterprise risk management. As part of their analytical tools they have implemented an IES (investment evaluation system). The IES prioritizes all capital and maintenance projects based upon several major factors including risk management, financial return and prudence, and impact on strategy using the BSC metrics.

STRATEGIC INITIATIVES AND BUDGETING   Over the past five years, PMG has transformed its business planning process to include benchmarking data that are used to include initiatives in its business plans that require capital expenditures. This approach drives the implementation of best practices and moves the company closer to achieving top deciles, top quartile strategic performance. PSE&G has been recognized by industry associations as a leading company in implementing best practices. PSE&G has shared its approach, both within and outside of the industry, though formal presentations and published magazine articles.

During the difficult financial climate that the economy is currently experiencing, PSE&G will invest over $1.7 billion in infrastructure projects that will drive its strategy. Examples of strategy translating into *innovative* strategic initiatives include:

- Solar panels on poles; world's first utility project to be installed on over 200,000 poles.
- Solar loans; over $105 million in loans.
- Solar 4 All project; renting roof space on government buildings, schools, and public housing to install solar panels.
- Deep-water wind farm; 96 turbines located 20 miles offshore to reduce visual signature.
- Upgrade and expand electric grid and construction of over 200 miles of new high-voltage transmission lines.
- Relamping street lights; the United States' first large-scale project to replace 100,000 street lights with high-energy-efficient units.

The entire initiative portfolio groups strategic initiatives by major category such as Smart Grid, Solar Loan Program, and so on. PSE&G then evaluates the impact of each initiative on the BSC measures by quadrant: people providing, safe and reliable, economic, and green energy. PMG conducts analytics to determine how this portfolio delivers on company strategy.

PSE&G STRATEGY MAP   PSE&G has adopted the Kaplan and Norton Strategy Map tool (see Exhibit 5.13) to translate its strategic plan and key strategies into operational terms to drive improvements.

PSE&G's strategy is to be the safe, reliable, and low-cost leading utility in the nation. PSE&G has defined those primary top three strategic objectives shown in the strategy map as:

1. Top decile performance in safety for its employees and customers
2. Top quartile in reliability
3. Top quartile in reliability and low cost

The strategy map reflects the company strategy by strategic objective across four perspectives, reading from bottom to top: People, Operations

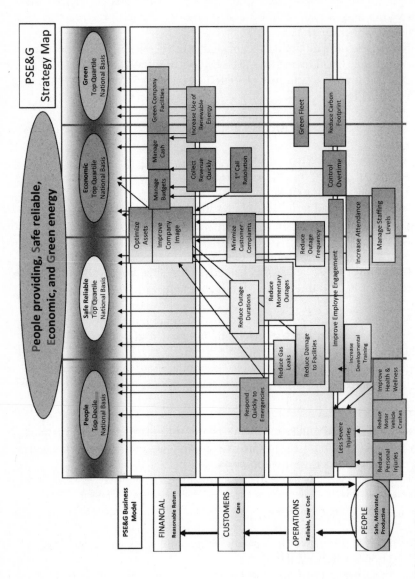

EXHIBIT 5.13 PSE&G Strategy Map

Courtesy of Public Service Electric & Gas.

(process), Customers, and Financial. These outcomes are met by strategic objectives, again noted in the four perspectives. The company has built on its success keeping employees first in the business model.

COMMUNICATING STRATEGY   The strategy map and BSC results have been successfully used as a primary communication tool, not only to the board of directors, but also when speaking to state regulators, shareholders, employees, and the investment community. The BSC is shared with the board of directors on a monthly basis

PSE&G has been able to articulate its strategy in a clear, simple manner in which all its employees understand where the company is heading and how their individual contribution is linked to achieving those ends. Senior leaders continuously communicate the strategy, the business model, and the performance results not only to employees but also at public forums, to state regulators, and with shareholders.

PSE&G leadership shares both the strategy and results with all employees through various media, such as being posted on the intranet on a BSC website, posters at field locations, group meetings, quarterly business outlook presentations, and union presentations.

CORE AND INNOVATIVE BEST PRACTICES   PSE&G exercises the core best practices identified earlier and has advanced knowledge in this area with new, innovative best practices.

Principle 2: Refresh and Communicate Strategy

- **Strategic planning.** PSE&G leverages the strategic planning process to understand changing market conditions including competitor, supplier, rival, and potential entrants and substitutes in the marketplace.
- **Core and adjacent products and services.** Define and determine core and adjacent products and services (e.g., solar panels and Energy Efficiency programs) to focus on highest probabilities for success.
- **Strategic plan.** Produce a comprehensive strategic plan.
- **Strategy mapping.** Develops a corporate level strategy map containing objectives along four perspectives including financial, customer, operations and people. It observes strategy map design parameters of 20 to 25 objectives.

(Continued)

- **Link strategic planning and budgeting processes.** Link strategic planning to the budgeting process, partner and budgeting with finance to provide for a seamless continuum.
- **Communications plan.** Communicate strategy throughout the organization using a comprehensive communications plan and multiple channels and media.
- **Innovative Best Practice.** PSE&G has integrated benchmarking into its strategic planning and target setting processes to fund major, strategic initiatives to close performance gaps and attain top deciles and quartile service levels.
- **Innovative Best Practice.** PSE&G integrates strategic planning and risk management. Its investment evaluation system prioritizes all capital and maintenance projects based upon several major factors including risk management, financial return and prudence, and impact on strategy using the BSC metrics.
- **Innovative Best Practice.** PSE&G has pioneered innovation strategy with placement of solar panels on over 200,000 utility poles, an industry first on this scale.
- **Innovative, Best Practice.** PSE&G has pioneered an innovative strategy of a deep-water wind farm consisting of 96 turbines located 20 miles offshore to reduce the visual signature.
- **Innovative, Best Practice.** PSE&G has successfully used the strategy map and BSC as primary communication tools, not only to the board of directors, but also when speaking to state regulators, shareholders, employees, and the investment community. This is far more wide-ranging than what is done by most award-winning utilities and organizations.

Sharp HealthCare: Best Practice Case

The Sharp Experience infuses Sharp's mission by reconnecting the hearts, minds, and attitudes of its almost 14,000 team members, 2,000 volunteers, and 2,600 affiliated physicians to purpose, worthwhile work, and making a difference.

STRATEGY DEVELOPMENT PROCESS Executive steering initiated a strategic planning effort in 1999 to refocus Sharp's direction and maintain and enhance its position as San Diego's health care leader. The board and senior management sought input from national health care and other best-practice service organizations to transform Sharp from a *good* health care system to a *great* one. This good-to-great focus became the cornerstone of Sharp's strategic planning process. The process focused first at the system level with a reassessment of Sharp's mission and values. Next, the forces that impact Sharp's success were evaluated through an extensive internal and external market assessment. The market assessment led to a SWOT at the system level. The system SWOT became the basis for developing Sharp's seven critical success factors (CSFs):

1. Vigorously define, measure, and communicate clinical and service excellence.
2. Build lasting relationships with/among physicians and affiliated medical groups.
3. Increase patient and community loyalty.
4. Attract, motivate, maintain, and promote the best and brightest health care work force in San Diego.
5. Pursue innovation in clinical programs, information/support services, and products.
6. Balance long-term capital availability and capital requirements.
7. Enhance the organization's ability to make timely, collaborative decisions to ensure progress on system goals.

This led to the development of six goal statements and a vision statement. Upon completion of system goals, corporate and operating entities initiated development of specific strategies and action plans to support Sharp's vision. Additionally, the hospital entities began a coordinated master site planning process to determine the long-range health care needs of their local communities. Entity planning teams also reviewed and provided input into the system's mission, vision, values, CSFs, and goals, ensuring a shared and supported strategic direction. Entity planning teams included management, physicians, volunteers, and boards.

- **Sharp HealthCare Mission Statement:** To improve the health of those we serve with a commitment to excellence in all that we do. Sharp's goal is to offer quality care and services that set community standards, exceed patients' expectations, and are provided in a caring, convenient, cost-effective, and accessible manner.
- **Sharp HealthCare Vision Statement:** Sharp will redefine the health care experience through a culture of caring, quality, service, innovation, and excellence. Sharp will be recognized by employees, physicians, patients, volunteers, and the community as the best place to work, the best place to practice medicine, and the best place to receive care. Sharp will be known as an excellent community citizen embodying an

organization of people working together to do the right thing every day to improve the health and well-being of those we serve. Sharp will become the best health care system in the universe.

- **Sharp HealthCare Core Values:** Integrity, caring, innovation, excellence.
- **Sharp HealthCare Six Pillars of Excellence:** Quality, service, people, finance, growth, community.
- **Sharp HealthCare Core Competency:** Transforming the health care experience through The Sharp Experience (as symbolized by the flame).

This strategic planning process (shown in Exhibit 5.14) resulted in "top-down" direction setting and identification of system goals, as well as "bottom-up" planning founded on the environmental analysis and identification of issues and opportunities for each entity.

Over the 12-month planning cycle, departments, entities, and the system prepare integrated plans, which include a five-year (long-term) horizon and an annual (short-term) focus. Executive steering selected the five-year horizon as its long-term planning period, as the industry is one of rapid change. A one-year planning period was chosen as Sharp's short-term planning horizon to coincide with annual budget process. To effectively align the organization with Sharp's goals, the six goal statements were transformed into the Six Pillars of Excellence. Measurable objectives are established within each pillar for each year of the five-year long-term planning horizon. Year One targets are defined and published in a system report card (shown in Chapter 6). Results are measured and analyzed monthly, quarterly, or annually, as applicable. For areas not improving, action plans are developed. The annual strategic planning process begins in June upon the release of Office of Statewide Health Planning and Development (OSHPD) hospital utilization information (Step A) in Exhibit 5.14. The system strategic planning department (B) updates the system and entity environmental assessments with OSHPD data, as well as other surveillance information, including an evaluation of Sharp's progress toward reaching short-term and long-term report card targets and customer and partner input from listening and learning tools.

Competitor assessments are made through publicly reported information and other reliable sources, including market evaluations, future growth plans, and operational reviews, to understand the five-year competitive market environment. The results of the environmental assessments are shared with system and entity leadership, who use the information to update their respective SWOT analyses (C). SWOTs address each pillar to ensure the organization considers all aspects of the internal and external environments including the identification of potential blind spots.

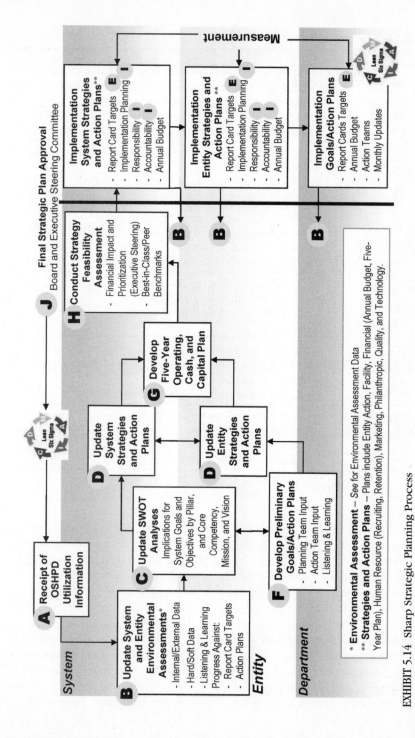

EXHIBIT 5.14 Sharp Strategic Planning Process

Courtesy of Sharp HealthCare.

173

EXHIBIT 5.15 Pillars of Excellence Strategies

Pillar	Fiscal 2007 – 2012 Strategies
Quality	▪ Enhance patient outcomes and safety (including enterprise-wide implementation of Six Sigma) ▪ Team training to create a culture of safety ▪ Enterprise-wide EMR, POE, and Ambulatory EHR
Service	▪ Focus on top patient satisfiers as identified by Press Ganey patient surveys ▪ Hospitals, Medical Groups, and SHP satisfaction ▪ Physician leadership development and satisfaction
People	▪ Sharp Experience Action Team initiatives ▪ EOS action plans by department ▪ New EOS tool to provide best-in-class benchmarking ▪ Recruiting initiatives for nurses and hard-to-fill positions
Finance	▪ Cash generated by operations improvement ▪ Employee safety improvement ▪ Initiatives to enhance Sharp's capital structure
GROWTH	▪ Six Sigma throughput projects ▪ Hospital and Medical Group expansion plans ▪ Contracting initiatives ▪ SHP revenue and profitability growth initiatives
Community	▪ Legislative initiatives ▪ Fundraising campaigns ▪ SHC community benefit initiatives ▪ Board discussion forums

Courtesy of Sharp HealthCare.

From the SWOTs, planning teams update system and entity strategies and action plans (D). Short-term and long-term report card targets are systematically evaluated and set annually by the accountability team to ensure progress is measured in meeting system and entity goals by pillar (E) as shown in Exhibit 5.15.

INTEGRATION WITH PLANNING AND BUDGETING The five-year plan balances long-term capital availability with capital requirements and determines the financial feasibility of Sharp's strategic initiatives. The five-year plan includes an extensive capital planning process. Strategic capital requests resulting from each entity's action plan development are evaluated by executive steering through a quantitative process that measures a project's financial benefit, quality results, and service excellence. Operations are forecasted with realistic inflationary and volume assumptions based upon current results and the expected business and legislative environment. Executive steering's quantitative capital evaluation process provides Sharp with the best strategic capital initiatives that meet the goals of the organization and the needs of the community. The process is collaborative to ensure community resources are directed to initiatives based on Sharp's strategic imperatives under the Six Pillars of Excellence. The five-year plan includes an evaluation of Sharp's financial ratios compared to its peers and the best-in-class, thereby determining the feasibility of the strategic direction and ensuring Sharp's ability to execute its strategic plan (H). Additionally, the plan provides five-year targets that focus on advancing the organization toward meeting its vision, while maintaining a strong competitive position and ensuring organizational sustainability.

Sharp ensures that resources are available to support its action plans through the five-year plan. During the five-year plan process, the system CEO and CFO, including strategic planning and finance management representatives, meet with each entity's CEO and CFO to evaluate the entity's five-year plan forecast, refine its projections, and ensure the system's ability to meet its five year planning targets and operational obligations. Upon finalization of the entity five-year plans and consolidation of the system's plan, a two-day executive steering session is held to review and refine the five-year plan projections and evaluate and approve entity strategic capital initiatives. In this session, executive steering evaluates Sharp's strategic capital projects stemming from each entity's strategies and action plan development. The capital evaluation process is quantitative and based upon equally weighted scoring criteria designed to target resources to strategies and actions that provide the most benefit for the community, as measured by the impact on Sharp's pillars. Financial and other risks are assessed through the capital evaluation process.

After reviewing each proposal, executive steering members score each strategic capital project. The collective scores are used to rank strategic capital initiatives based upon Sharp's available capital funding for the five-year projection. Once the five-year plan is approved by the board in the spring, entity strategies and action plans are finalized and presented to the board at its annual strategic planning retreat.

The plan's year one financial results become the targets for the annual budget process, which begins in May. In addition, Sharp includes a $65 million strategic capital funding pool in the five-year plan to provide agility to allow for new initiatives and investing activities based on significant market changes, health care innovations, and customer needs and preferences. Sharp's boards approve all budgeted capital expenditures prior to purchase, including separate review of items in excess of $750,000, ensuring appropriate capital expenditures are made to support community needs.

Human resource planning is an integrated part of the strategic planning process. During the environmental assessment, staff positions are evaluated (B). Human resource action plans are based on Sharp's mission, vision, values, and SWOT analyses, and from these action plans, human resource operating and capital needs are included in the five-year plan. Human resources' action plans, available onsite, focus on retention, recruitment, and expansion of the local employee market for hard-to-fill positions (D).

Compensation enhancements are determined based on review of Sharp's salary and benefit position within its marketplace, as compared to peers. The five-year plan (J) is completed and presented to the board in the spring.

Entity and system strategies and action plans are completed in draft form by January (F). Beginning in January, the capital and operating impact of each entity's strategies and action plans is forecasted in the five-year plan, which is developed for each entity and consolidated for the system (G).

INTEGRATING ETHICS AND RISK INTO STRATEGIC PLANNING AND MANAGEMENT

Numerous indicators are measured consistently to meet or surpass all requirements for regulatory, legal, and accreditation. Furthermore, community assessment and proactive thinking are integral to Sharp's system and entity strategic planning. When faced with the regulatory requirement to provide seismic retrofit at each acute-care hospital, Sharp expanded this effort to include a comprehensive strategic master plan.

From patient interactions to business transactions, ethical behavior is an imperative standard discussed in the *Commitment to Principles* handbook and managed by the compliance department. Compliance is communicated through policies, procedures, and staff training; achieved through audits, feedback mechanisms, and contracts and agreements; and reinforced through appropriate corrective actions and annually with all employees through computer-based training on ethics, compliance, and patient privacy. The process for managing ethical behavior is as follows:

- Identify areas at risk.
- Implement appropriate training and/or process improvement actions and controls to mitigate risks.
- Monitor and evaluate results through internal audits and the activities of safety and compliance officers.
- Respond to breaches with immediate corrective action, reevaluate the process, and monitor training.

Entity ethics committees actively participate with families/caregivers to address clinical ethics issues and patients' rights. Members educate and serve as a resource for clinical decision making by patients/families and health care providers.

INTEGRATING STRATEGY PLANNING AND SUPPORT OF KEY COMMUNITIES   Through the strategic planning process, Sharp identifies key communities in San Diego and key services important to health care maintenance within these communities. Supportive data for these analyses include demographic data and disease indices. Assessments are scientific and rigorous in their approach. Most methods include prioritization among competing health issues using objective rating scales corresponding to the seriousness, size, and level of community concern about the health issue. Year over year, there is consistent growth in the economic value of services provided by Sharp to the community.

STRATEGIC OBJECTIVES   As a component of Sharp's annual strategic planning process, the accountability team develops short-term, annual targets to measure Sharp's progress in meeting its pillar goals, as well as annual five-year targets to monitor Sharp's advancement toward attaining its vision. Monthly reporting on Sharp's annual progress is performed through the report card, which is disseminated throughout the system.

The short- and long-term report card targets are integrated throughout the system and are a balanced evaluation of Sharp's strategic planning success, where quality and service targets are each weighted 25 percent, people and finance are each weighted 20 percent, and growth and community are each weighted five percent. The pillars were designed to address challenges and opportunities of the organization based on its patient, community, and stakeholder needs. To achieve Sharp's vision, report card targets are assessed annually to ensure ongoing relevance and continual improvement under each pillar.

COMMUNICATING STRATEGY   Sharp's vision, values, and goals are formally documented and conveyed per the comprehensive communications plan (see Exhibit 5.16).

Communication follows a standard format with a consistent message. Quarterly LDS, employee forums, and monthly department/unit staff meetings afford leaders the opportunity to compare progress to system and entity goals and reinforce strategies to drive results. Employees, volunteers, and physicians celebrate their success at the annual all-staff assembly and renew their commitment to Sharp's mission, vision, and core values. Intranet postings, communication bulletin boards, e-mails, internal newsletters, and letters from the CEO reinforce the message of excellence. Upward

EXHIBIT 5.16 Strategic Communications Plan

When	How (↑↓Communication)	Audience	Message Points
Every Year	Off-Site Planning ↑↓	Senior Leaders, Board	Strategic planning assessment and direction
	All-Staff Assembly ↑↓	Employees, Physicians, Suppliers, Partners	CEO end-of-year Report Card update: best practice learning: Pillar of Excellence Award
	Employee Satisfaction Survey ↑	All Employees	Employees communicate likes dislikes to leadership in a safe, anonymous environment; recommendation for change
	Physician Opinion Survey ↑	All Physicians on Medical Staff	Physicians communicate likes/dislikes to leadership in a safe, anonymous environment; recommendation for change
Every Quarter	LDS ↑↓	Sharp Leaders	Performance update: best practice sharing: education; reward and recognition
	Supplier Partner Review ↑↓	Suppliers, Partners	Performance update; best practice sharing
	Employee Forums/ Communication Expos ↑↓	Employees	Performance update: best practice sharing: education; reward and recognition
Every Month	Department Meetings ↑↓	Employees	Performance update; best practice sharing: education: reward and recognition
	Quality Councils ↑↓	Employees, Physicians	Performance Improvement activities, progress on goals and action plans
	Report-Out ↑↓	Leaders, Teams	Performance update: best practice sharing: education
	Action Teams ↑↓	Employees	Plan updates, education initiatives, organisational improvement
	Medical Staff Leaders ↑↓	Physicians	Performance updates: operational Issues, clinical Issues
	Operations Meeting ↑↓	Leaders, Physicians	Best practice sharing and process Improvements: coordination of tactics

Frequency	Channel		Audience	Purpose
	Medlca1 Executives	→	Physicians	Governance of medical staff, peer review, and strategies coordination
	Board Meetings	↑↓	Board Members	Business of the health system; Pillar performance
	Entity Newsletters	↑↓	Employees, Physicians	Breaking news; performance updates; education
Bi-Monthly	*Experience Sharp* Newsletter	↑↓	Employees, Physicians	System and entity feature stories and news; employee of the month recognition; employee pulse survey on interesting topics
	Chiefs of Staff	↑↓	Physicians	System initiatives, best practices, and planning
Regular	CEO Letters	→	Employees	Company news and happenings
	Newsletters News Articles	→	Employees	Breaking news; event and class information; links to Sharp mentions in the news; new polices and procedures; recognition
	Global E-mails	→	Employees	Major announcements (re: clinical/operational updates)
	Sharp Internet, Web-based Tools	→	Employees	Regularly updated Information and resources (e.g., Policies and Procedures, Dashboards, benefits and payroll, and training)
	Thank-You Notes	↑↓	Employees	Regularly communicate appreciation to team members
Every Day	Rounding with Reason	↑↓	Customers. Partners, Employees	Walk units and connect with customers/partners; identity successes/concerns; reward and recognition

Courtesy of Sharp HealthCare.

communication and the evaluation of methods are fostered through ad hoc focus groups, annual opinion surveys, leadership sessions and employee forum evaluations, suggestion boxes, formal meeting evaluations, e-mail to CEOs, and department/unit–level staff meetings. The "Ask Mike" box located within the corporate office enables staff to submit questions they would like answered by the system's CEO or other senior leader. Annually, senior leaders identify and award the individuals, departments, and teams that exemplify The Sharp Experience by pillar with Center of Recognized Excellence (C.O.R.E.) Awards. From entity C.O.R.E. Award winners, a system team selects the annual Pillar of Excellence Award winners. These awards are given by the senior leaders at the all-staff assembly.

CORE AND INNOVATIVE BEST PRACTICES   Sharp exercises the core best practices identified earlier, plus it has advanced knowledge in this area with new, innovative best practices.

Principle 2: Refresh and Communicate Strategy

- **Strategic planning.** Leverage the strategic planning process as either owner or partner to understand changing market conditions including competitor, supplier, rival, and potential entrants and substitutes in the marketplace.
- **Core and adjacent products and services.** Define and determine core and adjacent products and services to focus on highest probabilities for success.
- **Strategic plan.** Produce a comprehensive strategic plan.
- **Strategy mapping.** Sharp does not use.
- **Link strategic planning and budgeting processes.** Link strategic planning to the budgeting process, partner and budgeting with finance to provide for a seamless continuum. Weighting point system used for capital expenditures.
- **Communications plan.** Communicate strategy throughout the organization using a comprehensive communications plan.
- **Innovative Best Practice.** Sharp has developed one of the most comprehensive, integrated bidirectional communications plans on strategy to its employees among dozens of companies reviewed, consisting of annual, quarterly, monthly, bimonthly, weekly, and daily formalized frequencies among multiple channels.

- **Innovative Best Practice.** In place of strategy maps, Sharp uses the Six Pillars containing strategic objectives covering quality, service, people, finance, growth, and community. This approach provides significant clarity to its strategic intent and to ease of understanding for employees.
- **Innovative Best Practice.** Sharp integrates ethics and risk into strategic planning and management to optimize their integration; most companies treat these key elements as separate events or work streams.
- **Innovative Best Practice.** Sharp integrates strategy planning and support of key communities and supportive services, thus factoring in key community requirements to its strategic plan, strategic objectives, and major initiatives.

CHAPTER 6

Principle 3: Cascade and Manage Strategy

When you can measure what you are speaking about, and express it in numbers, you know something about it; but when you cannot measure it, when you cannot express it in numbers, your knowledge is of a meager and unsatisfactory kind.

—Lord Kelvin

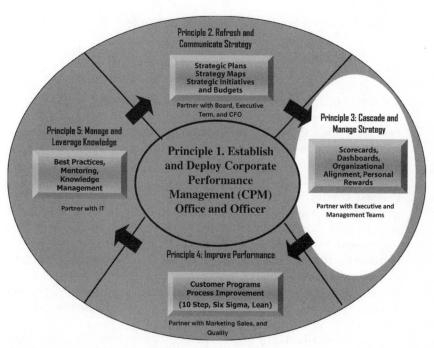

© Copyright 2010 Bob Paladino and Associates, LLC.

*P*rinciple 3, Cascade and Manage Strategy focuses on translating the outputs from Principle 2 into strategic objectives, measures, and targets that are actionable by employees. A key influence on development of these best practices derives from my experiences leading one of Kaplan and Norton's largest consulting divisions, leading the Crown Castle International BSC program to earn the BSC Hall of Fame award, and from collaborating with over 20 Hall of Fame organizations through the years. Award-winning organizations have been successful at cascading measures and linking and aligning them vertically and horizontally enterprisewide.

CPM Core Process Blueprint and Key Process Roles

Careful research of the cases in this book reveals they follow a discernible set of core CPM processes organized within the Five Key Principles. These processes are arrayed in Exhibit 3.1 to provide strategic context and a working framework to assist you in your organization. Please note that Principle 3: Cascade and Manage Strategy consists of four primary CPM processes. Some organizations have expanded beyond these core processes.

Corporate Balanced Scorecard Process Example

The CPM office members will play one or more of three key roles in executing the CPM core processes with the fourth, participants. We will focus on the strategic planning process at award-winning Crown Castle International where I functioned as the CPM officer to share an example.

1. **Process Sponsor.** The sponsor is typically the most senior executive accountable for the process outcomes and for overseeing the process owner. The process sponsor for the corporate BSC process at Crown was the CEO.
2. **Process Owner.** The owner is typically the senior leader accountable to the sponsor for managing the process and is usually a process subject matter expert (SME). As the CPM officer, I was the process owner for the corporate BSC process at Crown.
3. **Process Facilitator.** The facilitator is typically the individual who day to day interacts directly with process participants to drive the process and integrate the process with other key processes. The Crown BSC process facilitator was a BSC manager responsible for the corporate BSC process and ongoing reporting of BSC results.
4. **Process Participant.** The process participants are typically subject matter experts, those who will be accountable for the process outcomes

and/or are the recipients of the process outcomes. The process participants in the corporate BSC process were the executive and senior management teams.

Prior to turning our attention to in-depth cases, let us review the core best practices recognized by all the case companies. See each case that follows for their innovative new best practice, so you can appreciate the context and relevance of the practices to their organizations.

Principle 3: Cascade and Manage Strategy Best Practices

- **Partner with business owners.** Partner with line and staff leadership team members to gain support and influence as partners to help them achieve results.
- **Develop level 1 BSC.** Translate strategy into level 1 BSC measures and measure targets at the highest organizational level.
- **Leverage proven BSC or comparable method.** Observe BSC or comparable design parameters, assigning one to two measures to each strategy map objective.
- **Cascade BSC to lower levels.** Cascade and align level 1 BSC to levels 2, 3, 4, and so on, depending on organizational and accountability structures.
- **Align support services.** Identify and define measures for all support services that align with levels 1 and below.
- **Align teams and individual employees.** Define personal BSCs for teams and/or individuals that align with higher-level and support services' Balanced Scorecards.
- **Link compensation.** Align rewards, recognition, and compensation programs to the Balanced Scorecard.
- **Manage using measures.** Manage BSC meetings to address the appropriate mix of strategic and operational issues; link these issues with Principle 4: Business Improvement.
- **Automate measurement.** Implement CPM software to manage BSC program with links to other principles.

Cargill Corn Milling North America: Best Practice Case

Cargill Corn Milling's (CCM's) strategy deployment process provides CCM a BSC approach at the top level for measuring and monitoring business performance. The CCM BSC uses key performance measures aligned with key strategies and the annual business planning (ABP) process. The president's performance measures and incentives are aligned with CCM's key strategies and the fiscal commitment to Cargill through the linkage of the ABP process with the performance management process (PMP) for individual performance reviews. The PMP process includes a "one up" step to ensure that leadership performance and incentives are reviewed at upper management levels of Cargill.

MEASUREMENT, ANALYSIS, AND KNOWLEDGE MANAGEMENT   The CCM leadership system data and information are essential to all key work processes. Data and information requirements are driven by strategy and cascade from the BSC Level 1 at the top of the pyramid down three levels, which are described in the following sections.

BSC Level   The upper level of the pyramid consists of the overall performance metrics used by CCM, product lines, functional areas, PDGs, and facilities based on the ABP process. The SLT is the primary owner of these performance metrics, including the CCM BSC. Data at this level are aligned with initiatives on the annual business plans, which are tied to strategic objectives. The BSC level drives the metrics used at all other levels of the pyramid and is integrated into the performance management process through individual key result areas. The BSC level contains data and information collected from the financial reporting, business system, and process control levels.

Financial Reporting Level   Business plans and BSC metrics drive the financial management process. Data and information collected from both the process control and business system levels support the financial reporting process. This process provides reports to drive fact-based decision-making, analyze business performance in financial terms, and make longer-term strategic decisions. The SMT, facility leadership teams, and other managers, as appropriate, use information from this level.

Business System Level   The business system level includes multiple tools to manage data and information utilizing business applications and reports, decision support tools, enterprise databases, personal databases, Web communities, and electronic commerce. Data collected from the process control level are consolidated into information used to support fact-based decision making and to capture ideas for innovation. Enterprise tools used to capture innovative ideas reside at this level, such as *Ideas to Innovation (i2i)* and root cause analysis. Additionally, this level includes data and information from outside sources, such as customers, suppliers, and other stakeholders.

This level is used daily by the majority of CCM employees to perform process analysis, conduct short-term planning, and make course corrections when necessary.

Process Control Level   The process control level is the foundation and is critical to meeting customer requirements including consistent quality and optimized plant efficiencies. Data used to monitor and control plant operations are collected in real time or once per day depending on the criticality of the data and stability of the process. The majority of these data are generated and captured electronically through the distributed control system. Data at this level are used to make operational and product quality decisions by operators, engineers, and chemists.

PERFORMANCE MANAGEMENT PROCESS AND DEVELOPMENT PLAN PROCESS   The annual performance management process (PMP) and development plan process (DPP) are separate processes administered concurrently. PMP and DPP are used to align performance to business plans, evaluate individual performance, assess employees' abilities with respect to the Cargill leadership model (CLM), develop career goals, and define skills needed for high performance. Implementation and deployment are the responsibility of supervisors, who work closely with their direct reports through all steps of the process including the following: (1) After annual business planning, KRAs key results areas and individual development plans are created; (2) mid-year PMP progress review and discussion; (3) year-end PMP performance assessment; and (4) annual development plan discussion, which includes both career and skill development. In addition to these four steps, ongoing coaching and informal feedback discussions are encouraged throughout the year. KRAs are specific action-oriented objectives developed to ensure that individual employees focus on their personal contribution to business plans. At mid-year and year-end reviews, employees receive feedback on KRAs.

SELECTION OF COMPARATIVE DATA   The SLT identifies critical metrics to support operational and strategic decision making during the ABP process. Comparative data are used at every level of the data and information pyramid. These comparative data are obtained through both internal and external sources. Depending on the level of the data, different teams are responsible for obtaining comparative data. For example, at the process control level, process development group teams are responsible for identifying best practices and measures associated with these practices. Process steps used to select comparative data include (1) identify metric, (2) identify world-class comparison, and (3) start using metric and world-class comparison to support improvement and innovation. Approaches used by CCM in steps 1 and

2 to identify world-class comparisons include working with the Cargill Information Center to obtain information from the public domain, other Cargill business units, trade journals, surveys, independent market analysis, industry and professional organizations, EDT, process development groups, and other cross-functional improvement teams. The EDT is used for project analysis (e.g., deep-dive study of ethanol market), growth opportunities (e.g., grow existing business, mergers, and acquisitions), and strategic direction analysis. The data obtained come from external sources, which include *IndustryWeek* Best Plant database, customers, annual reports, Corn Refiners Association, membership in professional organizations, governmental sources, and MBNQA recipients. To ensure effectiveness of comparative information each PDG develops BSCs to measure performance.

KEEPING PERFORMANCE MEASUREMENT SYSTEM CURRENT   The data and information pyramid provides a framework for all levels of the organization to engage in the process of keeping the performance measurement system current with business needs. The ABP process drives initial changes to the performance measurement system. For example, to promote the *Be Innovative* value, the SLT decided that every business plan must include the metric implemented idea savings. The SMT monthly business performance review (BPR) process drives course corrections in metrics and goals based on performance to budget.

MEETING MANAGEMENT, BUSINESS ANALYTICS, PERFORMANCE ANALYSIS, AND REVIEW

Meeting Management   SLT Meeting: The SLT meets monthly as a leadership team to review the overall health of the business unit, evaluate strategy, discuss and decide policy issues, project future profitability, and make final decisions on anything impacting CCM.

SMT Meeting: The SMT holds monthly conference calls and meets face-to-face on a quarterly basis. This team reviews current performance, ensures alignment, sets priorities, and discusses projects and initiatives. The SMT cascades information from these meetings throughout the organization utilizing functional, facility, and product line meetings.

SLT Forum: The SLT sponsors a biennial process called the SLT Forum. This process includes approximately 200 managers and individual contributors, providing the SLT another method to communicate strategy, reinforce values, increase customer knowledge, promote team building, and recognize outstanding performance.

Business Performance Review Analytics Process   The BPR process starts at the monthly SMT meeting with a review of the CCM BSC. This examination of key performance measures utilizes methods such as deviation from goals, trend analysis, and comparisons to strategic measures to identify opportunities for *improvement or innovation*. If a deeper understanding of an issue or strategy is required, cross-functional product line teams or the EDT will be utilized to do the analysis.

Translation of Organizational Performance into Priorities for Improvement   SMT uses the following process steps to translate organizational performance review findings into priorities for improvement:

Step 1. Identify high-level opportunity.
Step 2. Perform and validate analysis.
Step 3. Identify specific opportunities.
Step 4. Charter a cross-functional improvement team or ad hoc team.
Step 5. Address barriers and monitor progress.

This process is used as appropriate depending on changes in the market, technology, industry, governmental policies, suppliers, and production capacity. In order to focus resources on strategic priorities with greatest opportunity for creation of distinctive value, the SMT uses a two-dimensional decision matrix. The matrix includes attractiveness versus strategic fit and net present value versus risk.

Incorporating Performance Review into Systematic Improvement   The SMT utilizes various methods to deploy priorities and opportunities for improvement from organizational performance reviews throughout the business unit. Exhibit 6.1 illustrates the various methods the SMT deploys to communicate priorities and opportunities for improvement throughout the organization.

Each approach allows two-way communication. Understanding why initiatives are being started or business plans are being changed is the key to gaining support and ownership at all levels. The SLT utilizes the SLT tours to communicate and review organizational performance.

ALIGN INDIVIDUALS AND REWARDS AND RECOGNITION   Targets are incorporated in managers' job performance goals for the year. The SMT emphasizes CCM values of *Expand Customer Focus*, *Promote Collaboration*, and *Be Innovative* using several formal recognition processes to reinforce high performance and customer focus. The CCM Leadership Award process recognizes both teams and individuals. Teams can nominate themselves for a customer focus, innovation, and high-performance award. The winning team(s) will exhibit leadership in sharing learning, transferability of results, and the success of the project. The winning individual(s) are those that best exemplify the leadership capabilities of the Cargill leadership model. The SLT selects the

EXHIBIT 6.1 Communication of Results

Method	Communication Message	Responsibility	Frequency	Audience
SLT Tour	Communicate business results, plans, and strategies while locations provide a progress report on key initiatives.	SLT	Annual	Facility management and plant personnel
E-mail	Communicate strategies, organizational changes, and performance results.	BU President	Varies	Depends on info
Com Milling Website	Communicate performance of CS measures.	SLT	Monthly	All CCM employees
Conference Calls	Cascade information and performance results at the functional level as it relates to overall business performance.	Functional area leader, PLL PDG leaders	Monthly or as needed	Department employees or team members
Town Hall or Quarterly Meetings	Cascade information and performance results at the functional level as it relates to overall business performance.	Facility manager and local management	Quarterly or as needed	All employees

Courtesy of Cargill Corn Milling.

award winners and recognizes teams and individuals during the biennial CCM awards ceremony held at the SLT Forum. The Corn Milling Innovation (CMI) Awards process recognizes *innovative ideas* and collaborative behaviors.

CCM uses multiple compensation, recognition, reward, and incentive processes to reinforce high performance.

Compensation: Salary Review Process   The annual salary review process (SRP) ensures that the highest-performing employees are rewarded at the highest levels through a merit-based compensation program. This SRP is managed by the SLT and CCM HR manager and includes exempt and nonexempt support employees.

Other factors that influence pay for performance decisions include achievement of business plans, business life cycle, internal factors (e.g., affordability), and external factors (e.g., economics).

Participation in Cross-Functional Teams   The SLT rewards high-performing employees by offering them opportunities to participate in high-visibility teams and projects as a method to encourage high performance, customer focus, and *innovation*. Examples include membership in process Development groups, cross-functional improvement teams (i.e., CCM Engagement Committee), and ad hoc teams (i.e., root cause analysis problem-solving teams).

Cargill and CCM Leadership Awards   The Cargill Corporate Leadership Team and SLT present three biennial recognition awards to individuals or teams exhibiting leadership in customer focus, innovation, and high performance.

Corn Milling Innovation Awards   The innovation team along with SMT leadership selects individuals and teams from nominations submitted by their peers for annual awards based on innovative ideas and collaborative behaviors.

Incentive Plan Process   The annual incentive plan process provides variable compensation for high-performing exempt employees and is based on CCM results and individual performance.

BSC SOFTWARE, DATA AND INFORMATION AVAILABILITY   CCM's goal is to provide accurate, timely, and actionable information to employees and other stakeholders for decision making. Data and information required to operate the business effectively are selected to support key processes, business plans, and strategies. Every CCM job function requires access to different levels of the data and information pyramid. Access to data and information is given to employees based on their job function.

CORE AND INNOVATIVE BEST PRACTICES   CCM exercises the core best practices identified earlier; it has advanced knowledge in this area with additional, innovative best practices.

Principle 3: Cascade and Manage Strategy

- **Partner with business owners.** Partner with line and staff leadership team members to gain owners' support and influence as partners to help them achieve results.
- **Develop level 1 BSC.** Translate strategy into level 1 BSC measures and measure targets at the highest organizational level.
- **Leverage proven BSC or comparable method.** Observe BSC or comparable design parameters, assigning one to two measures to each strategy map objective.
- **Cascade BSC to lower levels.** Cascade and align level 1 BSC to levels 2, 3, 4, and so on, depending on organizational and accountability structures.
- **Align support services.** Identify and define measures for all support services that align with levels 1 and below.
- **Align teams and individual employees.** Define personal BSCs for teams and/or individuals that align with higher-level and support services' BSCs.
- **Link compensation.** Align rewards, recognition, and compensation programs to the BSC.
- **Manage using measures.** Manage BSC meetings to address the appropriate mix of strategic and operational issues; link these issues with Principle 4: Business Improvement.
- **Automate measurement.** Implement software to manage BSC program with links to other principles.
- **Innovative Best Practice.** Comparative data are used at every level of the data on the information pyramid. Comparative data are obtained through multiple internal and external sources.
- **Innovative Best Practice.** Business performance review (BPR) analytics process utilizes methods such as deviation from goals, trend analysis, and comparisons to strategic measures to identify opportunities for improvement or innovation.
- **Innovative Best Practice.** Leadership Award process recognizes both teams and individuals where teams can nominate them for a customer focus, innovation, and high performance awards. The Corn Milling Innovation (CMI) Awards process recognizes innovative ideas and collaborative behaviors.
- **Innovative Best Practice.** SLT introduced the performance measure alignment matrix to identify measures that must appear on

business plans produced during the ABP process. For example, to promote the *Be Innovative* value, the SLT decided that every business plan must include the metric of implemented idea savings.

- **Innovative Best Practice.** CCM extends its performance model outside "horizontally" to benchmark against industry association results.

City of Coral Springs: Best Practice Case

The strategic plan, directional statements, and key intended outcomes are the basis for the development of the City of Coral Spring's business plan and individual departmental work plans that constitute the action plan for meeting strategic objectives. Performance measures relative to the action plans are selected by departments based on how well they support key intended outcomes (KIOs), business plan initiatives, and successful delivery of basic services, as well as how well they leverage core competencies.

In addition to the key intended outcomes and performance measures developed by the departments, the city also uses a Composite Index, the Financial Trend Monitoring System, an early warning system, benchmarking, and individual performance measures to track progress on action plans.

The Composite Index is a set of ten key performance indicators that are used as an indication of the value provided to city residents. Often referred to as the city's "stock price," the index not only serves as a basis for relative performance evaluation, but also as a leading indicator of the city's well-being.

1. School overcrowding
2. Volunteers in government
3. Nonresidential property values
4. Residential property values
5. Employee productivity
6. Customer satisfaction
7. Athletic league participants
8. Crime rate
9. Employee satisfaction
10. Accidents at major intersections

The *Financial Trend Monitoring System* is a set of measures, balanced between objective and subjective information, that provides a snapshot of the financial condition of the city, with long-term trends identified and an analysis of the "meaning" of the measures, whether positive or negative.

In contrast, the City Help Desk system is used as an in-process measure to monitor subjective changes in core business processes throughout the organization. In general, the city's level of performance compares favorably to best-in-class performers, local competitors, and national benchmarks. When performance gaps against competitors are identified, cross-functional task teams are created to research and implement best practices to improve performance.

LEVEL 1 CORPORATE BALANCED SCORECARD The city's seven strategic priorities consist of over 30 KIOs to monitor and manage performance (shown in Exhibit 6.2). For instance, the "customer priority" contains KIO measures such as customer service rating by residents and customer service ratings by business. The "Excellence in Education" priority contains a KIO measure on reading and math scale scores at the city charter school.

Coral Springs is subject to state and federal regulations applying to employment, the environment, occupational health, and safety. The city also chooses to comply with the rules and standards required for national and state police department accreditation.

MEETING MANAGEMENT AND BUSINESS ANALYTICS The City Commission holds itself directly accountable to Coral Springs residents for performance in each of the seven strategic priorities. These results are regularly reported to residents in *Coral Springs* magazine and are presented in detail at the annual State of the City event. Ultimately, commissioners are held accountable to the public through the election process. KIOs are also a contract between the city manager and the commission; department measures are contracts between the department directors and the city manager; employees have performance contracts as part of the incentive pay system. The city prepares an annual report, which is mailed to all residents each year. It is also the basis for the "State of the City" presentation. The annual report lists the city's performance in each priority area and KIO. The KIOs represent the city's "report card." They are not, however, the sole method of measuring success. Each department director also develops a set of departmental performance measures. Each director meets with the city. Department processes are expected to include in-process measures, which give an "early warning" if processes are not on track.

CASCADING BALANCED SCORECARDS, ALIGNMENT, AND INTEGRATION The city uses a performance management model to measure, analyze, and improve organizational performance. The model consists of multiple layers of performance agreements at all levels that are aligned and explicitly linked.

Fundamental to the measurement system is that it must link all activity to the strategic plan and the business plan; it must define success in

EXHIBIT 6.2

Key Intended Outcomes by Strategic Priority

Customer-Involved Government
- Number of volunteer hours denoted to the City of Coral springs each year ↑ c
- Percent of voter turnout ↑ a
- Overall rating of the City in terms of communicating with residents ↑ a
- Overall rating of the City in terms of communicating with businesses ↑ a
- Customer service rating by residents ↑ a
- Customer service rating by business ↑ a
- Number of mentors trained ↑ a
- Overall quality rating for City services and programs by residents ↑ a
- Overall quality rating for City services and programs by businesses ↑ a
- Employees satisfaction rating ↑ a

Financial Health and Economic Development
- Bond ratings ↑ a
- Commercial square cottage development inhibited within the Download CRA ↑ a
- Percent of plan reviews completed within 15 days ↑ a
- Non-residential value as a percent of total taxable value ↑ a
- Residents value rating (City survey) ↑ a
- Percentage increase of operating melange role ↓ a
- Add $2 million annually to financial reserves until policy is met ↑ c

Excellence in Education
- Percent of school overcrowding (normalized) ↓ a
- Number of students participating in partnering institutes of higher education ↑ a
- Achieve gains in reading, math, mean scale score at the Greater School ↑ a

Neighborhood and Environmental Vitality
- Number of formal and informal neighborhood partnerships each year ↑ c
- Number of cooperative projects and the number of different partners (public private and intra-city depts.) focused on enhancing the environment ↑ c
- City crime rate (crimes 100,000 residents—Calendar Year) ↓ a
- Percent of code cases brought into voluntary corpulence prior to judicial process ↑ a
- Number of trees Planted ↑ a

Youth Development & Family Values
- Number of youths involved in City-sponsored leadership opportunities ↑ c

(Continued)

(*Continued*)

- Number of teen volunteer hours donated so the City of Coral Springs   ↑ c
  each year
- Number of middle school after-school programs offered annually   ↑ a

Strength In Diversity

- Minority residents who feel that the City is a great place to live (City   ↑ a
  Survey)
- Citizen rating of City for respecting religious and ethnic diversity (City   ↑ a
  Survey)

Traffic Mobility, & Connectivity

- Achieve overall reduction of 10% of speeds or 15% reduction of volume   ↑ c
  on traffic calmed roads
- Number of accidents of 16 major intersections   ↓ a
- Number of riders in intercity bus routes   ↑ a

Key: arrows indicate positive direction, a = annual and c = cumulative

Courtesy of City of Coral Springs.

measurable terms; it must measure success; and it must use data analysis for improving processes. The KIOs from the strategic plan form the performance agreement between the city manager and the City Commission. Departmental performance agreements are negotiated between the city manager and each department director. In turn, performance agreements based on departmental performance measures and other internal department process/in-process measures are incorporated into each staff member's performance evaluation, process teams, and cross-functional process improvement teams. Process metrics include different dimensions of key work processes. Regular analysis (trends, outliers, variance, and root cause) of higher-level performance measures and process metrics relative to performance standards *fuels innovation* and improvement opportunities, and incorporates organizational performance reviews into the evaluation of key processes.

PERFORMANCE MANAGEMENT DATA TYPES AND INTEGRATION   The city leverages several different performance management data types, which are described next.

The first two categories, KIOs and department measures, are the organization's key performance measures and are part of the city's quarterly performance management reporting system. The system includes quarterly meetings between the city manager and individual department directors to review progress and determine if any course corrections are needed.

Key intended outcomes are the highest level "vital few" measures that are monitored by the city manager's office and reported to the commission. These measures (usually 30 to 35) are formulated by staff, adopted by the commission, and are a performance contract between the city manager and the commission for a given fiscal year, providing a basis for the city manager's annual review.

Departmental performance measures represent a performance contract between the city manager and the department for a given fiscal year. Department measures are typically output or outcome measures of key work processes, and they can also be a KIO if they are among the "vital few" being closely tracked by the senior administration team and the City Commission.

Process measures are tracked by process owners. Some are also department measures, but others are reported to the department director and are not on the senior management team's "radar screen" unless they become problematic. These measures are key in tracking operations (cycle time, cost, customer satisfaction). They also *support innovation*. If a process is not meeting its requirements, cross-functional process improvement teams are directed to develop and take corrective action.

In-process measures are aligned with process measures and are key in tracking daily operations. They are used to assess if processes are on track to meet requirements. The frequency with which in-process measures are monitored depends on the consequence of significant variation in process output. For instance, EMS response times are tracked daily to determine if there is unacceptable variation, and corrective action is taken if specific responses went over a specific threshold. Analysis of total response time includes reviewing the cycle time for the segments of emergency response—intake, dispatch, turnout, and travel. Each part has its own performance goal. This detail permits focused corrective action.

Transaction or event measures are captured in any one of these business applications; data are updated in multiple applications. For example, the process of paying a water bill updates databases used by the utility billing, cash receipts, and general ledger business applications. These transaction data become the primary source of internal data used for process and in-process measurements.

COMPARATIVE ANALYTICS AND BENCHMARKING The city participates in numerous comparative and benchmarking groups.

1. Data are also integrated through the GIS, which maps events to assist the user in discerning patterns and problem solving. Fire, EMS, police, community development, and public works are the principal users of GIS. One approach the city uses to select key comparative data to support decision making and innovation is the annual process of reporting data to the International City/County Managers' Association Center for Performance Measurement (CfPM).

2. A 2005 improvement cycle resulted in the city collaborating with ten other local Florida governments informing the Florida Benchmarking Consortium (FBC).The FBC was formed to create a source of comparisons for governments operating under the same state laws and in a similar climate.

3. Comparison data are also selected and collected at the department level based on the process management and process improvement needs identified by teams. Sources include professional associations and accreditation bodies that generate industry standards. Police and fire have extensive industry databases available to them, and comparisons are required for ratings and accreditation.

4. The Benchmark Cities Survey is another source of comparison data on police departments in terms of resources, crime rates, and level of sophistication.

5. Out of the first survey rose the first meeting of the Benchmark Cities Chiefs, who now come together annually to discuss the results and to share information on common problems and best practices.

6. Other financial and human resource comparisons are made with South Florida governments. These comparisons provide insight into the effects of the local economy, labor market, and environmental conditions such as recent hurricanes.

The analysis of the comparison data is systematic in that it is part of the strategic planning process. Observations from the CfPM database are included annually in the environmental scan, and comparisons and benchmarking are required as part of the city's approach to program development. When a cross-functional team project is complete, the process team continues to update and use the comparative data used in the team analysis. The effective use of comparative data is also ensured by sharing the results of organizational-level analysis with work groups through the deployment system.

PERFORMANCE REVIEWS The city has a robust approach to assessment of organizational performance, capabilities, and progress relative to strategic goals and action. Analyses to support performance reviews, ensure conclusions are valid, and assess success and competitive position also include periodic assessments using the Sterling/Baldrige criteria. These assessments, including Sterling and Baldrige site-visit teams and internal assessments by city staff members who are Sterling or Baldrige examiners, have been done seven times in the past 15 years.

Organizational performance review findings are translated into priorities for continuous and breakthrough improvement and *opportunities for innovation*. Priorities and opportunities are deployed to work groups. In summary, the results of performance review are incorporated into the environmental scan that is used as the basis of strategic planning and the development of business plan initiatives, which include action plans for process improvements.

INDIVIDUAL REWARDS AND RECOGNITION AND INNOVATION Workforce performance is managed through a set of systems that were designed to specifically link the attainment of stated city goals to individual employee work plans/objectives and to reinforce the city's core values and priority areas. The incentive pay system (IPS) evaluates employees on two levels. At the beginning of each fiscal year, an employee and a supervisor agree on a work plan and measurable objectives for the year. These objectives, which may be developmental in nature, are tied to departmental objectives, which in turn link to city KIOs.

Senior leaders recognize and reward high performance in a variety of ways. The IPS evaluates yearly performance based on established goals and objectives. Employees may earn up to 6 percent for high performance. "Applause" cards are an opportunity for any employee to recognize outstanding performance by presenting an applause card to any other employee. Through the Instant Employee Recognition program, employees may also be awarded gift certificates to local restaurants and shops for performance above and beyond the normal call to duty. Yearly, employees are nominated by their peers for Excellence Awards in each of the city's five core values. A panel of independent judges reviews all submitted nominations and selects a winner in each category.

Awards for excellence in each of the core value areas are awarded to outstanding employees each year to serve as role models in delivering high-quality customer focus, leadership, empowerment, continuous improvement, and sustainability. The awards are given at citywide celebrations that also have included team presentations and guest speakers. The city accomplishes individual goal setting through the IPS.

Incentive programs *encourage initiative and innovation* and include the Instant Employee Recognition program, the project and performance bonus program, and the gain sharing program. Fifty percent of the rating is based on the accomplishment of these objectives. The remaining 50 percent of the rating is based on specific job skills, which are tied to the city's five core values—customer focus, leadership, empowered employees, continuous improvement, and sustainability. An informal session is held midyear to assess how the employee is progressing relative to the goals set at the beginning of the year and adjusts objectives as required. Based on the results of the end of year IPS review, an employee will be eligible for awards ranging from 0 to 6 percent, depending on ratings received. In addition to the IPS, other recognition and incentive systems are in place to support high-performance work and workforce engagement. The Employee Excellence Awards are given out to employees and teams annually in each of the five core value areas. Specific recognition systems have been established to reinforce areas of particular importance to the city—customer service and employee safety.

Other recognition systems that reinforce the city's goals include the Instant Employee Recognition program, project and performance bonuses, certification bonuses, and gain sharing. The Instant Employee Recognition program provides department directors with the ability to give incentives in the form of restaurant certificates, movie tickets, and other awards to employees who display outstanding initiative. Project and performance bonuses are offered to reward employees who have excelled in their job performance above and beyond the call of duty, or have met extremely tight deadlines imposed by the city, or have participated on a team that completed a project deemed particularly significant by the city. Project and performance bonuses are paid in one-time lump sum cash bonuses that may either be a percentage of base pay or a set amount ranging from $500 to $5,000. Certification bonuses are available to employees who attain or increase certification levels in their professional area. The gain sharing program recognizes all employees through a cash bonus that is based on the city's positive budget variance. Ten percent of each year's variance is divided equally among all employees.

CORE AND INNOVATIVE BEST PRACTICES   The city exercises the core best practices identified earlier and has advanced knowledge in this area with new, innovative best practices.

Principle 3: Cascade and Manage Strategy

- **Partner with business owners.** Partner with line and staff leadership team members to gain owners' support and influence as partners to help them achieve results.
- **Develop level 1 BSC.** Translate strategy into level 1 BSC measures and measure targets at the highest organizational level.
- **Leverage proven BSC or comparable method.** Observe BSC or comparable design parameters, assigning one to two measures/KIO to each strategic priority.
- **Cascade BSC to lower levels.** Cascade and align level 1 BSC to levels 2, 3, 4, and so on, depending on organizational and accountability structures.

- **Align support services.** Identify and define measures for all support services that align with levels 1 and below.
- **Align teams and individual employees.** Define personal BSCs for teams and/or an individual that align with higher-level and support services' Balanced Scorecards.
- **Link compensation.** Align rewards, recognition, and compensation programs to the Balanced Scorecard.
- **Manage using measures.** Manage BSC meetings to address the appropriate mix of strategic and operational issues; link these issues with Principle 4: Business Improvement.
- **Automate measurement.** Implement CPM software to manage BSC program with links to other principles.
- **Innovative Best Practice.** The City of Coral Springs index is often referred to as the city's "stock price." The index not only serves as a basis for relative performance evaluation, but also as an innovative leading indicator of the city's well-being.
- **Innovative Best Practice.** City of Coral Springs incentive programs to encourage initiative and innovation; these include the Instant Employee Recognition program, the project and performance bonus program, and the gain sharing program.
- **Innovative Best Practice.** City of Coral Springs participates in several city-, department-, and process-level comparative benchmarking groups that leverage comparative analytics to identify potential innovation and improvements.
- **Innovative Best Practice.** City of Coral Springs has established process owners and process measure metrics (cycle time, cost, customer satisfaction) to identify variation and to initiate. In process measures, for instance, EMS response times are tracked daily to determine if there is unacceptable variation, and corrective action or innovation is begun.

Delta Dental of Kansas: Best Practice Case

Delta Dental of Kansas (DDKS) adopted Kaplan and Norton's method consisting primarily of the Strategy Map and Balanced Scorecard tools. Within the BSC construct the organization clearly articulates its objectives and progress against those objectives in both near- and long-term requisites. Conceptually and practically, the scorecard cascades through all levels of the organization specifically to oblige managers to direct data collection, measurement, and analysis in an integrated manner (see Exhibit 6.3).

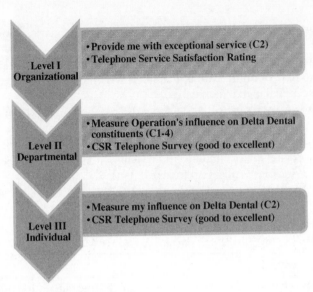

Level I Organizational
- Provide me with exceptional service (C2)
- Telephone Service Satisfaction Rating

Level II Departmental
- Measure Operation's influence on Delta Dental constituents (C1-4)
- CSR Telephone Survey (good to excellent)

Level III Individual
- Measure my influence on Delta Dental (C2)
- CSR Telephone Survey (good to excellent)

EXHIBIT 6.3 DDKS Scorecard Cascade
Courtesy of Delta Dental of Kansas.

At the corporate level 1, DDKS develops goals, corresponding measurements, initiatives, and action plans to support continued organizational performance improvements. Similarly, throughout the organization, using both top-down and bottom-up methodologies, functional departments develop corresponding synergistic, departmental-level business plans, set goals, establish measurements, and assess opportunities for tactical level performance improvements. The level 1 DDKS BSC contains financial, constituent, process, and learning and growth perspectives.

The BSC ensures DDKS is using those measurements that truly reflect the performance and direction of the organization based on the assessments made during the planning process. On BSC measure information collection, DDKS draws from several sources of data including the following:

- A large body of peer member company (MC) data
- Proprietary operational data and statistics
- Industry benchmarks
- Direct collection efforts that include custom data collection processes and/or project- or process-specific methodologies to collect the information necessary for analysis
- Constituent interchanges
- Competitive information during the RFP process

- Customer service inquiry statistics using advanced call-center software
- G.O.S.E. program
- Corporate training and outreach programs including the annual membership meeting, professional impact councils (PICs), key customer and customer advisory group meetings, and input

CASCADING BALANCED SCORECARDS, ALIGNMENT, AND INTEGRATION Alignment occurs as BSC goals developed during the LRP process become nested within departmental, unit, and individual scorecard development. LT members meet jointly as a group and collectively across dependent functional areas when corporate goals cross functional boundaries. Meetings ensure that departmental goals remain aligned and provide an environment where interrelated goals can be appropriately championed. Universally, action plans are approached in a teaming methodology where cross-functional teams form to support specific plans. Unambiguous ownership coupled with diligent measurements ensures project integration.

Department strategy maps also serve to align functional areas with company strategy and serve as another reference point for implementation purposes. Exhibit 6.4 shows the human resources strategy map. Human resources is well positioned strategically and retains a proactive business outlook as evidenced by:

- The company mission statement is placed at the top of its strategy map.
- Human resources customer perspective contains a broad array of both external customers (candidates, visitors, callers, business partners, community agencies) and internal customers (employees, management, and board members).
- HR core process themes and strategic objectives focus on solutions innovation and external influences.

The FOCUS team, comprised of frontline managers who meet biweekly, functions to further align and integrate ongoing subtasks of both corporate and departmental objectives. This committee is assigned the task of cross-coordination, prioritization, and allocation of internal resources. They engage in fact-based decision making regarding resource prioritization and interdepartmental considerations.

The BSC depicting the corporate goals and associated measurements continues to be central to alignment and integration. At every level of the organization scorecards are reviewed routinely, performance is evaluated against the measure, and adjustments are made continuously to ensure progress toward the goal. At the departmental, team, and individual levels a rigorous framework of performance review identifies performance gaps using departmental-level key performance indicators (KPI) or metrics,

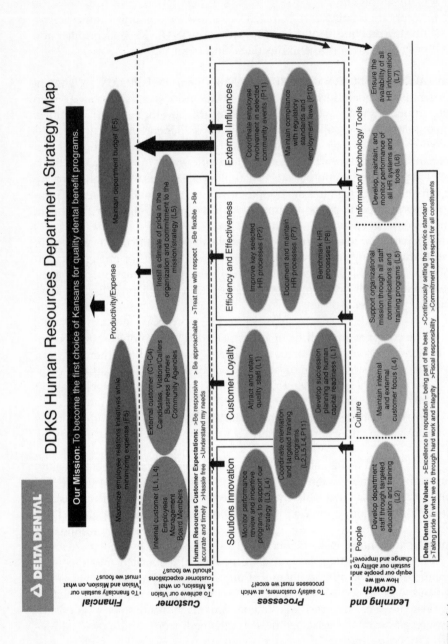

EXHIBIT 6.4 Human Resources Strategy Map

Courtesy of Delta Dental of Kansas.

204

seeking to adjust performance at the earliest sign of a gap to *encourage innovative* and timely approaches toward improvement.

Constituent satisfaction data are secured through several channels ranging from an annual survey of primary constituencies to professional impact councils to customer advisor group meetings.

DATA RELIABILITY Data reliability is extremely important to the organization, and accuracy is monitored in several ways:

- Multiple audits, both internal and external (Kansas Insurance Department, Delta Dental Plans Association, GAAP and statutory, SAS70, information system security audit, etc.)
- Comparison of data with that of Delta Dental Member Companies in other operating regions
- Claims adjustments/refund review process
- G.O.S.E. program service alerts and payouts
- Annual customer satisfaction surveys compared year-to-year
- Program testing at all levels of development

Linking the information and data directly to the BSC and maintaining the integrity of the data ensures its effective use. Performance measurement systems and the measures themselves are kept current with business needs and direction by linking them directly to the BSC.

MEETING MANAGEMENT AND BUSINESS ANALYTICS Performance review and analysis is an integral step within the LRP process, supported by the BSC management methodology. For every data collection effort, there are formalized review and analysis procedures, including formal review meetings, service performance committees (e.g., G.O.S.E.), departmental KPI reviews, and individual performance reviews. Each type of meeting has standardized agendas and draws on the data collected specifically to address the measure being evaluated. The meeting agenda provides insight into DDKS strategic thinking, for the first agenda item is focused on company strategy and corporate initiates to enable attainment of company strategic objectives.

The cascading of BSC through the depth and breadth of the organization drives consistency of analysis and review very much as it drives consistency of measurement.

Members of the leadership team are assigned to lead corporate initiatives for the scorecard. They are responsible for tracking, follow-up, and making sure activities are kept on target. A monthly status meeting is held to discuss progress and obstacles.

The weekly dashboard captures those measurements that best reflect the company's financial health, marketing success, network growth, support system availability, and customer satisfaction. Concise departmental updates are included as well as follow-up items that have target completion dates and a person responsible for each item. The dashboard is reviewed by the leadership team and distributed to the board of directors and all employees along with a business update on a weekly basis.

In addition to financial and learning and growth metrics, the dashboard includes a balance of results tracked for outside constituent and internal workforce focus, which ranges from claims processing turnaround time and network providers participation to IT help desk turnaround time. Sharing of employee survey results and discussion of subsequent initiatives takes place during employee departmental feedback meetings. Department heads are encouraged to invite other LT members to their departmental staff meetings, and focused cross-departmental meetings have been facilitated between departments that routinely work together on projects.

ALIGN INDIVIDUALS AND REWARDS AND RECOGNITION   A core values assessment supplements the individual's quarterly BSC results. Employees have access to a merit increase associated with their individual level of performance and an incentive bonus program has been implemented. The incentive program provides employees with an opportunity to share in the company's financial success if their individual BSC goals are met and the company's BSC goals are achieved at 100 percent. Known as "Hitting Grand Slams," this program emphasizes that top-notch performance is the goal and that all-star performers will be rewarded.

Team award winners are recognized at company functions attended by staff and board members. Service awards presented by the CEO recognize individual service accomplishments at all-employee meetings. The new Ideas from Delta Employees in Action (IDEA) program includes monetary rewards and involves organizationwide recognition as well. While employees are regularly commended through companywide e-mail communications, the monthly employee newsletter features some of these accomplishments as well.

Compensation, including incentive plan participation, depends on individual and company targets being met. The CEO's performance is based on Level I (company) scorecard progress. A Level I update, as well as departmental successes, is shared quarterly with the compensation committee of the board of directors and the entire board. Compensation committee duties specifically include the performance review and compensation recommendation for the CEO of the corporation, review and approve recommendations regarding compensation of the LT, and review of corporate attorney performance.

Leadership team members were the first level of management to have compensation linked to BSC results based on both individual and company measurements. Soon after, DDKS developed an incentive program for all employees. The organizationwide incentive program reinforced the relevance of strategy while rewarding its all-star employees. Changing the sales incentive program to align with targeted growth objectives and customer intimacy themes helped drive results. The alignment of compensation and incentive systems to strategic performance also served to increase awareness of organizational and cross-functional objectives and tie the individual and company performance together.

Effective career progression is managed through the use of the DDKS employee development plan. A documented DDKSs Succession plan for identifying and preparing appropriate employees to fill key positions within the organization has been developed and shared with the board of directors. "Key positions" at DDKS is defined as those whose strategic and operational impact would benefit from executive-level discussion, input, and collaboration, including critical or direct impact on the strategy of the organization and/or a significant or direct impact on the operational health or effectiveness of the organization. Therefore personal goals are linked to company strategy map objectives.

The employee development plans are completed by DDKS staff annually and refined with their managers during the performance review process. During quarterly reviews the development plans are reviewed to measure progress. Development plans are given serious consideration by the business unit managers, and BSC learning and growth objectives include some of these targets.

TARGET SETTING AND BENCHMARKING Targets are established through the Level I BSC in support of the company strategy map, as approved by the board of directors. Individual targets for the CEO are established in the same manner, with the organization and top leadership goals in alignment. LT compensation is tied to both individual and organizational results, with board of directors' oversight.

Through DDPA membership, DDKS has access to competitive analysis and competitor information on a national, regional, and local basis. Information is provided by each Delta Dental member company, which is responsible for providing and updating this information for its specific business territory. DDPA also assists in the collection of industry-specific competitor data for comparative analysis.

BSC SOFTWARE DDKS uses Microsoft Excel to house and report its BSC results, given that the entire organization consists of only 110 employees. Retention, retrieval, and management access to BSC tools and learning plans are important, and cost benefit analysis will be reviewed as new technology becomes available.

CORE AND INNOVATIVE BEST PRACTICES   DDKS exercises the core best practices identified earlier and has advanced knowledge in this area with new, innovative best practices.

Principle 3: Cascade and Manage Strategy

- **Partner with business owners.** Partner with line and staff leadership team members to gain owners' support and influence as partners to help them achieve results.
- **Develop level 1 BSC.** Translate strategy into level 1 BSC measures and measure targets at the highest organizational level.
- **Leverage proven BSC or comparable method.** Use of Kaplan & Norton method, assigning one to two measures to each strategy map objective.
- **Cascade BSC to lower levels.** Cascade and align level 1 BSC to levels 2 and 3.
- **Align support services.** Identify and define measures for all support services that align with levels 1 and below.
- **Align teams and individual employees.** Define personal BSCs for teams and/or an individual that align with higher-level and support services' Balanced Scorecards.
- **Link compensation.** Align rewards, recognition, and compensation programs to the Balanced Scorecard.
- **Manage using measures.** Manage BSC meetings to address the appropriate mix of strategic and operational issues; link these issues with Principle 4: Business Improvement.
- **Automate measurement.** Implement software to manage BSC program with links to other principles.
- **Innovative Best Practice.** Data integrity: DDKS uses multiple third parties to audit the integrity of BSC data, thus raising the reliability of information for decision making.
- **Innovative Best Practice.** DDKS draws from numerous external and inventive data sources to secure benchmark and competitive information to inform its BSC results.
- **Innovative Best Practice.** DDKS "Strategic HR" function has incorporated strategic thinking and design into its strategy map and strategic objectives to support and enable the corporate strategy.
- **Innovative Best Practice.** DDKS directly links employee development plans, strategic skills definition, and strategic objectives.

Lockheed Martin, Information Systems & Global Services: Best Practice Case

The Lockheed Martin (LM) Information Systems & Global Services (IS&GS)-Civil BSC program is modeled after Kaplan and Norton's research into both the BSC and building strategy-focused organizations. BSCs are established and formally managed in IS&GS-Civil at two levels, at the business unit (i.e., IS&GS-Civil) and one level down (i.e., line of business or function). The BU strategy is described in 22 objectives across the four perspectives, and these objectives are shared verbatim at the two levels to foster alignment. The BSC program is linked to the established LM CPM process, which cascades from the business unit president to every employee in the organization. Through this process line of sight to the business unit BSC is established for every employee. Each employee, in coordination with his or her immediate supervisor, will select an appropriate subset of objectives, measures, and initiatives linked to the IS&GS-Civil to be included in the annual objectives.

The BU objective in the BSC has one or more associated measures. Considering the quote "What gets measured gets done," the primary question for each objective in the strategy is "What must get done?" As the CPM team develops the measures it considers what must get done, and that yields the strategic focus for the objective for the next 12+ months. The measure is derived from there.

The business unit (corporate) BSC (see Exhibit 6.5) measures align with the strategy map strategic objectives.

EXHIBIT 6.5 Level 1 Business Unit (Corporate) BSC

	Objectives	Measures
Financial	F1: Improve EBIT, ROS, and cash	F1.1 EBIT
		F1.2 ROS
		F1.3 Cash
	F2: Deliver sales & generate on-contract growth	F2.1 Sales
		F2.2 On-Contract Growth
	F3: Win new orders and keep business sold	F3.1 Orders
Customer	C1: "Do what you say you're going to do"	C1.1 (C1) Customer Assessment
		C1.2 Award Fee Score (Avg)
	C2: "Help me save money to buy more mission"	C2.1 (C2) Customer Assessment
	C3: "Make my mission, our mission"	C3.1 (C3) Customer Assessment
	C4: "Help me succeed with my stakeholders"	C4.4 (C4) Customer Assessment

(Continued)

Exhibit 6.5 (*Continued*)

	Objectives	Measures
Process	P1: Deploy agile staffing processes	P1.1 Hiring cycle time
	P2: Maximize ROI by institutionalizing business acumen at all levels	P2.1 Business Acumen training
	P3: Bid to win, start up successfully & perform with excellence	P3.1 Program performance
	P4: Engage partners and suppliers	P4.1 Supplier Assessment
	P5: Deliver the full breadth of Lockheed Martin	P5.1 Program collaboration
	P6: Know our customer's challenges and opportunities, listen and know when to act	P6.1 CRM rhythm
	P7: Drive efficiency, ingenuity, innovation and select investment into our solutions	P7.1 R&D investment leverage
	P8: Selectively target, position, & win growth accelerating campaigns	P8.1 % of bids over threshold
	P9: Champion solutions for citizen-to-government interaction	P9.1 Customer solution awards
Workforce	W1: Be personally accountable for wellness, safety, security, and the environment	W1.1 Healthworks engagement W1.2 Close Call Reporting
	W2: Be responsible, collaborative, creative, and agile	W2.1 Culture Survey
	W3: Be accountable for ethical execution of business and strategy objectives	W3.1 % BSC targets achieved
	W4: Leverage FSL to fully develop our program and business leadership	W4.1 Mentoring W4.2 FSL assessments
	W5: Communicate respectfully, openly, and often to eliminate surprises and build trust	W5.1 Skip-level meetings
	W6: Provide challenging opportunities for each employee to be successful	W6.1 Career Development Plans

Courtesy of Lockheed Martin.

CASCADING BALANCED SCORECARDS, ALIGNMENT, AND INTEGRATION   IS&GS-Civil performs only one level of cascade, from the business unit level to the line of business and function level. It fosters alignment through the BSC by two primary means.

First, the leadership team decided to have only one strategy map for the entire business unit (IS&GS-Civil). In previous experiences in LM, specifically its former Enterprise Information Systems (EIS) business unit from 2004 to 2008, that BU created one strategy map at the business unit level and created slightly modified strategy maps at the line of business and function levels. It opted to do this so the maps would resonate more readily with employees. Sharing a common strategy map across the business unit has had a powerful effect by fostering a common culture through a common language around the strategy. A perfect example of this is that a few objectives become such a part of the organizational lexicon that people stop referring to the objective by its full statement as seen on the map; they instead use just the code (e.g., P9, C3, etc.) and the objective is understood.

Second, alignment is driven through common measures across the BSC. Each objective at the business unit level has one or more associated measures and as the strategy is cascaded at least one of the measures per objective is shared—even if the contribution is only indirect. For instance, the "Sales" measure will be found on the human resources BSC because they are a critical indirect contributor to delivering sales through personnel even though they are not directly accountable. Thus, alignment is facilitated by a common set of objectives for the entire organization (i.e., common ideas) and a common or shared set of measures (i.e., common action). This example illustrates that an effective BSC and strategy management process is comprised of actively socializing ownership and engagement.

MEETING MANAGEMENT AND BUSINESS ANALYTICS The primary review mechanism of the IS&GS-Civil strategy is the quarterly strategy review (QSR) (see Exhibit 6.6). Its purpose is to drive discussion of the strategy, foster accountability for commitments, and collectively agree on the path forward. The most valuable aspect of this review is the active engagement of the leadership team which instills a sense of teamwork and knowledge sharing.

The preparation for the QSR focuses first on data collection that is managed primarily by the strategy management organization. The strategy management team centralized the data collection responsibility for the vast majority of the measures and allowed exceptions only where it made clear sense. The team also recommends that for initial rollout of a BSC the measures selected focus on their availability versus designing the "perfect" measure. The team emphasized it would leverage "reasonable" indicators of progress so the organization does not become overwhelmed with the measurement and data processes. A related goal is to mature the measures over time.

Next, preparation for the QSR includes drafting the analysis of performance in categories including *What's Working, Key Challenges,* and *Actions.* Each is presented as sections on the report for each objective in addition to the measure data. The agenda for the meeting is set to cover approximately four hours.

W1-W4-P2-P3-P5-
C1-C2-F1

Performance Advocate: Ken Asbury
Core Team: Josh Stalker

Objectives	Measures	Period	Target	Actual	What's Working & Key Initiatives
W4 Leverage FSL to fully develop our program and business leadership	% leaders completed the FSL 360 with a reviewed Development Plan	EOY	100%		• A LM-wide tool is rolling out soon to help match Mentors and Mentees
		3Q	80%	79%	• "Taking Full Spectrum Leadership to the Next Level" dialogue sessions are continuing the attention on FSL
	% of development plans reviewed with leaders in last 6 months	EOY	35%		
		3Q	20%	27%	**Initiatives:**
	% of mentees	EOY	6%		Full Spectrum Leadership
		3Q	5%	5.3%	Mentoring Connections
	% of mentors	EOY08	4%		
		3Q08	3%	2.1%	

Ken Asbury

Key Challenges & Actions
• **(Challenge)** Need additional focus on engaging employees with tangible and action-oriented efforts to help internalize the concepts of FSL.
  • **(Action—In process)** Design and rapidly implement a communication approach to link selected FSL imperatives and competencies to specific actions

• **(Challenge)** The FSL 360s need additional participation by leaders and assessors
  • **(Action)** Drive communication and awareness for need for this participation (e.g., strategic value and LM's investment)

** Example Only **

EXHIBIT 6.6 Quarterly Strategy Review
Courtesy of Lockheed Martin.

Leadership reviews objectives by color thread (i.e., cause and effect theme) as indicated on the strategy map to reinforce appreciation for the relationships deemed important to monitor. Generally, discussion lasts between two and five minutes on objectives performing well with limited challenges and opportunities. Those objectives with more challenges may extend discussion from five to 15 minutes where warranted. In a few cases leadership may defer discussions that clearly necessitate additional discussion and preparation.

During the QSR a facilitator plays a modest role focused primarily on time management, engaging all leaders in the discussion and asking limited questions. Once the Performance Advocates (Pas) have been through one or two QSRs they generally manage the process naturally, handing off discussion from one person to the next. As the QSR progresses, a single slide of material is presented overhead; the presenter stands and covers the material and engages the team. Core team members are encouraged to attend the QSR with their PA so they stay closely attuned to the discussion, capture notes and actions, and can support questions in a limited fashion. An important aspect of this process is to assign no more than two actions for the upcoming quarter, one if possible. It forces the team to focus on important activities and get those done. IS&GS believes the key to strategy execution in its culture is consistency in execution. With one or two actions per objective being accomplished every quarter, collectively this amounts to 40 to 50 actions being accomplished.

ALIGN INDIVIDUALS AND REWARDS AND RECOGNITION Annually, individual performance incentives, in terms of annual pay increases, are linked to the BSC through the CPM process. At the beginning of the year the IS&GS-Civil BSC is the foundation of the business unit president's objectives, which are cascaded and aligned to every employee in the organization. At the conclusion of the year, supported by interim reviews during the year, employees are given an assessment of performance with respect to their level (e.g., director, manager, staff, associate), their peer group, and the characteristics of performance from the lowest to the highest level. Thus, the BSC measures and targets are key factors informing individual performance assessment and associated compensation. Further, additional rewards and recognition are provided through the year for exceptional performance through both cash and noncash means. Cash and cash-value mechanisms include cash awards and company stock generally. These awards go through a submission and review process. Noncash awards include written recognition, leadership recognition (e.g., visibility or recognition at major company events), compensatory time off, or other means to express the appreciation of the company for the exceptional efforts of an employee or team. These rewards are generally at the discretion of the employee's supervisor in accordance with any rules or regulations that may apply. Further, awards and recognition are available at the LM level. The NOVA Award is presented by the chief executive officer at a corporate event and is often accompanied by a press release.

TARGET SETTING AND BENCHMARKING   Targets for BSC measures are primarily set in two ways. First, financial goals are established by executive leaders through the long-range plan (LRP) based on shareholder commitments and allocated to the business units according to their annual plans, efficiency goals, and market opportunity. The major financial targets are then incorporated into the BSC (e.g., orders, sales, EBIT, cash, ROIC, ROS) primarily in the financial perspective. The BSC process has limited influence on establishing these targets.

Second, targets set for customer, process, and workforce perspective measures are established by the PA informed by historical results, aspiration goals, industry benchmarks, and intuition. The ability to set effective targets is multifaceted. In the case of many objectives and measures in the process perspective of the BSC framework, you often find many measures associated with established operational processes in areas such as human resources, engineering, customer service, and business development. An example human resources measure such as "hiring cycle time" has a long history. Target setting for any other measure should be primarily informed by the results it delivers, that is, the leading and lagging effects of the measure must be considered. In this case, the cycle time measure is common across LM, yet IS&GS-Civil recognizes that its ability to hire and place employees in programs is key to achieving both financial targets and competitive advantage in a services-oriented business. Thus, IS&GS-Civil tends to be more aggressive with its targets than corporate and industry norms. In many cases, especially for newer measures, without historical norms or benchmarking data available, the team will set purely intuitive targets with the purpose of observing the results for a couple of quarters to understand the dynamics and norms of the measure. After a few quarters, the team will set more informed targets. Benchmarking is also considered carefully. In some cases industry norms are very valuable, especially for some IT services, data center, and customer service arenas. However, it is important to be aware that benchmarks may mislead you into thinking the industry norm is competitive in your market.

BSC SOFTWARE   Currently IS&GS-Civil uses Microsoft PowerPoint to present the BSC results and facilitate discussion at QSRs. Raw data for historical purposes are captured in simple Microsoft Excel tables. Concurrently, the team has developed an online mechanism leveraging Microsoft SharePoint and Oracle and expects to mature this capability for use this year. However, IS&GS-Civil does envision the use of COTS BSC or business intelligence (BI) software in some manner at a future date as the strategy management processes mature and information and analyses needs grow.

CORE AND INNOVATIVE BEST PRACTICES   LM IS&GS exercises the core best practices identified earlier and has advanced knowledge in this area with new, innovative best practices.

Principle 3: Cascade and Manage Strategy

- **Partner with business owners.** Partner with line and staff leadership team members to gain owners' support and influence as partners to help them achieve results.
- **Develop level 1 BSC.** Translate strategy into level 1 BSC measures and measure targets at the highest organizational level.
- **Leverage proven BSC or comparable method.** Observe BSC or comparable design parameters, assigning one to two measures to each strategy map objective.
- **Cascade BSC to lower levels.** Cascade and align level 1 BSC to levels 2, 3, 4, and so on, depending on organizational and accountability structures.
- **Align support services.** Identify and define measures for all support services that align with levels 1 and below.
- **Align teams and individual employees.** Define personal BSCs for teams and/or individuals that align with higher-level and support services' BSCs.
- **Link compensation.** Align rewards, recognition, and compensation programs to the Balanced Scorecard.
- **Manage using measures.** Manage BSC meetings to address the appropriate mix of strategic and operational issues; link these issues with Principle 4: Business Improvement.
- **Automate measurement.** Implement CPM software to manage BSC program with links to other principles.
- **Innovative Best Practice.** LM IS&GS has innovated the use of the Strategy Map using a "lean" concept to align all level 1 and level 2 lines of business and functions to "one" centralized map to break down silos and engender cross-organizational cooperation.

(Continued)

> - **Innovative Best Practice.** LM IS&GS believes its employees identify with one strategy map to better internalize and recall the strategic objectives but allows differentiation and innovation through BSC measures at level 2.
> - **Innovative Best Practice.** LM IS&GS has embedded innovation into is BSC objectives and measures, Objective P9: Champion solutions for citizen-to-government interaction is measured by P9.1, the number of customer solution awards.

M7 Aerospace: Best Practice Case Study

M7 Aerospace adopted the BSC as its strategy deployment and execution framework in 2005. It has since built out the strategic planning process described in Chapter 5 and shown in Exhibit 6.7. Following the completion of strategy formulation and the strategic plan, the leadership team engages in refreshing its strategy maps and BSCs to align with existing and new strategies at all levels. M7 Aerospace has developed corporate, BU, inline BU, and in some cases individual BSCs throughout the organization.

LEVEL 1 CORPORATE BALANCED SCORECARD HIGHLIGHTS The corporate level BSC contains measures that link and align with the corporate strategy map strategic objectives. Consistent with best practices, the corporate BSC contains 20 to 25 measures, some of which are mandatory for each level 2 BU.

M7 Aerospace focuses strategically on its "common" or integrated service strategies; however, BUs also concurrently pursue dissimilar BU-specific strategies. M7 Aerospace therefore functions as a portfolio with numerous outcome or lagging indicators. Corporate has high-level leading indicators; however, the BU-specific leading indicators reside at the BU level 2.

CASCADING BALANCED SCORECARDS, ALIGNMENT, AND INTEGRATION M7 Aerospace has adopted an enterprisewide view to performance management and has cascaded the BSC to the level 2 core business units (profit centers) and support units (service centers). Selected corporate BSC measures such as revenue or DSO are required of all BUs and thus these measures appear at all level 2 BSCs.

INTEGRATION OF CUSTOMER AND BU BSCs A large portion of M7 Aerospace's business is focused on the DoD, which issues the "Customer Performance

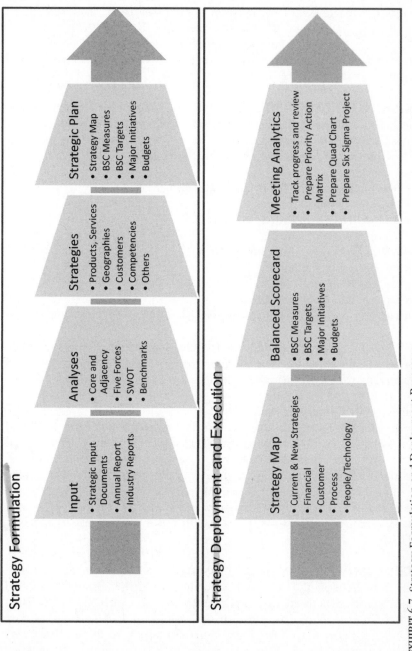

EXHIBIT 6.7 Strategy Formulation and Deployment Processes
Courtesy of M7 Aerospace.

Assessment Report" (CPAR) Card containing key elements of performance and satisfaction. CPAR BSCs cover quality, schedule, cost control, business relations, management of key personnel, and other areas. The CPAR ratings are directly aligned with the BU BSC measures. For non-DoD customers, M7 uses an Internet-based survey to gather customer feedback on customer satisfaction including questions on pricing, on-time performance, and quality.

VIRTUAL, CROSS FUNCTIONAL BSC   The government services BU provides contract logistics support (CLS) for certain military aircraft returning from conflict zones for repair and overhaul. For each aircraft, the following jobs and work orders must be addressed by a cross-functional team:

- Routine inspections (labor and material)
- Flying hour tasks
- Aircraft interior and exterior paint
- Troop seat refurbishment
- Airline passenger seat refurbishment
- Interior panel wallpaper
- Cockpit floor covering
- On condition engine overhaul
- Field service representative support, flying hours

The BU is primarily responsible for ensuring aircraft mission readiness, safety, and airworthiness. The program therefore is a BU with a dedicated strategy map and BSC. However, the program relies on other M7 Aerospace level 2 BUs and level 3 departments to provide services and support to deliver on its contract terms.

Exhibit 6.8 is an example of how the accountabilities are identified and assigned to all parties to create a shared or virtual BSC. Notice that the BU has revenue responsibility; however, the supporting finance, records reliability, materials management group, repair station and quality do not. Rather, these other functions provide process perspective services and BSC measures in the process section that support or enable the government services BU to deliver on its commitments to the U.S. military.

MEETING MANAGEMENT AND BUSINESS ANALYTICS   M7 Aerospace CEO Kevin Brown meets monthly with his leadership team consisting of BU and SU heads to review not only the corporate BSC but also each BU and SU BSC. Mr. Brown uses an exception-based approach to conduct meetings focused on underperforming (red or yellow) measure results, or those results with negative trends. This results in an efficient use of meeting time. BU and SU

EXHIBIT 6.8 Shared, Virtual BU Balanced Scorecard

Code	Objective	Measure	Ownership Matrix for DOD Reset Program						
			Application DOD Reset (Yes, No)	DoD Maint	Finance	SCM-Records Reliability	SCM Mat Maint Group	Repair Station	Quality
F2	**Drive Revenue Growth**	Revenue recognized ($)	Yes	Yes	No	No	No	Yes	No
		YTD Revenue recognized ($)							
F4	**Optimize WIP**	WIP Aging							
F5	**Continuously Improve Profitability**	Net Operating Margin Pre SG&A$							
		EBITDA ($)							
		EBITDA YTD($)							
		Non reimbursable Expenses							

Courtesy of M7 Aerospace.

219

leaders will prepare for meetings by completing a four-part solutions chart referred to as a quad chart, a priority action matrix, or launch a process improvement project.

Four-quadrant or "quad" charts and priority action matrixes are derivatives of quality tools that break out the issues into their component parts for management discussion and analyses. If an issue is significantly more complex, then a six sigma quality team is launched (this is discussed further in Chapter 7).

The quad chart contains four sections:

1. Objective: The strategic objective from the organization strategy map.
2. Measures: The BSC measure results that provide insight into progress toward attaining the strategic objective.
3. Specific Issues: These are root causes of the underperformance; their resolution will enable improvement in performance.
4. Actions/Discussions: Specific actions, one for each issue, and a timeline for resolution.

The priority action matrix provides several key components for problem resolution:

- Category: Contains definition for the issue or BSC measure.
- Who else: Who else or what organization will contribute.
- What: What measure or topic is being addressed.
- When: When the topic will be addressed.
- Issue status: Red, yellow, or green status indicating progress toward resolution.
- Comments/updates: Explanatory information to provide more insights.

ALIGN INDIVIDUALS AND REWARDS AND RECOGNITION   HR VP Phil O'Connor has designed and developed a BSC-based reward and recognition system for nonexecutive employees. The recognition of performance is primarily based on the BSC measures for each position. Executives are held responsible for both the consolidated corporate scorecard as well as their own departmental scorecard results.

The BSC-based performance management form contains three key components: (1) BSC measure results, (2) evaluation of executive and management performance traits, and (3) employee development plans.

TARGET SETTING AND BENCHMARKING   M7 Aerospace sets targets based on one of the following four methods:

1. Top-down targets: Targets are established or directly derived from goals set at the top of the organization or at the shareholder level. These types of measures are typically financial.
2. Benchmark targets: Targets are set to match competitive, best-in-class, or market-driven performance levels. These targets are typically for measures that follow from the business strategy, such as price position, market share, or industry leadership.
3. Rate of improvement targets: Targets are derived from a desired rate of improvement and might be calculated by computing annual performance necessary to reach an identified performance level. Target setting for measures of quality, time, or service levels can generally be derived in this manner.
4. Experiential targets: Certain measures will be new to an organization and a sufficient base of experience does not exist to establish targets. In this case, measures are tracked and discussed as part of the management process until sufficient experience is gained to establish targets.

The SCM team uses key industry data for benchmarking. Currently, M7 pulls data on the aerospace and defense industry from CAPS Research and creates a personalized M7 analysis.

From a practical standpoint, two BU leaders weighed in on target setting.

Steve Leland stated, "From a contractual standpoint, we have set targets for customer service (i.e., mission readiness rates). An example of a target is not having any aircraft fall below 80% percent MC (mission capability) rate. In 2004–2005 we had nine airplanes drop below 80 percent MC rate in the first year. In 2009, due to the collective BSC measures, we had 0."

Mark Provost stated, "The BSC forces you to establish very clearly defined targets and benchmarks. Before the BSC, our backlog and performance metrics were not clearly defined. An example of the day-to-day performance is frequently and many metro operators are serviced. BSC has helped us clearly identify our goals and define what we need to do to reach our goals."

BSC SOFTWARE M7 Aerospace has been using workbooks to collect and report on BSC results. Recently the company committed to deploying the integrated financial system to bring together data from disparate systems.

CORE AND INNOVATIVE BEST PRACTICES M7 Aerospace exercises the core best practices identified earlier and has advanced knowledge in this area with new, innovative best practices.

Principle 3: Cascade and Manage Strategy

- **Partner with business owners.** Partner with line and staff leadership team members to gain owners' support and influence as partners to help them achieve results.
- **Develop level 1 BSC.** Translate strategy into level 1 BSC measures and measure targets at the highest organizational level.
- **Leverage proven BSC or comparable method.** Observe BSC or comparable design parameters, assigning one to two measures to each strategy map objective.
- **Cascade BSC to lower levels.** Cascade and align level 1 BSC to levels 2, 3, 4, and so on, depending on organizational and accountability structures.
- **Align support services.** Identify and define measures for all support services that align with levels 1 and below.
- **Align teams and individual employees.** Define personal BSCs for teams and/or an individual that align with higher-level and support services' Balanced Scorecards.
- **Link compensation.** Align rewards, recognition, and compensation programs to the Balanced Scorecard.
- **Manage using measures.** Manage BSC meetings to address the appropriate mix of strategic and operational issues; link these issues with Principle 4: Business Improvement.
- **Automate measurement.** Implement CPM software to manage BSC program with links to other principles.
- **Innovative Best Practice.** M7 Aerospace utilizes an innovative shared or virtual BSC to link and align multiple BUs and supporting departments to deliver on customer requirements.
- **Innovative Best Practice.** M7 Aerospace extends use of the BSC outside the organization to include a mirror image of the customer CPAR requirements to deliver mission-ready planes.
- **Innovative Best Practice.** M7 Aerospace leverages multiple quality methods, quad charts, Priority Action Matrix (PAMs) and Lean Six Sigma (LSS), depending upon the severity of the issue, to rapidly resolve business issues. LSS governance and projects are discussed later and are reserved for more complex and impactful issues.

Mueller, Inc.: Best Practice Case

Mueller's strategy deployment process consists of a set of corporate and cascaded BSCs down to the team level. These are described in the following sections.

CORPORATE BSC   Mueller has a BSC with measures balanced across financial and nonfinancial perspectives. Mueller fundamentally believes this practice is essential to successful strategy execution and to a successful organization.

An example of a nonfinancial perspective includes the learning and growth perspective, which contains a strategic objective, "Develop a Climate for Action," to which Mueller applies its employee survey. The survey allows management to obtain a pulse on various factors from the employees, which in turn allows management to take measures to ensure there is a good climate for growth and empowerment for the employees.

Two financial perspectives that Mueller uses are the year over year sales growth and the return on assets (ROA). The balance of financial and nonfinancial perspectives reinforce each other and help to give a complete view of the organization.

CASCADING, ALIGNING, AND INTEGRATING WITH THE BSC   Mueller created its BSC at the highest level of the organization and cascaded it down throughout the rest of the company. Each area of the organization contributes to the execution of the strategy, ensuring alignment through integrated BSCs. In some cases, functional areas were added to the organization to fill in gaps required to meet the strategy. The BSC is used to communicate the defined purpose of the business and as a tool to communicate expectations and results throughout Mueller.

The BSC is used to communicate and guide the strategy of the business units at Mueller where predefined objectives cascade to lower levels to ensure alignment. These BSCs are all centrally provided through Lack's office.

The business process works well and has had excellent results. Previously, retail sales branches operated autonomously, which produced inconsistencies across the organization. There were unique cultures within each branch, and with nearly 30 branches, there was too much inconsistency for Mueller to have common services and reputation for its customers. Currently, the BSC enforces consistency. For example, the time a customer's order was sitting on the floor before deliver was up to 30 days at some locations and less at others. That meant there was inventory sitting on the floor that could cause problems for sales, security, and inventory, and possible damages. By focusing on the metric of "Days Sales in Inventory" across all sales branches, sales branches are now looking at the same goals and objectives, enabling internal benchmarking.

To further standardize, Mueller created what it calls its Branch Target system. The Branch Target system organizes Mueller branches into three groups: Calves, Heifers, and Cows. According to Lack, the system was inspired by the BCG matrix to determine priorities for allocating resources. One of the stages in the BCG matrix is "cash cows." According to Lack, "We decided to go all the way with the agricultural theme."

- The Calves group includes Mueller's newest and youngest branches as well as any branches that are underperforming.
- Heifers are the mid-sized branches and medium performers.
- At the top are the Cows, Mueller's best performers and usually the most mature.

The Branch Target system consists of models for each category of branch office that give managers guidance and direction on how their branches should be performing against a number of key financial metrics. Says Davenport, "We wanted to give our branch managers the responsibility and authority to run their branches like they are independent businesses, but we couldn't have them all going off and creating their own targets and systems for measuring performance. That might work when you have five branches, but what about when you have 50?"

CASCADED TO TEAMS The BSC is cascaded down through the organization. Each sales location may have different goals, but each is aligned with the overall goal of sales expectations. The manager in each department may assign different goals to each employee, but overall the manager is responsible for the entire group meeting the goal. Mueller does not yet formally align individuals to the strategy as the individuals are aligned through their team.

CASCADED TO POSITION TYPES, STRATEGIC JOB FAMILIES Strategic job families with personal development tools, such as training to reduce accidents, are aligned to achieve strategic results; however, it is a loose alignment. Lack's office supports the strategic levels, and a stronger tie to the BSC is the direction Mueller is taking for personal development plans.

Mueller's goals are under two themes, growth and efficiency, where sales (job family) is tasked with providing profitable revenue, and the rest of the job families are tasked with efficiency. Mueller's goal is to use the BSC to have personal development aligned with overall strategy.

COMPARATIVE DATA RESEARCH: TARGET SETTING AND BENCHMARKING Mueller has established targets for every measure across financial and nonfinancial perspectives because the target is what indicates whether the organization is executing on the strategy. Mueller measures targets and uses this insight to drill down and see where the problems are. Mueller can then focus on problem areas in order to improve upon its strategic executions, ensuring a consistent and collaborative view across the entire organization in terms of goals and measures. As noted earlier, the 30 branch office results are compared and quartile analyses are performed to benchmark performance.

MEETING MANAGEMENT, BUSINESS ANALYTICS, PERFORMANCE ANALYSIS, AND REVIEW Mueller reviews its strategic and operational performance through a series of four meeting frequencies and types:

1. Annual review of strategic priorities.
2. Quarterly meetings discuss longer-term performance and solutions to interim issues.
3. Monthly briefings highlight critical issues for immediate action.
4. Daily operating measures on an informal basis focus on task-level corrections.

Both the formal and informal reviews help ensure consistency and regular communication on the topic of strategy. These meetings are crucial to the maintenance of the strategy and contribute to Mueller's overall success through communication. Mueller reviews strategy formally because it holds meetings on a quarterly basis, ensuring that items are dealt with, the BSC and its strategy are kept top of mind, and any adjustments or corrections are made as needed.

Mueller's BSCs provide a complete view across all areas of the organization. They also provide financial and nonfinancial measure results, ensuring perspectives from all areas of the company are considered in strategy execution. Lagging financial and customer measure results are balanced with leading process and people measure results to help Mueller have a true look at its performance and improve decision making and predictive capabilities.

Mueller has seen some big leaps forward in terms of information speed and accuracy. Users have faster access to standard reports and more thorough sales analyses. In many cases, content is delivered in minutes instead of days. Mark Lack says one of the first things management noticed is the new level of insight and understanding people are sharing in company meetings. "People in the past would talk about process or strategy and say 'It would be great to know the percentage of this, or why that happened.' This kind of discussion would have been either rhetorical or would have to be taken offline to research. We now pull up the BSC system and can find the answers right away."

What's more, staff can drill into details and pull together different pieces of information to gain dimensional views they never had previously. The insight is a boon to decision making. "We can find information that we didn't even know existed before," adds Lack. "People are calling me and asking very advanced, complex questions, which means they are looking at the data in new ways. We've created a much more knowledgeable workforce that can now act on key information very quickly."

ALIGN INDIVIDUALS AND REWARDS AND RECOGNITION   Targets are incorporated in managers' job performance goals for the year. At first, Sales gave mixed reviews on using the BSC, so Mueller tied it to compensation in order to ensure it received priority within Sales. This produced incredible results, with a significant number of sales units coming into line with the rest of the organization in terms of consistency and uniformity.

Incentives as well as individual performance at Mueller are equally based on the achievement of the company's goals. This shows that while individual performance counts, overall company performance is equally important. This helps address the differences between sales goals and operational goals. For example, Sales wants good customer service, but Operations wants to reduce costs. With this incentive method both individual and company goals are balanced. Sales will be prudent with shipping costs, for example, and Operations would be more flexible with costs to meet customer service demands. This helps everyone in the company understand that the end user of the products are Mueller's customers, not just customers of one department or one salesperson.

Compensation, where an employee falls within a salary range, is partially based on achievements of BSC metrics. A salesperson would need to meet sales targets and BSC metrics in order to receive a raise in salary. Mueller also feels that having the compensation and incentive system linked to strategic performance has been a critical best practice. Mueller has structured its incentive program so that the company's goals are taken into consideration just as much as the individual's goals. This has ensured that overall company performance has become a priority for all employees. No matter what department an employee may work in, that employee understands that he or she must reach individual goals and encourage colleagues to do so as well, by sharing of best practices, in order for the company to meet its goals.

Compensation has also been linked to the strategic performance of the company to further communicate the importance of reaching targets. This important link between compensation, incentives, and performance has ensured that customer service and value add have become strategic priorities throughout the entire organization.

BSC SOFTWARE, DATA, AND INFORMATION AVAILABILITY Mueller uses IBM Cognos Planning and Cognos Business Intelligence (BI) along with BSC reporting to guide decision making, assess progress toward strategic objectives, and test strategic hypotheses. Mueller's system works like a feedback loop. Metrics are in green, yellow, or red depending on their status.

When items are yellow or red, reporting and BI tools are used to determine where the problem started. Then, planning evaluates whether to adjust to meet the metric's target. The cycle then returns to monitoring metrics. This BI environment also allows for testing strategic hypotheses to gauge outcomes.

CORE AND INNOVATIVE BEST PRACTICES Mueller exercises the core best practices identified earlier; it has advanced knowledge in this area with new, innovative best practices.

Principle 3: Cascade and Manage Strategy

- **Partner with business owners.** Partner with line and staff leadership team members to gain owners' support and influence as partners to help them achieve results.
- **Develop level 1 BSC.** Translate strategy into level 1 BSC measures and measure targets at the highest organizational level.
- **Leverage proven BSC or comparable method.** Observe BSC or comparable design parameters, assigning one to two measures to each strategy map objective.
- **Cascade BSC to lower levels.** Cascade and align level 1 BSC to lower levels.
- **Align support services.** Identify and define measures for all support services that align with levels 1 and below.
- **Align teams and individual employees.** Define personal BSCs for teams and/or individuals that align with higher-level and support services' BSCs.
- **Link compensation.** Align rewards, recognition, and compensation programs to the BSC.
- **Manage using measures.** Manage BSC meetings to address the appropriate mix of strategic and operational issues; link these issues with Principle 4: Business Improvement.
- **Automate measurement.** Implement CPM software to manage BSC program with links to other principles.

(Continued)

■ **Innovative Best Practice.** Mueller recognizes and leverages the value of leading indicators in its processes, and has defined requirements and measures for both core and support processes. This enables longer lead times to resolve issues that would later impact lagging measures of customer satisfaction and financial results.

■ **Innovative Best Practice.** Mueller uses a systematic and business intelligence–based approach in selecting comparative measures to support internal benchmarking.

NSTAR: Best Practice Case

One of the major changes NSTAR made was to have CPM work in conjunction with its executive team and the business planning process. The goal was to ensure NSTAR created, communicated, and achieved specific levels of performance in critical areas for the company. CPM established an NSTAR balanced scorecard framework for performance measurements, with customer service, operational excellence, employees, and financial/growth/regulatory dimensions.

The leadership team at NSTAR quickly embraced the performance framework and used the results of performance reporting and analytics to make needed improvements in the business. Once the performance goals began to be communicated, requests from many business units were made to CPM to develop even more measures and management reports to help managers understand the drivers of their performance.

As NSTAR's performance culture took hold and performance began to improve, CEO Tom May challenged CPM and the leadership team to establish "second-generation performance metrics." These new metrics help NSTAR drill down to the root causes of opportunity areas.

TARGET SETTING   Target setting for industry-standard operational metrics was NSTAR's first foray into establishing an initial set of performance metrics. NSTAR used benchmarking information to understand its own performance versus industry peers. The idea was to draw clear lines in the sand for desired performance levels over time, and set attainable targets based on the industry.

For newer and more company-focused performance measures it could not readily compare to the industry, NSTAR set preliminary targets until it could better track its own performance. Once the company could see the level at which it performed on a particular metric, it then set targets to maintain that level or improve it based on areas of priority. Today, NSTAR annually sets targets based on a philosophy of ongoing improvement, so the company continues to deliver great service and gain new operational efficiencies.

In addition to its internal system of performance measurement, NSTAR also works to meet customer service performance metrics set by the Massachusetts Department of Public Utilities (DPU). Called the Service Quality plan, these metrics help DPU monitor the performance of all public Massachusetts utilities. Utilities are required to meet performance benchmarks based on each company's past performance, or face potential financial penalties in the form of customer rebates. Since the Service Quality plan went into effect in 2001, NSTAR has outperformed DPU requirements each year.

CPM TOOLS, SOFTWARE, AND MONITORING All NSTAR performance metrics are managed and visualized using a performance reporting application from Actuate, internally called the NSTAR Performance System. Right from their desktop computers, the management team and all employees can view targets and actual performance values for each measurement, as well as breakdowns of the measure, such as time or location dimensions. The performance information is retained as a repository for historical performance data so that analyses are consistently presenting the same result – the same version of the truth.

Depending on the performance measure, actual performance is updated within the NSTAR Performance System on a weekly, monthly, or quarterly basis. Many operational metrics are updated weekly and most high-level business metrics are updated monthly. The NSTAR Performance System allows managers to understand how they are performing over time, showing progress and variance toward year-to-date targets, as well as trends in their leading indicators.

The CPM team monitors and controls the quality of the information used in the measurements, working with NSTAR's information technology department and other business areas to identify, access, validate, and sometimes create new sources for data used in measuring performance. A key driver for building confidence in a performance measurement system is data quality. To that end, NSTAR implemented new business processes and computer application changes to support the company's ability to accurately measure performance in several areas.

Standardized and custom performance reporting and scorecards are created from the NSTAR Performance System and by using tools such as Microsoft Excel or Crystal Reports. NSTAR leaders and their teams have come to rely on their scorecards, as well as other performance analytics and detailed management reports, to help them monitor their performance and pinpoint areas of opportunity.

MEETING MANAGEMENT AND BUSINESS ANALYTICS A key component of NSTAR's performance culture journey has been to ensure employees remain aware of the company's customer service, operational, and employee-centered performance goals and progress. Early on, CPM teamed up with human resources and corporate communications to execute a comprehensive communications campaign aimed at:

- Promoting the importance of improving NSTAR's performance
- Educating employees on the relationship between the work they do every day and overall company performance
- Regularly relaying NSTAR's progress toward meeting desired performance levels

CASCADING BSCs, ALIGNMENT, AND INTEGRATION Since this early campaign, NSTAR has implemented several other methods to increase employee engagement and awareness around performance. Each month, CPM creates the executive performance review and assembles other scorecard materials and analytics for key operating areas. Much of this performance information is made available corporatewide via NSTAR's company intranet, as well as through regular updates in NSTAR's daily newsletter.

Managers throughout the company also devote time at staff meetings to review performance, where leaders share information about local and company performance using the scorecards and other related information. Innovations and ideas surface at scorecard meetings, leading to further performance improvements at every level.

ALIGN INDIVIDUALS AND REWARDS AND RECOGNITION Each of NSTAR's non-represented employees (approximately one-third of all employees) has an individual performance plan, which includes goals aligned to their role in meeting the company's overall operating plan and focuses their work efforts. Development plans and leadership action plans for managers are also created, which include improvements individuals are working on to improve their own performance and specific steps managers will take to build employee engagement in their areas. Performance against business performance goals, individual development goals, and leadership goals are all tied to the allocation of annual incentives rewards for departments and eligible employees.

In addition, each month NSTAR creates updated performance posters for every company location, calling attention to the company's most important goals. CPM also takes advantage of a wide variety of corporate communications channels, such as daily newsletters, leadership team meetings, local employee meetings, and home mailings, to provide employees with up-to-date performance information. The CPM director and the entire executive team also meet monthly to review and discuss progress on key performance goals and business improvement initiatives.

CORE BEST PRACTICES   NSTAR exercises the core best practices identified earlier.

Principle 3: Cascade and Manage Strategy

- **Partner with business owners.** Partner with line and staff leadership team members to gain support and influence as partners to help them achieve results.
- **Develop level 1 BSC.** Translate strategy into level 1 BSC measures and measure targets at the highest organizational level.
- **Leverage proven BSC or comparable method.** Observe BSC or comparable design parameters, assigning one to two measures to each strategy map objective.
- **Cascade BSC to lower levels.** Cascade and align level 1 BSC to levels 2, 3, 4, and so on, depending on organizational and accountability structures.
- **Align support services.** Identify and define measures for all support services that align with levels 1 and below.
- **Align teams and individual employees.** Define personal BSCs for teams and/or individuals that align with higher-level and support services' BSCs.
- **Link compensation.** Align rewards, recognition, and compensation programs to the Balanced Scorecard.
- **Manage using measures.** Manage BSC meetings to address the appropriate mix of strategic and operational issues; link these issues with Principle 4: Business Improvement.
- **Automate measurement.** Implement CPM software to manage BSC program with links to other principles.

Omaha Public Power District: Best Practice Case

Omaha Public Power District (OPPD) has elected to leverage Kaplan and Norton's Balanced Scorecard methodology, referred to as Performance Scorecard (PSC) to deploy its corporate strategy. The program entails a defined hierarchy of PSCs three levels deep into the organization. The three levels include:

1. President and CEO W. Gary Gates manages the entire company.
2. Five vice presidents manage portfolios of functions:
   - Vice President and Chief Financial Officer Edward E. Easterlin
   - Vice President Nuclear Chief Nuclear Officer David J. Bannister
   - Vice President Employee and Customer Relations Timothy J. Burke
   - Vice President Essential Services Adrian J. Minks
   - Vice President Operations Dale F. Widoe
3. Division managers and direct reports lead functional divisions consisting of multiple departments.

CASCADING PERFORMANCE SCORECARDS, ALIGNMENT, AND INTEGRATION The corporate PSC contains numerous measures that are required for cascading down through core and support organizations to ensure alignment both vertically at all levels 1 through 3, and horizontally across the organizational units. An illustrative example of one such goal is "P3, Support the Community." This is being tracked and managed by two measures: (1) volunteer hours per employee, and (2) percentage of employees volunteering. The goal and both measures can be viewed throughout the organization. For example, the nuclear business unit has been managing with measures for years. The strategic goal "P9, Continuously Improve Generation Asset Performance" also aligns with the corporate strategy map and PSC. The two measures provide focus on the plant (1) capability factor and (2) capacity factor.

STRATEGY-FOCUSED MEETING MANAGEMENT OPPD PSC organizational leaders meet monthly to review the PSC and deploy an exception-based management approach to leverage precious meeting time. The CPM corporate team ensures timely updates of all measures on the corporate Performance Scorecard each month. The updated PSC is then shared with the senior management and division management teams via e-mail prior to the leadership meeting to allow time for review prior to the meeting. The CPM corporate team then facilitates short, high-impact meetings of an hour or two in duration that focus on strategic goals. The same format is also used at the monthly division managers meeting. This focused approach typically results in lean meeting agendas that address between two to four strategic and operational issues per meeting.

BUSINESS ANALYTICS/INTELLIGENCE AND SOFTWARE The core CPM team responsible for designing and rolling out dozens of PSCs throughout the organization were careful to clearly define the metadata or information about data for each measure. As we continue the example focused on strategic goal "P3, Support the Community" with the measure "Percent of Employees Volunteering," a description of this objective worksheet containing the following measure information:

- CPM metric name.
- Status, trend, actual, target, variance, owner, last updated.
- Reporter, technical and functional descriptions.
- Owner contact information.
- Permission table for access.
- PSCs that contain the measure so there is understanding about horizontal and vertical usage.
- The tolerance and target(s) are established on the measure history detail.

ALIGN INDIVIDUALS AND REWARDS AND RECOGNITION OPPD HR division is responsible for deploying personal goal setting and personal development plans. Personal goals are aligned with corporate, business unit, division, and/or department strategy map goals and PSCs. In 2009, recognition for PSC performance was provided by members of the leadership teams to their respective teams. The communications plan provided highlights of success stories to provide linkages and alignment between performances and the company strategic goals and PSC measures. OPPD planned to link rewards to the PSC in 2010.

TARGET SETTING AND BENCHMARKING OPPD target setting primarily focused on a single target for each measure. A select grouping of measures also provided for minimum and stretch targets as well. Targets could be established based on the frequency of the measures (monthly updated could have distinct targets for each month). Tolerances to determine color coding were established around the target for each measure. For instance, in our continued example of P3 volunteer hours, if a division shows performance yellow, that means it is between 90 to 99 percent of target. The threshold for a red light is attaining below 90 percent of target. Green performance is 100 percent or higher of target.

PSC SOFTWARE OPPD has deployed Cognos Metrics Studio to enable enterprisewide permission-based access to strategy maps, Performance Scorecards, and their components (goals, measures, measure history, targets, etc.).

CORE AND INNOVATIVE BEST PRACTICES OPPD exercises the core best practices identified earlier.

Principle 3: Cascade and Manage Strategy

- **Partner with business owners.** Partner with line and staff leadership team members to gain support and influence as partners to help them achieve results.
- **Develop level 1 PSC.** Translate strategy into level 1 PSC measures and measure targets at the highest organizational level.
- **Leverage proven PSC or comparable method.** Observe PSC or comparable design parameters, assigning one to two measures to each strategy map objective.
- **Cascade PSC to lower levels.** Cascade and align level 1 PSC to levels 2, 3, 4, and so on, depending on organizational and accountability structures.
- **Align support services.** Identify and define measures for all support services that align with levels 1 and below.
- **Align teams and individual employees.** Define personal PSCs for teams and/or individuals that align with higher-level and support services' Balanced Scorecards.
- **Link compensation.** Align rewards, recognition to the PSCs.
- **Manage using measures.** Manage PSC meetings to address the appropriate mix of strategic and operational issues; link these issues with Principle 4: Business Improvement.
- **Automate measurement.** Implement CPM software to manage PSC program with links to other principles.

Poudre Valley Health System: Best Practice Case

Overall, key performance measures for tracking achievement of SOs populate the system BSC. Senior leaders select these measures through SDD and a systematic process. Reviews by the leadership team and SMG throughout the process ensure that targets are set to achieve or surpass performance projections and realistically address strategic challenges. The GPS model, incorporating the BSC process, ensures systematic deployment of the SOs, guides appropriate goal-setting, and ensures that the measurement system covers key deployment areas and stakeholders.

Through the BSC, PVHS has established a process for selecting, collecting, aligning, and integrating data to track organizational performance, including progress relative to the strategic plan. As described in the organization's formal BSC policy, the annual process begins with SDD, when

SMG identifies (1) strategic goals and action items in support of each SO; and (2) key performance measures indicating progress toward the strategic plan. These key performance measures, including short- and longer-term financial measures, populate the BSC system aligned with the top SOs.

BSC MEASUREMENT STANDARDS REVIEW BSC measures go to a multidisciplinary knowledge management team, where each measure is assigned to a "point person" with relevant expertise for standards review consisting of the following questions:

- What is the purpose of the measure?
- Why was the measure chosen?
- How was the measure chosen?
- How should the measure be defined?
- How often should this item be measured?
- What is the format of the measure?
- What are acceptable and unacceptable values for this measure?
- Are the definition and range acceptable for all levels of the organization?
- What sources were consulted for possible industry benchmarks?
- Is there an industry benchmark?
- Is there a data source and benchmark for this measure?
- If a benchmark is not appropriate, why not?
- Are there other factors to consider?

BSC MEASUREMENT TARGET RANGES AND FOUR COLOR CODES Each "point person" sets performance goals and ranges, using blue, green, yellow, or red tolerances for quick visual identification. Monitoring these measures regularly helps *drive innovation* and performance improvement, based on comparative data for the top 10 percent of U.S. organizations or an internal stretch goal determined by trending historical data:

- Blue: The best practice or world-class stretch goal
- Green: An indicator of acceptable performance
- Yellow: An indicator that performance is in transition and warrants monitoring
- Red: An indicator that performance falls outside the acceptable range and warrants immediate action

SMG gives final BSC approval, and the system BSC is created in PVHS' innovative electronic BSC system. From the *system BSC*, individual SMG members create BSCs with *division*-specific measures and goals that support the system BSC. Directors then create *department* BSCs with service area–specific measures and goals that support the division and system BSCs.

Each month, managers of data related to HR, patient satisfaction, financials, market share, and key clinical process/outcome measures globally populate the electronic BSCs. SMG and directors populate additional key measures on their respective BSCs. At a glance, system BSC users can gauge organizational progress relative to the strategic plan. It is common to see departmental and system BSCs printed and posted in staff lounges or meeting areas as a constant visual image of how the organization is progressing toward meeting its goals.

If key performance measures are blue or green, PVHS is on track to accomplish the corresponding strategic plan items; if key performance measures are yellow or red, the organization is not on track to accomplish these items. On the system BSC, if a measure is red for one month or yellow for three months, the point person for that measure determines why the measure is not on track and develops a BSC improvement/action plan, which is approved and monitored by the appropriate SMG member and hyperlinked to the electronic BSC. The result is continual performance improvement and progress toward the organization's strategic plan. In addition to using the BSC to track organizational performance and drive innovation and performance improvement, PVHS also analyzes data for information to make fact-based decisions at both strategic and operational levels. One critical tool across the organization is the monthly key performance indicator (KPI) reports that go to each director. The KPI reports roll up from department to division to facility to system. The resulting system monthly financial results report goes to all directors, SMG, and the board of directors.

BSC COMPARATIVE DATA SETS PVHS uses comparative data to set goals that *drive innovation* and performance improvement at both strategic and operational levels. For instance, year after year, PVHS has set increasingly aggressive goals for patient satisfaction scores and systematically implemented initiatives to achieve them. To select and ensure the effective use of comparative data, the organization requires identification of comparative data through formal, systemwide processes, including (1) SDD; (2) BSC; (3) the feasibility analysis step of the business decision support process; (4) the process for monitoring, evaluating, and improving the organization's key processes; and (5) PDCA improvement model.

With all applications of comparative data, the organization asks the following questions:

- What comparative data are available in (1) external and world-class sources; (2) external sources but not world-class; (3) internal sources; or (4) none?
- Are the data truly comparative?
- Do the data drive performance improvement and stimulate innovation?

PVHS' key sources of comparative and competitive data in the health care industry include:

- Thomson Healthcare Database
- National Database of Nursing Quality Indicators (NDNQI)
- Quality Indicator Project (QIP)
- Colorado Health and Hospital Association (CHA)
- Ingenix
- Avatar
- VHA
- Vermont-Oxford
- National Trauma Data Bank (NTDB)
- HealthGrades
- Relevant Baldrige award recipients
- Hospital Consumer Assessment of Healthcare Providers and Systems (HCAHPS)

Comparative data from outside the health care industry come from sources such as American Society for Training and Development (ASTD), Moody's financial ratings, and relevant Baldrige award recipients. If external comparative data are not available, PVHS uses internal, historical data to perform trend analyses and set stretch goals that will drive performance improvement and innovation.

The annual learning process prompted creation of a formal BSC policy, a strategic decision to use national comparative databases rather than comparative results from individual high-performing organizations, and implementation of an electronic BSC. The most recent Baldrige-based cycle of improvement to PVHS' performance measurement system is implementation of the Thomson Reuters health care database for benchmarking of risk-adjusted clinical outcomes against more than 3,000 U.S. hospitals. To ensure that the performance measurement system is sensitive to rapid or unexpected organizational or external changes, the BSC policy allows SMG to add or remove BSC measures and adjust BSC goals outside the annual SDD process.

CASCADING AND MANAGING USING THE BSC   From the *system BSC*, individual SMG members create BSCs with *division*-specific measures and goals that support the system BSC. Directors then create *department* BSCs with service area–specific measures and goals that support the division and system BSCs. The BSC system can also be used to set individual BSCs, if desired.

Reviews and adjustments happen at all levels of the organization. Performance review findings help the organization prioritize opportunities and resources for improvement and innovation through (1) the SDD process, which sets goals and action plans for achieving the SOs and identifies opportunities for innovation; and (2) the BSC review process, which directs improvement/action plan development aimed at getting low-performing areas back on track. For instance, at PVH, increasing emergency department (ED) wait times and decreasing ED patient satisfaction prompted PVHS to drill down into ED performance measures and determine that mental health and substance abuse patients were significantly impacting ED processes.

Organizational performance reviews drive systematic evaluation and improvement of key processes by SMG, steering committees, and directors throughout PVHS. Measures not performing to goal can prompt corrective actions such as (1) initiation of a system PDCA team; (2) development and implementation of new/updated policies and procedures; (3) workforce training/re-training; (4) process redesign; and (5) resource allocation through SDD.

BSC AND PROCESS MANAGEMENT   PVHS has identified key core and support work processes and defined requirements and BSC process level measures to manage and improve the business. A few core examples include patient intake, clinical assessment, and discharge.

INDIVIDUAL GOAL SETTING AND REWARDS AND RECOGNITION   Annually, through the performance review process staff members set individual goals in support of the SOs and outline resources they will need to accomplish those goals. Employees and volunteers record those goals on individual goals cards, which they wear attached to their I.D. badge.

The organization celebrates initiative through reward and recognition (see Exhibit 6.9) of individuals and teams; supports professional and personal development; and regularly promotes from within.

All staff members undergo an annual performance review using a standardized and innovative review instrument developed within PVHS to further communicate the strategy of the organization. Managers and peers evaluate a staff member based on the behavior standards, values, and key customer and staff requirements. Staff members set individual goals to align their work with the PVHS strategic plan, drive high performance, and engage them in the organization's success. The staff member and manager review the staff member's job description and identify education/training needs. On an ongoing basis, HR coordinates evaluation and improvement of the performance review process to more fully engage the workforce and support high performance.

The Optional Performance Plan (OPP) is an incentive program designed to engage staff and reinforce innovation, high performance, and patient/customer focus linked to achievement of organizational goals. Payout is based on (1) attaining a net gain on the budget; (2) achieving

EXHIBIT 6.9 Rewards and Recognition

REWARDS AND RECOGNITIONS	STAFF	PHYSICIANS	VOLUNTEERS	GIVEN BY	FREQUENCY
Hospital Week & Nurses Week Celebrations	•	•	•	SMG	Yearly
Summer Picnic and Holiday Parties/Gifts	•	•	•	SMG	Yearly
Founders Day	•	•	•	SMG	Yearly
Employees of the Year	•			Workforce	Yearly
Volunteer Week Celebration			•	Management	Yearly
Physician Thank You Dinner		•		SMG	Yearly
Spotlight Volunteers and Traveling Thank You Cart			•	Directors	Ongoing
Special Meals in Physician Lounge		•		Management	Ongoing
Service Awards	•		•	Management	Ongoing
Theme Days	•	•	•	SMG	Ongoing
Birthday Certificates	•		•	Management	Ongoing
Peer-to-Peer Coupons	•	•	•	Workforce	Ongoing
R&R Certificates ($5–$500)	•			Workforce	Ongoing
Thank-You Notes	•	•	•	All	Ongoing
Retail and Entertainment Discounts	•	•	•	All	Ongoing

Courtesy of Poudre Valley Health System.

75 percent participation in the Employee Culture Survey; and (3) attaining established patient satisfaction goals (currently set at 80 percent Top Box, systemwide). All staff members share equally in the OPP, with individual payout amounts determined by number of hours worked, not organizational rank. SMG annually evaluates and adjusts OPP to drive continuing performance improvement.

In the Reward & Recognition (R&R) program, managers may request an R&R certificate for staff who demonstrate (1) high performance, innovation, and patient/customer focus toward achievement of the SOs; or (2) behavior standards and values. The certificates are redeemable for $10 to $500 at a diverse list of area businesses that support the PVHS Foundation. Peer-to-peer coupons, redeemable for $3, allow staff, volunteers, and physicians to reward each other for actions supporting behavior standards and values. Members of the workforce nominate staff "Employees of the Year" for consistently supporting SOs and VMV. PVHS uses numerous other informal and individualized rewards. However, federal law limits rewards hospitals can give independent physicians. Thus, PVHS cannot extend many of its reward programs to physicians.

Compensation includes an hourly rate plus benefits worth an additional 27 percent of salary. HR adjusts salaries annually based on market analysis. Managers may also make individual equity adjustments. Evening or night workers receive generous shift differentials, and staff who are called in to work with less than 24 hours notice receive short-notice pay. To retain and engage the workforce, PVHS offers referral bonuses for individuals who recruit critical-to-recruit employees, as well as benefits based on length of service: increasing vested interest in matched retirement investments and increasing paid-time-off (PTO) hours and health benefits.

BSC AND INNOVATION   PVHS fosters *innovation* in the work environment:

- Through the BSC process and performance management system, PVHS sets and deploys goals to drive innovation throughout the organization.
- The SDD process includes extensive information gathering so that the organization stays current on work environment innovations internal and external to the health care industry.
- PVHS engages staff, physicians, and volunteers in workplace design of remodels, additions, and new facilities, so that work layout and location support innovative and patient-focused processes. With MCR, staff and physicians joined the design team in site visits to innovative facilities across the country and then tested mock patient rooms, an elevator, a trauma resuscitation suite, and an operating room, all built out of Styrofoam and cardboard in a local warehouse. As a result, MCR now incorporates innovations such as (1) the Disney design concept that separates public spaces from patient flow pathways to ensure patient privacy and optimize workforce productivity; (2) streamlined pathways for trauma patients to maximize critical patient care minutes and allow the entire trauma team to stay with the patient at all times; (3) intensive care beds with power, data ports, and medical gases coming from free-standing columns rather than mounted headwalls to facilitate 360-degree access to the patient by the care team; and (4) surgical imaging technology available at only 14 other hospitals in the country.

- As part of the business decision support process and performance improvement system, interdisciplinary teams research internal and external best practices to drive innovation. For instance, PVHS was the first hospital or health system in Colorado to improve productivity and patient safety with complete lab automation, and PVHS' in-house counsel adapted the purchasing department's RFP process for legal applications and continues to save the organization over $500,000 a year in insurance premiums.
- The annual Quality Festival, which invites members of the workforce to highlight quality improvement projects, promotes and rewards sharing and implementation of innovations across the organization.
- The Employee Culture Survey (now conducted annually) helps leaders and staff monitors how conducive the work environment is to innovation.

CORE AND INNOVATIVE BEST PRACTICES   PVHS exercises the core best practices identified earlier and has advanced knowledge in this area with a new, innovative best practice.

Principle 3: Cascade and Manage Strategy

- **Partner with business owners.** Partner with line and staff leadership team members to gain support and influence as partners to help them achieve results.
- **Develop level 1 BSC.** Translate strategy into level 1 BSC measures and measure targets at the highest organizational level.
- **Leverage proven BSC or comparable method.** Observe BSC or comparable design parameters, assigning one to two measures to each strategy map objective.
- **Cascade BSC throughout organization.** Cascade and align level 1 BSC to division, department, and process levels (levels 2, 3, and 4) depending on organizational and accountability structures.
- **Align support services.** Identify and define measures for all support services that align with levels 1 and below.
- **Align teams and individual employees.** Define personal BSCs for teams and/or individuals that align with higher-level and support services' Balanced Scorecards.

- **Link compensation.** Align rewards, recognition, and compensation programs to the Balanced Scorecard. It contains both annual and ongoing elements to more closely link desired behavior to rewards.
- **Manage using measures.** Manage BSC meetings to address the appropriate mix of strategic and operational issues; link these issues with Principle 4: Business Improvement.
- **Innovative Best Practice.** PVHS uses a systematic approach in selecting comparative data sources by looking for data in (1) external and world-class sources; (2) external sources but not world-class; (3) internal sources; or (4) none.
- **Innovative Best Practice.** PVHS fosters and reinforces innovation in the work environment through the BSC and a range of programs; such as BSC process and performance management system and the Disney design concept.
- **Innovative Best Practice.** PVHS Measurement Standards Review includes 14 key questions to continuously improve BSC information value.

Public Service Electric & Gas: Best Practice Case

The BSC has metrics that clearly link strategy to measurement. The BSC contains measures that include both financial and nonfinancial measures. Public Service Electric & Gas (PSE&G) level 1 corporate BSC contains measures across the four quadrants of its BSC People, Safe and reliable, Economic, and Green; each with five-year targets. Included in the target-setting process are five years of historical performance, a three-year average, five years of external benchmark history along with current performance, current benchmark data, and a five-year projected benchmark trend. All factors are used to determine where the target is to be set.

In 2002, former president Ralph Izzo (now CEO) built on the success he had in one of the business areas as a vice president, launched a similar approach, and expanded the use of the BSC across all the business areas in PSE&G.

He selected the five principles of a strategically focused organization to align and focus this leadership team. In July of that year, a series of discussions were held with senior leaders including vice presidents and directors. They reviewed the income statement and company strategy to identify 27 key drivers that affected performance. From that document a working group was formed to develop measures based upon the drivers.

The working group was comprised of members from each business area focused on an aggressive journey of developing measures for each of the 27 drivers. They identified 520 BSC measures in their first iteration, and then reduced it to 135, then to the 26 currently used as shown PSE&G BSC in Exhibit 6.10.

BSC results and methodology have been successfully used as a primary communication tool, not only to the board of directors, but also when speaking to state regulators, shareholders, employees, and the investment community. The BSC is shared with the board of directors on a monthly basis.

CASCADING BSCs, ALIGNMENT, AND INTEGRATION Coupled with this effort the organizational structure was aligned in a manner that clearly defined accountability and, for the first time, one set of measures was applied across the utility. Additional BSCs that supported the utility-level BSC were also produced and, in many cases, down to the functional level in a four-tier structure from holding company PSEG, PSE&G, BUs and divisions/departments. Efforts were also underway to translate strategy to day-to-day operations. By making strategy everyone's day-to-day job it allowed employees see how they contributed to the bottom line.

By the end of 2002 a fully integrated BSC was completed and the first utility-level BSC was published in January 2003. The publication of the BSC was further enhanced with data being presented using a variety of formats: tabular, graphical, and written. Monthly meetings were held to discuss results and to further reinforce the linkage between the BSC, day-to-day operations and achieving company strategy. A BSC intranet website, open to all PSE&G employees to view, was launched sharing how the business is performing. An employee can view performance either at the utility or business area level.

The PSE&G BSC is a roll-up and includes the business area contribution toward those roll-up results. It shows the individual business performance and aggregates each component to the overall company results. The measures are directly linked to the business strategy. Each business area has supporting BSCs that align with corporate BSC.

SUPPORT FUNCTIONS AND SUPPLIER BSCs Support units such as HR, IT, and finance ensure alignment with business unit and enterprise strategy. The support processes as defined above are part of the Services Company, a separate entity from PSE&G. The Services Company is part of Public Service Enterprise Group (the parent holding company). Enterprise is just beginning to implement the BSC and is currently aligning its strategies across the businesses. However, there are smaller support groups of this nature within PSE&G that are represented and included as part of the PSE&G BSC.

Employee Safety and Development National Top Decile	System Safety and Reliable Service National Top Quartile	Financial Return National Top Quartile	Environmentally Friendly National Top Quartile
People providing	• OSHA Recordable Rate • OSHA DAFW Rate • Total MV Accident Rate • **Staffing Levels** • **Employee Availability** • **Employee Development**		
Safe and reliable		• Frequency of Outages • Duration of Outages • Facility Damages • Gas Leak Rate • Emergency Response Rate • Inquiry Service Level • Perception Survey • Transactional Survey	
Economic			• Total CapEx • Total O&M • ROIC • Net Write-Off • Days Sales Outstanding • Capital Project Results
Green energy			• Renewable Energy Generated • Fleet MPG • Reduce Hazardous Waste • Recycle Non-Hazardous Waste

EXHIBIT 6.10 PSE&G Balanced Scorecard

Courtesy of Public Service Electric & Gas.

Supplier performance results are part of the lower level supporting BSCs that measure performance on the process levels.

The BSC has been in place for the past seven consecutive years. One of the most successful developments has been the integration of the BSC with both the benchmarking and business planning processes.

DATA RELIABILITY   Since PSE&G BSC results are directly linked to both the shared savings program for the unions and the performance incentive plan that for nonunion employees, data reliability, accuracy, and integrity are critical. The results are also used by the board of directors, shareholders, and investment groups. All the data collected are scrutinized and go through a thorough validation process. While each operating area is ultimately responsible for their data submittal, the PMG has specific controls built into the process to further validate the data that are submitted. PSE&G corporate internal auditing completed in December 2009 their full review of the BSC, target setting, and benchmarking process and data results with no significant weaknesses in the process or inconsistencies in the data results.

MEETING MANAGEMENT AND BUSINESS ANALYTICS   The current president of PSE&G, Ralph LaRossa, has built upon the BSC progress first launched by Ralph Izzo when he was president. Ralph LaRossa meets with his leadership team each month to discuss BSC results and to determine the impact on overall strategic performance. He then meets with each vice president, along with their direct reports, quarterly to review and discuss, in detail, the status of specific initiatives vital to the success of company strategy. In addition, he also meets with the union leadership on a quarterly basis to share results and to gain their insights and recommendations.

While PSE&G believes top leaders driving strategy execution is a vital attribute to success, it has fostered a culture in which leadership at all levels of the organization drives company strategy.

In addition, there is also a quarterly business outlook meeting of the top 100 leaders of the company, including union leaders. The presentations from these meetings are posted on the BSC intranet site and shared with all employees. This approach increases top-level visibility and commitment across the businesses, both vertically and horizontally, to drive the BSC as a tool to improve company performance and reinforce the business strategy to all employees. Included in all these meetings and discussions are external benchmarking comparisons. This continual external view of performance unites the individual departments of the business and gives them a broader perspective of company performance.

For example, during the meeting, measure analytic pages are presented and discussed in depth. Exhibit 6.11 is such a page for safety measure OSHA recordable incident rate that includes several key measure elements.

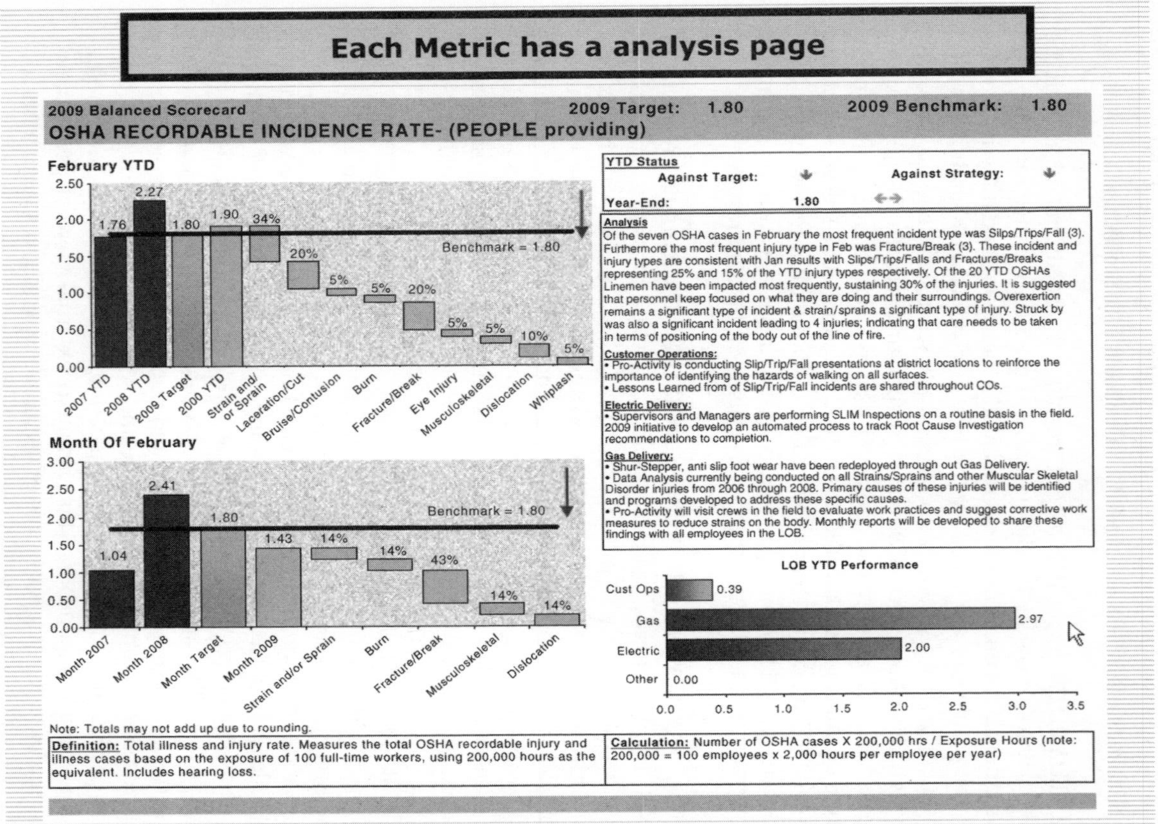

EXHIBIT 6.11 Balanced Scorecard Measure Analytics Page

Courtesy of Public Service Electric & Gas.

ALIGN INDIVIDUALS AND REWARDS AND RECOGNITION   Each executive is responsible for the execution of his or her operating plans including strategic initiatives. Compensation is directly impacted as a result of successful completion of the operating plans. Individual goals are measured through the performance partnership system in which employee individual or group goals have to be directly supporting products and services that align with the business strategy. Additionally, all employees, including union employees, are linked to the BSC through PSE&G Performance Incentive Plan (PIP).

The PIP payout is based and calculated on four sections:

1. (20 percent) EPS compared to a benchmark of peer companies
2. (20 percent) on operating company financial factor
3. (50 percent) operating company BSC performance
4. (10 percent) strategic initiatives

Part 3 operating company BSC performance (50 percent) above is further broken down into Parts A and B, each weighted at 50 percent.

- Part A is paid out if the metric is achieving performance that meets or is better than the strategic target of either top decile or quartile.
- Part B is achieving performance that is better than the previous year.

The rate of payout is based upon the specific pay grade of each employee. Each section has a multiplier performance target set at:

- 0.5 to 0.9 (worse than target)
- (at target)
- to 1.5 (better than target)

The PIP metrics are aligned to the strategy and also aligned throughout the levels of the company, so incentive metrics for an employee at the apprentice level are the same as for the president of the company. There are a few minor differences, but for the most part all employees are working toward the same end.. Employees are able to view quarterly performance results, including projected year-end results and expected incentive compensation, on the PSE&G intranet BSC website.

TARGET SETTING AND BENCHMARKING   PSE&G has a very mature and integrated benchmarking process used to identify performance gaps in metrics between current performance and desired benchmark performance. A business case is then prepared and a strategic decision is made to close the performance gap by dedicating required funds and needed resources to implement major improvements.

All measures across the four quadrants of the BSC (People providing, Safe and Reliable, Economic, and Green Energy) have five-year targets. The target setting template has been developed for the each of the business areas, and it incorporates a variety of data points beyond the traditional historical trend data that is used to set targets including:

- Three-year historical average
- Current year to date performance
- Current year-end projection
- Target performance that was placed into the five-year plan for the current year
- Current benchmark performance (either top decile or top quartile)
- Projected three- to five-year benchmarks

These factors are the basis for discussion in determining the proper level for setting the coming year target. PMG and individual business areas perform analyses of the data points and independently arrive at a proposed target along with the logic used to arrive at that figure. Discussions are held between the two groups and a joint proposed target is submitted to the president for review and approval. The use of external benchmarks has resulted in driving targets and actual performance to levels previously viewed as unattainable.

BSC SOFTWARE   PSE&G has developed an intricate process that coordinates, validates, and reports the results in an efficient and accurate manner each month. PMG leverages the intranet website to post and distribute BSC results throughout the entire company.

CORE AND INNOVATIVE BEST PRACTICES   PSE&G exercises the core best practices identified earlier and has advanced knowledge in this area with new, innovative best practices.

Principle 3: Cascade and Manage Strategy

- **Partner with business owners.** PMG partners with line and staff leadership team members to gain support and influence as partners to help them achieve results.
- **Develop level 1 BSC.** Translate strategy into level 1 BSC measures and measure targets at the highest organizational level.

- **Leverage proven BSC.** PMG leverages proven Kaplan & Norton BSC and design parameters, assigning one to two measures to each strategy map objective.
- **Cascade BSC to lower levels.** Cascade and align level 1 BSC to levels 2, 3, 4, and so on, depending on organizational and accountability structures.
- **Align support services.** Identify and define measures for all support services that align with levels 1 and below.
- **Align teams and individual employees.** Defines personal BSCs for teams and/or individuals that align with higher-level and support services' BSCs.
- **Link compensation.** Align rewards, recognition, and compensation programs to the BSC.
- **Manage using measures.** Manage BSC meetings to address the appropriate mix of strategic and operational issues; link these issues with Principle 4: Business Improvement.
- **Automate measurement.** Implement CPM software or intranet website to manage BSC program with links to other principles.
- **Innovative Best Practice.** PSE&G includes supplier performance results as part of the lower level supporting BSCs that measure performance on the process levels.
- **Innovative Best Practice.** PSE&G has developed a flexible BSC-based Performance Incentive Payout structure for both union and nonunion employees.
- **Innovative Best Practice.** PSE&G PMG not only verifies BSC information integrity, but also PSE&G corporate internal auditing completes a full review of the BSC data results, target setting, and benchmarking processes to verify there are no significant weaknesses in the process or inconsistencies in the data results.

Sharp HealthCare: Best Practice Case

As strategic context for measurement, in March 2007 the California Hospital Assessment and Reporting Task Force (CHART) launched CalHospitalCompare.org, a comprehensive, online report card that provides consumers with information about the quality of care provided by California hospitals in a number of clinical areas. More than 200 California hospitals—including Sharp HealthCare—are voluntarily participating in CalHospitalCompare.org. Most of the hospital systems and the majority of larger individual hospitals, representing more than 70 percent of all hospital admissions in the state, are included in the report card. CalHospitalCompare.org rates hospitals on

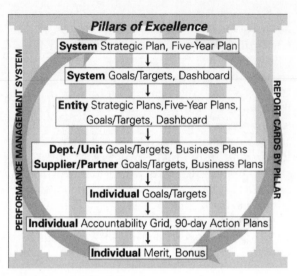

EXHIBIT 6.12 Strategy Deployment Process
Courtesy of Sharp HealthCare.

50 "performance indicators"—measurements that are commonly accepted as valid assessments of the quality of clinical care provided to patients. Cardiac care, maternity services, compliance with surgical infection standards, treatment for pneumonia, as well as patient satisfaction are among the yardsticks.

STRATEGY DEPLOYMENT AND MANAGEMENT   Sharp's strategy deployment process shown in Exhibit 6.12 provides for the alignment and integration of goals across all levels of the system from staff member to Sharp leader, department to entity, senior leader to entity, and entity to system.

Using the results of the annual environmental assessment and SWOT, entity and corporate planning teams develop strategies and action plans to support Sharp's goals by Pillar. Champions are assigned to each action plan by entity and corporate leadership teams to ensure progress toward goals. Champions and leadership teams develop action plans that include completion dates, results-driven targets, and, if appropriate, market share goals, volume projections, capital requirements, and human resource needs.

HOSPITAL SYSTEM REPORT CARD: LEVEL 1 CORPORATE   Sharp's Report Card is used to monitor the success of strategic initiatives. With the exception of quality measures that change from year to year to stimulate breakthrough improvement, the targets are broad measures of Pillar success. Accomplishment

EXHIBIT 6.13 Strategic Pillars and Measures of Success

Pillar/Measure Description	Improvement %/Measure of Success
Quality Pillar	
• Surgical Infection Prevention	9%
• ROMACC	170%
Service Pillar	
• Inpatient Satisfaction	>150%
• Medical Group Patient Satisfaction	>100%
• Physician Satisfaction	Top Quartile System wide
People Pillar	
• Employee Satisfaction	Exceeds Best in Class
• Employee Turnover	36%
Finance Pillar	
• EBITDA	80%
Growth Pillar	
• Net Revenue	68%
Community Pillar	
• Manager Hours of Community Service	>400%

Courtesy of Sharp Healthcare.

of Sharp's organizational strategy is demonstrated in Exhibit 6.13 in the year-over-year success of the system Report Card measures.

Each champion develops operational implementation and monitoring plans and mobilizes necessary resources and knowledge to ensure strategic objectives are achieved and sustained. The targets associated with action plan items provide the tool to monitor success and make rapid corrections when needed. Champions report progress on action plans to respective entity or corporate leaders. Quarterly, 90-day plans are developed and reviewed to ensure progress. Success and sustainability are monitored through ongoing measurement of key dashboard indicators.

CASCADING BALANCED SCORECARDS, ALIGNMENT, AND INTEGRATION Sharp's Report Cards and dashboard indicators measure and track monthly progress in achieving action plan goals. Entity Report Cards are aligned with the system's Report Card targets, while taking into account the unique aspects of each operating entity. Managers incorporate the entity and system Report

Card and dashboard indicator targets into their annual management goal-setting process by establishing department-specific targets in concert with their supervisors.

PROCESS-LEVEL PERFORMANCE MEASUREMENT Performance measures that monitor operations and other priorities are identified by breaking down key work processes into subprocesses and then associating indicators that reflect the process' performance. For example, the reconciliation completion indicator is associated with the medication reconciliation subprocess within the discharge work process. Indicators for key processes are aligned by Pillar and tracked and trended on Pillar-specific dashboards. Dashboard indicators are reviewed weekly, monthly, quarterly, or annually depending upon the nature of the data and the need for an agile response. Sharp's key work process requirements and measures are listed in Exhibit 6.14. The key work processes comprise the essential elements of the product Sharp delivers, health care, along with business and support processes required to provide health care. How Sharp delivers this product is determined by its core competency. The Sharp Experience drives the cultural environment, priority setting, strategic execution, and structure for evaluation of success across the Pillars. Integration across the partner and regulatory feedback uses listening and learning tools as well as best practices and benchmark performance.

Gaps in performance measures drive decisions about where to focus PI efforts through the PI process. In this process, finding innovative solutions is a top priority and systematically achieved through the DMAIC problem-solving process described in Chapter 7.

COMPARATIVE DATA RESEARCH: TARGET SETTING AND BENCHMARKING Sharp uses a systematic approach, comparative data selection process in selecting comparative data sources to determine the appropriate targets for Report Card indicators and other performance indicators.

When a performance measure is identified, evidence-based literature, regulatory organizations, health care and non–health care organizations, competitors, and Baldrige winners are examined. If an optimal comparative database exists, it is evaluated for size, validity, reliability, organization/service type, usability, and cost. When no relevant comparative data exist, comparison is made between Sharp entities and departments and/or between historical and current performance. Common external comparative data sources for each Pillar are listed in Exhibit 6.15.

Executive steering and the accountability team collaborate to determine aggressive targets. Targets are set at the top comparable performance metric, as applicable and available, to achieve Sharp's vision of becoming the best. Comparative analyses by disease states are accomplished through Sharp's

EXHIBIT 6.14 Sharp Key Process Requirements and Measures

Manage Health Care		
Process	**Key Requirements**	**Process Measures**
Screening	Safe, timely	Blood sugar, cholesterol, cancer screening, and glucose levels
Admission/ registration	Safe, timely	Patient satisfaction, accredited, privacy, and door to doctor
Assessment and diagnosis	Safe, evidenced-based, efficient, timely	Patient satisfaction, skin care, Stroke care
Treatment	Safe, evidence-based, efficient, timely, patient-centered, equitable	Glycemic control, AMI (heart attack), beta blockers, CAP antibiotics, cancer, treatment measures
Discharge/ education	Safe, patient-centered, timely	AHRQ patient safety, AMI mortality, bariatric program, smoking cessation
Manage Business and Support		
Process	**Key Requirements**	**Process Measures**
Revenue cycle	Timely, accurate	EBITDA, days in AR, billing cost, payment
Strategic planning	Timely, accurate	Net revenue, market share, growth
Knowledge management	Timely, safe, and accurate	Internal promotion, training expenditure, out of network, critical values
Supply chain management	Timely, accurate, efficient, safe	Pharmacy turnaround, sales outstanding, and automated orders
Key suppliers and partners management	Efficient, accurate, timely satisfaction	Provider survey and denials

Courtesy of Sharp HealthCare.

EXHIBIT 6.15 External Data Comparative Sources

Pillar	External Comparative Data Source
Quality	AHRO, CHART, CMS, NCI, STS, Vermont Oxford
Service	Press Ganey (service company)
People	HR Solutions
Finance	Standard & Poor's, BBB+ rated facilities
Growth	Region Public Data
Community	Region Government Data

Courtesy of Sharp HealthCare.

MedAI subscription, which uses inferential statistics to compare clinical outcomes with national benchmarks. Evidence-based standards of care are used to set clinical targets. Sharp has a culture of innovation and continuous improvement that is systematically supported by the DMAIC process. Other industries are often examined to find translatable solutions; for example, the team resource management curriculum was adopted from the aviation industry, and the LSS performance improvement strategy and tool set was adopted from the automotive manufacturing industry. Sharp also engages its suppliers, collaborators, legislators, brokers, and payors on the challenges and opportunities in the health care industry and collaborates on innovative solutions by hosting semi-annual educational sessions. Additionally, innovative solutions are discovered through the attendance of local and national conferences by Sharp.

Annual targets are set based on Sharp's performance as compared to benchmarks, peers and competitors, while considering the unique aspects of the organizations within Sharp's market. When available, Sharp sets targets based upon a percentile ranking to ensure continual improvement to best-in-class levels. If percentile rankings do not exist, targets are set to applicable benchmarks, with specific thought to competitor positions. Sharp has defined Report Card targets for year-end at the system and entity level, as well as five-year and vision attainment targets for the system. Best-of-class comparison information is shown for each Report Card indicator where available, as well as a description of the benchmark source. Sharp's historical Report Card performance for fiscal 2002 through 2006 compared to baseline and Sharp's annual goals under each Pillar are available for review onsite, as are competitor assessments. Sharp has made significant improvements in all of its Pillar goals. As performance gaps are identified, Sharp leaders prepare strategies and action plans to improve Sharp's position and further its journey to become the best place to work, best place to practice medicine, and best place to receive care.

CHANGE CONTROL, CONTINUOUS IMPROVEMENT The board, executive steering, entity leaders, suppliers, partners, and collaborators assist in the continuous evaluation of the performance measures for relevance and sensitivity. When metrics are no longer relevant, they are retired. The sensitivity of the performance measurement system is achieved by using a combination of leading, real-time, and lagging indicators. For example, real time status of medication reconciliation was determined to be a patient safety priority by Sharp leaders; therefore, an electronic data entry system was developed collaboratively with nursing, physicians, CDS, and LSS. Now, users have real-time feedback to support their decision making. Relevance with health care service needs is achieved by using listening and learning tools. On an annual basis, the accountability team obtains examples of dashboard reports from recognized health care systems and uses best practice findings (such as those published by The Advisory Board) to review the continued relevance and strength of Sharp's Report Card measures.

MEETING MANAGEMENT, BUSINESS ANALYTICS, PERFORMANCE ANALYSIS, AND REVIEW The performance measurement system describes the process for reviewing organizational performance and capabilities. As described earlier the strategic deployment process determines the structure so that key performance measures and progress relative to report cards and action plans are systematically reviewed throughout the organization by the board, executive steering, entity leaders, employees, suppliers, partners and collaborators, and integrated across the system. Numerous forums including board meetings, LDS, quality councils, and employee forums support the propagation of these performance measures via Sharp's communication plan. The review of key performance measures and other performance measures to monitor operations and priorities at all levels of the organization creates alignment of priorities and drives decision making about resource management and prioritization of process improvement efforts. Executive steering meetings, entity leadership meetings, and other forums are held, such as quality councils and LSS Report Outs about the organization's ability to respond rapidly to identified gaps and changing organizational needs and challenges. When organizational needs change or performance trends demand mid-course correction, priorities are continuously reevaluated by senior leaders. When targets are exceeded, results are celebrated to ensure changes endure. Descriptive and inferential statistical analyses are performed to ensure appropriate interpretation of performance measurement data to support decision making.

SUPPLIER SCORECARD   Key supplier performance metrics and supply chain benchmarking is conducted via the Premier Supply Focus Scorecard, which provides performance indicator comparisons of hundreds of peer hospitals. As outlier indicators are identified, research is conducted to isolate and reduce variability. Results are discussed with each entity's CFO and materiel manager, and action plans are developed. The process for translating performance review findings into continuous and breakthrough improvement and innovation is accomplished through the PI prioritization process and will be discussed in Chapter 7.

ALIGN INDIVIDUALS AND REWARDS AND RECOGNITION   Targets are incorporated in managers' job performance goals for the year. Annual management evaluations occur in November and are fully aligned with Sharp's Pillars. The management merit system is results-driven, in that 100 percent of a manager's merit pay is based on goal attainment. Additionally, management is held accountable to entity and system Report Card results through Sharp's annual incentive system. Quarterly, managers develop 90-day action plans in support of department, entity, and system goals. Staff is held accountable to Report Card and dashboard indicator targets that relate to its respective area of responsibility. Annual goals, which align with department, entity, and system targets, are established for all staff members by the employee and his or her supervisor. Goal attainment represents a percentage of an employee's annual merit raise. Staff also are evaluated on performance relative to Sharp's 12 Behavior Standards, which also comprise a percentage of an employee's annual merit raise. Key vendors are held accountable to Report Card and dashboard indicators, as applicable to the services provided.

BSC DATA COLLECTION AND REPORTING   The strategic planning development and deployment processes determine key performance measures within the *Performance Measurement System.*

Common enterprise information systems including clinical, financial, human resource, and supply chain systems enable the collection of data and information to support daily operations and organizational decision making. Electronic data collection is used whenever available. However, if specific process inputs or in-process metrics are not available electronically, those data may be collected manually through 16 chart review, check sheets, or direct observation. Data are aggregated at the unit, department, entity, and system level. Data are segmented according to factors determined to be contributing to variation in the process. The clinical decision support and financial decision support departments clean up, aggregate, segment, statistically analyze, and evaluate data against targets on a monthly, quarterly, and annual basis. Results are presented in easy-to-read, color-coded formats, highlighting key findings and significant variances. Results are regularly published on SharpNet and disseminated in multiple formats via Sharp's communication plan. Progress is tracked and shared, and achievements and learnings are recognized and deployed across the system. The boards, executive steering, entity leadership, quality councils, managers, suppliers, partners, and collaborators review the Report Cards and other pertinent dashboards, which provide a common, measurable focus to monitor action plan progress, gauge success, and empower decision making for continued alignment with strategic goals, the mission, and the vision.

Sharp continuously improves the IT infrastructure and processes to measure performance and manage knowledge. Sharp has a single network and standardized IT products across the system. Sharp is recognized as one of only nine health care organizations to receive the 100 Most Wired awards for nine consecutive years.

CORE AND INNOVATIVE BEST PRACTICES Sharp exercises the core best practices identified earlier; it has advanced knowledge in this area with new, innovative best practices.

Principle 3: Cascade and Manage Strategy

- **Partner with business owners.** Partner with line and staff leadership team members to gain support and influence as partners to help them achieve results.
- **Develop level 1 BSC.** Translate strategy into level 1 BSC measures and measure targets at the highest organizational level.
- **Leverage proven BSC or comparable method.** Observe BSC or comparable design parameters, assigning one to two measures to each strategy map objective.
- **Cascade BSC to lower levels.** Cascade and align level 1 BSC to levels 2, 3, 4, and so on, depending on organizational and accountability structures.
- **Align support services.** Identify and define measures for all support services that align with levels 1 and below.
- **Align teams and individual employees.** Define personal BSCs for teams and/or individuals that align with higher-level and support services' Balanced Scorecards.
- **Link compensation.** Align rewards, recognition, and compensation programs to the Balanced Scorecard.

- **Manage using measures.** Manage BSC meetings to address the appropriate mix of strategic and operational issues; link these issues with Principle 4: Business Improvement.
- **Automate measurement.** Implement CPM software to manage BSC program with links to other principles.
- **Innovative Best Practice.** Sharp extends its performance model outside "horizontally" through voluntarily participating in consortia group that rates hospitals on 50 "performance indicators" or measurements that are commonly accepted as valid assessments of the quality of clinical care provided to patients.
- **Innovative Best Practice.** Sharp extends its performance model "upstream" and uses supplier scorecards to evaluate and manage their performance.
- **Innovative Best Practice.** Sharp recognizes the value of identifying leading indicators in its processes and has defined requirements and measures for both core and support processes. This enables longer lead times to resolve issues that would later impact lagging measures of customer satisfaction and financial results.
- **Innovative Best Practice.** Sharp uses a systematic approach in selecting comparative data sources to determine the appropriate measures and targets for Report Card indicators and other performance indicators.

CHAPTER 7

Principle 4: Improve Performance

*Major failures in business come not so much from unmet goals, as
from lack of response to unforeseen changes.*

— O. L. Duff

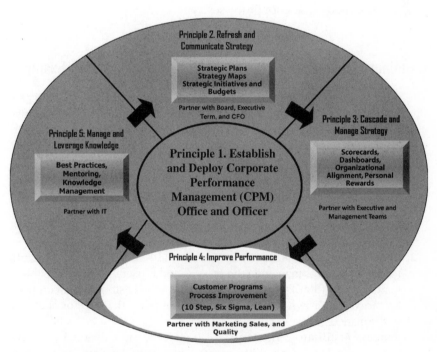

Principle 4, Improve Performance, focuses on improving customer and competitor intelligence and business improvement processes. In concert with Principle 3, if your balanced scorecard (BSC) indicates underperformance, then it would be incumbent on you to launch an initiative to improve performance. Principle 4 business improvement teams provide best practices and innovations for inclusion in Principle 5, Manage and Leverage Knowledge, discussed in the next chapter.

CPM Core Process Blueprint and Key Process Roles

Careful research of the cases in this book reveals they follow a discernible set of core corporate performance management (CPM) processes organized within the Five Key Principles. These CPM processes, arrayed in Exhibit 3.1, provide strategic context and a working framework to assist you in your organization. Note that Principle 4, Improve Performance consists of three consistent CPM processes, though some organizations have expanded beyond these core processes.

Customer and Competitor Survey and Intelligence Process Example

The CPM office members play one or more of three key roles in executing the CPM core processes with the fourth, participants. We will discuss *customer and competitor survey intelligence process* roles my CPM office deployed at award-winning Crown Castle International to illustrate the roles:

1. **Process Sponsor.** The sponsor is typically the most senior executive accountable for the process outcomes and for overseeing the process owner. The process sponsor for the customer and competitor intelligence process at Crown was each country president, United States, United Kingdom, and Australia.
2. **Process Owner.** The owner is typically the senior leader accountable to the sponsor for managing the process and is usually a process subject matter expert (SME). The process owner for the customer and competitor process at Crown was one of my direct reports, the director of global performance.
3. **Process Facilitator.** The facilitator is typically the individual who day to day interacts directly with process participants to drive the process and integrate the process with other key processes. The process facilitator of the Crown customer and competitor intelligence process was my direct report, the director of global performance.

4. **Process Participant.** The process participants are typically SMEs, those who will be accountable for the process outcomes and/or are the recipients of the process outcomes. The process participants in the Crown customer and competitor intelligence process were the U.S. vice president of marketing, the U.K. director of marketing, and the Australian managing director; their respective staff organizations; numerous customers; and, quite literally, competitors.

Prior to turning our attention toward the in-depth cases, let us review the core best practices recognized by all the case companies in this book. See each case that follows for their innovative new best practice, so you can appreciate the context and relevance of them to their organizations.

Principle 4: Improve Business Core Best Practices

- **Prioritize improvement projects.** Identify and prioritize strategic and operational initiatives projects to improve organization's performance along financial, customer or constituent, process, and people dimensions.
- **Leverage customer facing processes.** Develop and exercise customer and constituent facing processes to understand and recalibrate processes around changing customer needs. Gather customer and competitor intelligence using regular customer surveys, focus groups, call centers, and related methods and approaches. Leverage process improvement methods.
- **Leverage process improvement methods.** Design and maintain an ongoing process improvement methods and problem-solving to identify and eliminate root causes of issues.
- **Realize value from benchmarking.** Leverage benchmarking and comparative methods to identify and regularly improve core and support processes.
- **Create a performance culture.** Create a virtual community of practitioners to coordinate initiative completion.

Cargill Corn Milling North America: Best Practice Case

CCM leverages its customer processes to secure, track, and trend customer satisfaction and requirements. These customer processes in turn provide insight and requirements for innovations to processes for sustainable improvements.

CUSTOMER AND MARKET KNOWLEDGE

Customer Segmentation The Cargill Corn Milling (CCM) value of Expand Customer Focus is demonstrated in the delivery of products, services, and unique customer solutions in the food, feed, and fermentation market segments. These three market segments and ten product lines serve a diverse customer base of over 3,000 customers with a thousand product shipments each day. Because of this diversity, each product line's approach to customer segmentation is adapted to fit its specific industry.

Customer segmentation for the corn sweeteners product line adds objectivity to the customer segmentation process. The customer segmentation matrix includes all existing sweetener customers, customers of competitors, and potential customers. Every customer and potential customer is evaluated based on four major categories: (1) sweetener portfolio, (2) corporate culture, (3) complexity, and (4) financial. Each major category is further subdivided into subcategories. Each customer is ranked from one (low) to five (high) for each subcategory based on historical data, EDT analysis, and the sales group's experience with the customer. These rankings allow CCM to sort, analyze, and report the matrix information for decision making. This provides direction on where to focus resources with regard to existing customers, competitors' customers, and potential customers.

Listening and Learning to Determine Key Customer Requirements and Innovations
The CCM leadership system addresses the delivery of customer value through the key work process of *Manage Customer Service*. With this key work process, listening and learning methods are closely linked to strategy process in order to effectively translate the voice of the customer into strategies and actions that will create distinctive value. As input to the SR process, CCM utilizes a variety of methods to listen and learn and determine the relative importance of key customer requirements and expectations. Sales and customer service personnel interact with the customers daily to determine the most appropriate approaches for listening and learning as well as ways to improve these methods. CCM uses primary and secondary methods to obtain customer information pertaining to product, service, and delivery requirements, competitive factors, strategic direction, future requirements, and relative importance of purchasing decisions resulting in value-sharing opportunities. Exhibit 7.1 defines customer listening and learning processes.

CCM serves customers and markets in three markets segments: food, feed, and fermentation. Listening and learning methods have common elements as well as distinct approaches that are appropriate for each of the segments. Common elements include dedicated sales resources led by product line leaders. The feed product line utilizes these common approaches

EXHIBIT 7.1 Listening and Learning Mechanisms

KEY LISTENING METHODS	Product Requirements	Service Requirements	Delivery Requirements	Competitive Factors	Strategic Direction	Future Requirements	Relative Importance of Purchasing Decision	When?	How requirements are deployed?	Who uses the data?	How data are used?
Direct Sales Contact	P	P	S	P	P	P	P	Varies Based on Customer	Call Reports. MasterCard updates; Specific communication to plants. 95% Sure List. Contracts	Commercial Operations, Product Line Leaders, QA, Operations, Credit	Planning products and services, marketing, and new business opportunity
Customer Service Rep Contact	P	P	P	S	N	S	N	Daily/Weekly	Procedure changes, MasterCard Update	Operations, QA, Commercial Operations, Credit	Planning products and services, making process improvements, issue resolution
Technical Service and R&D Contact	S	S	S	P	S	P	P	Project Basis	Contact Report and Master Report	Sales Management, Product Line Leaders	Strategic planning, sales strategy, evaluate new products

(Continued)

EXHIBIT 7.1 (Continued)

KEY LISTENING METHODS	Product Requirements	Service Requirements	Delivery Requirements	Competitive Factors	Strategic Direction	Future Requirements	Relative Importance of Purchasing Decision	When?	How requirements are deployed?	Who uses the data?	How data are used?
Expert Panels	N	N	N	P	P	P	P	Product Basis	Strategic and Business Plans	Product Line Leaders, Sales	Strategic direction and future direction
Customer Audits	P	P	P	N	N	N	N	Based on Customer	Audit Feedback Report, Verbal Communication	Operations, QA, Commercial Operations	Planning products and services

P-Primary way to gather info   S-Secondary way to gather info   N-Not a source

Courtesy of Cargill Corn Milling.

264

along with the distinct approach of employing scientists to interact with the customers' technical counterparts in the animal nutrition industries.

Customer touch points occur at all levels of the organization and are key to listening and learning about customer requirements and expectations. This process is used by CCM to promote customer interaction at all levels of the organization. Processes are used to collect and transfer data from these interactions. For example, senior leadership team members regularly visit key customers. Corporate account leaders are instrumental in gathering and interpreting data and information regarding the customer's industry. CCM invites customers to its facilities to share information regarding their business with its employees. CCM's technical department and research and development group interact with customers to develop new formulations and new products. Customer audits of the manufacturing facilities and terminals are important methods of learning about customers' expectations and requirements. Product lines commonly host annual customer appreciation events for the key customers, focused on thanking customers for their business and exchanging ideas.

Voice-of-the-Customer CCM uses the core competencies of technical support and supply chain management to drive the development of innovative solutions and create distinctive value with voice-of-the-customer ideas and suggestions. Being customer focused by providing innovative solutions to customers has resulted in a number of customer awards.

Keeping Listening and Learning Methods Current with Business Direction During the annual business planning (ABP) process, quarterly business reviews, and sales and product line meetings, the senior leadership team and product line leaders evaluate and improve listening and learning methods based on voice-of-the-customer data and employee suggestions. These review processes have led to multiple improvements in CCM listening and learning methods and resources.

Direct Sales Contact As the business strategy shifted and CCM recognized the opportunity to diversify into new markets such as branded feed and fermentation, CCM's need for specialized knowledge increased. Based on these new business needs and directions, CCM hired direct sales specialists including technical experts enabling effective communication, learning, and understanding of customers' needs in these highly technical markets. CCM collaborated with other Cargill food ingredient and systems business units to develop a go-to-market strategy to enhance the overall customer experience. In addition, CCM has hired experts from the feed, sugar, fermentation, biofuels, and corn sweetener industries to augment the market knowledge and provide customer insight.

Customer Service Rep Contact   In 2001, the customer service department was restructured to put more focus on the customer. The new customer service team provided an enterprisewide focus and systematic approach for listening to customer concerns, handling complaints, and utilizing processes such as root cause analysis and process development groups to increase learning and sharing across the enterprise. Previously, this process was more plant level and internally focused. In 2005, the CCM supply chain department was reorganized to align customer service representatives, logistics, and terminal operations with the direct sales group to improve efficiencies based on geographic regions of the country. In 2007, CCM centralized sweetener customer service to make it easier for customers to do business with CCM.

Technical Service and Research and Development Contact   Technical service refinements are focused on improving the learning from customer contact and sharing the knowledge gained across the business unit and across the Cargill food ingredient and systems platform in a more systematic process. A new process called Project Portfolio Management organizes and prioritizes customer-driven opportunities for all business units within the Cargill food ingredient and systems platform, including CCM. This approach enables greater collaboration and supports the development of more complex solutions to create distinctive value for the customer. In addition, a new training process is focused on equipping technical service personnel with a breadth of information about Cargill products, services, applications, and contact information to provide a more complete answer in addressing customer concerns.

BUILDING CUSTOMER RELATIONSHIPS   The CCM purpose, "To be the partner of choice of the customers it serves," is achieved through building relationships with the products, services, and customized solutions offered to its customers. The senior leadership team has structured the organization and designed processes to deliver distinctive value for customers in the food, feed, and fermentation market segments. Recent additions to the CCM product line structure, namely dry corn ingredients, sugar, and acidulants, along with greater collaboration with other business units, such as the ethanol producer services alliance, have further strengthened relationships with existing customers through a broad portfolio of product offerings. The CCM approach can be characterized as deploying customer-focused people with the right skill sets and technical knowledge to interact directly with the target customer's organization to build relationships and develop business insight. This approach is repeated at all levels. For example, the CCM president and product line leaders make direct customer contact a priority by spending time with customers at sales meetings and industry conferences and hosting customers. The senior leadership team, on average, spends

25 percent of their time visiting customers. Product line leaders and the sales force are responsible for this ongoing relationship-building process with customers. The senior leadership team developed a structure to support the ten unique product lines.

KEY ACCESS MECHANISMS   CCM customers have various access mechanisms to select from based on need and expectations in order to seek information and conduct business.

Customer service reps (CSR) use a customer set-up process with new customers to identify preferred key access mechanisms. The steps of this process include the following: (1) Sales submits a new customer to the CSR; (2) CSR contacts customer to verify requirements, expectations, and preferred access mechanism; and (3) customer requirements are entered into the MasterCard system. The MasterCard system is used to communicate expectations to all personnel involved in customer contact. Employees are trained on how to locate customer information, resolve customer issues, and whom to contact in the customer's organization based on particular customer issues. To ensure that customer information is current, the Master-Card system automatically prompts the CSR to verify requirements annually. Key access mechanism requirements are reviewed when customer requirements change or when a new access mechanism is added or enhanced. For example, electronic data interchange (EDI) enhancements were added in 2007 to allow for a broader deployment of the EDI mechanism to CCM customers, resulting in less manual intervention in the ordering process. The CCM access mechanisms are reviewed annually during the annual business planning process.

Customer Complaint Process   CCM uses a customer relationship tracking (CRT) system for managing customer complaints. The basic steps are to record the incident, investigate, identify, review, and implement correction actions. Throughout the complaint process CCM contacts the customer to seek information and verify that the corrective action was effective. Complaint information, corrective action investigations, and customer information are tracked in the CRT system.

All incidents must be entered into the CRT system within 24 hours of notification to raise awareness of potential failures within CCM. If the incident is a rejection or repeat failure requiring a root cause analysis, the process must be initiated within 24 hours of notification. The system allows CCM to review data by times, types of nonconformances, product, customer, location, department, or functional area. Any nonconformance is classified into one of three categories: customer incidents, complaints, and rejections. Customer incidents occur when CCM proactively alerts the customer of a potential nonconformance (i.e., potential late delivery). The data in the

CRT system are used to aggregate and analyze customer nonconformances through a key metric called the Customer Quality Index. This is a weighted index based on customer incidents, complaints, rejections, and total shipments, and is a useful metric for trend analysis and comparison of product line and plant performance. The Customer Quality Index and total rejections are aggregated daily by facility, product line, and business unit and compiled as monthly measures on the CCM BSC. Prioritizing issues, using root cause analysis to identify causes, and implementing effective solutions enables CCM to minimize customer dissatisfaction. Since the CRT system was introduced in 1999, numerous improvements have been made. For example, in 2004 the CRT system was modified to include the Carrier Rating Index to measure and track shipment performance. In 2007, a new Web-based reporting system was implemented.

Keeping Relationship-Building Approaches Current   The food, feed, and fermentation market segments represent dynamic industries with growing customer needs. Product line leaders are responsible for ensuring that their approaches are effective in building successful customer relationships. In 1999, the senior leadership team transformed CCM from an individual facility design to an enterprise design to improve service and relationships with customers. Subsequently, customer service and the supply chain were reengineered to address the enterprise approach. In 2004, CCM and other Cargill food ingredient and systems business units embarked on a major strategic initiative called "Go to Market." This initiative addressed consolidation in the food market segment and the need to take costs out of the system while maintaining quality and service. CCM could create synergy among other business units in the development of customer relationships that enable it to more effectively collaborate and create complex customer solutions. In 2007, this initiative further led to the centralization of CCM's sweetener customer service in Eddyville, Iowa.

Customer Satisfaction, Dissatisfaction, and Loyalty   CCM considers customer retention and loyalty with key customers as the most important customer satisfaction measures. CCM invests resources in direct customer contact; as a result, its primary method to evaluate customer satisfaction is through direct daily dialogue with customers. Sales personnel communicate regularly and directly with key customer personnel. In addition, CSRs facilitate direct communication among the appropriate quality assurance (QA), technical service, operations, and purchasing personnel. The result is communication at multiple levels and functions with key customer organizations. This communication and resulting information is used throughout the organization to identify and remove barriers to customer satisfaction and loyalty and improve both service and product quality. For example, technical service representatives compile a monthly report on their customer activities. These reports are consolidated into a master report of customer activities and issues. The resulting master report identifies common themes for improving the customer experience with products.

Likewise, the branded feed team conducts daily conference calls involving multiple functions to discuss any outstanding customer incidents, operational challenges, and any business change that may impact the ability to deliver to the customer. To gain further insight into customer satisfaction, dissatisfaction, and loyalty, CCM deployed a Customer Engagement Survey across the food businesses in 2008. Customer satisfaction is tracked using the customer relationship tracking system and measured by the Customer Quality Index. This system is deployed across all product lines and all customers. Through ad hoc problem-solving teams and CRT review teams, using processes such as root cause analysis, they identify and implement effective solutions to address the causes of customer dissatisfaction. Some large customers provide performance information from their viewpoint. These measures provide customer satisfaction information. In 2007, CCM received several major customer recognition awards supporting the relationship-building, satisfaction, and loyalty processes. Product line leaders use customer satisfaction and dissatisfaction data and information in the ABP process and include goals and improvement initiatives in their annual business plans.

Follow-Up with Customers on Product, Services, and Transactions The CCM key work process of Manage Quality requires feedback from customers to assure requirements and expectations are being met. Customer feedback is obtained during customer visits and discussions regarding order or delivery opportunities. Sales and CSRs communicate customer feedback to the appropriate personnel to drive discussions and foster continuous process improvement. CCM's customers receive feedback within 24 hours regarding corrective action to a concern or complaint. A customer delivery assessment process is utilized to seek opportunities and solutions with existing truck customers. This process is owned by the commercial operations manager and utilizes cross-functional teams consisting of operations, QA, and commercial operations personnel to address multiple contact points with the customer. Delivery assessments are performed at customer locations upon first deliveries or where there were delivery problems, as appropriate.

CUSTOMER SATISFACTION AND COMPETITIVE INTELLIGENCE CCM obtains comparative satisfaction information for its business and competitors through close working relationships with customers at multiple levels, supported by frequent face-to-face meetings. Comparative data and information on customer satisfaction are evaluated with opportunities identified for improvement. If it is determined short-term action is needed, a cross-functional ad hoc team is formed to address the issue. If a long-term approach is required, the opportunity is included in the annual product line business plan. Analysis of results from CCM's Customer Engagement Survey will provide additional insight for competitive benchmarking, identifying key drivers of value and how CCM compares to competition. CCM engages with customers at an intimate working level daily. Product line leaders are responsible for ensuring that CCM is listening to the voice of the customers in their markets and making necessary changes as part of their annual business plans.

The following sections link prior customer processes to ongoing process improvement methods and processes to improve the business performance and achieve key outcomes.

PROCESS MANAGEMENT AND CORE COMPETENCIES Core competencies are reviewed during the annual strategy review process. The EDT and senior leadership team perform a capability inventory assessment in the three market segments (food, feed, and fermentation) to identify critical knowledge, assets, people, and technology factors that influence the ability to fulfill the mission of creating distinctive value. The senior leadership team further analyzes these factors and utilizes a three-dimension core competency scoring matrix to determine the core competencies of the business unit.

Each key process has a SMT owner, who reviews the process annually and determines whether CCM has the internal capability to meet the process requirements. CCM's strategy drives the creation of new processes, which may require specific expertise not available within CCM. For example, in the key work process *Manage Idea and Concept Generation*, CCM utilized an external resource to help create the innovation process and to provide a database for tracking innovative ideas. After its implementation CCM internalized all aspects of this profitability key work process for creation of distinctive value.

BEST PRACTICE MODEL DISCIPLINED APPROACH TO PROCESS IMPROVEMENT
CCM has developed the best practice model (BPM) to innovate work processes to meet key requirements. The BPM includes the key steps and the requirements for each step (see Exhibit 7.2).

This process is owned by the senior leadership team and deployed by process development group leaders and is used to design processes and modify processes for efficiency, effectiveness, agility, and cost control improvements. As illustrated in the final step in Exhibit 7.2, the management of change process is used to ensure product quality; implementation of new technology; service, safety, food safety, consistency, reliability and environmental protection are built into each process design or refinement. In the

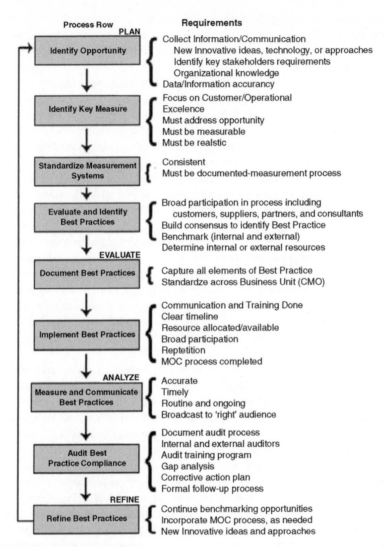

Process Row

PLAN

Requirements

Identify Opportunity
- Collect Information/Communication
  - New Innovative ideas, technology, or approaches
  - Identify key stakeholders requirements
  - Organizational knowledge
- Data/Information accurancy

Identify Key Measure
- Focus on Customer/Operational Excelence
- Must address opportunity
- Must be measurable
- Must be realstic

Standardize Measurement Systems
- Consistent
- Must be documented-measurement process

Evaluate and Identify Best Practices
- Broad participation in process including customers, suppliers, partners, and consultants
- Build consensus to identify Best Practice
- Benchmark (internal and external)
- Determine internal or external resources

EVALUATE

Document Best Practices
- Capture all elements of Best Practice
- Standardze across Business Unit (CMO)

Implement Best Practices
- Communication and Training Done
- Clear timeline
- Resource allocated/available
- Broad participation
- Reptetition
- MOC process completed

ANALYZE

Measure and Communicate Best Practices
- Accurate
- Timely
- Routine and ongoing
- Broadcast to 'right' audience

Audit Best Practice Compliance
- Document audit process
- Internal and external auditors
- Audit training program
- Gap analysis
- Corrective action plan
- Formal follow-up process

REFINE

Refine Best Practices
- Continue benchmarking opportunities
- Incorporate MOC process, as needed
- New Innovative ideas and approaches

EXHIBIT 7.2 Best Practice Model
Courtesy of Cargill Corn Milling.

same step of the model, new and *innovative* ideas and approaches initiate a refinement cycle for the process. The use of new technology and organizational knowledge is incorporated into several steps of the BPM either directly or through the management of change process. For example, in 2006 CCM innovated the key sustainability work process *Manage Corn &*

Energy Risk by creating the customer relationship management system for improving interactions with farmers followed the best practice process and was developed as a result of changing requirements from employee and farmer stakeholders.

For new work processes standard operating procedures (SOPs) are created and used for training employees. Modifications to work processes require updating SOPs and training employees affected in the new procedures and requirements. Process owners are responsible for maintaining SOPs. Key process measures are identified to control and monitor processes. Methods used for the implementation of new or modified work processes include pilot testing or parallel processing. For example, in 2003 CCM started a total cost of ownership implementation process as part of the manage IT services key work process. Total cost of ownership is an initiative to lower cost by standardizing computer hardware and software. Measures are defined for all key work processes and are used for control and improvement. Process owners monitor key work process performance measures on a routine basis (daily, weekly, or monthly). In addition, product line, functional area, and operations personnel routinely monitor in-process measures hourly, daily, weekly, or monthly based on the cycle time of data. For example, quality testing in the manage quality key work process occurs in-line, in the production areas, and in the laboratory depending on the cycle time needed to control quality and process parameters.

The process quality database system is used to track and monitor quality attributes the distributed control system does not monitor. The distributed control system monitors real-time processing data such as flow rates, temperatures, and pressures. Operators use these in-process measures to monitor and control the process to ensure product quality and quantities meet requirements. Deviations from expected results in all processes are addressed through standard operation procedures and through the development of action plans. Root cause analysis is used to create action plans addressing rejections, lost-time accidents, environmental incidents, significant property damage, and major maintenance repairs or repeat issues. For example, an in-process measure for the key profitability works process *Manage Manufacturing Strategy* is a behavioral-based safety process index. This metric is a leading indicator of safety performance measured by the safety index. Customer, supplier, and partner input are gathered using the listening and learning mechanisms. Process owners are responsible for monitoring and evaluating this information and for keeping the process current with the needs of the business. Process owners communicate changes in requirements with stakeholders, as appropriate. These requirement changes can result in utilization of the BPM to develop new or improved processes. Pilot processes utilize customer feedback in the design stages to ensure customer requirements are achieved.

Continuous Improvement: Reducing Unnecessary Process Steps   The follow represent numerous approaches to reducing unnecessary process steps.

- Process development groups, in conjunction with the quality assurance
  department, review testing and inspection frequencies to determine
  where they can be reduced or eliminated. These reviews are completed at least once per year in all operational areas and occur more
  frequently when opportunities are identified by the process development groups. Additional in-line instrumentation, capability studies, and
  improved process control logic in the distributed control system are
  examples of refinements that have reduced inspection cost efforts. In
  addition, the preferred supplier process has allowed the company to
  reduce inbound testing of chemicals and processing aids. CCM prevents
  defects and service errors, minimizes warranty costs, and reduces customer productivity losses primarily through process design and process
  refinements made using the BPM, through standard operating procedures as well as prevention-based processes including: use of predictive
  maintenance technologies to identify potential equipment problems and
  to plan and schedule maintenance activities.
- Monthly or quarterly (as appropriate) performance reviews are performed for the major road and rail carriers.
- Annual utility outages at facilities to inspect boilers, motors, circuits, and
  install new equipment.
- Daily calibration and preventive maintenance for lab instrumentation.
- Daily, weekly, and monthly required control points monitoring, verification, and validation for food safety.
- Behavioral-based safety observations are used to prevent potential acci-
  dents caused by unsafe employee behaviors.
- Use of railcar preload checklists by operators to prevent accidental filling
  of contaminated vessels or use of non-food-safe cars.
- Annual audits of truck wash stations and terminals (Cargill owned and
  third party) for compliance to food safety regulations.
- Annual third-party inspections for housekeeping, sanitation, and food
  safety.
- Annual process development groups and corn milling operation audits
  for compliance to best practices.
- Order confirmations with customers to ensure order accuracy.

CCM improves work processes to achieve better performance and
reduce variability using the BPM. This model addresses how CCM plans,
evaluates, analyzes, and refines work processes. This process is owned by
the senior leadership team and deployed by the process development group
leaders. The key work process owners are responsible for monitoring and

evaluating their processes and keeping them current with the needs of the business. Process development group leaders meet to review the BPM and make improvements to the model by including additional tools to help support this model. For example, root cause analysis was incorporated into the planning stage of the model.

Three Organizational Learning and Innovation Processes   CCM utilizes (1) process development groups, (2) Ideas to Innovation (i2i), and (3) root cause analysis, three distinct but integrated processes, to improve organizational performance and learning, reduce variability, and improve products and services.

Process Development Groups   The SMT first introduced the process development groups process during the transition from an individual plant-focused work design to an enterprise-focused work design in 1999. The original intent of the process development groups process was to encourage the behaviors of cooperation and collaboration, *promote innovation,* and expand organizational learning and expertise. Process development groups are now used to provide sources of sustainable competitive advantage through continuous development of the technology base. Process development group teams utilize the steps illustrated in the BPM. The SMT is responsible for the process development groups process and process development group leaders are responsible for deployment and implementation of best practices across the CCM for their process development groups. This deployment model creates a culture of continuous process improvement and standardization. The benefits CCM has realized from the process development groups model include cost savings, reduced variability, documentation, and standardization of procedures (corn milling operations), promoting collaboration through implementation of best practices, increased employee training and organizational learning, *innovation*, and employee skill development. Process development groups were expanded throughout CCM between 2000 and 2006. In 2006, a process development groups steering team was created including all process development group leaders to review the BPM, identify top initiatives for each location, and prioritize initiatives based on savings potential.

Ideas to Innovation (i2i) Process   i2i is a formal approach used in a key profitability work process, *Manage Idea & Concept Generation,* and is owned by the innovation manager. The i2i process supports CCM's values of *Be Innovative and Promote Collaboration.* i2i captures and tracks innovative ideas relating to new discoveries, cost efficiencies, process improvements, and ways to help meet business goals and objectives through a computer-based system. The steps for this process include: (1) Employees enter ideas into the i2i system; (2) ideas are reviewed by cross-functional innovation review teams; (3) innovation review teams classify ideas using an idea prioritization matrix or through the team's knowledge of the feasibility and effectiveness of the idea; and (4) idea mentors are assigned to either nurture the ideas through the system or inform the ideator why the idea is not being advanced at this time. The idea mentor along with automatic system updates (through e-mail) keep the ideators informed as their ideas advance through the process. The i2i process has benefited from multiple evaluation and improvement cycles. In 2004, CCM started utilizing formal business unit idea campaigns to generate focused ideas on a specific opportunity. In 2005, a common website tool was implemented in order to share knowledge and ideas throughout Cargill. In 2006, CCM initiated annual *recognition awards for innovation.* In 2007, formalized standard operating procedures were created to define the process and the responsibilities of the ideator, mentor, and innovation review team members.

Root Cause Analysis Process   CCM has utilized root cause analysis (RCA) as a formal approach to analyze problems and implement solutions for improvement since 2000. The key steps are: (1) The problem owner forms an ad hoc RCA team once a threshold limit has been reached (such as a rejection, injury, environmental incident, etc.); (2) this team meets and develops a cause-and-effect chart; (3) team gathers evidence to determine the root causes of the problem; (4) team brainstorms effective solutions to eliminate the root causes; (5) team implements the solutions; and (6) team follows up to ensure resolution. The cross-functional RCA steering team meets annually to review threshold triggers for the business unit. The RCA coordinator is the owner of this process. This process has been improved through many refinements. In 2004, an RCA database was created to track RCA completion and solution implementation. In 2007, the RCA steering team modified the RCA database to provide automatic monthly reports for facility managers and department managers in order to monitor and track the implementation of RCA solutions supporting the demand accountability value.

CORE AND INNOVATIVE BEST PRACTICES   CCM exercises core best practices discussed earlier and has advanced knowledge in this area with new, innovative best practices.

Principle 4: Improve Performance

- **Prioritize improvement projects.** Identify and prioritize strategic and operational initiatives projects to improve organization's performance along financial, customer or constituent, process, and people dimensions.

- **Leverage customer facing processes.** Develop and exercise customer and constituent facing processes to understand and recalibrate processes around changing customer needs. Gather customer and competitor intelligence using regular customer surveys, focus groups, call centers, and related methods and approaches.
- **Leverage process improvement methods.** Design and maintain an ongoing process improvement methods and problem-solving to identify and eliminate root causes of issues.
- **Realize value from benchmarking.** Leverage benchmarking and comparative methods to identify and regularly improve core and support processes.
- **Create a performance culture.** Create a virtual community of practitioners to coordinate initiative completion.
- **Innovative Best Practice.** CCM leverages customer survey processes and a plethora of listening methods clearly linked to each customer segment and their respective strategies to determine customer satisfaction and dissatisfaction levels and new customer requirements. This is more advanced than what most companies do.
- **Innovative Best Practice.** The CCM customer relationship process formalizes deploying customer-focused people with the right skill sets and technical knowledge to interact directly with the target customer's organization to build relationships and develop business insight.
- **Innovative Best Practices.** CCM invites customers to its facilities to share information regarding their business with its employees. CCM technical department and research and development group interact with customers to develop new formulations and new products.
- **Innovative Best Practices.** CCM has developed the Best Practice model (BPM) to innovate work processes to meet key requirements. The BPM includes the key steps and the requirements for each step.
- **Innovative Best Practices.** Being innovative is a CCM value. CCM utilizes three formal methods: (1) process development groups; (2) i2i to systematically capture and track innovative ideas relating to new discoveries, cost efficiencies, and process improvements; and (3) root cause analysis.
- **Innovative Best Practices.** CCM has formalized innovation in its key work process "Manage Idea and Concept Generation" utilizing an external resource to help create the innovation process and to

provide a database for tracking innovative ideas before bringing this capability in-house. The process supports CCM's values of Be Innovative and Promote Collaboration.

- **Innovative Best Practices.** CCM supports a culture of innovation through quarterly and annual recognition, monthly BSC communications, an innovation website, sponsoring location innovation champions, and a business unit innovation team.
- **Innovative Best Practices.** CCM prevents defects and service errors and minimizes warranty costs and customer productivity losses primarily through process design and process refinements through standard operating procedures as well as over ten prevention-based processes.

City of Coral Springs: Best Practice Case

The City of Coral Springs leverages its customer facing surveys and listening and learning methods to secure, track, and trend customer satisfaction. These customer processes in turn provide insights and requirements for innovations to processes for sustainable improvements.

CUSTOMER SEGMENTATION   Coral Springs has defined two customer groups: residents and businesses. Residential customers are segmented by owners/renters, length of residence, location/"slice" of residence, children/no children at home, and ethnicity. Residential customers' expectations include high overall quality of services from the city, a safe community, an aesthetically pleasing community, low taxes, quality schools, and recreational opportunities. Business customers are segmented by location, type, and size of business. Their expectations include high overall quality of services from the city, a healthy economic environment, a safe community, and low taxes and business fees. For purposes of customer segmentation, "slice" refers to one of six geographical segments. Annually, the city hosts "Slice of the Springs" meetings in each of these geographic regions to give residents up-to-date information about the city as well as to solicit feedback on city issues. A special "Business Slice" is also held annually.

Coral Springs competes regionally—in a tri-county area for residents, and nationally for businesses. In fiscal year 2002 residential build-out was achieved (meaning that 95 percent of available residential land within the city had been developed).

CUSTOMER LISTENING METHODS   Residents rely on the city to provide services to meet their daily needs, such as police, fire and emergency medical services, street repairs, code enforcement, and recreational activities. Businesses located within the city rely on the city for such services as building permits, inspections, occupational licenses, and police and fire services. The city does not determine or select its customers; rather, customers select the city by deciding to live or own a business within its legal limits. The city attracts new customers because of its great reputation for schools, low crime rate, parks programs, and customer service. Using customer knowledge developed through surveys, focus groups, and "Slice of the Springs" meetings, the city pursues potential customers through a variety of marketing strategies including showcasing the city through its website and television channel, the Coral Springs Chamber of Commerce, the Economic Development Foundation, word-of-mouth by current satisfied customers, advertising and publications produced by communications and marketing staff, and national awards recognition.

The city reviews its sources of feedback from three perspectives to enable it to listen and learn, build relationships, and/or manage complaints. Exhibit 7.3 maps the source of one or more of these three perspectives.

Based on information from listening and learning mechanisms (see Exhibit 7.3), residential customers are segmented by owners/renters, length of residence, location/"slice" of residence, children/no children at home, and ethnicity. Businesses are segmented by type, size, and location. Customer segmentation is used to identify gaps in service programming and special needs for customer satisfaction. This information is used to design service programs, improve existing programs, and fund new programs and services, and is targeted to specific segmented groups as identified. Customers of competitors (other cities) are included through reviews of comparative data noted in Chapter 5. A variety of methods are used to determine key customer requirements, needs, and changing expectations. The primary method is the biannual resident and business surveys conducted by an independent research company.

The questions focus on assessment of performance in relation to the city's key intended outcomes (KIOs). This information is used to provide direction for future planning and action. Individual operating departments also survey residents to get actionable feedback on requirements. Some departments use phone surveys immediately following a transaction. Others use written surveys, opinion cards, and online surveys at various sites. For example, the Parks and Recreation Department uses survey methods to gather information to make improvements (e.g., hours of operation, new equipment) and retain its customers at the Tennis Center, Gymnasium, and Aquatics and Fitness Center. Another primary way to learn about resident requirements, needs, and changing expectations, segmented by neighborhoods within the city, is the "Slice of the Springs" meetings. The Development Services Department conducts six neighborhood meetings for

EXHIBIT 7.3 Customer Listening Methods

Method	Listen and Learn	Building Relationships	Complaint Management
Customer Surveys	✓	✓	
"Slice of the Springs" Meetings	✓	✓	✓
Public Hearings	✓	✓	✓
Advisory Committees	✓	✓	✓
Focus Groups	✓	✓	✓
City Hall in the Mall	✓	✓	✓
CCR Tracking	✓	✓	✓
coralsprings.org	✓	✓	✓
Monthly eNews		✓	
Coral Springs Magazine		✓	
Customer Care Center	✓	✓	✓
CityINFO Line		✓	
CityBlog	✓	✓	✓
CityTV		✓	
CityRadio		✓	
CityPageAds		✓	
Podcasts		✓	
State of the City		✓	
Annual Report		✓	
Community Forums	✓	✓	✓
Police Substations	✓	✓	✓
Community-Oriented Policing	✓	✓	✓

Courtesy of City of Coral Springs.

residents and a commercial meeting for businesses yearly. Residents are invited for face-to-face communication with city staff on issues important to them in their neighborhoods and the city. Residents and businesses are asked for realistic solutions to their concerns and are invited to improve their community through the Neighborhood Partnership Program and downtown redevelopment. Commercial Slice of the Springs meetings are also conducted to address business issues regarding signage, codes and regulations, and ways to attract and keep businesses in the city. Staff contacts former businesses through phone contact to determine the reason for relocating. The city's Communications and Marketing Department also gathers information from customers through the city's website. As well as being able to learn about the city, customers can use the website to request or comment on city services using the City HelpDesk tracking system, and complete the "Slice of the Springs" meeting surveys. Due to the highly visible nature of communications and marketing output, feedback is usually immediate and specific. E-mails, phone calls, and media reports serve as *early warning indicators* of topics or issues that might need additional attention.

The city keeps its *listening and learning methods* current with business needs and directions through an annual/periodic review of key methods including customer surveys, Slice of the Springs, City Hall in the Mall, and City HelpDesk. These reviews include specific customer feedback, survey and other data, as well as staff input. Depending on issues identified, either problem-solving or process improvement approaches will be implemented.

BUILDING CUSTOMER RELATIONSHIPS   Employees at all levels are dedicated to building relationships with customers and exceeding their expectations. The city implemented a state-of-the-art Premier Customer Service program to assist in this endeavor over the past decade. This is not just a training program; it is a system that includes training, accountability, recognition, reinforcement, measurement, and improvements.

An "Applause Card" recognition program was developed to recognize and reward employees for modeling desired behaviors. In addition, the city has an annual Excellence Award for Customer Service, for which the employee wins a trophy and a cash prize. Employee focus groups are periodically convened to review the Premier Customer Service program and make improvements. For example, standards have been updated to include e-mail response time and to use a community *A-to-Z Guide* and a *Guide to Doing Business* to assist customers. Transaction-based phone surveys were also added to get immediate and actionable feedback. Customer relationships are further enhanced by providing many avenues to listen and respond to customer needs. These avenues include the city's website, CityTV, CityRadio, the Customer Care Center, the quarterly *Coral Springs* magazine, the annual report, Slice of the Springs neighborhood and business meetings, and advisory boards and committees. The Police Department is committed to establishing close ties with and responding to community needs through the philosophy of community policing. Four police substations are in place within targeted areas to further build relationships. The programs and partnerships that have been established as a result of these substations helped earn the department the 2004 Crime Prevention Award.

The city's key access mechanisms enable customers to seek information, conduct business, and make complaints through convenient mechanisms that meet the needs of different stakeholders. Key customer contact requirements for each mode of access are determined by the Premier Customer Service focus group comprised of consultants, frontline employees with customer contact, and other employees throughout the city. Customer contact standards cover five value dimensions and examples include updating voice mail regularly, returning all phone and e-mail messages the same day, and using the customer's name. The standards are improved as a result of customer comments, department surveys, the resident survey, and focus group meetings. These contact requirements are deployed to all employees through performance reviews, customer service training, new employee orientation, payroll stuffers, e-mails, and staff meetings. These contact requirements are also included in processes involved in the customer response chain including complaint management, vendor contracts, code enforcement, recruitment, and water billing.

CUSTOMER COMPLAINT MANAGEMENT PROCESS The city's complaint management process, called the City HelpDesk system, collects comments, complaints, and requests from residents and businesses that are received from multiple portals—directly into the Internet-based City HelpDesk, from e-mails, in person, by phone, or through the city commissioners. Each department has a lead City HelpDesk person and a back-up on the system, and all employees who cover phones or front desks are trained on the system. The City HelpDesk process owner reviews all entries within one business day of entry and assigns the entry to a category. The categories permit the owner to compile reports on community concerns, priorities, and interests. The owner assigns a lead department to respond to the City HelpDesk. Tracking numbers are assigned to all entries, and the lead department responds within two business days either with the final resolution or the schedule for resolving the matter. The process owner reviews reports monthly from the City HelpDesk, the Public Works and Code Work order system, commission citizen comments, and Slice of the Springs meetings and reports significant trends to the city manager's office. Trend information is used to identify process changes and training necessary for customer satisfaction. The process owner, along with staff users of the City HelpDesk, recommends and implements system modifications as needed.

When individual processes are being reviewed, cross-functional process improvement teams often assemble customer focus groups to pinpoint features of processes that are satisfiers and elements that are dissatisfiers.

Many improvements have been made, including redesigning surveys to include open-ended questions to receive more actionable feedback, the addition of "key driver" analysis, the periodic use of focus groups to ensure questions are directed to customer requirements, expanded measurement scales to contain more forced choice answers, and follow-up focus group meetings with customers. One of the most meaningful improvements came when the city increased the sample size to allow for segmenting responses by geographical location and some key demographic measures.

PROCESS IMPROVEMENT SYSTEM The city has a comprehensive performance improvement system. As discussed in prior chapters at the strategic level, an environmental scan supplies data and information for the strategic plan and business plan. The business plan lists specific new services and service improvements that will be affected by teams. As shown in Exhibit 7.4, Design Process for Services and Delivery Systems, there are several sources of data service specifications. Once the process is approved, refinements to the service are based on stakeholder input. Measure, outcomes, and reporting systems provide direction to the team to pilot improvements. Pilot programs are reviewed to either refine process requirements or proceed to full implementation. Process outcomes are continuously monitored through listening methods and included in the following planning cycle. This closed loop

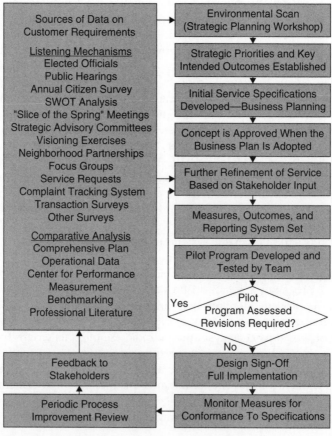

EXHIBIT 7.4 Design Process for Services and Delivery Systems
Courtesy of City of Coral Springs.

learning model enables prioritization of initiatives and process improvement projects.

At an operational level, during new employee orientation all employees are introduced to the "plan/do/check/act" and embedded six-step approach to problem solving.

BENCHMARKING The city participates in cooperatives that provide the majority of comparative and competitive data from within the municipal government industry. The first is through participation in the International City Managers Association Center for Performance Measurement. Just 80 to 100 municipalities across the nation participate in this process each year. Participation involves the completion of questionnaires covering performance measures in various functional areas of local government. However, because only a few municipalities participating in the Center for Performance Measurement CPM are located in Florida, the city has helped found the Florida Benchmarking Consortium (FBC) to encourage benchmarking and to develop standard definitions of performance measures. In addition, the city benchmarks with specific cities that are recognized for general overall excellence or identified best practices.

WORK SYSTEM AND INNOVATION: INSOURCING AND OUTSOURCING Work system design is based on four principles that support city values and encourage innovation. They are customer focus, empowerment, continuous improvement, and team-based operations. These design features are covered in new employee orientation since employees at all levels are involved in design.

1. Customer focus encourages innovation because government systems traditionally focus on documenting regulatory compliance.
2. Empowerment encourages minimal layers of bureaucracy.
3. Continuous improvement promotes innovation.
4. Diversity in teams stimulates creativity.

The decision to operate a process with internal resources is based on two criteria: whether the process is a key work process and whether an external resource can do it cheaper while sustaining quality standards. Key work processes are central to public trust and therefore are operated with internal resources. The city needs to directly manage these areas to monitor the quality of outputs on a daily basis and to have the agility needed to adapt to changing customer requirements and civic emergencies. Occasionally, processes that are not fundamental to local government are subject to a request for proposal process to determine if city staff can perform the function better and at a lower cost than the private sector. Fleet maintenance, operation of the Tennis Center, and water billing are examples of functions assessed through a request for proposal process. In Florida, the determination of a city government's key work processes is broadly based on state law authorizing cities to provide "municipal services." These services traditionally include law enforcement, fire/EMS services, parks and recreation programming, street maintenance and utilities, code enforcement, and economic development.

Key work processes of the city involve the majority of Coral Springs employees and are the processes most critical to adding value. However, city governments are like holding companies, and the key work processes are a subset of a collection of over 50 processes. The city's key work processes relate to the core competencies in that they all employ the core competency processes in their operation. For instance, police patrol uses customer service data to assess the human relations approach of the Police Department. The core competencies and key work processes contribute to profitability and organizational success, and sustainability in those results in these areas create the credibility necessary for voter support of city programs and *innovations*. The core competencies are also tied to the city's strategic priorities, which are carefully crafted based on the annual environmental scan that includes several data sets on community priorities. The design process provides an overview of how customer, supplier, and partner input is used in determining requirements. Processes are designed to meet all key requirements through multiple phases of testing and revision before a process or significant process change is fully implemented and through involvement of customers in the design. Implementation is affected when a process consistently produces the required output or outcome.

PROCESS INNOVATION AND BEST PRACTICES   Teams develop innovations when existing processes fail to meet changing requirements or research on best practices shows that existing approaches are inadequate to meet new requirements. In addition, the city's budget manual includes a "Jump Start Review Process." It is used in the development of proposals and stimulates nonincremental thinking. New technology is incorporated into processes through Information Services staff who serve on all development teams. They research best practices and scout and critique new technology through professional associations, user groups, and networks of local governments. The design process requires research into best practices and benchmarking. At this time, Web-based applications are a major focus of local governments across the nation, affording many opportunities to share experience with technology. Coral Springs has recently incorporated Web-enabled applications into the building permit process, the employment process, and water bill payment. Incorporating organizational knowledge does not require a complex system in a small, flat organization like Coral Springs. An improvement cycle created the new Knowledge Network that includes team stories and lessons learned. Ongoing teams post their activities on the Active Strategy system; the teams' progress and approach are available to all departments for input. Further, to facilitate knowledge sharing among departments, in 2006 a comprehensive review of processes was conducted through process management training presented to senior management at team meetings.

The need for agility is acknowledged and incorporated into process design by requiring that processes have a means of monitoring changes in customer requirements and the environment. Monitoring performance measurements creates a "feedback loop" that enables design refinements if cycle-time performance is not up to standard. Upgrades in Fire Rescue response were achieved through these mechanisms. Each phase of emergency response has time standards that are monitored. If the system design does not perform to specification, detailed data are available on what part of the process is causing delays.

Process improvements are focused on process segment(s) that account for the problem and the design is perfected.

NEW PROCESS DEVELOPMENT The system for designing new processes ensures that design requirements are implemented through tests and measurement before full rollout of processes and through feedback from users. For example, *a new express permit* system is being tested by a team in consultation with a focus group of developers. They want quick turnaround and no lines for small routine permits. The quick turnaround requirement led to a performance measurement of issuing small plan permits in 24 hours. The "no lines" requirement dictated that all hands work on the express permits during set periods. The same focus group consulted on system specifications and is helping to test the "alpha" approach and provide feedback on the new delivery system. The performance measures are used for control and improvement of key work processes and the associated in-process measures. These measures, based on process requirements and training on requirements, are the principal way the city ensures requirements are met in day-to-day operations. System requirements are deployed and reinforced in department, unit, and employee objectives used for evaluation; in periodic reports on operations; in formal training, particularly training on customer service; and in discussion and problem solving during staff meetings. To minimize the cycle time for corrective action, line staff are trained to interpret and access data on performance and can bring problems to the attention of their team at any time.

CULTURE OF PROCESS IMPROVEMENT The costs associated with inspections, tests, and process audits are minimized by involving employees in the development of processes, clearly defining process requirements and monitoring of in-process measures. All employees receive training in process operation and process improvement and are empowered to initiate improvements in collaboration with the members of their unit. Equipped with highly accessible performance data, a full understanding of the rationale behind process design, and the use of data to identify process deficiencies, problems are quickly identified and corrected. Department directors and supervisors are trained in process management and process improvement and guide improvement activities without having to negotiate with "think tank" staff units that are not part of the process. Defects are avoided by using a design model that prescribes stakeholder involvement in service and delivery system development, testing, and phased implementation. Also, central to "defect" prevention are systems employed to assure employees maintain all their required certifications. Prevention is accomplished through team research on best practices and the experience of other cities that employ the systems being evaluated.

Warranty, liability, and rework costs are managed by focusing inspections and tests in areas in which the consequences of error are most significant. All employees receive training on Plan/Do/Check/Act at employee orientation. Training on process improvement stresses the analytical power of segmenting performance data both in identifying the problem and analyzing the problem. For instance, response time statistics for a month might appear to meet requirements, but segmented by day of week, time of day, or sector of the city, deficiencies might be identified. Segmenting the data also permits a targeted and effective approach to generating solutions. If response time is slower than required during one period of the day, solutions are different than if the deficiency is around the clock. Further, periodic input from customers on all key and core processes keeps the processes current with community change.

CORE AND INNOVATIVE BEST PRACTICES   The city exercises the core best practices identified earlier and has advanced knowledge in this area with new, innovative best practices.

Principle 4: Improve Performance

- **Prioritize improvement projects.** Identify and prioritize strategic and operational initiatives projects to improve organization's performance along financial, customer or constituent, process, and people dimensions.
- **Leverage customer facing processes.** Develop and exercise customer and constituent facing processes to understand and

recalibrate processes around changing customer needs. Gather customer and competitor intelligence using regular customer surveys, focus groups, call centers, and related methods and approaches.

- **Leverage process improvement methods.** Design and maintain ongoing process improvement methods and problem-solving (six step Plan, Do, Check, and Act, PDCA) to identify and eliminate root causes of issues.
- **Realize value from benchmarking.** Leverage benchmarking and comparative methods to identify and regularly improve core and support processes.
- **Create a performance culture.** Create a virtual community of practitioners to coordinate initiative completion.
- **Innovative Best Practice.** City Premier Customer Service Program is not just a training program; it is a system that includes training, accountability, recognition, reinforcement, measurement, and improvements. It is based on five value dimensions.
- **Innovative Best Practice.** City of Coral Springs has expanded scope of process improvement to include an ongoing assessment of outsourcing key work processes to reduce costs, reduce cycle time, or increase outcomes.
- **Innovative Best Practice.** City of Coral Springs goes beyond traditional training on performance improvement methods to encourage innovation. Its work system design is based on four principles that support city values and encourage innovation. They are customer focus, empowerment, continuous improvement, and team-based operations.

Delta Dental of Kansas: Best Practice Case

Delta Dental of Kansas (DDKS) leverages innovative constituent segmentation and listening and learning approaches. These processes in turn provide insight and requirements for innovations to processes for sustainable improvements.

CONSTITUENT SEGMENTATION   DDKS recognizes four key external constituent groups: group purchasers, enrollees, participating dentists, and brokers as shown in the following list. DDKS also includes employees as an internal stakeholder.

- Key requirements of DDKS' *group purchasers*: include affordable rates, large provider network, fast and accurate claims payment, ease of administration and responsive customer services.

- *Enrollees*, who are the end users of DDKS' products, require an adequate dental network, responsive customer service, no balance billing and prompt, hassle-free claims payment.
- Participating *dentists* maintain contracting relationships with DDKS and are considered a key supplier, member, and partner. The elements critical to DDKS maintaining a positive relationship with its dentists include adequate fee reimbursement, sufficient enrollee/patient base, respect for the dental profession, and open, honest communication.
- *Brokers, consultants and agents* are distributors of DDKS' products. They expect fair commissions, comprehensive product information, and quality products and dental networks to offer their customers.

Each constituent desires something different from partnering with DDKS. For example, group purchasers want the lowest price while still receiving the best plan, yet the participating dentists desire greater payouts for dental services. DDKS attempts to minimize organizational tension and satisfy both constituent groups by balancing fees, costs, and competitive pricing. The addition of the BSC formalized DDKS' four key external constituent groups. Due to parameters established by Delta Dental Plan Association (DDPA), DDKS' market is limited to businesses headquartered in or having the benefits buying decision in Kansas.

To keep abreast of the key requirements of potential groups, DDKS staff regularly reviews newspapers, periodicals, trade publications, and networks with associates at business, community, and social functions. Subscribers are the individual employees covered under the group dental insurance provided by group purchasers. Enrollees are end-users and beneficiaries of benefit programs administered by DDKS, which recognize that enrollee satisfaction is an important influence in the benefits decision-making process. According to an independent survey conducted in 2006, 93 percent of benefit managers consider employee influence and approval when selecting a benefits carrier. Depending on the size of the company, it is common for groups of enrollees to collectively lobby their company benefits decision maker in order to influence the decision process. Within the study, 44 percent of respondents said they would suggest an alternative carrier if they had a negative experience.

Participating dentists maintain contracting relationships with DDKS and are considered a key partner, as well as a constituent group. Dentists were the driving force in the founding of DDKS and continue to be represented on the board. Brokers are distributors of DDKS products, especially in the Kansas City Metro area where a significant amount of group business is written through brokers. DDKS utilizes brokers to help market its products to group purchasers, and therefore is able to maintain a lean sales force. In addition, many large companies do not contract directly with benefits vendors, and instead negotiate products through brokers. The broker selling process provides DDKS the opportunity to build relationships with the brokers and be responsive to their needs, which in turn makes it more likely the brokers will submit requests for proposals to DDKS during the renewal process

CONSTITUENT LISTENING METHODS   DDKS uses a variety of listening and learning approaches to gain an external view of the company, to develop mutually beneficial relationships, and to understand and respond to the drivers of satisfaction and loyalty for its key constituents (see Exhibit 7.5).

The company actively seeks information from all constituents regarding their changing needs. An independent research firm administers unique annual surveys to company constituent groups. Personal 30-minute telephone interviews are conducted with its top 100 brokers. Surveys, in addition to personal interaction and multiple additional qualitative methods, are used to understand future needs or identify a shift in constituency. Results are presented to the board of directors and leadership team where comments and suggestions are viewed and considered. Based on the feedback obtained from its constituents, necessary modifications to strategy can be made by the leadership team during LRP sessions as these data are essential in establishing an accurate strengths, weaknesses, opportunities, and threats (SWOT) analysis and formulating initiatives. Documenting this information enables DDKS to grasp external market factors affecting group purchaser decision making and the competition plus it allows the company to make changes and improvements as necessary.

The flexibility of various listening methods enables DDKS to quickly analyze feedback and respond to market demands including key product enhancements and innovations or process improvements. For example, when a new group is taken through the implementation process a cross-functional team of sales, operations and information technology employees meets with group purchasers to ascertain needs and respond accordingly. Suggestions and concerns are discussed in FOCUS team meetings and elevated to the leadership team.

Monthly, the manager of customer service and chief operations officer aggregate results of paper-based customer service survey cards and the comments received during approximately 7,000 customer service calls to identify opportunities for improvement and innovation. Multiple value-added projects have emerged from the examination of current procedures.

DDKS market listening and learning methods are continuously being analyzed and improved to stay current with business needs and to react to changes in the marketplace. For example, a recent significant improvement came with the addition of a new phone system. The proprietary call

EXHIBIT 7.5 Constituent Listening Methods

Constituent	Key Requirement	Listening Methods
Group purchasers ■ Benefit managers ■ HR professionals ■ Decision makers	■ Responsive customer service on all issues ■ Affordable rates ■ Large network of licensed and credentialed providers ■ Fast and accurate claims processing ■ Detailed and customizable reporting ■ Easy to understand billing	■ Annual survey ■ Finalist presentations ■ Web page hits
Subscribers ■ Employees of enrolled groups ■ End-users	■ Limited out-of-pocket expense ■ Little or no paperwork to submit claims ■ Numerous Participating Dentists to select from ■ Live person answering the phone and responsive service ■ Timely receipt of ID cards ■ Easy to understand benefits information ■ Fast claim payments ■ No balance billing	■ Annual survey ■ CS line ■ CS survey cards ■ Benefit fairs ■ Web page hits ■ Enrollment meetings
Brokers ■ Distributors	■ Fair commissions ■ Quality products ■ Large network of licensed and credentialed providers ■ Comprehensive product information ■ Responsive service	■ Annual survey ■ Meetings ■ Web page hits
Participating Dentists ■ Kansas-based dentists	■ Adequate fee reimbursement ■ Responsive service ■ Knowledgeable staff ■ Sufficient patient base ■ Offer value-added services ■ Fast and accurate claims processing	■ Annual survey ■ PICs ■ Office visits ■ Annual Meeting ■ Online services survey ■ Web page hits

Courtesy of Delta Dental of Kansas.

capturing system enables DDKS to monitor, capture, and analyze customer service phone calls each week to drive opportunities for innovation.

PROCESS IMPROVEMENT AND INITIATIVE PRIORITIZATION   Process improvement teams (PIT teams) are created to suggest and research innovative opportunities for the company. With team members chosen to address a particular process improvement challenge, these teams play a valuable role in improving DDKS' internal and customer facing processes.

PIT teams support a corporate or cross-functional initiative and have an executive sponsor from the leadership team. The company methodology incorporates "public domain" techniques such as flowcharting, process mapping, and process simulation techniques to facilitate an accelerated improvement tool with "implementable" recommendations and active participant involvement.

A new "Ideas from Delta Employees in Action" (I.D.E.A.) program encourages and rewards suggestions to support all perspectives of company strategy and innovation at the individual level. Annually the company recognizes performance by team effort, with shared monetary incentives. Team awards have recognized such efforts as PIT team results in streamlining the cross-functional customer group set-up process to facilitating a building move and phone system technology upgrade with minimal disruption to customer service efforts.

DDKS translates performance BSC review findings into priorities for improvement and innovation through the development of corporate, departmental, and individual improvement initiatives.

These initiatives result from the long-range plan process, from specific issue identification resulting from data collection, from risk assessment or audit opportunities, from the Guarantee of Service Excellence (GOSE) process, or from performance gap analysis at the process level. At the corporate level, the CEO assigns initiative responsibility directly to one of the leadership team members. Based on the scope and scale of the initiative, the executive sponsor organizes an interdisciplinary team necessary to accomplish the objective. DDKS works to encourage varied experiences across any interdisciplinary team in order to better advocate an innovative and open-minded approach to problem resolution. Seeding teams with fresh ideas and perspectives invariably fosters a climate of innovation.

Given the resources dedicated to reviewing and analyzing results, DDKS empowers teams to drive process improvements directly into the everyday operations and key processes of the business. While strategic-level initiatives drive higher level business improvements and adjustments, GOSE team, FOCUS team, and PIT programs systematically bond results to key business process improvements. A PIT initiative will have broad-reaching interdepartmental or multifunctional considerations. A PIT team will also consist of a multidisciplinary team capable of addressing cross-functional considerations for process improvement.

The leadership team reviews corporate initiative action plans monthly; reallocation of resources can be deployed to either reprioritize or shift responsibility to obtain results. The initiative tracking tool is used to review progress regarding corporate initiatives.

For corporate initiatives, detailed business plans and timelines chart individual tasks with assignment of responsibilities coordinated by the executive sponsor. The initiative tracking tool provides a means to quickly determine if the plan is on target, ahead of schedule, or behind schedule. While numeric targets are set on the Level I BSC for each quarter, the performance measure for corporate initiatives is on a "progress to plan" basis, with department and individual BSC goals established to provide accountability with all key deployment areas. Numeric goals are established for objectives once implementation is complete. The BSC methodology ensures the alignment of the action plan with the strategy of the organization. Targeted communications with stakeholder groups impacted by corporate initiatives are identified in these business plans.

Historic metrics are in place for claims turnaround time, average speed to answer, participating dentist network size, and other key performance measures and indicators (KPI). Weekly updates of the dashboard enable DDKS leadership to review KPI for all stakeholders and deployment areas as seen in the dashboard. The Level I BSC reflects performance measures for corporate initiative action plans and key numerical performance indicators for DDKS quarterly.

BENCHMARKING   Through DDPA membership, DDKS has access to competitive analysis and competitor information on a national, regional, and local basis. This information is provided by each Delta Dental member company; the MC is responsible for providing and updating this information for its specific business territory. Through DDPA, DDKS is able to benchmark business results against other Delta Dental peer members, based on revenue, enrollee, claims, and/or expense thresholds. DDPA also assists in the collection of industry-specific competitor data for comparative analysis.

DDKS obtains competitive and benchmarking data through information garnered from annual external constituent surveys, competitor websites, and through benchmarking and best practice sharing with other Delta Dental member companies. DDKS conducts annual constituent surveys of every external constituent group. The results of these surveys are analyzed and initiatives are developed to address areas where improvement is needed. Quantifiable measurements for key initiatives are incorporated into the company's corporate, departmental, and individual BSCs.

CORE AND INNOVATIVE BEST PRACTICES DDKS exercises the core best practices identified earlier and has advanced knowledge in this area with new, innovative best practices.

Principle 4: Improve Performance

- **Prioritize improvement projects.** Identify and prioritize strategic and operational initiatives/projects to improve organization's performance along financial, customer or constituent, process, and people dimensions.
- **Leverage customer facing processes.** Develop and exercise customer and constituent facing processes to understand and recalibrate processes around changing customer needs. Gather customer and competitor intelligence using regular customer surveys, focus groups, call centers, and related methods and approaches.
- **Leverage process improvement methods.** Design and maintain an ongoing process improvement methods and problem solving to identify and eliminate root causes of issues.
- **Realize value from benchmarking.** Leverage benchmarking and comparative methods to identify and regularly improve core and support processes.
- **Create a performance culture.** Create a virtual community of practitioners to coordinate initiative completion.
- **Innovative Best Practice.** DDKS has a very well-defined set of requirements for each of its four constituent segments.
- **Innovative Best Practice.** DDKS participates with member companies and other sources to benchmark and provide the basis for process improvements.

Lockheed Martin, Information Systems & Global Services: Best Practice Case

Lockheed Martin (LM) Information Systems & Global Services (IS&GS)-Civil segments its customers and secures customer feedback.

CUSTOMER CONSTITUENT SEGMENTATION LM IS&GS-Civil has multiple constituencies, each of whom is addressed in the strategy. This section references the strategy map in Chapter 5.

- The company is a publicly traded corporation, so shareholders are a key customer. Their needs are primarily addressed in the financial perspective and are based on the ability to deliver financial results consistent with LM commitments.

- Direct customers (i.e., those the organization contracts with, such as NASA, FBI, FAA, and the Department of Health and Human Services) are another major customer constituency. Their needs are primarily addressed in the BSC customer perspective in terms of delivering on promises in a manner that encourages repeat business.
- A related constituency, as indicated by objective C4 ("Help me succeed with my stakeholders") reflects an appreciation for LM customers' customers (i.e., whom they are accountable to). These stakeholders range from a customer's immediate supervisor, to the authorities who set appropriations (e.g., Congress), to citizens they directly serve.
- Another constituency IS&GS-Civil recognizes is its partners, including fellow LM businesses and outside suppliers. Their needs and focused engagement with them are indicated in the process perspective in objectives P4 (Engage partners and suppliers) and P5 (Deliver the full breadth of LM capabilities).
- Another customer constituency includes communities in which LM operates and its employees live. This focus is reflected in strategic measures around community service and volunteerism in W6 (Provide challenging opportunities for each employee to be successful).
- Finally, at the foundation of all success, company employees are a critical customer constituency. Leaders believe and espouse that they "serve" employees and that the organization must remain focused on energizing and empowering the workforce. This focus is reflected in the workforce perspective of the strategy.

CUSTOMER SATISFACTION DETERMINATION   Direct customer insight is secured in numerous ways. Customers provide written assessments of performance in the form of Award Fee Feedback and the Contractor Performance Assessment Reporting (CPAR) system, so it is important not to confuse these assessments with the complete picture of customer satisfaction. This is especially certain in government business because it boils down to stewardship and trust of the taxpayers. This stewardship is evidenced in part by the statement of strategy: Compete Citizen Services.

To secure further insights customer surveys (online, written, face-to-face, etc.) and customer visits are used. Determining the elements of value core to differentiated customer relationships boils down to how well the business unit knows its market, customers, and its customers' environment. Generally, the core team holds interviews with leadership and solicits suggestions from all employees. This generates a comprehensive list of factors people deem important to customer satisfaction. Through analysis of the unstructured data (i.e., written text) recurring comments start to emerge. These comments are narrowed down to a handful of ideas and discussed as part of the strategy map workshop, resulting in the objectives that will make up the customer perspective of the BSC model. At the IS&GS-Civil level, these elements are C1, C2, C3, and C4 on the strategy map. IS&GS-Civil uses quotes around these objective statements, referred to as the "voice of the customer," to reinforce the idea that this is how customers describe what it is like doing business with the business unit. It reflects the customer's desired customer experience for every program across the business unit. It also reflects the experience desired for internal relationships among and between lines of business and the functional organizations supporting them.

PROCESS IMPROVEMENT LM has been actively applying Lean and Six Sigma practices for process improvement for well over a decade. These practices are integrated across the corporation through a program called LM21 Operating Excellence. IS&GS-Civil actively manages these efforts and has robust sets of trained and experienced professionals called Green Belts and Black Belts. Progressively their efforts are being aligned with the strategy through the BSC in a very logical and intuitive manner. Since the BSC model describes the internal activities that the organization must excel at, per the process and workforce perspectives, these objectives serve as a catalyst for identifying where operating excellence investments should be focused. This focus serves two alignment functions. It drives bottom-up discussion around the strategy within the operating excellence organization (i.e., "Where are process improvements needed?"), and it drives leadership top-down discussion "Can we apply operating excellence efforts on this objective?"

The result of these two aligning forces, are a series of Lean and Six Sigma initiatives, many of which are considered initiatives in the BSC model as specific investments of organizational resources to improve the performance of objectives. Ideally, these investments are focused on closing the performance gap between actual and target BSC measure performance. From an alignment perspective, the linkage between strategy, measures, targets, and initiatives reinforces the operating excellence team's "seat at the table."

INITIATIVE PRIORITIZATION AND ONGOING MANAGEMENT Generally, internal initiatives are prioritized using business cases with levels of detail deemed commensurate with the desired investment. Initiatives are sourced and managed in three primary ways. First, investments are identified and reviewed within a line of business or function and funding is allocated within their budget. These initiatives often reflect efforts to effect change that fits within the unique charter of the organization, making it logical and effective for this management approach.

Second, initiatives are identified that clearly have benefit across multiple lines of business and functions. In these cases, a portion of costs are allocated across groups. Effectively, they each contribute funds that would otherwise be used for their own initiatives. This approach can be effective because it ensures that such investments are vetted and agreed to by all the leaders.

Third, more technically oriented initiatives are vetted and managed through the research and development process as indicated in earlier sections.

Significant internal initiatives are indicated on the BSC, associated with the specific related objective. The PA becomes a stakeholder in the initiative because of its influence on his or her strategy and strategic objective. The PA briefly discusses the initiative in each QSR so the full leadership team is informed of the investment and its purpose. Initiative management is one of the key areas of focus as its overall strategy management process matures. Since significant initiatives are a major mechanism to advance the strategy in a visible manner across the business, the team sees this as an important aspect of strategy management in terms of both strategy execution and to demonstrate results of the process.

BENCHMARKING   Benchmarking is used in some operational areas, especially in information technology where such comparative data are readily available. Informally, there are several measures where industry and competitive benchmarks are applied. In some cases competitors are publicly traded companies and selected financial data are readily available to gauge overall industry growth (e.g., compounded annual growth rate). The more important benchmarks, from a competitive standpoint, often deal in the efficiency of program management, innovation, and customer relationship processes. In some of these areas benchmarks are available and estimated based on industry conferences and associations. Additionally, the nature of publicly funded programs presents multiple opportunities to develop a reasonable understanding of competitor performance levels.

CORE AND INNOVATIVE BEST PRACTICES   LM IS&GS exercises core best practices identified earlier and has advanced knowledge in this area with new, innovative best practices.

Principle 4: Improve Performance

- **Prioritize improvement projects.** Identify and prioritize strategic and operational initiatives projects to improve organization's performance along financial, customer or constituent, process, and people dimensions.

- **Leverage customer facing processes.** Develop and exercise customer and constituent facing processes to understand and recalibrate processes around changing customer needs. Gather customer and competitor intelligence using regular customer surveys, focus groups, call centers, and related methods and approaches.
- **Leverage process improvement methods.** Design and maintain an ongoing process improvement methods and problem solving to identify and eliminate root causes of issues.
- **Realize value from benchmarking.** Leverage benchmarking and comparative methods to identify and regularly improve core and support processes.
- **Create a performance culture.** Create a virtual community of practitioners (green and black belts) to coordinate initiative completion.
- **Innovative Best Practices.** IS&GS-Civil has defined requirements for a complex, expanded definition of customers and stakeholders that include direct and (end) customers' customers, partners and suppliers, and fellow LM business units, which range from a customer's immediate supervisor, to the authorities who set appropriations (e.g., Congress), to citizens they directly serve.
- **Innovative Best Practices.** IS&GS-Civil closely aligns its process improvement (e.g., Lean Six Sigma) investments to its strategic objectives and BSC measures.

M7 Aerospace: Best Practice Case

A large portion of M7 Aerospace's business is focused on the Department of Defense (DoD), which issues the "Customer Performance Assessment Report" (CPAR) containing key elements of performance and satisfaction. The CPAR evaluates quality, schedule, cost control, business relations, management of key personnel, and other areas that show their past rating, current rating and trends. The CPAR ratings are directly aligned with the business unit BSC measures described in the prior chapter.

Steve Leland states, "We have scheduled CPAR surveys the government gives us (billing efficiency/accuracy, mission capable rates, performance of contracts). We have sent out an annual customer service survey at different symposiums to receive not only information from our direct customer (the government) but from the government's end user as well."

BSC ratings are reviewed during weekly and monthly management meetings where improvements are brought about through priority action matrices, quad charts, and Six Sigma projects described later in this case. All survey results are posted on the intranet so government contract employees see everyone's shortcomings and successes.

CUSTOMER SALES MANAGEMENT PROCESS   An effective and transparent sales management process is the underpinning of M7's overall revenue growth engine. The ability to carry an identified sales opportunity through the life cycle of lead generation to contract award not only provides a tried and true method to generate sales revenue, but it provides a very strategic tool in terms of applying resources to the marketplace where required to be successful, both long- and short-term with the overall corporate business development efforts.

The scope of the sales management process is all new or organic business opportunities that may exist across all M7's business units. The process objective is to provide the transparent management tool that intelligently identifies M7 business opportunities, assesses for reasonableness and product fit, clearly coordinates internal and external capture requirements, proactively monitors customer response, and tracks award performance to facilitate future follow-on opportunities. The sales management process consists of seven steps.

Step 1: Lead Generation   M7 competes in a very complex marketplace where integrated aerospace services are at the pinnacle of the aerospace aftermarket. M7's overarching strategy is to pair and bundle the products and services of its seven business units and bring to market integrated solution sets. Given that it competes in both commercial and government arenas, the sources for sales leads and business development opportunities come from many wide and varied sources.

These sources include, but are not limited to, government Web-based solicitations, teaming and partnering agreements, trade shows and conferences, visits to military and governmental agencies, sales calls, and unsolicited requests for proposals and requests for quotes. Given that all of these sources are very much different in terms of identifying the lead, M7 needed one repository (Web-based on its internal extranet) that could break down the lead into a few basic elements: *Matching to Core Capabilities, Current Capacity*, and/or *Is it a strategic-based opportunity?* If it fits one of these three criteria, the opportunity is pushed to the second step, lead qualification.

Step 2: Opportunity Assessment and Qualification   The second step of the process starts the internal qualifying and gating process. *Gating* is the hurdles and assessment tools that are used to qualify an opportunity. The key areas in this step are determining if there is investment required, and if so, what is the return on investment, net present value, or RONCE. If the financials are sound and viable, the company begins to identify the required resources or budgetary items that may be impacted. More important in this step of the process, M7 determines the strategic value of the opportunity. It is key for M7 to apply resources to opportunities that have the higher potential or "win percentage" and at the same time either enables a strategic initiative or pulls the organization closer to meeting a strategic target.

Step 3: Assignment of Opportunity   Once the opportunity is vetted and qualified for pursuit, the next step is to assign the opportunity for capture. Assignment is a critical function in terms of accountability and ownership. What M7 has found is that many times, opportunities were not "owned" by either an individual or one of its business units. When this occurred, there were cases when the opportunity lapsed (time sensitivity response). Depending on the size, complexity, and strategic value of a qualified opportunity, the opportunity is either assigned to an individual business unit leader, a cadre of business unit leaders (an integrated services opportunity), or kept within the business development team. Along with the assignment, expectations are set in terms of actions, timelines, resources, and so forth. All of these actions are tracked within its Web-based CRM system linked to the company and BU BSCs.

Step 4: Team Capture   After assignment of the opportunity, the pursuit strategy is initiated. If the assignment was a sole individual or business unit, the pursuit is monitored against agreed on milestones (agreed to in the assignment process step) and reviewed on a weekly basis with senior management. If the opportunity is a joint pursuit (more than one business unit and/or the involvement of the business development team), it too will be monitored against set milestones, but there will also be the expectation of joint team meetings and briefings when required.

Step 5: Proposal, Quote, and Response   As part of the pursuit and capture strategy, the assigned business unit or business development team member will be responsible for ensuring a simple quote response or a very complex (in some cases with government business a proposal can be hundreds of pages in length) proposal response. This response is reviewed by multiple functions to ensure that pricing, products, and services being offered, innovative approach to the solution set, and so forth are of the highest quality.

Step 6: Opportunity Tracking   Proactively tracking an opportunity response is a step in the process that many companies take for granted. When M7 reaches out to the customer its win percentage increases dramatically. The opportunity is tracked until one of two events take place: (1) M7 is awarded the contract, or (2) it can unequivocally determine that it did not win the award. If it happens to lose, it performs a past event analysis to understand why it was not successful. Was it price, product quality, terms and conditions, or other contributing factors? From this analysis M7 will adjust accordingly for future competitions.

Step 7: Award Performance   After being awarded the contract, continually monitoring the performance of the contract through the BSC is at the foundation of driving organic growth. The business unit's ability to deliver quality product, on time, and within agreed-on terms and conditions drives customer goodwill and ultimately, follow-on opportunities to assess and feed back into the sales management process.

BUSINESS AND PROCESS IMPROVEMENT   Business unit and service unit (SU) leaders, as discussed in Chapter 6, will prepare for meetings and address BSC underperformance by completing either a four-part solutions chart referred to as a quad chart, a priority action matrix, or a process improvement project.

Quad charts and priority action matrices are derivatives of quality tools that break out the issues into their component parts for management discussion and analyses. If an issue is significantly more complex, then a Lean Six Sigma quality team is launched.

Quad Chart   The quad chart contains four sections:

1. **Objective.** The strategic objective from the organization strategy map.
2. **Measures.** The BSC measure results that provide insight into progress toward attaining the strategic objective.
3. **Specific Issues.** These are root causes of the underperformance; their resolution will enable improvement in performance.
4. **Actions/Discussions.** Specific actions, one for each issue, and a timeline for resolution.

Priority Action Matrix   The priority action matrix provides several key components for problem resolution:

- **Category.** Contains definition for the issue or BSC measure
- **Who else.** Who else or organization will contribute
- **What.** What measure or topic is being addressed
- **When.** When the topic will be addressed
- **Issue status.** Red, yellow, or green status indicating progress toward resolution
- **Comments/updates.** Explanatory information to provide more insights

Lean Six Sigma Governance and Project Prioritization   M7 Aerospace utilizes an executive committee to oversee the Lean Six Sigma process improvement program for the entire corporation. This committee is called Executive Committee for Internal Processes. The charter for this committee includes the accredited action board, Lean Six Sigma program, and review of all internal processes and procedures. Regarding Lean Six Sigma and process improvement, the executive committee gathers the pool of candidate projects, makes sure the programs are quality programs to go after and are true process improvement programs, and then assigns the project to a Lean Six Sigma trained Black Belt. The board then powers the black belt with a project team. The executive committee acts as a committee to oversee the project progress.

Lean Six Sigma   The use of Lean Six Sigma is reserved for more focused process projects. We will illustrate this method through a brief case study focused on streamlining the timely receiving and stocking of supplier goods in the warehouse. This process is critical since accurate and timely parts replenishment impact sister manufacturing, maintenance repair operations (MRO), spares, supply chain, and engineering business unit customer satisfaction ratings for on-time delivery and quality, to name a few.

The dock to stock team leveraged the Lean Six Sigma DMAIC (Define, Measure, Analyze, Improve, and Control) approach shown in Exhibit 7.6. Each project utilizes either the full set or a subset of the detailed DMAIC steps. The DTS project leveraged the steps in bold print in Exhibit 7.6, some of which will be described in the following paragraphs.

In the Define Stage, the charter statement was developed by the executive committee and the team. The DTS team targeted reducing work-in-process (WIP) inventory and reducing cycle time, or process lead times.

One of the first Define steps was to develop a SIPOC (Suppliers, Inputs, Process, Outputs, & Customers) chart. The purpose of the SIPOC chart is to define customer requirements and understand the value chain necessary to deliver on those requirements. The Lean Six Sigma team reviewed the process and reverse engineered it from the customer perspective. M7 internal customers are BUs and SUs such as MRO, manufacturing, engineering, IT, government programs, and so on. The Lean Six Sigma team looked at the outputs customers are looking for: percentage of parts received in 24 hours, process lead time, supplier ratings, and so on. The team is therefore working from its customers' needs back to M7 outputs, M7 inputs, and finally back to the supplier.

The C in SIPOC is also further broken down into a customer segmentation matrix to further define customer requirements, to understand who the customers are and what they bring into this process and the effects of

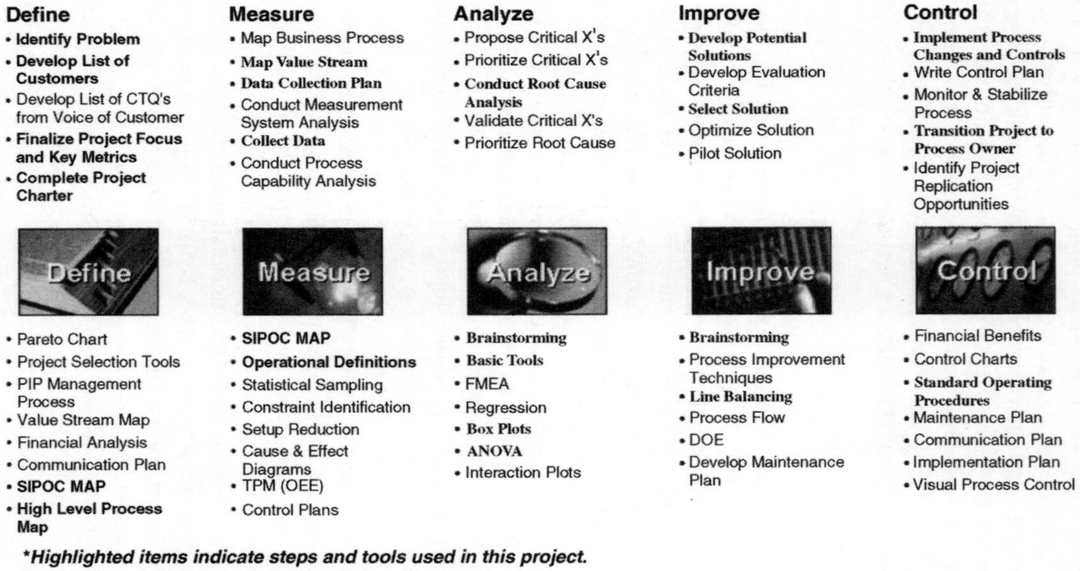

Define
- **Identify Problem**
- **Develop List of Customers**
- Develop List of CTQ's from Voice of Customer
- **Finalize Project Focus and Key Metrics**
- **Complete Project Charter**

- Pareto Chart
- Project Selection Tools
- PIP Management Process
- Value Stream Map
- Financial Analysis
- Communication Plan
- **SIPOC MAP**
- **High Level Process Map**

Measure
- Map Business Process
- **Map Value Stream**
- **Data Collection Plan**
- Conduct Measurement System Analysis
- **Collect Data**
- Conduct Process Capability Analysis

- **SIPOC MAP**
- **Operational Definitions**
- Statistical Sampling
- Constraint Identification
- Setup Reduction
- Cause & Effect Diagrams
- TPM (OEE)
- Control Plans

Analyze
- Propose Critical X's
- Prioritize Critical X's
- **Conduct Root Cause Analysis**
- Validate Critical X's
- Prioritize Root Cause

- **Brainstorming**
- **Basic Tools**
- FMEA
- Regression
- **Box Plots**
- ANOVA
- Interaction Plots

Improve
- **Develop Potential Solutions**
- Develop Evaluation Criteria
- **Select Solution**
- Optimize Solution
- Pilot Solution

- **Brainstorming**
- Process Improvement Techniques
- **Line Balancing**
- Process Flow
- DOE
- Develop Maintenance Plan

Control
- **Implement Process Changes and Controls**
- Write Control Plan
- Monitor & Stabilize Process
- **Transition Project to Process Owner**
- Identify Project Replication Opportunities

- Financial Benefits
- Control Charts
- **Standard Operating Procedures**
- Maintenance Plan
- Communication Plan
- Implementation Plan
- Visual Process Control

Highlighted items indicate steps and tools used in this project.

EXHIBIT 7.6 Six Sigma Improvement Process Roadmap

Courtesy of M7 Aerospace.

failure of this process to them (economic effects, work stoppage, external customer requirements).

In the Measure Phase, the Lean Six Sigma team developed a top-down process flowchart consisting of the major steps: receive, inspect, and stock broken down into substeps. The team broke down the "Receive" major step into three major subsections: (1) receive from shipper, (2) determine priority, and (3) process parts. These subsections in turn were broken down further into subprocess steps. The flowchart depicts the major step, receive, its major subsections and steps, from when the product comes off the truck to the time that it is on the shelf for the inspectors to do their job.

Similarly, the major steps "Inspect" and "Stock" were flowcharted down to all the steps and organized by the system requirements.

But the team discovered in the process that it did not measure the time the product came off the truck to the time the product was on the shelf (stocked), so the Lean Six Sigma team established new BSC measures.

An important point to bring up is that the Lean Six Sigma team did not wait for the entire DMAIC process before it reaped benefits from Lean Six Sigma. The team, as it went through DMAIC phases, identified some quick wins and immediate actions. The first quick win centered on a short-coming in the process where damaged product boxes would go through a subroutine called *damaged product processes*. The team made sure the parts would be placed into the priority process so that M7 customers would know immediately and could formulate alternative plans if desired.

In a second quick win, 4 to 5 percent of products come through *buyer hold* and were not entered into the system. Similarly, now receivers immediately enter products into the system.

In the Analyze Phase, the Lean Six Sigma team leveraged data collection system and Lean Six Sigma Black Belt tools to analyze the data.

For the data sampled, a mean time of 54.9 hours of dock-to-stock time was too long and the team goal was to reduce this time. Further breaking it down, the team found inspection span time and stock span time. The inspection span time was averaging 0.2 hour per part, which is impressive. But the products were in queue for too long. The subprocess covering the *time from the inspection to the time it is on the shelf* has a total mean time of 17.6 hours, an opportunity for improvement.

One of the things the team found was that the inspection span time, which everyone initially thought was the problem, really was not a problem. When the team broke the inspection step out to about 25 separate steps, it found there was not much time to take away from this process. One of the things the team found was they were spending too much time in inspection queue time at 28 hours.

The Lean Six Sigma team looked closer at the shipping inspection that verifies the condition of the parts on the shelf that were previously inspected by the receiving inspector or the fabrication inspector who put it on the shelf. *In the Improve Phase*, the solution was to allocate inspector time to the receiving side and arrange for other less-skilled personnel to take more on the shipping side. The team assigned the stock clerk to inspect the shipping items, and in the event that the item looked damaged, they could still go to the inspector to determine if it was okay to ship or not. This freed the inspectors to spend more time on receiving products and ultimately reducing inspection queue time.

In the Control Phase, the focus is on how to make the process improvement permanent. The team focused on new SOP work instructions and employee training.

The ISO-compliant work instruction authorizes qualified warehouse personnel to perform basic shipping inspection and explains the new procedures that happen. To enforce these procedures, training is critical.

DMAIC Results   The Lean Six Sigma team successfully reduced work-in-progress from 206.1 jobs to 38.3 jobs, an 81 percent decrease, and reduced process lead time from 30 hours to 5.2 hours, an 82 percent decrease! These improvements were so successful that M7 was able to move parts through the system so fast that it only needed one inspector and had free time to start scanning records into the system.

CORE AND INNOVATIVE BEST PRACTICES   M7 Aerospace exercises the core best practices identified earlier and has advanced knowledge in this area with new, innovative best practices.

Principle 4: Improve Performance

- **Prioritize improvement projects.** Identify and prioritize strategic and operational initiatives projects to improve organization's performance along financial, customer or constituent, process, and people dimensions.
- **Leverage customer facing processes.** Develop and exercise customer and constituent facing processes to understand and recalibrate processes around changing customer needs. Gather customer and competitor intelligence using regular customer surveys, focus groups, call centers, and related methods and approaches.
- **Leverage process improvement methods.** Design and maintain an ongoing process improvement methods and problem solving to identify and eliminate root causes of issues.

- **Realize value from benchmarking.** Leverage benchmarking and comparative methods to identify and regularly improve core and support processes.
- **Create a performance culture.** Create a virtual community of practitioners to coordinate initiative completion.
- **Innovative Best Practice.** M7 Aerospace's comprehensive sales process includes not only the front-end relationship management but also includes the complete life cycle of a program through delivery of customer results.
- **Innovative Best Practice.** M7 leverages multiple quality tools including quad charts, priority access matrices, and Lean Six Sigma depending on the nature of the issue being resolved.

Mueller, Inc.: Best Practice Case

Strategically, Mueller is committed to creating long-term loyalty from its customers. Each sales location is measured on service to the targeted customer.

The approach used to determine customer satisfaction and dissatisfaction consists of a survey sent to every end user that purchases a major project from Mueller 30 days after the completed sale. The surveys use a 5-point scale and include questions on employees, product quality, and overall experience. The final question, "Would you recommend Mueller?" is the most watched result. The surveys are reviewed and scored, and feedback to the organization is immediate.

BENCHMARKING AND BEST PRACTICES   Customer surveys give feedback on sales in each location and these metrics are used to benchmark or rate the sales organization. Each sales group then has its target set at the "median of the top half" for everyone in the group. This is a self-correcting method, as the groups who are performing at the top are setting the standard, and the ones underperforming now have to reach that higher target. Each year the bar is reset to meet the new top performers, to reinforce meeting customer commitments by bringing the lower performers up to the goal. This is illustrated in Exhibit 7.7.

Peer groups are used to set targets at the "median of the top half" within the group. For instance, the top half starts with the New Braunfels branch and goes above. The median result of the top group target lies with West Fort Worth at 92.86 percent of target. Therefore the branches in the bottom half would set their target consistent with West Fort Worth. Through repetitive cycles this method raises the bar across the whole branch system. The

EXHIBIT 7.7 Customer Survey Benchmark Report

	2007 YTD	**2008 Target**
Ballinger	93.21%	92.86%
West Fort Worth	92.86%	92.86%
	92.65%	92.86%
Temple/Waco		
Amarillo	91.75%	92.86%
Conroe	91.37%	92.86%
New Braunfels	88.89%	92.86%
Orange	93.50%	91.96%
Waxahachie	92.41%	91.96%
Lubbock	91.51%	91.96%
Baton Rouge	90.00%	91.96%
Kilgore	89.61%	91.96%
Albuquerque	85.99%	91.96%
El Paso	85.71%	91.96%
Sherman	84.38%	91.96%

Courtesy of Mueller, Inc.

underperforming branches then engage in improvement projects to raise performance.

"I'm a big believer in standardization," says Davenport. "But as we added branch offices, every one of them started to look a little different. Before we got too big, I wanted to *adopt a set of best practices* that we could use indefinitely and anywhere in the country to ensure that our branch offices were being well managed by the local managers." Mueller created what it calls its Branch Target System.

STRATEGIC LINKS TO ONGOING PROCESS IMPROVEMENT At Mueller, initiatives are tested against the BSC and are added as part of the process if they are in alignment with overall goals and strategy. Initiatives are defined and aligned with the BSC and prioritized according to their value to the organization. Mueller will not change the strategy to fit an idea, unless it is a major business foundation changing idea. Initiatives that do not provide a level of increased value add to the end user of Mueller's products are not considered.

When an initiative can help improve process and add value to the end user, a research task is assigned to look into the profitability, process, viability, and cost. At a future meeting Mueller then decides if that particular initiative fits with the strategy and whether to implement it. The BSC and the strategic initiatives are reviewed every quarter in a formal meeting and performance, existing initiatives, and any challenges are discussed and worked on.

IMPROVEMENT INITIATIVES AND ACCOUNTABILITY   Every initiative at Mueller is assigned to an executive who is responsible for communicating formal status updates to the rest of the executive management. Depending on the strategic initiative, there may be a partnership between two groups, IT and Operations, for example, to deliver on the initiative. Mueller believes it to be critical to its success to ensure to match accountability and responsibility for each strategic initiative, whether it is a successfully implemented initiative or one that is discontinued if it is found to not fit with the overall goals of the organization.

PROCESS QUALITY IMPROVEMENT METHOD   Mueller uses business intelligence (BI) along with BSC reporting to guide decision making, assess progress toward strategic objectives, and to test strategic hypotheses. Mueller's system works like a feedback loop. Metrics are in green, yellow, or red depending on their status.

When items are yellow or red, reporting and BI tools are used to determine where the problem started. Then, planning evaluates the process improvement project or change required to improve performance.

CORE BEST PRACTICES   Mueller exercises the core best practices identified earlier.

Principle 4: Improve Performance

- **Prioritize improvement projects.** Identify and prioritize strategic and operational initiatives projects to improve organization's performance along financial, customer or constituent, process, and people dimensions.
- **Leverage customer facing processes.** Develop and exercise customer and constituent facing processes to understand and recalibrate processes around changing customer needs. Gather customer and competitor intelligence using regular customer surveys, focus groups, call centers, and related methods and approaches.
- **Leverage process improvement methods.** Design and maintain an ongoing process improvement methods and problem solving to identify and eliminate root causes of issues.

(Continued)

> - **Realize value from benchmarking.** Leverage benchmarking and comparative methods to identify and regularly improve core and support processes.
> - **Create a performance culture.** Create a virtual community of practitioners to coordinate initiative completion.

NSTAR: Best Practice Case

NSTAR regularly surveys its customers to understand their overall perception of the company and obtain information on levels of satisfaction and links these to its process improvement processes.

CUSTOMER SURVEYS NSTAR has implemented a multidimensional survey process that enables them to measure customer transactions including bill payments; questions about a bill; reporting an outage; making account-related changes like name or phone number; new service connections; learning about energy efficiency programs; and field construction or maintenance services.

Within one week of a customer transaction, NSTAR randomly surveys customers to check in with them on their experience, capturing their comments and asking for satisfaction ratings via standardized questions. In addition, after a field visit by an NSTAR technician to maintain or connect a new service, NSTAR also surveys customers about that particular face-to-face experience.

As customers are surveyed, if they are unhappy with NSTAR's performance for any reason, NSTAR requests permission to follow up with them to get additional insight into what could have been done to make the experience better. This opportunity to get direct feedback one-on-one has uncovered the specific concerns of customers which is helpful for NSTAR to use in the design and improvement of the company's customer service processes.

NSTAR has conducted customer focus groups, where small groups of customers review and react to specific areas of NSTAR's service, facilitated by a professional focus group service. In addition, NSTAR has organized employee focus groups on numerous occasions to find ways to improve customer service from employees whose daily jobs involve customer interactions. Both of these methods of research have provided a rich source of input that has been used in making numerous changes to NSTAR's customer service processes.

IMPROVING NSTAR's CORE BUSINESS: PROCESS IMPROVEMENT NSTAR has focused a significant amount of management attention and investment in customer satisfaction results and what is driving them. Changes the company has made to business processes and performance has resulted in improved customer satisfaction ratings in each of the past four years as measured by J.D. Power & Associates, as well as per results of customer surveys conducted. Some of the major improvements NSTAR has implemented in recent years based on customer feedback are:

- Customer relationship management technology to better equip call center representatives with the tools they need to respond well to customer inquiries.
- Natural-language interactive voice response system to eliminate the "press 1" menu style of automation that many customers dislike.
- Updated summary bill format and online e-billing options to make it easier for customers to understand and pay their energy bills.
- Creation of a call center focused specifically on the unique needs of business customers.
- Customer service representative (CSR) skills training and monitoring to improve knowledge, courtesy, and responsiveness.
- Reengineered "New Customer Connects" process.
- Reengineered outage communications process, which now provides restoration time estimates, information about the cause and scope of the outage, and customer call backs to confirm their power is back on.
- Customer surveys that focus specifically on the communications process for planned and unplanned outages.
- Reengineered customer commitment management process to ensure the company always closes the loop in a timely fashion on customer requests.
- Self-service technology for customers to complete commonly needed transactions by telephone and Web.
- Streamlined process for customers reporting information about service interruptions.

PRIORITY INITIATIVES As a part of the business planning process, CPM coordinates with the NSTAR senior team to develop a set of "Priority Initiatives" to further drive NSTAR's efforts to deliver great service to customers, improve performance, reduce costs, and meet the strategic and operational plans. They are cross-functional and often cultural initiatives, well publicized throughout the company. Each month, progress toward each of these priority initiatives is reported and discussed among the executive team using the monthly scorecard package NSTAR calls the Executive Performance Review.

Over the past five years, NSTAR has made considerable investments in its electric infrastructure, resulting in top quartile reliability performance. Customers now go an average of 16 months between service interruptions, compared to nine months just five years ago. This translates into a 40 percent reduction in the number of customers experiencing an outage. NSTAR has also reduced the average time it takes to restore power from 77 minutes to 59 minutes.

NSTAR's electric system is one of the most automated in the country, with 1,400 pole-mounted switches, each with three voltage sensors and three current sensors. If the sensors detect a problem, such as a broken component or damaged power line, the switch opens automatically and notifies dispatchers back at the office that a problem exists. A first responder can then be dispatched to correct the problem. For a subset of these switches, NSTAR uses additional technologies for self-healing processes, automatically rerouting the flow of electricity to as many customers as possible. Using recent grants from economic stimulus funding, NSTAR will be expanding these technologies to a majority of its electric distribution system. These technologies will improve a customer's experience by greatly reducing the number and frequency of interruptions and speeding up service restoration, while at the same time reducing NSTAR's operational costs.

Recent investments in computer technology have enabled the company to pinpoint the source of outages and dispatch trouble crews faster than ever. In fact, NSTAR can now analyze 90 percent of outages in less than ten minutes. NSTAR also manages a comprehensive emergency response plan, allowing the company to efficiently respond to major storm damage and restore power quickly.

In addition, automated meter reading technology now helps NSTAR read 99 percent of customer meters on time, which results in faster, more accurate billing. These and other customer experience improvements have led to higher-than-ever customer satisfaction rates.

In 2009, NSTAR embarked on an initiative to further reduce costs and improve performance. This new process augments the business planning process in three major ways: enhancing the use of benchmarking and best practices; improving cross-organizational planning and prioritization at the vice president level; and using a common methodology and approach to project management and process improvement.

Enhanced Benchmarking Plan   NSTAR is now improving its benchmarking process by increasing the functions and processes that are benchmarked and seeking out best practices using a focused approach. In the past, the company obtained benchmarks for some key metrics and used them for senior-level target-setting. Results from benchmarking studies were shared with the internal groups managing the functions being evaluated, and best practices were periodically sought out.

In order to create a comprehensive continuous improvement process, the company has expanded its approach to measuring benchmarks for a broader spectrum of performance indicators across the entire business. It uses the results of benchmark comparisons to identify areas of greatest opportunity to improve performance, or reduce the cost of doing business.

NSTAR is now proactively conducting research with other companies to understand other practices or technologies that would be feasible for NSTAR to take advantage of in the future. To develop its plan for what to research, NSTAR is capturing and prioritizing among the following inputs:

- Key metrics where NSTAR performs below second quartile compared to peers or where it missed internal performance targets or regulatory expectations
- Aspects of the business that NSTAR's management team believes could be improved
- Areas where other companies are known to be best performers

As an example, one of the study projects is called the Gas and Electric Utility Peer Panel, sponsored by PSE&G, an electric and gas utility in New Jersey. The data are collected from numerous other utilities, and reports are prepared via Web-based technology. These panel groups meet twice a year, once in the fall to review and revise the data collection package for the coming year, and once in the spring to focus on the identification of best practices. NSTAR also regularly participates in other benchmarking studies, such as the J.D. Power & Associates customer satisfaction studies and the EEI/AGA Datasource annual survey of customer care functions.

In addition to understanding how NSTAR's performance compares to its peers, best practices are researched to uncover ideas for ways current business processes could be altered to achieve better performance. Through a Best Practices forum offered via the Utility Peer Panel, NSTAR has been able to learn about how other utilities approach key business functions, such as electric circuit remediation, storm response, and more. The EEI/AGA Datasource group holds annual Best Practices workshops where numerous utilities vendors meet to exchange best practices and ideas. At these workshops, NSTAR has learned about new trends in customer billing, meter reading, and customer contact options.

The various utility benchmarking groups bring together a large number of electric and gas utilities, as depicted in Exhibit 7.8 illustrating the participants in the PSE&G sponsored Utility Peer Panel Groups.

Key electric and gas utility benchmarks include comparisons of standard operating metrics that are normalized based on the demographics of each

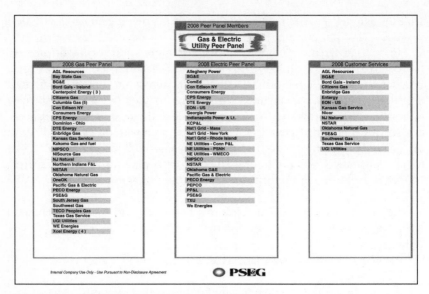

EXHIBIT 7.8 PSE&G Sponsored Benchmarking Studies
Courtesy of Public Service Electric & Gas.

company, such as number of customers, miles of circuits, and design of electric system.

Vice President Cross-Organization Planning and Prioritization

In 2009, CPM led the NSTAR team of vice presidents in a new process to identify and select cross-functional cost reduction initiatives. Cost efficiency is extremely important to regulated electric and gas delivery utilities, as their revenues are dependent on the amount of electricity or gas sold to customers.

Using this new process, every organization was asked to contribute ideas for ways the company could reduce the cost of business while maintaining high-quality customer service. Then, NSTAR vice presidents embarked on a multiweek initiative to select several cross-functional initiatives to reduce NSTAR's cost of doing business. In addition to the cross-functional initiatives, the vice presidents selected numerous other cost improvement action items that they separately implemented within their own business units.

To select the key cost reduction initiatives, the vice presidents first reviewed NSTAR's spending history and allocations, and specific cost benchmarks where NSTAR appeared more costly than its peers in key functions. The team created a set of evaluation criteria to prioritize the various cost reduction ideas, paring down the list to keep the team focused on the most significant, cost reduction ideas. As a result of this process and additional research on the narrowed list of opportunities, recommendations for four new cross-organizational initiatives relative to reducing the cost of doing business were chosen. NSTAR's Senior Team approved each initiative, selected executive sponsors for each one, and incorporated them into NSTAR's set of priority initiatives.

Project Management and Process Improvement Methodology   In 2009, CPM led a cross-functional team to select a common methodology for project management and process improvements. NSTAR realized it was the right time to invest in capabilities to improve the management of business improvement initiatives and achieve expected benefits. The company's current process lacked consistency, and projects sometimes did not meet the original expectations. NSTAR recognized that improvement in project execution was needed and set about learning how others were achieving success in this area. The project team interviewed executives at several companies to understand how they improved their process improvement process and gained much insight as to a workable approach.

Ultimately NSTAR decided to implement the Project Management Institute's methodology and selected process improvement tools based on a combination of Six Sigma and lean manufacturing methods. It created an NSTAR tool box of process improvement analytic tools to support project teams in determining the best solutions to achieve desired results. The tools NSTAR selected are geared toward the types of initiatives the company typically employs to effect change and used to uncover and correct root causes of problems in business processes.

NSTAR also wanted to obtain proper training, so project managers, key team leaders, and the NSTAR executive team were trained in the project management and process improvement methods the team selected. It was critical for project managers and executive sponsors of improvement initiatives to understand phases of projects, key deliverables, and roles and responsibilities to successfully manage each initiative.

Pulling from the newfound project management and process improvement skills, NSTAR then formed a two-tiered process for oversight and improvement. First, a subset of the cross-functional methodology and training selection team formed an ongoing Project Management/Process Improvement Council. The role of this team, which is made up of skilled project managers from across the company, is to coach and mentor new project managers, measure use of the trained skills, and make recommendations for continued improvement in the company's use of methods and tools.

Second, an executive advisory group was created. The executive advisory role is to provide high-level and visible support for the use of these methods. This executive advisory team meets every other month with the sponsor and project manager for each key business improvement. Using a combination of specific checklist items and open dialogue, the meeting's purpose is to assess the use of the training methods and to provide immediate support to project teams as needed. Both the executive advisory team and the improvement council are set up to support the success of project teams and promote consistent use of the project management practices, not as punitive entities.

CORE BEST PRACTICES NSTAR exercises the core best practices identified earlier.

Principle 4: Improve Performance

- **Prioritize improvement projects.** Identify and prioritize strategic and operational initiatives projects to improve organization's performance along financial, customer or constituent, process, and people dimensions.
- **Leverage customer facing processes.** Develop and exercise customer and constituent facing processes to understand and recalibrate processes around changing customer needs. Gather customer and competitor intelligence using regular customer surveys, focus groups, call centers, and related methods and approaches.
- **Leverage process improvement methods.** Design and maintain an ongoing process improvement methods and problem solving to identify and eliminate root causes of issues.
- **Realize value from benchmarking.** Leverage benchmarking and comparative methods to identify and regularly improve core and support processes.
- **Create a performance culture.** Create a virtual community of practitioners to coordinate initiative completion.

Omaha Public Power District: Best Practice Case

Omaha Public Power District (OPPD) serves three primary rate-paying customer segments: residential, small commercial, and large commercial (usually industrial companies or large commercial campuses). OPPD key accounts are grouped by industry type and served by OPPD representatives who are well versed in the energy-using equipment and technologies used in the industry. Residential segments vary by building type (single-family home or apartment) and type of heating and cooling technology. The business planning and strategy division and the load forecasting and rates department evaluate the current and prospective growth of these segments and their specific needs.

CUSTOMER LISTENING METHODS AND COMPETITIVE INTELLIGENCE   OPPD leverages several channels to secure customer intelligence including its website, transaction or event based surveys, as well as outside organizations such as J.D. Power & Associates.

OPPD has an ongoing program of transaction surveys that continuously collects opinions from customers who interact with OPPD. These interactions may be a service request (such as a billing question or starting electric service) as well as an experience with other OPPD programs or products. Several OPPD surveys closely monitor customer perception of the service they receive on a range of attributes. Comments are collected regarding how service can be improved. If any aspect of the customer service process is changed, the survey results are analyzed for the customer reaction. If a positive response is noted, the change in process may be extended to other customer service processes. The survey results provide the basis of performance measures for customer service organizations.

In addition to transaction surveys, OPPD conducts a series of general perception surveys. These surveys measure general opinion about OPPD including price, reliability, citizenship, communications, advertising awareness, and environmental issues.

SPOTLIGHT ON J.D. POWER SURVEY   J.D. Power & Associates, an independent outside organization, conducts a consistent survey to the customers of virtually every large and mid-sized utility in North America. This provides an industry benchmark for comparison. The key output of the J.D. Power Survey is the Customer Satisfaction Index. The index is a weighted average of approximately 33 questions that represent the best predictors of overall customer satisfaction. The questions are divided into six categories: (1) customer service, (2) price, (3) reliability, (4) citizenship, (5) communications, and (6) billing and payment.

The Customer Satisfaction Index is a customer model that weights each question to most closely correlate with a customer's overall satisfaction. Therefore it not only measures overall satisfaction, it also indicates which aspects are the key drivers of satisfaction. Therefore it is possible to determine which changes to your operation have the most potential for moving your customer satisfaction score.

The benchmark offers a way to compare every aspect of your operations to other utilities. Best practices are shared among utilities. OPPD has been ranked first for Midwest, mid-sized utilities for nine consecutive years (many years it was ranked #1 for the entire country). Even so, there are aspects of the business that rank relatively low when compared to others. OPPD therefore seeks out the highest-scoring utility in this particular area to better understand their operation.

J.D. Power has a residential and a business survey. Customers are surveyed continuously through the year, with the residential survey reporting quarterly and the business survey reporting semiannually. This offers the opportunity to refresh comparisons and trending analysis often.

PROCESS MANAGEMENT AND PROCESS IMPROVEMENT The operation analysis team is responsible for:

- Conducting process mapping and ensuring process standardization
- Deploying process improvement methods linked to PSC results
- Facilitating other business improvements and special projects using the PMM framework

OPPD did not have a sustained culture of continuous process improvement. While process improvement initiatives were often undertaken at OPPD, they were usually isolated and unique events initiated at the division or department level. There was little formal training or consistency in the improvement processes. Furthermore, the process improvement generally lacked sustained measurement and follow-up.

As part of OPPD's strategic plan, operation analysis was tasked with developing an ongoing culture of continuous process at OPPD.

PROCESS IMPROVEMENT METHODOLOGY OPPD chose to use lean principles and a hybrid version of the DMAIC (Define, Measure, Assess, Implement, and Control) process improvement methodology.

THE LEAN APPROACH Lean uses various tools (value stream mapping, Kaizen events, metrics-based process mapping, 5S/visual workplace, etc.) to avoid "analysis paralysis," tying improvement to a larger strategy, and involving all the necessary perspectives to create relevant, measureable, and sustainable improvement. For example, the Kaizen Event is typically a two- to five-day focused improvement activity during which a sequestered, cross-functional team maps out the as-is process, designs the to-be process, and fully tests and implements the stated improvements.

The initial challenge was to identify all of the processes at OPPD. The American Productivity and Quality Center (APQC) developed a framework for classifying all the processes occurring within an electric utility. The APQC framework is comprehensive and was used as the starting point, but later was customized to fit all OPPD specific processes.

PROCESS IMPROVEMENT TEAM APPROACH   Each business unit/division with the assistance of operations analysis was responsible for:

- Defining all their critical processes (self-centered within the business unit).
- Defining other noncritical/subprocesses (self-centered within the business unit).
- Defining processes that cross business units.
- Prioritizing each group of processes (needs significant improvement, needs fine tuning, working well, and just needs monitoring). Those that cross business unit lines should be prioritized by the business units that have pieces of the process.
- Providing a process owner for each process.

Each process improvement project included:

- Project sponsor (senior manager, division manager, or department manager)
- Lead facilitator and possible co-facilitator
- Project team
- Project charter/scope document/expected deliverables
- Performance measures
- Timeline

Each process intervention was a collaborative effort between the operations analysis and planning and budgeting divisions. An implementation action plan and tracking document was established for each process review and included such information as actions to be taken, primary and support responsibilities, identified savings broken down by head count, activity code, and a timeline. Specific measures of success were identified for each of the initiatives. Operations analysis, planning and budgeting, and a selected team conducted a periodic assessment to ensure that the implementation was moving forward and that the true cost savings were being realized and reflected.

CONTINUOUS PROCESS IMPROVEMENT GOING FORWARD   Continuous improvement at OPPD is considered a journey, not a destination. OPPD believes it may take upward of three to five years to realize and sustain the necessary culture and behaviors of continuous improvement. Bottom-line impacts will be felt more quickly, but the cultural transformation and leadership development necessary for the company to adopt the lean way of thinking may take some time.

CONTINUOUS PROCESS IMPROVEMENT AND PSC   In an example, operations analysis partnered with the CPM Performance Scorecard (PSC) core team to document the human resources processes to link and align process maps with PSC measures.

The CPM team applied standardized process documentation methods and tools to the "Employee Time Reporting Process."

The process map provided the framework for the core CPM team to identify seven potential process measures at key process steps to enhance performance: (1) time sheets on time, (2) time sheets completed accurately, (3) number of adjustments, (4) cost of overtime, (5) sick leave, (6) number of check stubs, and (7) cost of stubs.

The direct link between the PSC and process mapping and improvement enables focused improvement efforts.

BENCHMARKING   OPPD sponsors and participates in numerous industry benchmarking and best practice sharing forums to assist in the target setting process. The most notable is with J.D. Power & Associates, described before.

CORE AND INNOVATIVE BEST PRACTICES   OPPD exercises the core best practices identified earlier; it has advanced knowledge in this area with a new, innovative best practice.

Principle 4: Improve Performance

- **Prioritize improvement projects.** Identify and prioritize strategic and operational initiatives projects to improve organization's performance along financial, customer or constituent, process, and people dimensions.
- **Leverage customer facing processes.** Develop and exercise customer and constituent facing processes to understand and recalibrate processes around changing customer needs. Gather customer and competitor intelligence using regular customer surveys, focus groups, call centers, and related methods and approaches.
- **Leverage process improvement methods.** Design and maintain an ongoing process improvement methods and problem solving to identify and eliminate root causes of issues.

- **Realize value from benchmarking.** Leverage benchmarking and comparative methods to identify and regularly improve core and support processes.
- **Create a performance culture.** Create a virtual community of practitioners to coordinate initiative completion.
- **Innovative Best Practice.** OPPD has deployed a comprehensive process classification framework from APQC to guide its process taxonomy definition and improvement efforts.

Poudre Valley Health System: Best Practice Case

Poudre Valley Health System (PVHS) uses several processes to segment customers, secure customer requirements, and effectively engage its customer base. Customer processes provide inputs into its performance excellence journey, to improve its performance along multiple dimensions.

CUSTOMER SEGMENTS AND VOICE OF THE CUSTOMER   PVHS has identified its two key customers as patients and community, and PVHS has segmented patients into inpatient, outpatient, and emergency department (ED), based on the location of their care, and the community into primary and secondary service areas, based on geography and service utilization. PVHS defines its market areas by geography, based on a detailed analysis of zip code–based service utilization data that incorporates customers of competitors and other potential customers.

PVHS uses an integrated listening and learning process to hear the voice of the customer.

Voice of the customer information continuously comes to PVHS through the (1) patient satisfaction process; (2) relationship-building process; (3) comment management process; (4) community needs assessments; (5) access mechanisms; and (6) SDD. PVHS customizes listening methods for different customers, with further customization as appropriate. For instance, PVHS hosts focus groups for various customer groups, gathering information about key customer requirements. Members of an inpatient focus group may talk about their Poudre Valley Hospital (PVH) experience with nurse responsiveness, room cleanliness, and meal delivery, while a community focus group tested furniture during construction of MCR. The customer service steering committee, with representatives from PVH and MCR inpatient, outpatient, ED, community health, marketing, volunteer services, and quality resources, is responsible for aggregating and analyzing voice of the customer information.

To determine key customer requirements for patients and community, the customer service steering committee relies on the Avatar patient satisfaction survey and community health survey with verification from other voice of the customer information. Monthly, the customer service steering committee reviews voice of the customer information such as (1) Avatar patient satisfaction, dissatisfaction, loyalty, and retention data from former patients; (2) Avatar priority matrix, which ranks patient survey items by their relative importance to customers' health care purchasing or relationship decisions; (3) complaints and compliments from current and former patients; and (4) market data related to health care service utilization, consumer preferences/loyalty, and community health needs. This review enables the organization to identify changing expectations. PVHS uses voice of the customer data in (1) health care service design, (2) the business decision support process, (3) the strategy development and deployment (SDD) process, (4) evaluation and improvement of key access mechanisms, and (5) evaluation and improvement of work systems and processes discussed later in this chapter.

PVHS uses voice of the customer information and feedback to become more patient- and family-focused and community-focused, satisfy patient/customer needs and desires, and identify *opportunities for innovation*.

To support systemwide goals, customer service steering committee team members meet with directors in patient care units and departments and use the Avatar priority matrix to identify improvement opportunities, set goals for department BSCs, and write unit improvement initiatives.

Annually, the customer service steering committee establishes and deploys systemwide, customer service–focused improvement initiatives in support of the SOs, with resource allocation through SDD. The customer service steering committee also monitors action plan progress for customer service–focused improvement initiatives. For 2008, the major customer service improvement initiative focused on reengaging staff in the "We're Here for You" campaign and achieving top box patient satisfaction scores of 80 percent. In 2009, the initiative focused on engaging physicians and medical providers in achieving top box and Hospital Consumer Assessment of Healthcare Providers and Systems goals.

PVHS continually strives to keep its listening and learning methods current with health care service needs and directions.

BUILD PATIENT AND OTHER CUSTOMER RELATIONSHIPS   For PVHS, building relationships with patients and other customers begins long before they come to the organization seeking services and continues throughout their care and after their discharge.

Relationship-building efforts aimed at acquiring patients and other customers are initiated through the marketing, outreach/business development, and community health departments in support of the strategic plan. These departments identify key target audiences in the primary and secondary service areas and develop relationship-building initiatives, which may include the following:

- Establishing partnerships
- Providing community health services, such as the free, 24-hour Poudre Valley Nurse Line and Nurse-Is-In program
- Offering specialty clinics and other clinical and administrative services in rural areas
- Providing community health education and continuing medical education
- Creating community health organizations, such as the Healthy Kids Club and Aspen Club
- Participating in community organizations, such as the Mental Health and Substance Abuse Partnership

Three years prior to the scheduled opening of MCR, PVHS began relationship building with potential customers in the Loveland area. The MCR president conducted town hall meetings, and a permanent gazebo at the construction site allowed the community to watch project progress and gain information about PVHS. PVHS regularly hired the Loveland Optimist Club to grill lunch for construction crews and continues to provide free emergency medical coverage for athletic events in Loveland schools. Hospital officials also established a physician advisory committee and multiple community advisory groups.

Once customers enter PVHS, the organizational vision guides the workforce to offer services in a manner that exceeds customer expectations and secures future interactions; builds loyalty, and gains positive referrals. Fewer than 2 percent of hospitals are able to achieve and maintain improvement in customer satisfaction for three consecutive years, according to Press Ganey Associates. Yet PVHS has sustained continued improvement since 2001, earning Avatar's Overall Best Performer Award, Five Star National Award, Most Improved Inpatient and Outpatient Scores at the national level, and numerous innovation awards, including four for 2007.

INNOVATIVE SERVICE EXCELLENCE Innovative systemwide service excellence initiatives that support the organization's continuing success in this area include the following:

- Staffs use Key Words at Key Times to enhance customer interactions.
- Volunteer patient liaisons make rounds monitoring current patient satisfaction, logging complaints/comments, and forwarding them for follow-up.

- Guest Services helps family members find affordable accommodations at local hotels or one of the PVHS-owned hospitality houses (Pitkin Houses).
- The concierge service meets individual patient and family needs prior to and during hospitalization.
- GetWell Network, an in-room, interactive patient education program in each patient room at PVH and MCR, offers a real-time customer satisfaction component that allows patients to (1) obtain information about their care team; (2) access the Internet and e-mail; (3) communicate complaints and compliments; and (4) order on-demand movies.
- Operating room nurse liaisons update family members on patient status, with continual updates from an electronic status board, an Avatar.
- PVH operates the Lemay Bistro adjacent to surgery waiting rooms so family members can get convenient refreshments, including PVHS' own coffee blend, and, based on community focus group input; the MCR ED offers vending machines with hearty, healthy snacks for late-night visitors.
- PVHS was an early adopter of patient room service.
- MCR patient rooms are all private and equipped with sleeper sofas and windows that open to let in fresh air. PVH has only three remaining semiprivate rooms.
- MCR also offers showers, changing rooms, full kitchens, and healing gardens for family use.
- Caregivers wear color-coded identifiers on their name badges because patients and families wanted to quickly identify nurses, physicians, and other caregivers.
- MCR departments wear color-coded scrubs.
- PVH and MCR have implemented bedside registration and checkout. Patients go straight to their room rather than having to stop in Admitting and fill out paperwork, and the final bill is delivered to the patient room the morning of discharge to avoid delays as the patient is leaving.
- PVHS patients receive follow-up phone calls from a nurse after certain outpatient procedures or discharge from the hospital.
- Many units also send personal thank-you notes.

MULTIPLE KEY ACCESS MECHANISMS AND SERVICE RECOVERY PVHS has established multiple access mechanisms enabling customers to seek information, obtain services, and share complaints and compliments. (Seeking information, PVHS provides extensive information to patients and the community related to health care services, disease management, and health and wellness.)

- Access to service: PVHS ensures customer access regardless of customer finances or location.

■ Complaints/compliments: PVHS reaches beyond traditional complaint management by establishing a comment management system for gathering and trending complaints and compliments. This formal comment management system has key mechanisms for receiving complaints and compliments described more fully in the following paragraphs.

The workforce focus team established, deployed, and annually evaluates the behavior standards, which outline the organization's key customer contact requirements for all access mechanisms. During development of the behavior standards, this team looked at best practices from Baldrige recipients and then reviewed patient feedback for guidance on how to operationalize PVHS values and the key customer requirements into specific staff behaviors. The systematic deployment strategy includes:

■ Formal training for all managers and supervisors through the Learn and Lead program, with tool kits to facilitate staff meeting discussions
■ An acknowledgment to abide by the behavior standards signed by all job applicants and members of the workforce
■ Adherence check at annual staff performance review
■ Linkage of reward and recognition (R&R) program to behavior standards
■ SMG presentations at NEO and employee/volunteer forums
■ Visual displays throughout health system facilities, including computer screen savers
■ "How We're Making PVHS World Class" information, distributed and posted throughout the health system
■ Reengagement of staff through "We're Here for You" campaign

To reinforce the behavior standards, the customer service steering committee also established and deployed Key Words at Key Times, which outlines specific customer contact requirements related to customer access (e.g., answering the phone and welcoming customers to facilities). The customer service steering committee determined Key Words at Key Times through its extensive data aggregation and analysis activities.

PVHS' comment management system collects, tracks, aggregates, and trends complaints to ensure prompt, effective resolution and a better understanding of what drives customer satisfaction and dissatisfaction. As a cycle of improvement, PVHS also collects, aggregates, and trends compliments. Comments may enter the system through any of the key access methods. To minimize customer dissatisfaction and secure future interactions and referrals, PVHS trains and empowers front-line staff members and volunteer patient liaisons to (1) proactively address concerns before they become complaints; and (2) resolve complaints immediately before they escalate.

Staff and volunteer patient liaisons use (1) a *service recovery process*, which is taught through the Learn and Grow series and distributed throughout the health system in the "How We're Making PVHS World Class" information sheet; and (2) the Splash of Sunshine program. Splash of Sunshine authorizes staff members to offer a voucher to patients or family members for food or gifts to help ease concerns. A patient representative tracks and trends voucher distribution to look for improvement opportunities and to better understand dissatisfaction. If staff members or volunteers cannot resolve an issue on their own, they contact their supervisor and/or director. Complaints received through physicians go directly to the appropriate director.

The director promptly assists in resolving the complaint. If resolution is not possible at the director level or if the director ascertains that the complaint puts the organization at risk, the director contacts a patient representative, who works with the director to resolve the complaint. Despite top box scores exceeding the organization's stretch goals, PVHS tasked a subset of the customer service steering committee to develop and deploy a comprehensive Service Excellence and Recovery Training program. Titled "Every Person, Every Time," the program was conducted over a three-month period in 2009, and was attended by 98 percent of staff and volunteers. CARE service recovery includes:

- C: Clarify the customer's concerns and expectations.
- A: Apologize and acknowledge the problem.
- R: Resolve the problem.
- E: Explain how the problem will be fixed.

If the patient representative cannot resolve a patient complaint, the patient/customer lodging the complaint can enter a formal grievance process involving the CEO of PVH, MCR, or PVHS. The CEO has seven days to respond and attempt to resolve the complaint. Patient representatives trend, track, and review grievances quarterly with their CNOs.

To maintain a strategic advantage and ensure world-class health care, PVHS monitors customer satisfaction relative to competitors, other organizations offering similar health care services, and health care industry benchmarks. PVHS also relies on comparative data from Baldrige award recipients and participates in the VHA Superior Performance Improvement Initiative.

COLLABORATIVE RESULTS The VHA Superior Performance Improvement Initiative is a collaboration among 36 participating hospitals that have standardized a series of Avatar and Press Ganey patient satisfaction survey questions. For the first time, CMS' new Hospital Consumer Assessment of Healthcare Providers and Systems are providing a nationally standardized survey instrument. Additional information on local competitors is collected through a variety of mechanisms, including the annual consumer awareness survey; local media; competitor websites, advertisements, and press releases; and visits to competitor facilities by staff and the CEO. PVHS uses comparative satisfaction data for setting world-class goals during SDD, BSC development, and improvement initiatives.

To keep its approaches for determining customer satisfaction current with health care service needs and directions, PVHS annually and as needed evaluates and improves its approaches. A significant improvement occurred when PVHS converted to the Avatar satisfaction-survey system, which increased statistical reliability and frequency of satisfaction determination (weekly updates). At the same time, PVHS began surveying patients from all care areas. The customer service steering committee continues to identify new data needs and requests Avatar adjustments, including customized reports and new questions, or new information-gathering tools. For example, the customer service steering committee is currently working with Avatar on a database component to pull patient satisfaction data related to specific physicians. PVHS stays up to date on the latest available information gathering tools through participation in conferences and trainings.

PERFORMANCE EXCELLENCE JOURNEY PVHS has been on a multiyear performance excellence journey choreographing a multitude of tools and methods to improve performance. PVHS' innovative, team-based performance excellence cycle (see Exhibit 7.9) drives improvement of organizational effectiveness.

PROCESS MANAGEMENT PVHS' key work processes build on the organization's core competencies. Health care processes provide value to the customer through direct patient or community services; support processes enable the health care processes to operate effectively and efficiently. Together, they ensure organizational success and sustainability, enabling the organization to achieve SOs; meet key customer requirements; and address competitive advantages and challenges.

PVHS determines key work process requirements based on extensive voice of the customer data input from patients and the community. For support processes, voice of the customer information comes from workforce, supplier, and partner surveys, interviews, and/or focus groups, as well as stakeholder representation on process design teams. Based on customer requirements, design teams identify in-process and outcome indicators and goals to ensure that the process is performing to target.

PROCESS DESIGN AND INNOVATION IN SIX STEPS PVHS has a systematic process for designing and innovating key work processes:

1. An oversight committee or director identifies a need for process design and forms a multidisciplinary design team representing stakeholders, such as the workforce, suppliers, and partners.

EXHIBIT 7.9 Performance Excellence Cycle

2000	2001	2002	2003	2004	2005	2006	2007
1st Baldrige Feedback Report	Performance Review	Optional Performance Plan	60 New Managers	Leadership Rounding	Definition of World-Class Customer Service	Leadership Priorities Template	Employee/Volunteer Forums
Balanced Storecard	Peer Evaluations	Patient Focus Group	Thank You Notes	Learn and Lead Key Words at Key Times	Must-Haves	Global Path to Success and Personal Goals	Personal Goal Cards
Balanced Staffing Model	Employee Suggestion Program	Volunteer Patient Liaisons	Discharge Phone Calls	IS Steering Committee Structure	Splash of Sunshine	BSC Action Plan Process	Strategic Planning Timeline
Value Model	PDCA	Customer Champions	Walk Don't Point	Proactive Ergonomics	Concierge Service	Strategic Planning Timeline	Increased Physician Participation in SDD
		Referral Bonus Program	VIC (Intranet)	Performance Excellence Team Coordination	Provider Identification	Customer Service Steering Committee	We're Here for You
		PDCA Training	Physician Connectivity	CPEx Peak Award	Electronic Health Record	Top Box Lemay Bistro OR RN Liaison	GetWell Network
			Mentor Program		Behavior Standards	Definition of System BSC Measures	Private Rooms
					Learn and Grow Training on Process Improvement	Management Orientation	Electronic ESC
						New PDCA Process	Thomson Healthcare Database
						Business Decision Support Process	Volunteer Performance Review
							Stay Interviews
							New Exit Interview Process
							Peer Recognition for Volunteers and Physician
							PDCA Facilitation

Courtesy of Poudre Valley Health System.

2. The design team determines process requirements, such as efficiency and effectiveness measures and the need for agility.
3. The design team identifies internal and external best practices and opportunities for innovation, including new technology, through organizational knowledge, literature reviews, site visits, and/or experts.
4. The team maps the process.
5. If possible, the team performs a pilot process to make sure that the process meets requirements.
6. If the process does not perform to goal, the team revises the process.

Medical Center of the Rockies (MCR) provides a unique glimpse of process design and implementation in action. The MCR steering committee, led by the MCR president and guided by organizational learning from throughout PVHS and partner Regional West Medical Center (RWMC), identified key processes that needed to be in place when MCR opened and assigned each process to a design team (Step 1). To determine process requirements (Step 2), the teams looked at PVH's voice of the customer data and convened focus groups to reach new communities that would be served by MCR. Based on these requirements, the teams visited world-class organizations around the country, mapped service delivery processes, and piloted those (Steps 3 to 5). For instance, teams worked with suppliers to build and test mock-ups of key spaces planned for the facility; one team invited city transportation officials to be "patients" in the back of ambulances and tested proposed street and driveway design; and the teams worked with partners and suppliers to hold a series of "Day in the Life" events where community members posed as "patients" and "family members" in numerous possible scenarios. The teams revised facility or process design based on these pilots (Step 6), documented processes in policies and procedures, and trained the workforce.

PROCESS MANAGEMENT AND QUALITY IMPROVEMENT   PVHS also uses the PDCA quality improvement model, which consists of:

- Plan. Form PDCA team to analyze data, identify root cause, research best practices, and develop improvement plan to meet customer and process requirements. Identify outcome or in-process measures for determining whether the process is performing to goal (e.g., cycle time, patient satisfaction).
- Do. Implement improvements, possibly through a pilot.
- Check. Check results against measures of success. If results are not attained, return to plan step.
- Act. Institutionalize change through change management process, policy/procedure revisions, and training. Monitor performance to make sure the process is functioning to plan.

To ensure that processes are meeting key requirements in day-to-day operations, PVHS designs processes to incorporate automation, error proofing, and alert systems, and monitors in-process measures as early indicators of potential problems. The organization also monitors monthly, quarterly, and yearly audits through oversight committees (Clinical Quality Improvement Council). If a process is not meeting established requirements, the PDCA process may be initiated. To reduce variability and response time, PVHS uses unit-specific collaborative-practice guidelines and protocols. Quality Resources performs real-time audits to ensure that guidelines are followed. Processes incorporate patient feedback and in-process measures, such as those gathered hourly by caregivers or throughout the day as physicians make rounds. These measures are particularly important in the timely control and improvement of health care processes, as they allow care providers to make immediate adjustments to patient care plans. In-process measures are also critical for timely responses by the environmental health and safety team. Suppliers assist in managing work processes by training on new equipment, advising on design and remodel, ensuring product availability and effectiveness, and participating in process improvements. Major suppliers meet regularly with appropriate directors to assess service standards and product availability.

Also, SMG and directors serve on supplier advisory boards and provide direct input into decisions that will impact design and delivery of future products and services. The role of partners in managing work processes varies with the nature of the partnership but may include (1) participation in process implementation; (2) collection and monitoring of key process performance measures; (3) identification of opportunities for process improvement; and (4) participation in improvement initiatives, including sharing of best practices. Collaborators may identify opportunities for process improvement and participate in improvement initiatives.

PVHS minimizes overall costs associated with inspections, tests, and process or performance audits by incorporating automation and error proofing into process and service design and identifying in-process measures that give early indications of potential problems. Part of the design process includes investigating whether automated alert systems or other error-proofing tools are available to ensure vigilant monitoring. PVHS has invested significantly in automated alert systems that minimize constant checking and rechecking of vital systems. For example, computerized monitoring systems—such as lab delta checks, drug interaction notifications on medication orders, flow meter alarms on patient IVs, and temperature monitoring of medication, lab, and blood bank refrigerators—save caregiver time that can be better spent on direct patient care needs. Support processes have similar mechanisms: Computerized systems alert staff to supply outdates and Food and Drug

Administration recall; Charge Master Committee assists revenue-generating departments in routine audits of billing procedures that assure appropriate and timely charges; Claim Scrubber and Grouper software functions ensure that reimbursement is complete and that data have no conflicts; required fields in the admissions process collect billing information and reduce insurance claim rejections; and compliance software performs a medical-necessity check.

A focus on performance excellence and organizational learning is embedded in the culture of PVHS, with formal and informal approaches driving continual work process improvement. Process improvement begins at the front line with staff that is empowered to identify improvement opportunities for simple problem solving by unit or department teams. Complex, costly, or far-reaching improvement opportunities identified by staff or through the PVHS performance measurement system escalate to system PDCA initiatives based on defined criteria and a formal scoring process. Tools for determining when a formal PDCA initiative is appropriate are available on the intranet. The PIT approves and monitors system PDCA initiatives to ensure strategic alignment and resource optimization:

- The PDCA initiator completes a Team Purpose form that quantifies the improvement need, defines the scope of the proposed PDCA initiative, recommends team membership, and establishes measures of success.
- The initiator presents the Team Purpose form to the PIT.
- The PIT evaluates the proposed PDCA initiative using a formal scoring tool based on implications for patient safety, regulatory compliance, the strategic plan, and other defined factors.
- Approved teams receive a trained facilitator, post summary information on the intranet, and report quarterly progress to PIT. PIT annually evaluates the organization's PDCA system and recently, as part of the performance excellence cycle, completed a PDCA on PDCA, which improved PDCA deployment, standardization, and knowledge management. PIT is one of seven multidisciplinary performance excellence teams, which also play a key role in PVHS' performance improvement system. These teams, organized around the Baldrige categories, function as systemwide oversight committees with defined roles in the annual performance excellence cycle and monthly monitoring of key performance measures. Process improvement staff belong to each team and coordinate improvement efforts between the teams, as well as quarterly learning opportunities for all team members.

CORE AND INNOVATIVE BEST PRACTICES PVHS exercises the core best practices identified earlier and has advanced knowledge in this area with new, innovative best practices.

Principle 4: Improve Performance

- **Prioritize improvement projects.** Identify and prioritize strategic and operational initiatives projects to improve organization's performance along financial, customer or constituent, process, and people dimensions.
- **Leverage customer facing processes.** Develop and exercise customer and patient facing processes to understand and recalibrate processes around changing customer needs. Gather customer and competitor intelligence using regular customer surveys, focus groups, call centers, and related methods and approaches.
- **Leverage process improvement methods.** Design and maintain ongoing process improvement methods (e.g., PDCA) and problem solving to identify and eliminate root causes of issues.
- **Realize value from benchmarking.** Leverage benchmarking and comparative methods to identify and regularly improve core and support processes
- **Create a performance culture.** Create a culture of quality, virtual community of practitioners to coordinate performance improvement
- **Innovative Best Practice.** PVHS starts building relationships with patients and other customers long before they come to the organization seeking services and continues throughout their care and after their discharge.
- **Innovative Best Practice.** PVHS customer service questions collect information that covers the full "life cycle" of patient interaction, from admission to discharge.
- **Innovative Best Practice.** PVHS has fully integrated its BSC measurement approach and its process improvement methodology.
- **Innovative Best Practice.** PVHS has augmented its process improvement method with quality audits and reviews to ensure process integrity and results.

Public Service Electric & Gas: Best Practice Case

Public Service Electric & Gas (PSE&G) leverages several methods for gathering voice of the customer information including:

- Ongoing customer surveys of residential, small business and large business customer segments. PSE&G uses two external survey companies to continually conduct voice of the customer surveys. One survey is a perception survey of how customers perceive PSE&G whether or not they had any recent interaction with the company. The other survey is a transactional survey conducted with customers who recently had interaction with the company. The perceptions focus on image, cost of services, corporate citizenship, and so on. The transaction survey focused on all key processes and employee engagement questions. The results are based upon a 10-point scale with 0 to 6 as not satisfied, 7 and 8 satisfied, 9 and 10 very satisfied. Customer verbatim comments are also captured along with identified areas for improvement, which are shared with the process areas for corrective or improvement actions.

- Benchmarking. Participation in ongoing benchmarking consortia projects through sharing of information on customer peer panels. Benchmarking will be described more fully later in this section.

PROCESS IMPROVEMENT Based on the foregoing benchmarking and best practice data gathering, PMG, in coordination with business unit leaders, determine if an improvement initiative is warranted.

PSE&G has evolved over the past 25 years from a company that had a formal corporate quality organization to one that has process improvement embedded within the business areas. All team efforts must be linked to its strategy and directly impact one or more of the metrics on the BSC. Benchmarking efforts, including site visits and/or conference calls to other companies, are a key part of the process improvement efforts. PSE&G participates in numerous benchmarking studies each year. For the past 15 years PSE&G has been the sole sponsor of two major industrywide benchmarking consortiums: one that measures the electric delivery business and the other, the natural gas delivery business. The data collected use the BSC balanced approach. PSE&G has also hosted several best practices sharing sessions at its facilities, which have included companies both within and outside the utility industry. Dozens of best practices have been implemented to bring about measureable improvement in performance; these are discussed further in the following chapter.

PSE&G has three levels of improvement: (1) a formal quality program, (2) a metric recovery plan, and (3) initiatives. Each will be discussed in the following paragraphs.

QUALITY IMPROVEMENT PROGRAM, COMPANY AND NUCLEAR PSE&G operates the Salem and Hope Creek Nuclear Generating Stations and has extensive quality experience related to these operations. PSE&G's quality program enables compliance with the Institute of Nuclear Power Operators (INPO), the World Association of Nuclear Operators (WANO), and the U.S. Nuclear Regulatory Commission (NRC). PSE&G also participates in benchmarking and best practice sharing with INPO and WANO. PSE&G's generating stations

METRIC RECOVERY PLAN—General Inquiry Service Level

Reason for not achieving Goal:

Increased call volume due to high level of storm activity in earlier months impacted results along with an increase in unknown customers

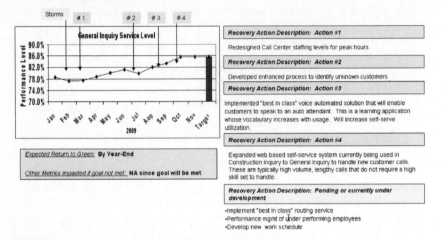

EXHIBIT 7.10 Metric Recovery Plan: General Inquiry Service Level
Courtesy of Public Service Electric & Gas.

are regularly inspected by the NRC and its nuclear BSC provides direction on improvement projects.

METRIC RECOVERY PLAN Each metric that is below target has a recovery plan included in the BSC meeting report. The owner of the measure provides reasons for not meeting the goal, essentially a root cause analysis. From this analysis, specific recovery actions are defined by function with an estimate of when the performance will turn back to green, or be in line with targeted performance levels. Exhibit 7.10 is an example of a metric recovery plan for general service inquiry. Notice the four recovery actions taken and overlaid on the BSC measure. One clearly sees measureable improvement after each action. The performance level steadily improved from 78 percent to 86 percent over the course of ten months.

INITIATIVE PRIORITIZATION AND ONGOING MANAGEMENT If more significant remediation is warranted, the business unit leader in concert with PMG will prepare an initiative template. PSE&G has developed an initiative template that clearly demonstrates the linkage from the strategy to the initiatives and accountabilities. Key initiative milestones are reviewed on a quarterly basis with leadership to monitor progress and to make any mid-course corrections.

Two examples of key strategic initiatives are (1) solar panels for utility poles and (2) replacing street lights.

Solar Panels on Utility Poles   PSE&G, one of the country's largest utilities, is outfitting 200,000 utility poles with solar panels, part of New Jersey's embrace of a strategy that has made it the nation's second-biggest producer of solar energy behind California. This project is the world's first such project of its kind.

Instead of bemoaning what it does not have—bright sunshine, high winds, and empty land—PSE&G has looked for places where solar capacity can be squirreled away inconspicuously. In addition to utility poles, the company is installing solar panels on both public and private locations.

FedEx Corporation, for example, has begun installing solar panels atop its distribution hub in Woodbridge, New Jersey, covering about three acres, and it is now the largest rooftop solar facility in the United States.

Replacing Street Lights   PSE&G has begun replacing 100,000 streetlights with new energy-efficient units that could save municipalities a combined $1 million a year in electricity costs. This is the largest relamping effort in the nation.

The new units will increase light with less glare and less "light pollution" than the mercury vapor units they will replace and last four times longer. The new induction fluorescent lights will be installed on municipal roads and residential streets in towns that sign up for the no-cost replacement program.

PSE&G worked with a California company to design the new units. The fixture, dubbed "The Jersey," is painted a pastel green to denote its environmental benefits. Forty-six New Jersey towns have signed up for the program.

BENCHMARKING: PEER GROUPS, CONSULTANTS, AND ASSOCIATION INPUTS   Over the past five years, PSE&G has transformed its planning process to include benchmark data from peers for its targeted top decile and top quartile performance. PSE&G has this data available ahead of the budgeting process, which allows PMG to include any initiatives that require increased funding. This ability to plan on timely data helps ensure implementation of best practices and moves the company closer to achieving its strategy. The panels meet twice a year, once in the fall to review and revise the data collection package for the coming year and once in the spring to focus on the identification of best practices.

The benchmarking consortium is called the Gas and Electric Utility Peer Panel and is solely sponsored by PSE&G at no cost to participating members. The data are collected and reports are prepared via Web-based technology (see www.utilitypeerpanel.org/peerpanel.asp).

PSE&G also gathers data through participation with PA Consulting and associations EUCG, Inc. and EEI. The measures are similar to the Electric Peer Panel Study. PSE&G gathers and shares information through industry associations American Gas Association, Edison Electric Institute, EUCG, Inc., and AGA/Edison Electric Institute.

All the benchmarking and best practices results are posted on the PSE&G intranet benchmarking clearinghouse website.

CORE AND INNOVATIVE BEST PRACTICES   PSE&G exercises the core best practices identified earlier and has advanced knowledge in this area with new, innovative best practices.

Principle 4: Improve Performance

- **Prioritize improvement projects.** Identify and prioritize strategic and operational initiatives projects to improve organization's performance along financial, customer or constituent, process, and people dimensions.
- **Leverage customer facing processes.** Develop and exercise customer and constituent facing processes to understand and recalibrate processes around changing customer needs. Gather customer and competitor intelligence using regular customer surveys, focus groups, call centers, and related methods and approaches.
- **Leverage process improvement methods.** Design and maintain an ongoing process improvement methods and problem solving to identify and eliminate root causes of issues.
- **Realize value from benchmarking.** Leverage benchmarking and comparative methods to identify and regularly improve core and support processes.
- **Create a performance culture.** Create a virtual community of practitioners to coordinate initiative completion.
- **Innovative Best Practice.** PSE&G is at the forefront of industry benchmarking, having led or pioneered establishment of utility and gas industry consortia.
- **Innovative Best Practice.** PSE&G has innovated performance management in the utility and gas industries, and is the ongoing best practices clearinghouse for multiple participating companies.
- **Innovative Best Practice.** PSE&G, in addition to formal quality programs, has innovated to create two tools, the Metric Recovery Plan and the Initiative Template, to drive performance.

Sharp HealthCare: Best Practice Case

Sharp has developed sophisticated patient and customer processes that inform the organization and that use a portfolio of quality methods to enable business improvement.

PATIENT AND MARKET KNOWLEDGE During the strategic planning process, a customer/partner-driven environmental analysis is produced. On an annual and ad hoc basis, Sharp assesses key customer groups, competitor activities, market share distribution, population health indicators, demographic data, customer group feedback, and industry trends data. This assessment provides the foundation for system and entity marketing plans that delineate customer-focused key business and marketing strategies, which are deployed to achieve the organization's short- and long-term goals. Customer satisfaction priorities also are assessed annually and integrated into the planning process, from which goals, strategies, and action plans are developed. Analyses of employer, demographic, discharge, and marketing data identify Sharp's primary target segments:

- Women (age 25–54), who make an estimated 80 percent of the buying decisions in health care
- Seniors (age 65+), who currently represent 31 percent of Sharp's discharges and are forecasted to represent 40.4 percent of Sharp's discharges by the year 2020
- Hispanics, who are forecasted to grow from a current 29.6 percent to 35.7 percent of the San Diego County population by 2020.

The Sharp Experience's customer focus facilitates an infrastructure of educating and mentoring Sharp's leaders to use a wide range of methodically selected listening and learning tools (see Exhibit 7.11) to provide different information sets by customer segments; inpatient (IP), outpatient (OP), emergency department (ED), brokers (B), and payors (P).

These tools empower employees to identify needs, expectations, and preferences of former, current, and potential customers/partners at the system, entity, department, and individual levels. For instance, employees are provided data, training, and tools to respond to customer/partner likes, needs, desires, and complaints with prescribed process improvement tools, service recovery methods, service experience mapping and design, and new product/service development. At leadership development sessions, leaders learn to analyze patient/customer satisfaction data, develop and implement process improvement initiatives, hardwire service and experience elements, and develop new product and service offerings. Additionally, *innovative* strategies to attract and retain customers are shared across the system. Sharp

Listening and Learning Tools (Including Processes)	Rate	Primary Users	Use	Customer		
Former and Current Patients and Families				IP	OP	ED
Patient Satisfaction Surveys (Press Ganey) for IP, OP, ED, urgent care, home health, hospice, skilled nursing, mental health, rehabilitation, and physician office visits. (7.2)	Real-time surveys monthly	Hospital/Medical Group, PFS, Managers, Staff	IP, OP, ED/ PI	▲	▲	▲
Primary/Secondary Market Research. (Includes awareness/ perception/utilization research, focus groups, mystery shopping, predictive health care segmentation) Secondary data: OSHPD, Solucient, JC. Primary data collected by Sharp agents and employees via interviews (available for analysis at any time).	Annually, Quarterly, Ad Hoc	Strategic Planning and Business Development, Marketing and Communications	IP, OP, ED/ Planning Services, Marketing	▲	▲	▲
Encounter and Enrollment Data. Data from ambulatory, inpatient, and outpatient electronic records are uploaded to the CRM database. (7.2)	Monthly	Finance, IT, System Marketing, Business Dev.	IP, OP, ED, P/ Business/ Planning Services	▲	▲	▲
Customer Contact Centers (82-Sharp, Sharp Nurse Connection®, Web Center). Call Center and Web Center data are uploaded monthly into the CRM database. Demographics are collected for target marketing and campaign effectiveness measurement. (7.5)	Monthly	Call and Web Center, Marketing and Communications	All Customers/ Planning Services, Marketing	▲	▲	▲
Other key elements include: AIDET, 12 Behavior Standards, Five "Must-Haves," and Key Words At Key Times	Ongoing	Leaders, Staff	IP, OP, ED	▲	▲	▲
Rounding with Reason/Rounding Logs. Managers are trained and accountable via performance standards, action plans, Accountability Grids, and Rounding Logs. Information is shared at LDS and Employee Forums or Communication Expos.	Ongoing	Leaders	IP, OP, ED PI	▲	▲	▲
Comment Cards and Interdepartmental Surveys. Data are aggregated by unit managers and shared at staff meetings.	Ongoing	Leaders, Staff	All Customers/ PI	▲	▲	▲
Complaint System and Informal Feedback. Most complaints are responded to immediately at point of service with empowered staff performing service recovery. Information is shared at unit meetings. Data are rolled up across the system for trending and action. (7.2)	Ongoing	Leaders	IP, OP, ED/ Planning Services, PI	▲	▲	▲
Selected Patient Follow-up Calls. Post-discharge and post-office visit telephone calls are made to assess outcomes and satisfaction.	Ongoing	Leaders, Staff	IP, OP, ED/ PI	▲	▲	▲
SHP Member Surveys. Consumer Assessment Health Plan Surveys mailed to random member sample to assess satisfaction/ needs. Brokers and employer groups are surveyed (Fig. 3.2-2). (7.2)	Annually	SHP Leaders, Risk/Quality Mgmt., SHP Staff	B, P/ Planning Services, Marketing, PI		B, P	
Potential Patients and Future Markets						
Primary/Secondary Market Research (awareness, perception, and utilization research, quantitative/qualitative/predictive health care segmentation). Sharp applies Solucient's Household View™ life-stage segmentation system and other research methods when planning marketing campaigns. Primary data are collected by Sharp employees and agents via interviews.	Annually and focused, Ongoing	Marketing/ Communications, Business Dev, Sharp Leaders	IP, OP, ED/ Business/ Planning Services	▲	▲	▲
Customer Contact Centers (e.g., 82-Sharp, Sharp Nurse Connection®) Data uploaded monthly into the CRM database. (7.5)	Ongoing	Call/Web Center, Marketing and Communications	IP, OP, ED/ Business/Planning Services	▲	▲	▲
Brokers/Payors. Dedicated Web page and annual meetings. (7.2)	Ongoing	Medical Groups and Contracts	B, P/ Business/ Planning Services		B, P	

EXHIBIT 7.11 Listening and Learning Tools

Courtesy of Sharp HealthCare.

uses marketing methods tailored to the diverse needs of Sharp's target segments, including language, gender, age, race, and disease-specific needs. Sharp differentiates its services from competitors by responding to patient contact requirements, such as allowing patients to pay their bill and request an appointment online, and providing same-day and next-day access to their primary care physician.

Listening and learning methods are kept current by ensuring accuracy of data, improving efficiency, cross validating data sources, comparing past predictions to actual performance, validating against industry benchmarks, conducting annual executive steering assessments of key strategic challenges, and performing industry analyses and outmigration studies by the strategic planning department.

PATIENT AND CUSTOMER SATISFACTION Strategically, Sharp is committed to creating long-term loyalty from its customers/partners across the continuum of care. Key mechanisms for relationship building with customer/partners who are seeking information; receiving, providing, or supporting care; making complaints; or obtaining other services include the following:

- Branding efforts
- Broker/payor meetings
- Community events
- Community health collaboratives and programs
- Customer relationship management database
- Customer contact centers
- Multicultural services
- Sharp Experience action teams
- Senior resource and information centers
- Web center

Sharp leaders determine key contact requirements for patient and customer access. Key customer access mechanisms include the following:

- Face-to-face contact
- Customer contact centers
- 82-SHARP
- Sharp.com (Web)
- SharpEnEspañol.com (Web)
- SRS call center (physician appointment scheduling)
- Sharp Nurse Connection® (offering 24-hour telephone medical triage)
- Health fairs
- Community events
- Written materials
- Letter/fax/e-mail
- Conferences
- Community education classes

For instance, customer contact centers exist as the "answer place" for customers/partners. These customer contact centers provide information by phone about 13,000 times per month and online over 275,000 times per month. Customer contact centers track customers by gender and age to determine how Sharp is serving its target segments. Sharp tracks online comment topics. Sharp empowers its employees to resolve complaints at the point of service through resolution and service recovery programs and by monitoring unit-level patient satisfaction data. Sharp's comprehensive patient relationship system includes organizational beliefs and proactive input, and a feedback/complaint process.

Sharp believes in ongoing learning for continuous improvement, and uses a variety of proactive tools to solicit formal and informal feedback. The process includes aggregating feedback/complaints by type, analyzing the learning, and instituting process change if necessary. Employees are trained to use a four-step service recovery process: **A**pologize, **C**orrect the situation, **T**rack, and **T**ake action (ACTT) immediately upon identifying a service gap to ensure that the customer service issue does not happen again.

The following sections link prior customer processes to ongoing improvement tools to improve the business performance and to achieve key clinical outcomes.

PROCESS QUALITY IMPROVEMENT METHODS: A SNAPSHOT Sharp HealthCare uses Six Sigma tools to improve quality as part of The Sharp Experience. Six Sigma is an important part of its journey to make Sharp the best place to work, the best place to practice medicine, and the best place to receive care. Six Sigma is defined as a method that uses data to make smart decisions to improve financial and operational performance; or a statistical term that represents near-perfect levels of performance. The Six Sigma method uses a set of tools to achieve excellence. They include:

- **DMAIC.** Define, Measure, Analyze, Improve, and Control is a systematic problem-solving approach, here defined with 12 steps, to quality improvement.
- **Lean Six Sigma.** A set of tools that helps identify and eliminate waste in a process in order to achieve a high level of efficiency.
- **Change Acceleration Process.** An organizational change method designed to accelerate progress of the human side of change.
- **Work-Out.**™ An improvement method that uses a concentrated (6- to 16-hour) decision-making session involving the people who do the work to solve the problems.

Sharp is consistently looking for ways to improve the care it provides to its patients. Six Sigma helps Sharp identify areas that need improvement and more importantly, fix them. Sharp uses the 12-step DMAIC problem-solving process. Sharp also uses the change acceleration process, a model for managing change; SIPOC/COPIS, a method for designing processes; and root cause analysis. Depending on problem complexity and the amount and type of engagement needed, projects are managed using the rigorous measurement of the Six Sigma method (usually six to eight months) or a rapid action project method (usually 30 to 90 days). Other strategies that are used as appropriate include Kaizen bursts and Work-Out™.

Process Improvement Prioritization Process The process for translating performance review findings into continuous and breakthrough improvement and innovation is accomplished through the PI prioritization process. The performance measures are regularly reviewed and the accountability team sets the annual Report Card targets. When performance gaps are noted throughout the year, Executive Steering, CEO Council, and quality councils determine the need for mid-course corrections and propose Lean Six Sigma projects. The Lean Six Sigma department scopes projects and places them into the project funnel.

When resources are available, Executive Steering scores PI projects using the weighted project selection criteria (i.e., alignment with strategy, resource availability, data complexity, scope/change management complexity). Projects that are not selected for Lean Six Sigma are analyzed for other PI methods, and monitored for reconsideration in the next project selection round. The project selection criteria incorporate evaluation of suppliers' and partners' priorities and level of engagement needed to drive improvement. Other methods for addressing opportunities for improvement not classified as a Lean Six Sigma PI project include leadership development session topics, centralized training through Lawson, departmental training, and revision of standard orders and job competencies. To emphasize the importance of management by fact to drive improvement, Sharp committed to data-driven performance improvement using the Lean Six Sigma approach enterprisewide.

Key Business and Support Processes Key work processes that are central to Sharp's core competency are determined and reevaluated during the strategic planning process. The decision making regarding the use of internal systems versus external resources is made through the strategic planning process using the outsource decision process.

The key work processes (see Exhibit 7.12) comprise the essential elements of the product Sharp delivers, health care, along with business and support processes required to provide health care. How Sharp delivers this product is determined by its core competency. The Sharp Experience drives

EXHIBIT 7.12 Key Business and Support Processes

Process	Key Requirements	Process Measures
Manage Health Care		
Screening	Safe, timely	Blood sugar, cholesterol, cancer screening, and glucose levels
Admission/registration	Safe, timely	Patient satisfaction, accredited, privacy, and door to doctor
Assessment and diagnosis	Safe, evidenced-based, efficient, timely	Patient satisfaction, skin care, stroke care
Treatment	Safe, evidence-based, efficient, timely, patient-centered, equitable	Glycemic control, AMI (heart attack), beta blockers, CAP antibiotics, cancer, treatment measures
Discharge/education	Safe, patient-centered, timely	AHRQ patient safety, AMI mortality, bariatric program, smoking cessation
Manage Business and Support		
Revenue cycle	Timely, accurate	EBITDA, days in AR, billing cost, payment
Strategic planning	Timely, accurate	Net revenue, market share, growth
Knowledge management	Timely, safe, and accurate	Internal promotion, training expenditure, out of network, critical values
Supply chain management	Timely, accurate, efficient, safe	Pharmacy turnaround, sales outstanding, and automated orders
Key suppliers and partners management	Efficient, accurate, timely, satisfaction	Provider survey, and denials

Courtesy of Sharp HealthCare.

the cultural environment, priority setting, strategic execution, and structure for evaluation of success across the Pillars.

These aforementioned quality tools enable continuous performance improvement driven by rapid responsiveness, rigorous data analysis, and reduction in variation and waste across the system. Ongoing assessments along with continuous performance improvement efforts assure the following:

- Current service offerings are aligned by Pillar with Sharp's Mission and Vision.
- New customer needs are identified.
- Key customer assessments are based on Press Ganey surveys, including verbatim and focus groups, along with employee input, and performance monitoring to validate that services provided are safe, evidenced-based, patient-centered, timely, efficient, and equitable.
- Existing service lines use evidence-based guidelines and in-process metrics, outcomes analyses, and listening and learning tools to drive improvements. Sharp's key work processes span the continuum of care, providing all basic patient care services, and focus on a patient-centered experience.

These processes contribute to the following:

- Improved health care service outcomes through ongoing performance improvement efforts using DMAIC
- Value and satisfaction for patients based on improved health outcomes
- Financial growth and efficiencies to continue organizational infrastructure investment
- Business growth for partners/brokers/payors/suppliers

The key requirements of Sharp's work processes are safe, evidenced-based, accurate, patient/customer-centered, timely, efficient, and equitable.

The design process uses customer, outputs, process, inputs, and suppliers (COPIS, right to left in Exhibit 7.13). Conversely, the process management uses suppliers, inputs, processes, outputs, customers (SIPOC, left to right in Exhibit 7.13).

Sharp's customers, partners, leaders, and the community demand effective and efficient work processes to ensure continued attainment of Sharp's mission and vision. Sharp's key work processes are determined based on these needs, aligned with system goals through the annual strategic planning process, and reviewed through the performance measurement system and system quality improvement efforts. Design and implementation requirements are ensured through the use of COPIS described earlier and the rigorous 12-step DMAIC process (see Exhibit 7.14).

For example, during the pilot phase of DMAIC (i.e., Step 9), process design requirements are validated and modifications made, if needed. Customer requirements used in DMAIC are from patients, partners, suppliers, or collaborators as determined by the customer of the process under

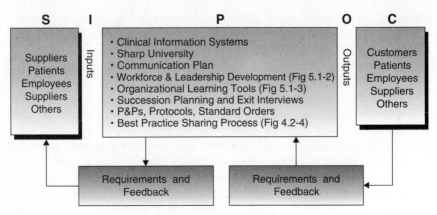

EXHIBIT 7.13 Process Design and Management SIPOC
Courtesy of Sharp HealthCare.

consideration. Key performance measures are identified and used. Additional day-to-day process metrics used for the control and improvement of work processes are listed in each Pillar dashboard available onsite. Measurement and control of day-to-day operations and key work processes are accomplished through the performance measurement system. Action teams and quality councils are charged with designing performance improvement plans using DMAIC to address each goal. These plans are reviewed at least

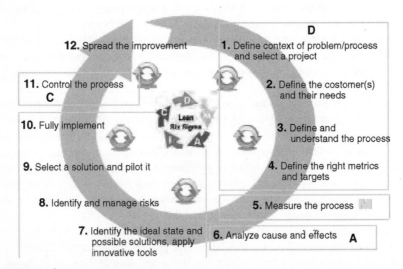

EXHIBIT 7.14 12 Step DMIAC Process
Courtesy of Sharp HealthCare.

monthly and identify the day-to-day changes needed to improve a process not meeting requirements.

In addition to fostering a culture of safety, a preventive approach is used to minimize overall costs associated with inspections and audits, avoiding failures in key work processes and medical errors by:

- Leveraging information technology in process surveillance and improvement such as smart pumps, bar coding, and On Watch. On Watch generates a list of patient care safety issues in real time on the EMR for caregiver action.
- Monitoring with control charts, the quarterly report by MedAI that identifies statistically significant variables across 35 disease states and 1,500 measures.
- Establishing and disseminating systemwide internal and external benchmarked process measurements, and conducting regular process reviews and random analyses of readiness/safety.
- Fostering a culture of safety at the unit level through team resource management and open communication to avoid costly and dangerous errors.
- Establishing a nonpunitive reporting policy and culture, staff education, and leader role modeling and mentoring.
- Providing a confidential reporting process for employees to submit quality concerns and patient safety near-misses.
- Deploying quality improvement methodologies, tools, and projects across the system including failure modes effects analysis (FMEA), team resource management, and Lean Six Sigma, which anticipate failure modes and reduce errors and defects.
- Routinely evaluating suppliers/partners and contractual requirements.
- Ongoing focus on leader/staff training and education.
- Timely RCA with resultant action plans.
- Safety steering committee actions for systemwide prevention based on industry alerts, anticipated errors, or entity experience (e.g., removal of risk-related supplies/equipment).

Quality variance reports are electronically delivered to the appropriate managers and quality departments. Trended quality reports with recommendations are reviewed regularly with entity quality directors in the Clinical Effectiveness department and at entity quality councils for organizational learning. Intervention or prevention steps are outlined and shared with managers for collaboration and implementation.

CORE AND INNOVATIVE BEST PRACTICES Sharp exercises the core best practices identified earlier; it has advanced knowledge in this area with new, innovative best practices.

Principle 4: Improve Performance

- **Prioritize improvement projects.** Identify and prioritize strategic and operational initiatives projects to improve organization's performance along financial, customer or constituent, process, and people dimensions.
- **Leverage customer facing processes.** Develop and exercise customer and constituent facing processes to understand and recalibrate processes around changing customer needs. Gather customer and competitor intelligence using regular customer surveys, focus groups, call centers, and related methods and approaches.
- **Leverage process improvement methods.** Design and maintain an ongoing process improvement methods and problem solving to identify and eliminate root causes of issues.
- **Realize value from benchmarking.** Leverage benchmarking and comparative methods to identify and regularly improve core and support processes.
- **Create a performance culture.** Create a virtual community of practitioners to coordinate initiative completion.
- **Innovative Best Practice.** Sharp leverages customer survey processes and listening methods clearly linked to each customer segment and their respective strategies to determine patient and other customer satisfaction and dissatisfaction levels. This is more advanced than what most companies do.
- **Innovative Best Practice.** Sharp has leveraged a "portfolio" of quality tools (Lean Six Sigma, DMAIC, Change Acceleration Process, Work-Out, etc.) to address differences in the scale, scope, and timing of process and business improvement needs.
- **Innovative Best Practice.** Sharp uses SIPOC and COPIS approaches to design and improve, and to manage their processes; both are disciplined approaches to viewing core and support processes. This is an innovative approach to leveraging the traditional SIPOC approach.
- **Innovative Best Practice.** Sharp has fully integrated its measurement approach including shared technology platform and common dictionaries across the system for use in collecting and aggregating performance data and its process improvement methodology.

CHAPTER 8

Principle 5: Manage and Leverage Knowledge

Hide not your talents, they for use were made.
What's a sun-dial in the shade?

—Benjamin Franklin

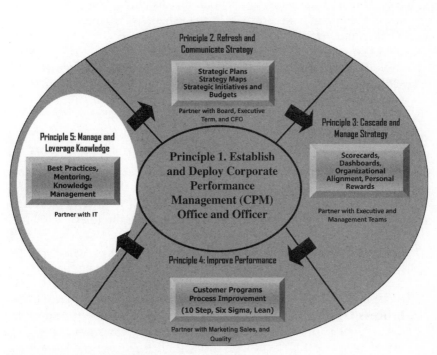

©Copyright 2010 Bob Paladino Associates LLC.

*P*rinciple 5, *Manage and Leverage Knowledge,* focuses on capturing and reusing enterprisewide intellectual property to leverage the organization's best minds, best practices, and of course innovations. As enterprises increasingly rely on knowledge workers, it is essential to have core knowledge management (KM) processes embedded in the organization to capture and propagate best-in-class and world-class results. These processes are augmented by mentoring, high potential, and employee development programs. Key influences for development of this section were my Crown KM or enterprise content management (ECM) program, but particularly the KM expertise shared selflessly by Carla O'Dell, president of APQC, and her talented KM team. In concert with Principle 3, if your Balanced Scorecard (BSC) informs you of a location that performs in the top quartile or decile, then it is advantageous to understand, document, and replicate this location's winning formula and realize the multiplier of many locations. Similarly, Principle 4, Improve Performance team outputs will provide innovations and best practices to raise performance.

CPM Core Process Blueprint and CPM Key Process Roles

Careful research of the cases in this book reveals they follow a discernible set of core corporate performance management (CPM) processes organized within the Five Key Principles. These CPM processes were shown in Exhibit 3.1 to provide strategic context and a working framework to assist you in your organization. Note Principle 5, Manage and Leverage Knowledge consist of two primary core CPM processes, though some organizations have expanded beyond these core processes.

Best Practice and Innovation Sharing Example

The CPM office members play one or more of three key roles in executing the CPM core processes with the fourth, participants. We will discuss *Best Practice and Innovation Sharing* process roles my CPM office deployed at award-winning Crown Castle International to illustrate the roles:

1. **Process Sponsor.** The sponsor is typically the most senior executive accountable for the process outcomes and overseeing the process owner. The process sponsor for the best practice and innovation sharing process at Crown were the U.S., U.K., and Australia company presidents.
2. **Process Owner.** The owner is typically the senior leader accountable to the sponsor for managing the process and is usually a process subject matter expert (SME). The process owner for best practice and innovation sharing process at Crown was one of my direct reports, the director of KM global performance.

3. **Process Facilitator.** The facilitator is typically the individual who day-to-day interacts directly with process participants to drive the process and integrate the process with other key processes. The process facilitator of the Crown best practice and innovation sharing process was one of my direct reports, the director of KM global performance.

4. **Process Participant.** The process participants are typically SMEs, those who will be accountable for the process outcomes and/or are the recipients of the process outcomes. The process participants at Crown were the Crown employees who formed numerous centers of excellence (COEs), communities of practice (COPs) analogous to face book groups for specific topics (engineering, accounting, etc.). Best practice sharing forums were extended outside the company with its participation in consortia learning groups at APQC, the Conference Board, industry and trade groups, and other think tanks and information clearinghouses.

Prior to turning our attention toward the in-depth cases, let us review the core best practices recognized by all the case companies in this book. See each case that follows for their innovative new best practice, so you can appreciate the context and relevance of them to their organizations.

Principle 5: Manage and Leverage Knowledge Best Practices

- **Develop KM processes.** Establish and leverage best practice identification, gathering and sharing processes, and technology solutions.
- **Leverage technology.** Partner with the information technology (IT) function to launch and maintain KMS.
- **Develop expert locator systems.** Design and use expert locator systems to capture systems employee skills inventory within the enterprise to accelerate problem solving in Principle 4 and to optimize human capital.
- **Link KM with improved process performance.** Link best practice or KM processes with Principle 4 processes to capture solutions and innovations.
- **Share best practices.** Share best practices with strategic planning processes to better understand core competencies and possible strategic advantages.
- **Maintain a virtual KM network.** Establish and maintain a virtual network of KM experts throughout the enterprise to optimize results.

Cargill Corn Milling North America: Best Practice Case

Cargill Corn Milling (CCM) is structured to promote enterprise thinking by sharing knowledge and innovation (as discussed in prior chapters) across functional and process development groups. Knowledge obtained from employees, customers, suppliers, and partners is shared across the organization, enabling CCM to operate as a single enterprise, emphasizing continual performance improvement. CCM utilizes many processes and tools to manage organizational knowledge.

COLLECTION AND TRANSFER OF WORKFORCE KNOWLEDGE, BEST PRACTICES Process development groups are the primary approach used to collect and transfer employee knowledge. Corn Milling Operations regularly documents process development groups' best practices through the BPM process. In addition to Corn Milling Operations, standard operating procedures (SOPs) are used to collect and transfer knowledge on how to operate specific unit operations. For example, a centrifuge SOP explains the steps required to start, stop, and run this piece of equipment. Corn Milling Operations and SOPs are available through the Cargill network or hardcopy based on employee job requirements. In addition, other CCM employee knowledge and knowledge collection and transfer approaches include employee training processes, employee suggestion systems, and team participation. Training processes include orientation, on-the-job, mentoring, specialized vendor, and train-the-trainer training sessions. Besides process development groups, employees participate on cross-functional improvement teams, ad-hoc teams, core user groups, functional areas, and department teams.

TRANSFER OF RELEVANT KNOWLEDGE FROM AND TO CUSTOMERS, SUPPLIERS, AND PARTNERS CCM transfers relevant knowledge to and from its key customers using cross-functional customer focus teams. These teams build relationships over time with peers and networks of employees in major strategic accounts. These relationships lead to insights that enable the discovery, creation, and delivery of customer solutions. In addition to customer focus teams, CCM deploys several applications to collect and transfer customer knowledge. Knowledge gleaned at customer touch points is collected and shared using the MasterCard system. Sales personnel and customer service reps are responsible for collecting and adding relevant customer knowledge into a customer database. Corporate account leaders and strategic account leaders are responsible for supporting the transfer of knowledge to and from key customers across multiple business units and product lines. CCM exchanges information with key suppliers on multiple levels. On a basic level it exchanges performance information. In addition, key suppliers are asked to provide insights into potential solutions being addressed by process development groups and are sometimes involved with improvement teams. Suppliers are also involved in providing training and knowledge during the implementation of new processes and systems or the introduction of new supplier products.

RAPID IDENTIFICATION, SHARING, AND IMPLEMENTATION OF BEST PRACTICES

As described previously, CCM uses process development groups and cross-functional improvement teams to identify and share the best-known practices within and outside of CCM. For example, the mill-feed process development group team works with Cargill Sweeteners Europe to collect, transfer, and share best practices for mill and feed operations for 31 worldwide mills. The Malcolm Baldrige National Quality Award (MBNQA) and Cargill Business Excellence (BE) are used to identify best business processes. CCM utilizes a systematic strategic planning process requiring inputs from many sources including customers, suppliers, partners, expert panels, and the workforce. The enterprise development team (EDT) leads strategic reviews and is responsible for assembling all information.

CORE COMPETENCIES, STRATEGIC CHALLENGES, AND ACTION PLANS The development and learning system used for workforce and leaders is the same for how they relate to core competencies, strategic challenges, and action plans. Depth and breadth of information shared will vary depending on the job function.

Managers in strategic roles within CCM receive formal training in Cargill or specific assignments to gain experience in leading organizational change and innovative improvement. Both the development plan process and succession planning processes are used to identify potential managers for training or assignments. For example, in 2007, several senior management team members worked with Cargill-wide teams on an *innovative* initiative to standardize all business processes across Cargill. They are now pivoting expertise into development of key leaders.

CCM leaders identify desired training needs through the development plan process. Education opportunities can include external or internal classes (HPLA, NourishingU, or Cargill) or growth opportunities. Growth opportunities include training, coaching, mentoring, and work-related experiences such as working on projects, assisting another facility with troubleshooting or startups of new processes, or being a member of business unit–wide cross-functional team. For higher-level leaders strategic assignments are provided to increase exposure, breadth of knowledge, and diverse experiences.

CORE COMPETENCIES AND SUCCESSION PLANNING PROCESS Prior to 2007 CCM utilized the Cargill leadership and talent management process for succession planning. This process applied only to leaders at the senior leadership team (SLT) level. In 2007, a refinement to the leadership and talent management processes was implemented. The key steps in this process include (1) identification of key strategic roles for each group based on business objectives; (2) identification of critical competencies for each role; (3) development of a list of potential candidates for each role; (4) discussion and agreement on readiness or developmental requirements for each potential candidate; and (5) work with candidate's supervisor on potential skills and growth opportunities to prepare the candidate for the future role. Through this systematic process, succession planning is linked to the performance management process and development plan process and is owned by the SLT. The succession planning process drives the career progression discussion between a succession candidate and his or her manager.

The SLT product line leaders and functional area managers focus on development of all their employees including the identification and support of high performers and key talent supporting the value of *Develop Talent*.

BEST PRACTICE SHARING Best practice sharing is evidenced within the organization, including cross-functional, departmental, and interdisciplinary sharing within member companies and the business community.

CCM has developed the best practice model (BPM) to innovate work processes to meet key requirements. The BPM includes the key steps and the requirements for each step (see Exhibit 7.2).

This process is owned by the senior leadership team and deployed by process development group leaders and is used to design processes and modify processes for efficiency, effectiveness, agility, and cost control improvements. As illustrated in the final step in Exhibit 7.2, the management of change process is used to ensure product quality, implementation of new technology; service, safety, food safety, consistency, reliability, and environmental protection are built into each process design or refinement. In the same step of the model, new and *innovative* ideas and approaches initiate a refinement cycle for the process. The use of new technology and organizational knowledge is incorporated into several steps of the BPM either directly or through the management of change process. For example, in 2006 CCM innovated the key sustainability work process *Manage Corn & Energy Risk* by creating the customer relationship management system for improving interactions with farmers followed the best practice process, was developed as a result of changing requirements from employee and farmer stakeholders.

IDEA TO INNOVATION (i2i) PROCESS i2i is a formal approach used in a key profitability work process, *Manage Idea & Concept Generation*, and is owned by the innovation manager. The i2i process supports CCM's values of *Be*

Innovative and Promote Collaboration. i2i captures and tracks innovative ideas relating to new discoveries, cost efficiencies, process improvements, and ways to help meet business goals and objectives through a computer-based system. The steps for this process include: (1) Employees enter ideas into the i2i system; (2) ideas are reviewed by cross-functional innovation review teams; (3) innovation review teams classify ideas using an idea prioritization matrix or through the team's knowledge of the feasibility and effectiveness of the idea; and (4) idea mentors are assigned to either nurture the ideas through the system or inform the ideator why the idea is not being advanced at this time. The idea mentor along with automatic system updates (through e-mail) keep the ideator informed as the idea advances through the process. The i2i process has benefited from multiple evaluation and improvement cycles. In 2004, CCM started utilizing formal business unit idea campaigns to generate focused ideas on a specific opportunity. In 2005, a common website tool was implemented in order to share knowledge and ideas throughout Cargill. In 2006, CCM initiated annual *recognition awards for innovation*. In 2007, formalized standard operating procedures were created to define the process and the responsibilities of the ideator, mentor, and innovation review team members.

CORE AND INNOVATIVE BEST PRACTICES   CCM exercises the core best practices identified earlier; it has advanced knowledge in this area with new, innovative best practices.

Principle 5: Manage and Leverage Knowledge

- **Develop KM processes.** Establish and leverage best practice identification, gathering and sharing processes and technology solutions.
- **Leverage technology.** Partner with the IT function to launch and maintain KMS.
- **Develop expert locator systems.** Design and use expert locator systems to capture systems employee skills inventory within the enterprise to accelerate problem solving in Principle 4 and to optimize human capital.
- **Link KM with improved process performance.** Link best practice or knowledge management processes with Principle 4 processes to capture solutions and innovations.

(Continued)

- **Share best practices.** Share best practices with strategic planning processes to better understand core competencies and possible strategic advantages.
- **Maintain a virtual KM network.** Establish and maintain virtual network of KM experts throughout the enterprise to optimize results.
- **Innovative Best Practice.** In a more sophisticated, expanded model than used by most award-winning companies, CCM transfers relevant knowledge and best practices from and to not only customers but also suppliers and partners.
- **Innovative Best Practice.** CCM leverages numerous forum and approaches to best practice sharing including Centers of Expertise, Process Development Groups, and cross-functional improvement teams to share BPM and i2i results.

City of Coral Springs: Best Practice Case

Results and learning are shared through staff meetings at all levels. Quarterly city manager communications meetings and the Supervisory Forum (a quarterly meeting of supervisors) are used to transfer learning. Organizational knowledge is collected and transferred through team competitions, employee celebrations and awards, after-action reports, and through the Knowledge Network and Active Strategy systems. Some of the most successful cross-functional task teams in the city have participated in quality competitions, where careful documentation of the problem, process, and solution is required. This documentation is available on the city website and the internal Knowledge Network.

All cross-functional teams share their "lessons learned" on the Knowledge Network. This system also includes "blogs" on problems and issues and can be used to tap into the institutional knowledge and memory of the entire workforce. The Knowledge Network is also used to disseminate policies, procedures, forms, and information on best practices. The status of ongoing high-profile teams is posted on the Active Strategy system. Management can "drill down" in Active Strategy to get a briefing on team progress and data on any analysis completed. Human resources staff act as a nexus for team-related knowledge and process management expertise. Using business analysts and cooperating with the performance measurement analyst, the human resources staff helps departments learn and deploy the problem-solving process and process design system. The organizational development coordinator (ODC) HR staff also ensures lessons learned in work teams and cross-functional tasks teams are captured and reported at the Supervisory

Forum and related to customers, suppliers, partners, and collaborators as appropriate.

Cooperation, effective communication, and skill sharing within and across work units, operating units, and locations is achieved through various methods including weekly senior management team meetings, weekly departmental staff meetings, quarterly city manager communication meetings, quarterly Supervisory Forums, cross-functional teams, and human resources liaisons.

The emergency medical response process improvement team was the state's team showcase winner and placed fourth overall in the nation in 1998. The citation system improvement team was the state's team showcase winner in 2005 and competed in the nationals in May 2006.

CORE AND INNOVATIVE BEST PRACTICES The city exercises the core best practices identified earlier and has advanced knowledge in this area with a new, innovative best practice.

Principle 5: Manage and Leverage Knowledge

- **Develop KM processes.** Establish and leverage best practice identification, gathering and sharing processes and technology solutions.
- **Leverage technology.** Partner with the information technology function to launch and maintain KMS called Knowledge Network.
- **Develop expert locator systems.** Design and use expert locator systems to capture systems employee skills inventory within the enterprise to accelerate problem solving in Principle 4 and to optimize human capital.
- **Link KM with improved process performance.** Link best practice or knowledge management processes with Principle 4 processes to capture solutions and innovations.
- **Share best practices.** Share best practices with strategic planning processes to better understand core competencies and possible strategic advantages.
- **Maintain a virtual KM network.** Establish and maintain virtual network of KM experts throughout the enterprise to optimize results.
- **Innovative Best Practice.** City of Coral Springs process improvement teams not only drive city organizational innovation, but also share nationally (and win awards). For example, the emergency medical response process improvement team was the state's team showcase winner.

Delta Dental of Kansas: Best Practice Case

Delta Dental of Kansas (DDKS) looks outside of its industry for innovative approaches used by other businesses. Executives participate annually in conferences, providing them a broad and comprehensive opportunity to see how others are executing their strategy management model. These sessions invariably result in a robust opportunity to share best practices across the full spectrum of U.S. and international business. Managers and supervisors are both encouraged and required, as part of their learning and growth imperative, to attend industry, functional, and association meetings to maintain technical currency and develop broader business-based views of their areas of responsibility. As a learning-focused organization, DDKS encourages higher education through tuition reimbursement. Mentoring on an informal level is encouraged, and currently there is a series of facilitated group discussions of the topic underway. Participation in the United Way loaned executive program, which provides a 12-week outside work assignment, and other community professional involvement encourages role-model leadership as well.

BEST PRACTICE SHARING FORUMS DDKS has sponsored the "Best Places to Work" competition through the *Wichita Business Journal*, and participation in that event has led to best practice sharing regarding the work environment. DDKS was recognized by the *Wichita Business Journal* as "Best in Business" in 2006 for its financial results, community involvement, and innovation. *Innovation* cited in the WBJ recognition also supports the agility of the organization in responding to the marketplace: "Delta Dental of Kansas recognizes that small businesses must continue to search for ways to keep costs low while providing a level of health benefits to employees that keeps them competitive in the marketplace." DDKS' team undertook a number of initiatives to provide a variety of dental products to small businesses. Specifically, DDKS introduced "Community Rated" dental plans for small businesses that have better rates, more flexibility, and were innovative. The plans enable small business customers to choose from three dental networks; change deductibles, maximums, and benefits; increase the annual maximum; and add composite (white) fillings, orthodontic services, and select riders for special services.

The BSC approach emphasizes learning and growth for the organization as a whole, and development is a focus at the individual and organizational levels. The learning and growth initiatives reflect DDKS's foundation in stressing that its people, culture, and technology/tools are foundations of company success. The DDKS online learning system was implemented to provide increased opportunities for learning to supplement other programs and provide flexibility in delivery. Training modules have been developed to increase knowledge of the dental field. Through the alignment of corporate strategy communication, career path planning, and workforce professional development, DDKS paints a very clear picture for employees on the company's direction for growth as a whole, as well as each one professionally. DDKS participates in best practice sharing with other member companies (MCs). These sharing opportunities occur at on-site conferences, conference calls, e-mail threads, and social media tools. Delta Dental Professional Association (DDPA) hosts an intranet for all MCs that also serves as an online sharing tool.

SUCCESSION PLANNING   Key position succession planning for the organization is an annual focus, followed by department succession planning documented during the process and reviewed by the CEO and vice president of human resources (see Exhibit 8.1). The development of this plan initiated an increased focus on development across the organization, and resulted in more structured employee development plans being implemented for quarterly update and discussion with managers.

INFORMATION AND KNOWLEDGE MANAGEMENT SYSTEM   DDKS uses a full spectrum of resources to ensure data and information are available to its workforce and stakeholders on a continuous cycle. User-facing systems are standardized across the workforce with application access tailored to meet each user's unique access requirements; controlled through a combination of software and hardware tools. Access restrictions ensure compartmentalization of data as necessary to protect sensitive information from inadvertent or deliberate disclosure. Access is further controlled by the combination of policies and processes instituted corporatewide and reinforced through repetitive training requirements. Web technology is leveraged, where appropriate, to broadcast common use information and to provide access to enterprisewide knowledge management resources. This includes access to Delta Dental Plan Association (DDPA) information available through their exclusive Web portal, and general Internet knowledge bases available on the World Wide Web. E-mail serves as a tertiary internal direct information-sharing modality, following face-to-face and telephonic exchanges. E-mail supplements DDKS external outreaching providing an additional modality for external constituents to communicate with workforce and leadership. DDKS publishes and adheres to strict response standards for this mode of communication to ensure its projects the same customer service persona as any other direct form of communication.

Outside stakeholder access generally takes one of two forms: pushed information or scheduled pulls of information, and may take one of several channels to ensure availability and utility of the shared information. In non-production processes (e.g., knowledge and information-sharing processes),

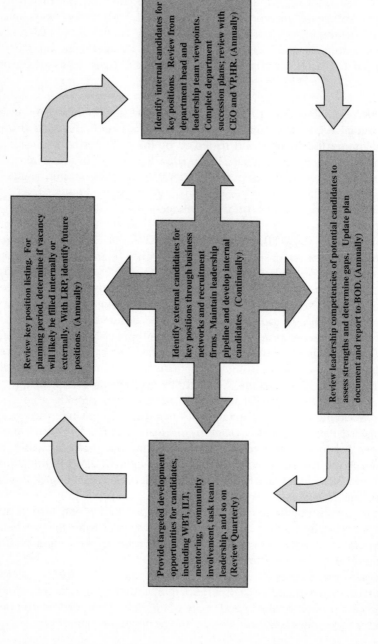

EXHIBIT 8.1 Succession Planning

Courtesy of Delta Dental of Kansas.

information and data are made available through the DDKS Internet portal on its proprietary website, and also through e-mail exchange as previously discussed. DDKS actively encourages constituents to use the Web portal for most of their information requirements. DDKS may elect to push information onto the Web portal for general information-sharing purposes; but in many cases information and data are available and used by DDKS constituents on their own schedule and for their own purposes. DDKS evaluates and tailors the site based on the information provided in constituent surveys to ensure the information and its accessibility meets their needs and desires.

Employees from several departments make up the DDKS Web Committee, whose mission is to provide an influence so organizational knowledge is shared and maintained with a visionary view. The primary function of the Web Committee is to make sure that the information that is placed on the company's Intranet, as well as the DDKS website, is relevant, accurate, reliable, and timely. The committee achieves this by closely monitoring each of the sites.

Workforce and organizational knowledge is collected, shared, and transferred through many channels. Developed to provide a centralized portal for employees to access organizational knowledge, the DDKS intranet was developed to drive organizational efficiency and productivity, and serve as reinforcement for internal communications.

The FOCUS team consisting of DDKS supervisors and middle managers, who meet biweekly to discuss company initiatives and prioritize programming requests, encourages cross-departmental communications and best practice sharing within the management group and between the leadership team (LT) and other employees. Best practices are also shared during these meetings.

The FOCUS team, with guidance from the LT, makes the decision if best practices are to be adopted and implemented by another department or companywide. Operation "Walk Throughs" are scheduled periodically for employees. The objective of these informational sessions is to expose employees, who are either new to DDKS or from a department outside of a particular operational process; this instills a culture of effective communication and skill sharing within and across work units so that a team culture is felt companywide.

Cross-training and employee "shadowing" also helps DDKS employees gain a better understanding of the organization as a whole, which also helps to pave an avenue of best practice and skill sharing across work units and give an opportunity for retiring and/or departing workers to transfer their knowledge to remaining DDKS employees. Best practice sharing is evident within the organization as well as externally, with presentations in several different venues providing an opportunity to exchange ideas and best practices and further the development of the organization. Each quarter all employees gather at the corporate office to attend a presentation delivered by the DDKS LT to create a state of awareness about corporate and departmental initiatives and to help build an informed workplace by transferring knowledge from the LT level to all employees.

The focus of these meetings is on making everyone aware of what is about to be implemented and the status of previously advised initiatives, with some high-level commentary on why it is important. These meetings provide an organizational knowledge forum where all employees receive the same message, at the same time, from the same people and provide opportunities for organizational knowledge and best practice sharing.

From a development perspective, the knowledge management system provides an information resource with early implementation of basic dental and vision terminology.

PEOPLE DEVELOPMENT, INTELLECTUAL PROPERTY To better position the organization for future development of its people and to provide more options for training and delivery methods, DDKS partnered with an online learning company. Originally developed as a learning management and learning content management suite, the platform was built to help manage the learning plans for all employees and to facilitate not only the delivery of online programs but to encourage supervisory interaction in the process by using one database of record.

DDKS' online learning system is instrumental in helping to support strategic objectives, deliver training for skill enhancement, and document results. This online learning system was designed to feature strategy components and core values and to emphasize the company's commitment to learning and growth. Learning is not a single event at DDKS; it is a continuous cycle where employees are offered countless learning and development opportunities. Aside from cross-training, shadowing, and networking with peers, formalized internal instructor-led training courses (ILTs) are also offered.

DDKS employees also have opportunities to voluntarily attend a variety of Lunch and Learns delivered throughout the year. The Lunch and Learns and Town Halls provide an opportunity for DDKS employees to showcase their talents and/or develop their presentation skills.

Since the DDKS on boarding process normally only involves one new hire at a time, the departmental training curriculum and agenda is developed, and delivered by departmental SMEs, specifically for each new employee. The training methods used are demonstration, mentoring and coaching, review of procedure manuals, one-on-one discussion, and hands-on exercises. The employee's skill and knowledge gaps are closely monitored by the hiring manager and the departmental SME to ensure that necessary training and development opportunities are provided and discussed at review time.

A committee of SMEs identifies gaps in employee knowledge and skills and develops articles and training documents that are accessible through the KMS or the mainframe computer system.

The KMS serves as a training tool. Its development by the CPM office and SMEs across the organization has served as a mechanism to explore other resources in the company to best house and retrieve learning resources in the most expedient manner. The initial process for developing the KMS resources is shown in Exhibit 8.2.

DDKS's website is an external portal for people to access organizational knowledge about DDKS. The purpose of the site is to communicate the brand to the external world, providing information to current and potential constituents.

Other examples of customer, organizational knowledge sharing includes but is not limited to wellness kits to all of its customers, sales and marketing presentations to DDKS current and potential groups, Professional Impact Councils (PICs), and Professional Relations (PR) dental office visits. Managing organizational knowledge to accomplish the assembly and transfer of relevant knowledge in the strategic planning process is done by presenting a summary of the outcomes of the strategic planning process in a long-range plan booklet presented to the entire staff at the January all-employee meeting. The FOCUS team encourages cross-departmental communications and best practice sharing within the management group, and between the LT and other employees. The employee newsletter provides updates on strategy implementation, and quarterly all-employee meetings share successes of the company and business units. Process improvement teams also enable learning and best practice sharing across the organization.

Best practice sharing is evidenced within the organization, including cross-functional, departmental, and interdisciplinary sharing within member companies and the business community.

The employee IDEA program (Ideas from Employees in Action) fosters innovation by providing an avenue for DDKS employees to share ideas, suggestions, and feedback regarding the organization. Ideas are eligible if they support the organizational strategy, goals, and objectives of DDKS; are specific; and propose suitable solutions that enhance efficiency of DDKS operations. Eligible submissions may qualify the employee for a monetary reward if the idea is considered.

CORE AND INNOVATIVE BEST PRACTICES DDKS exercises the core best practices identified earlier and has advanced knowledge in this area with new, innovative best practices.

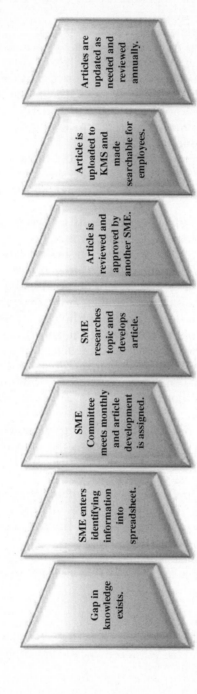

EXHIBIT 8.2 KMS Article Development Process

Courtesy of Delta Dental of Kansas.

The stages shown in the figure read:

- Gap in knowledge exists.
- SME enters identifying information into spreadsheet.
- SME Committee meets monthly and article development is assigned.
- SME researches topic and develops article.
- Article is reviewed and approved by another SME.
- Article is uploaded to KMS and made searchable for employees.
- Articles are updated as needed and reviewed annually.

Principle 5: Manage and Leverage Knowledge

- **Develop KM processes.** Establish and leverage best practice identification, gathering, and sharing processes and technology solutions.
- **Leverage technology.** Partner with the information technology function to launch and maintain KMS and explore other user-friendly options for knowledge access.
- **Develop expert locator systems.** Design and use expert locator systems to capture systems employee skills inventory within the enterprise to accelerate problem solving in Principle 4 and to optimize human capital.
- **Link KM with improved process performance.** Link best practice or knowledge management processes with Principle 4 processes to capture solutions and innovations.
- **Share best practices.** Share best practices with strategic planning processes to better understand core competencies and possible strategic advantages.
- **Maintain a virtual KM network.** Establish and maintain virtual network of KM experts throughout the enterprise to optimize results. DDKS has identified SMEs by department to brief company employees.
- **Innovative best practice.** DDKS personal development plans and learning are linked to succession planning forming sustainable organization capabilities.
- **Innovative best practice.** DDKS has considerably expanded the scope of best practice sharing beyond that of most companies to include external customers and constituents.
- **Innovative best practice.** DDKS leverages KMS with knowledge and skills gaps currently being identified and documented including an article development process where articles and training documents will be made searchable to all employees.
- **Innovative best practice.** The employee IDEA program fosters innovation by providing an avenue for DDKS employees to share ideas, suggestions, and feedback regarding the organization, tied to the company's strategy map.

Lockheed Martin, Information Systems & Global Services: Best Practice Case

Lockheed Martin (LM) has a classic knowledge worker environment organized with tens of thousands of highly trained, highly skilled, technically oriented personnel. Additionally, the complexity and scope of many services require that the best practices of the organization are brought to bear in an effective manner so as not to reinvent the wheel. Further, the competitiveness of this sector requires they maximize the leverage of best practices on a corporate scale. This is clearly a challenge for the corporation, Information Systems & Global Services (IS&GS)-Civil, and within it. It is evidenced on the IS&GS-Civil strategy map (see Chapter 5) in objective P5 (Deliver the full breadth of LM capabilities). This is an explicit recognition that the organization has likely seen and solved just about any challenge, technical or otherwise. A key example of this and a demonstration of the LM-wide focus on best practice sharing is the LM Connect conference. Formerly branded as the LM Mission Critical Enterprise Solutions Symposium, 2009 was the tenth annual LM Connect conference. The event brings together business leaders from across the corporation as well as several business partners to share expertise and solutions to improve business performance and deliver customer value.

LM IS&GS-Civil has a robust employee knowledge development infrastructure consisting of Institute for Leadership Excellence, Executive Leadership Program, Senior Leadership Development Program, Management Strategies Program, Management Fundamentals Program, and Foundations for Leadership Program. Additional functional programs include Business Management Institute, Capturing New Business Institute, Customer Relations Seminar, Effective Coaching, and Program Management Institute for Leadership Excellence.

BEST PRACTICE SHARING FORUMS   Best practice sharing is fostered across LM with active engagement from IS&GS-Civil in several ways. One approach is to invite keynote speakers to BU events to hear ideas and perspectives from speakers within LM (e.g., other business areas and corporate leaders), industry experts and thought leaders (e.g., Clayton Christensen on disruptive innovation), and others. One of the most significant forums is the annual LM Connect conference. Here, best practices and overall industry insights are shared from some of the brightest technical minds across the corporation, key business partners and suppliers, and esteemed guests with invaluable customer insights (e.g., military and political experts). Hosted over several days, in close proximity to major LM centers, dozens of presentations are shared across multiple tracks aligned to current challenges and opportunities seen across the corporation. The face-to-face nature of this event cannot be overappreciated. The contacts and resulting collaboration have led to performance improvements across the corporation.

INFORMATION AND KNOWLEDGE MANAGEMENT SYSTEM The primary information and knowledge management systems employed across LM IS&GS-Civil is called "Unity." Unity is an example of applying Web and Enterprise 2.0 concepts to provide a combination of social networking capabilities with an operational intent to support project interactions (e.g., perform document repository functions). Built on Microsoft's SharePoint and Active Directory, along with a Google search appliance, the Unity system's social networking capabilities supported by blogging, Wiki functions, personal pages and group forums allow people to post personal information about themselves, such as hobbies, interests, bios, and then link with others who have common interests. Operationally, these social media building blocks have begun to transform collaboration on programs and projects and share knowledge on a global scale. IS&G-Civil believes adoption of social media tools will lead it to innovative improvements in processes and reductions in costs. Currently, Unity is widely used within the IS&GS business area, comprising over 50,000 employees, and its use has been steadily broadening across LM over the past several years. At a corporate level, employees leverage a Web portal that extends across the entire corporation called PASSPORT. Powered by SAP tools, employees can use PASSPORT to find information about every business area across the corporation and find links to such tools as Unity. Beyond Unity and PASSPORT, there are many systems used to support information and knowledge sharing, including many of the common COTS tools used by many organizations, especially when it comes to unique needs and in some cases customer requirements for such tools.

SUCCESSION PLANNING FROM TALENT MANAGEMENT Succession planning, referred to as talent management within IS&GS-Civil, is a proactive effort led by senior leadership, including the business unit president. This process occurs on a quarterly cycle and embeds a focus on talent management as part of the business rhythm of the organization. This process is supported by multiple mechanisms used to develop people to ensure a consistent and effective pipeline of talent to support both robust growth (i.e., hundreds of millions of dollars a year within the business unit) and the evolving needs of its customers. These methods will be described in the upcoming section on People Development. Full Spectrum Leadership, the framework for leadership in LM, plays a significant role in talent management. As part of this process, prospective leaders are selected using a panel that assesses the leadership candidate based on questions directly linked to the five Full Spectrum Leadership imperatives: shape the future, build effective relationships, energize the team, deliver results, and model personal excellence, integrity, and accountability. These questions result in an overall score for the candidate and play an important role in the overall decision. This underscores recognition that the best leaders, the ones desired for LM, can both put numbers on the board and inspire customers and employees.

MENTORING: SHARING LEARNING   Mentoring is viewed as a key part of building an inclusive environment across the corporation. It has been a part of LM's organizational culture for several years and is part of the formal leadership model, Full Spectrum Leadership. IS&GS-Civil has recognized that the growth of the business requires it develop and train the next generation of leaders with a sense of urgency. Therefore, mentoring has become one of the strategic priorities in the IS&GS-Civil strategy—and measured in the BSC to ensure that leaders are actively engaging in the mentoring program as mentors; and equally important, mentees actively search out and engage mentors that can help them learn and grow. These relationships, which often last for years and even careers, provide a great way for all employees to gain insight and advice from leaders and technical experts. This also helps transfer the knowledge and expertise of an experienced workforce in a manner that cannot easily be replicated—especially with tacit knowledge. LM also encourages mentoring at all levels and offers further executive mentoring opportunities. A good example of this is through LM's Institute for Leadership Excellence. The institute provides a foundation for management development and is structured into a curriculum mandatory for each level of leadership. In some areas the Institute for Leadership Excellence promotes *reverse mentoring* where more senior leaders are mentored by more junior personnel in an effort to bridge generational gaps. This is especially helpful in some areas of technology (e.g., social media tools that the newer generations consider status quo and later generations consider somewhat foreign). This also helps disperse perceptions that groups may have of one another.

KNOWLEDGE WORKERS—PEOPLE DEVELOPMENT   LM has some of the most significant portfolios of programs committed to people development in business today and IS&GS-Civil actively engages in all of them. Over the past ten years LM has been cited as one of the best places to work, from more local sources like *Baltimore Magazine* to more nationally noted *Fortune* magazine. Additionally, LM has been consistently among *BusinessWeek*'s "Top Ten Places to Launch a Career" over the past ten years, where generous educational assistance policy was noted as one of its differentiators.

LM's approach to knowledge worker people development is a multilayered set of processes and opportunities that engage the individual employees and their leaders at all levels of the organization. Opportunities include tuition reimbursement in fields that have a clear benefit to the business objectives and on-demand online courses offered through the in-house learning management system, in subjects ranging from information technology to business management, in addition to classroom training at LM's Center for Leadership Excellence facility in Bethesda, Maryland. These types of opportunities are not necessarily part of any development program. Formal technical and leadership development programs cover entry-level, mid-level, and executive level programs. At entry-level, the mission of the leadership development program is to attract and develop high potential employees, providing a pipeline for future positions in business and technical leadership. These participants gain experience through two to three years of rotational assignments, technical training, and leadership development training. To ensure strong leadership in the future, LM needs people of all functional backgrounds with diverse educational and life experiences. At the mid-level and executive level several Institute for Leadership Excellence programs and goals are focused on building an understanding of the LM values, goals, requisite competencies, team-building skills, and business acumen appropriate to leadership roles.

CORE AND INNOVATIVE BEST PRACTICES LM IS&GS exercises the core best practices identified earlier and has advanced knowledge in this area with new, innovative best practices.

Principle 5: Manage and Leverage Knowledge

- **Develop KM processes.** Establish and leverage best practice identification, gathering and sharing processes (e.g., LM Connect conference) and technology solutions (e.g., Unity and PASSPORT).
- **Leverage technology.** Partner with the information technology function to launch and maintain KMS.
- **Develop expert locater systems.** Design and use expert locater systems to capture systems employee skills inventory within the enterprise to accelerate problem solving in Principle 4 and to optimize human capital.
- **Link KM with improve process performance.** Link best practice or KM processes with Principle 4 processes to capture solutions and innovations.
- **Share best practices.** Share best practices with strategic planning processes to better understand core competencies and possible strategic advantages.
- **Maintain a virtual KM Network.** Establish and maintain virtual network of KM experts throughout the enterprise to optimize results.
- **Innovative Best Practice.** LM IS&GS-Civil leverages multiple best practice and knowledge social media sharing platforms including Unity, which provides a combination of social networking capabilities with an operational intent to support project interactions.

(Continued)

Built on Microsoft's SharePoint, and Active Directory, along with a Google search appliance, Unity's social networking capabilities supported by blogging, Wiki functions, personal pages, and group forums allow people to post personal information about themselves, such as hobbies, interests, bios, and then link with others who have common interests. Operationally, these social media building blocks have begun to transform collaboration on programs and projects and share knowledge on a global scale

- **Innovative Best Practice.** LM IS&GS-Civil has a robust employee knowledge development infrastructure consisting of Institute for Leadership Excellence, Executive Leadership Program, Senior Leadership Development Program, Management Strategies Program, Management Fundamentals Program, and Foundations for Leadership Program. Additional functional programs include: Business Management Institute, Capturing New Business Institute, Customer Relations Seminar, Effective Coaching, and Program Management Institute for Leadership Excellence.
- **Innovative Best Practice.** LM IS&GS-Civil Institute for Leadership Excellence provides a foundation for management development and mentoring and is mandatory for each level of leadership. In some areas the Institute promotes reverse mentoring where more senior leaders are mentored by more junior personnel in an effort to bridge generational gaps.

M7 Aerospace: Best Practice Case

M7 has created executive committees that are responsible for strategy, internal processes, and human development. These committees meet on a regular basis to set goals and targets that are in line with creating an organization that is focused on the growth and success of M7. Each committee has a charter that spells out its mission within M7. The Human Development Committee (HDC) meets twice weekly and its mission statement is: To provide suggestions, guidance, direction, analysis, implementation assistance, performance monitoring, and recommendations to M7 Aerospace Executive Management Team (EMT) with respect to the human development, performance, and what is needed to attract and retain high potential employees.

HDC will ensure strategy and operations linkage is maintained between the people improvement activities and corporate employee improvement objectives on the M7 strategy map: (P3) Develop High Performing Organization.

COMPETENCY DEVELOPMENT AND SUCCESSION PLANNING The core strength of any organization is to have a workforce of knowledge workers who have superior competencies in their area of expertise. It takes a continuous program to maintain up-to-date methods and skills improvement; it is an ongoing process that is developed jointly by the business/support unit leader in mentoring his or her staff with stretch goals of improved performance and career development through online, offsite, or internal company classes and/or on-the-job training.

Human resources and senior-level executive staff identify "high potential" and high professional employees that are selected from this group of knowledge workers and are invited and encouraged to participate in a structured development program that can prepare these employees for future higher-level professional and management level positions.

This structured personal developmental process is the path to having opportunities available as vacancies in key positions become open. This employee management development program assures the stability of business operations and this learning program is individualized based on the needs of the company and the position(s) targeted for the individual.

The identification and selection of these superior individuals into this high potential, high professional program starts with a review of their individual BSC measures and performance traits assessment and historical scores. The next step would be to observe their leadership and their personal behavior traits; looking for excellent communication skills (written and verbal), and finally have a consensus on those selected for the program by the senior executives and assign a specific mentor(s) from the senior executive staff to monitor their individualized "fast track" developmental management program. These "High Potential/High Professional" employees will have a set training and development program established in a formalized manner.

The Behavior Zones is a bell-shaped curve that has identified quantifiable traits and examples for each sector of the curve. For example, the top 5 percent has superior traits/results expected listed; the next 20 percent has high standards and expected traits quantified listed, but less than the top 5 percent, and so on. The purpose is to try to take out of the decision making on awards, selections, high potentials, and so forth, the individual bias or halo effect (see Exhibit 8.3).

Those selected will have individual mentoring and coaching by assigned senior-level executives. The program objectives for the individual will be SMART (i.e., Specific, Measurable, Achievable, Realistic, and Time Oriented).

Succession planning is the lifeline of any successful company. That is the ongoing superior performance of their management team and a plan to maintain that high performance continuity as some retire, pursue other careers, or get promoted within the organization.

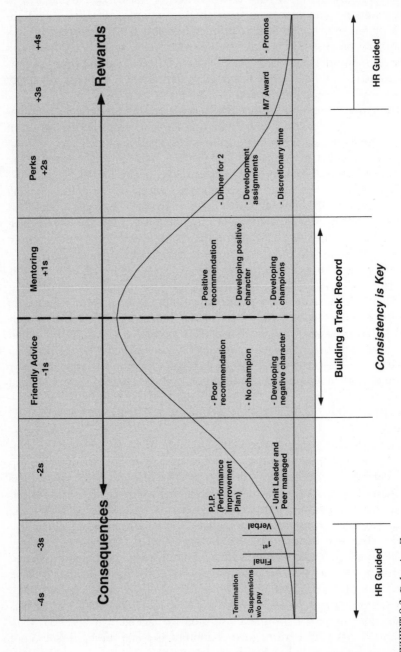

EXHIBIT 8.3 Behavior Zones
Courtesy of M7 Aerospace.

When searching for a "top performer" successor, human resources will analyze the open position, review requirements, and search its database of those within the company that have met the requirements as discussed by the senior executive committee. Those individuals selected for final consideration are professional or managers who have already been identified in prior exercises to be promotable within two years or less.

Based on the premise that existing management positions are essential for success, a formal replacement planning procedure is needed to ensure management continuity. In addition to maintaining current assessments of each incumbent's performance problems, development requirements, and potential for promotion, the system must identify successors by identifying the few top performers who are or will be ready for promotion in the near term (within two years), and designating one or more target positions for their candidacy.

Designated positions are the basis for providing highly promotable individuals with special assignments and executive training, which encourages their further development and retention with the company while waiting for the next higher position. To facilitate the planning process, the use of a succession planning chart system is used. The chart provides the basis for depicting each management position.

CORE AND INNOVATIVE BEST PRACTICES   M7 Aerospace exercises the core best practices identified earlier and has advanced knowledge in this area with new, innovative best practices.

Principle 5: Manage and Leverage Knowledge

- **Develop KM processes.** Establish and leverage best practice identification, gathering and sharing processes and technology solutions.
- **Leverage technology.** Partner with the information technology function to launch and maintain KMS.
- **Develop expert locater systems.** Design and use expert locater systems to capture systems employee skills inventory within the enterprise to accelerate problem solving in Principle 4 and to optimize human capital.
- **Link KM with improve process performance.** Link best practice or knowledge management processes with Principle 4 processes to capture solutions and innovations.

(Continued)

- **Share best practices.** Share best practices with strategic planning processes to better understand core competencies and possible strategic advantages.
- **Maintain a virtual KM Network.** Establish and maintain virtual network of KM experts such as Lean Sigma Black Belts in the enterprise to optimize results.
- **Innovative Best Practice.** M7 Aerospace uses depth chart grids, professional profiles, behavior zones, and mentoring to identify, nurture, and promote employees with the appropriate knowledge into leadership positions.
- **Innovative Best Practice.** M7 Aerospace has developed a strategic human resources function that closely aligns with and enables corporate and BU strategies and is developing a high-performance organization.

Mueller, Inc.: Best Practice Case

Mueller University is the name for the education and training program for all Mueller employees. Salespeople are taught to sell, warehouse employees learn about managing inventories, and customer orders and managers participate in continuing compliance and education.

The business purpose of Mueller's corporate human resources function is to utilize human resources to achieve organizational objectives through standardized and automated processes. This is accomplished by managing key areas including recruitment and selection, compensation and benefits, training and development, safety and health, and workforce management governance.

Once an individual is onboard and during employment within the organization, his or her development is an important aspect. An employee's development directly impacts the results achieved with daily contributions to the organization and its customers. It is Mueller's philosophy that all employees are responsible for taking the initiative and leading their development by relying on the resources, processes, and opportunity afforded by the organization.

As a support to training and employee development, Mueller's human resources function provides opportunities to participate in Mueller University. Mueller University's purpose is to make available course offerings that provide knowledge and skill development in the areas of customer education and specification development, Mueller products and services, technology applications, business processes, and regulatory compliance. Course offerings are provided in both the classroom and by the use of a learning management system. Mueller University currently provides training courses and modules to all new hires segmented by job type. Retraining is required for select courses.

A BEST PRACTICE CENTERED CULTURE Mueller ensures communication; learning, and best practice sharing is engrained in its culture. Every employee knows it is in his or her best interest to ensure the entire company is performing well, and so sharing successes and failures is important to everyone's success.

For example, Mueller separates each sales location into a group of like size and compares the higher sales numbers to the lower ones within that location. Discussion among sales managers is encouraged so that employees can share best practices. This fosters an environment of information sharing, and because incentives are based on company performance in addition to individual performance, it is in everyone's best interest to help others meet their goals as well.

"I'm a big believer in standardization," says President Davenport. "But as we added branch offices, every one of them started to look a little different. Before we got too big, I wanted to *adopt a set of best practices* that we could use indefinitely and anywhere in the country to ensure that our branch offices were being well managed by the local managers."

DATA, INFORMATION, AND KNOWLEDGE Mueller has seen some big leaps forward in terms of information speed and accuracy. Users have faster access to standard reports and more thorough sales analysis. In many cases, content is delivered in minutes instead of days. Mark Lack says one of the first things management noticed is the new level of insight and understanding people are sharing in company meetings. "People in the past would talk about process or strategy and say 'It would be great to know the percentage of this, or why that happened.' This kind of discussion would have been either rhetorical or would have to be taken offline to research. We now pull up the IBM Cognos system and can find the answers right away."

What is more, staff can drill into details and pull together different pieces of information to gain dimensional views they never had previously. The insight is a boon to decision making. "We can find information that we didn't even know existed before," adds Lack. "People are calling me and asking very advanced, complex questions, which means they are looking at the data in new ways. We've created a much more knowledgeable workforce that can now act on key information very quickly."

CORE BEST PRACTICES   Mueller exercises the core best practices identified earlier; it has advanced knowledge in this area with a new, innovative best practice.

Principle 5: Manage and Leverage Knowledge

- **Develop KM processes.** Establish and leverage best practice identification, gathering and sharing processes, and technology solutions.
- **Leverage technology.** Partner with the information technology function to launch and maintain KM and business intelligence capabilities.
- **Develop expert locater systems.** Design and use expert locater systems to capture systems employee skills inventory within the enterprise to accelerate problem solving in Principle 4.
- **Link KM with improve process performance.** Link best practice or KM processes with Principle 4 processes to capture solutions and innovations.
- **Share best practices.** Share best practices with strategic planning processes to better understand core competencies and possible strategic advantages.
- **Maintain a virtual KM Network.** Establish and maintain virtual network of KM experts throughout the enterprise to optimize results.
- **Innovative Best Practice.** Mueller workforce and leadership development and Mueller University have required skills development that includes review of best practices sharing.

NSTAR: Best Practice Case

NSTAR participates in benchmarking and best practice sharing consortia groups facilitated by PSE&G, Southern Company, Edison Electric Institute (EEI), the American Gas Association (AGA), and others. By building and maintaining good relationships with other utilities NSTAR gains input on a wide range of business topics important to the company.

INFORMATION AND KNOWLEDGE MANAGEMENT SYSTEM   NSTAR has deployed several information and KM systems ranging from comprehensive, in-person training sessions to online learning programs.

NSTAR manages full-range technical training centers where employees can learn the technical components of their jobs in a combined classroom and hands-on environment.

Employee safety is NSTAR's number one priority, so a significant focus of all training programs is on injury prevention, use of personal protective equipment, and specific procedures designed to ensure a safe working environment. NSTAR also supplements its safety, refresher, and compliance training with online programs to ensure field employees remain aware of all requirements for their jobs. Using specially designed workstations installed in all of NSTAR's regional service centers employees are able to balance training needs with their daily work. NSTAR uses a software product called VIVID for this training, which enables managers to keep track of test results and test completion rates for each employee.

To support employees learning to use new technology for their jobs, NSTAR has purchased and created eLearning modules, which train employees on specific computer tools and applications. These modules can even be tailored for a specific employee position. For example, a new employee hired to initiate customer requests for service will use NSTAR's eLearning program about customer information systems. NSTAR business analysts will use eLearning modules geared toward developing skills in creating business reporting using Crystal Reports or Microsoft Office applications. eLearning is an excellent resource and is available to all employees via the corporate computer network and the Internet.

SUCCESSION PLANNING Succession planning is critical for any company to ensure effective business continuity and success. At NSTAR, formal succession planning is led by the senior vice president of human resources and involves specific input and activities from the senior management team. A key component is NSTAR's Key Talent program, which helps identify, select, and retain high-potential leaders. Each year, senior executives identify specific individuals that have the drive and capabilities to become tomorrow's NSTAR executives, as well as those individuals with specific technical talents needed now and into the future.

Investments in these employees' ongoing development are made via special training and work opportunities aimed at personal and professional growth. The Key Talent program is limited to just 5 percent of NSTAR's management team to ensure focus remains on the top tier of performers, Specific performance targets for the Key Talent program are set each year to measure the percentage of employees in the program who are promoted, realize job growth, or transfer to a new or developmental role. The retention rate among these employees is also measured.

Mentoring is viewed as a key part of building an inclusive environment across the corporation. For the past several years, NSTAR has sponsored mentoring programs internally to support Key Talent employees, pairing them with more seasoned and successful managers. These mentoring programs build new skills, and offer a learning experience the individual might otherwise not have been able to achieve.

CORE BEST PRACTICES NSTAR exercises the core best practices identified earlier in this book.

Principle 5: Manage and Leverage Knowledge

- **Develop KM processes.** Establish and leverage best practice identification, gathering and sharing processes (e.g., safety training initiatives) and technology solutions (e.g., eLearning).
- **Leverage technology.** Partner with the information technology function to launch and maintain KMS (e.g., piloting collaboration tools).
- **Link KM with improve process performance.** Link best practice or knowledge management processes with Principle 4 processes to capture solutions and innovations (e.g., best practices research and cross-organizational sharing).
- **Maintain a virtual KM Network.** Establish and maintain virtual network of KM experts throughout the enterprise to optimize results (e.g., Project Management Improvement Council).

Omaha Public Power District: Best Practice Case

OPPD has strategically innovated through its best practices Following are a few highlights.

- Employees of Omaha Public Power District's (OPPD's) Fort Calhoun Station have received the nuclear energy industry's B. Ralph Sylvia Best of the Best Award, beating out more than 200 other nominees for the Top Industry Practice honor.
- The OPPD research team devised a method to accurately assess the susceptibility of stainless steel and other alloys to stress corrosion cracking. Their research will make it possible to find tiny flaws in metal that can take 20 years to develop. Results include:
  - Avoidance of unnecessary replacement of expensive components, saving $7 million since 1999

- Reduction in radiation exposure, cutting 10 to 50 person-rem of combined exposure to workers
- Improved safety and efficiency across the entire nuclear energy industry, if adopted by other utilities

MENTORING: SHARING LEARNING The impetus for a formal companywide mentoring program came from Gallup Q12 survey results, which suggested that OPPD employees with tenure in the range of five to ten years tend to be less engaged in their work than either employees with less than five years of service, or employees who have worked for the company for more than ten years. Once the program need was identified, numerous focus groups were conducted with employees and managers to gauge interest in a company mentoring program.

The resulting OPPD *Career Connections* program is a formal, company-sponsored mentoring program. The program matches protégés with management mentors. The program targets employees who have worked at OPPD for five to ten years. More than 40 protégé/mentor pairs currently participate in the program. Protégé eligibility for the *Career Connections* program includes two or more years of company service, "Meets Expectations" performance ratings for the previous two performance evaluations, and approval to participate from the protégé's immediate supervisor. A day-long mentoring skills-building session is a prerequisite for protégés and mentors who wish to participate in the mentoring program.

The *Career Connections* program takes protégés and mentors through an interactive process to learn about:

- Different types of development
- The P-I-E Formula for success (Performance, Image, and Exposure)
- The importance of and the roles in the mentoring relationship
- How to create a more effective, targeted career development plan for oneself
- OPPD's corporate culture—especially the "unwritten" rules

MENTORING CASE STUDY Proactive, targeted mentoring designed to ensure the transfer of critical knowledge also plays an important role at OPPD. In one case, as the incumbent maintenance manager in one of the fossil power plants was approaching retirement, his successor was appointed to the role several months in advance. The incumbent was assigned the full-time role of mentoring the new maintenance manager to ensure that he had a working knowledge of all aspects of his new role—before his mentor retired.

Measures

- While *Career Connections* is a new program, it is anticipated that outcomes of this formal mentoring program will include both increased employee engagement and employee retention.
- This proactive mentoring process helped to ensure a systematic transfer of knowledge and smooth transition of responsibilities when the mentor retired.

SUCCESSION PLANNING   The basic objective of the corporate succession planning process at OPPD is to ensure that skilled leaders are available from within the company to fill critical positions when needed (i.e., Right Leader, Right Skills, Right Role, Right Time). OPPD's formal, corporate succession program evolved over several years into a process with the following goals:

- Ensure continuity of leadership, operational excellence, and financial strength
- Increase in productivity, retention, and stakeholder satisfaction
- Enhancement of the corporate reputation and image

The corporate succession planning process is premised on an internally developed "Leader of the Future" competency set. The competencies are used to identify, evaluate, and develop high-potential leaders for 25 targeted "critical positions" in the company. The senior management team meets annually to review and confirm the critical position list and the succession candidate list. The corporate succession planning process is described in Exhibit 8.4.

SUCCESSION PLANNING CASE STUDY EXAMPLE   The succession planning process was recently used successfully to fill the vice president of transmission & distribution (T&D) engineering and operations position from within the internal succession candidate pool. The two internal candidates for the position were both identified as critical position succession candidates for the role and were developed for the position over a period of years. When the role became vacant, a rigorous selection process incorporating formal competency assessments and behavioral interviews was used to evaluate the candidates. The *Leader of the Future* competencies mentioned above formed the basis of the interview questions and assessments.

PEOPLE DEVELOPMENT   OPPD training and development functions tend to be decentralized by business unit. Each business unit is generally responsible for the technical training of its employees. The Safety and Technical Training

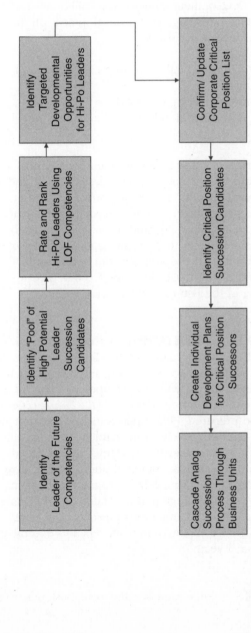

EXHIBIT 8.4 Corporate Succession Planning

Courtesy of Omaha Public Power District.

division has oversight of "generic" technical training such as first aid/CPR, confined space, fall protection, forklift training, and so on.

The corporate talent management function is responsible for the targeted development of company high-potential managers and supervisors. The strategic talent development framework is called the "Ladder of Development." The leader groups targeted for development on the four "rungs" of the Ladder of Development include:

1. Executives and high potential succession candidates
2. Mid-level managers
3. Supervisors (and those being groomed for the role)
4. Union leaders and other nondegreed, bargaining unit leaders (crew leaders)

Separate internal and external development experiences based on the Leader of the Future competency set are designed for and target each group. Development experiences include formal classroom training, job shadowing/rotation, project teams, serving on community boards, group and individual assessment and coaching, and so on. OPPD uses three internally administered assessment tools to drive manager and employee development coaching and feedback: the *Emergenetics* brain profile, Gallup Clifton *StrengthsFinder*, and an in-house developed 360-degree assessment tool based on the Leader of the Future competencies.

PEOPLE DEVELOPMENT CASE STUDY EXAMPLE   Based on internal needs assessment findings, and using the Leader of the Future competencies, OPPD talent management staff designed, developed, and delivered a new development program targeting the supervisor development "rung" of the Ladder of Development. The custom eight-day *Leaders of the Future (LOF)* supervisory series is designed to prepare OPPD supervisors and high-potential individual contributors to lead effectively in their roles. The curriculum includes such topics as aligning performance to strategy, customer focus, operations, innovation, change management, communication, talent management, and decision making. Participants in the LOF program are nominated by their division managers. The LOF program is facilitated by OPPD talent management staff and is enhanced by numerous presentations, panel discussions, and Q&A sessions from company line managers and executives. The program is offered twice a year.

CORE BEST PRACTICES   OPPD exercises the core best practices identified earlier.

Principle 5: Manage and Leverage Knowledge

- **Develop KM processes.** Establish and leverage best practice identification, gathering and sharing processes and technology solutions.
- **Leverage technology.** Partner with the information technology function to launch and maintain KMS.
- **Develop expert locator systems.** Design and use expert locator systems to capture systems employee skills inventory within the enterprise to accelerate problem solving in Principle 4 and to optimize human capital.
- **Link KM with improved process performance.** Link best practice or KM processes with Principle 4 processes to capture solutions and innovations.
- **Share best practices.** Share best practices with strategic planning processes to better understand core competencies and possible strategic advantages.
- **Maintain a virtual KM Network.** Establish and maintain virtual network of KM experts throughout the enterprise to optimize results.

Poudre Valley Health System: Best Practice Case

Poudre Valley Health System (PVHS) has received national recognition for its innovative use of information technology to improve patient care and safety, its efforts to provide physicians electronic access to patient records from their offices, and its use of information technology in business practices. PVHS' ability to meet and exceed the expectations of quality care, prompt service, and friendly staff is dependent on the timely availability of information for the workforce, suppliers, partners, collaborators, patients, and the community. To optimize the flow of accurate, real-time information, PVHS has established a secure, user-friendly network that is appropriately accessible to all stakeholders, regardless of geography or time of day.

More than 3,000 networked computers throughout PVHS facilities provide role-specific information access for authorized users, and secure portals give these users electronic access from outside the organization:

- **Physician/Partner Portal.** The *3M Care Innovation* clinical data repository system enables more than 99 percent of area physician offices, as well as appropriate partners, to retrieve patient information on a timely basis via off-site computers. With this system, authorized providers may access real-time patient information through the secure PVHS Web access site.

- **Staff Portal.** With Web access, authorized staff members can remotely access e-mail, shared drives, VIC (intranet), and Kronos (employee time clock).
- **Patient Portal.** The PVHS website provides information about the organization and its services, as well as patient education information and general health resources.
- **Community Portal.** The PVHS website provides information about the organization and its services, as well as patient education information and general health resources. HealthLink provides dedicated public access computers and printers throughout PVHS to help community members' access health information
- **Supplier Portal.** Vendor-specific electronic data interchanges provide automatic supply tracking, ordering, and billing with nearly 100 percent of PVHS vendors.

STANDARDS AND ORGANIZATIONAL KNOWLEDGE To facilitate integrity, reliability, timeliness, accuracy, security, and confidentiality of information and organizational knowledge, PVHS relies on industry standards for hardware, software, interfaces, and network protocols, with additional support including:

- **Accuracy.** PVHS relies on automation and audits to ensure accuracy of data and information. The Meditech-based network links clinical data from disparate applications and locations via a uniform patient identifier that assists clinicians in selecting the correct patient and supports the organization's patient safety initiative. Systems also have data input control mechanisms.
- **Integrity and Reliability.** The process for maintaining information integrity and reliability begins with data entry. System controls allow only authorized, trained individuals to input data, and systems have built-in data input control features, as well as extensive security measures.
- **Timeliness.** PVHS has devoted significant resources to developing an innovative electronic information system that ensures authorized users secure, user-friendly access to clinical and financial information, decision support, and the physician, employee, and patient information centers, regardless of geography or time of day
- **Security and Confidentiality.** PVHS established confidentiality as one of the organization's values, so the behavior standards and code of conduct emphasize confidentiality for all stakeholders. The workforce receives annual training on this topic.

PVHS manages organizational knowledge to ensure *knowledge transfer* to and from its key stakeholders:

- **Workforce.** Members of the workforce are key sources of clinical, operational, and organizational knowledge. Collection and transfer of clinical knowledge happens largely through the Meditech-based network, which allows authorized caregivers to enter and access real-time clinical information remotely or from any computer in the PVHS system. Nursing supervisors also get daily written and verbal reports, and caregivers provide real-time written and verbal reports when transferring patients between departments and shifts. Staffs who attend outside conferences share their learning at the department level. Appropriate oversight committees, including the performance excellence teams, systematically review key learnings to identify best practices and deploy them across the organization.
- **Patients.** In addition to listening and learning methods described earlier PVHS begins collecting information from patients prior to or immediately upon arrival. Results are available to staff, physicians, and other local health care organizations for use in evaluating existing services and designing new ones. PVHS transfers knowledge back to patients and the community.
- **Suppliers.** PVHS' electronic data interchange facilitates rapid information exchange with suppliers.
- **Partners and Collaborators.** Key mechanisms for transferring information to and from partners are through joint venture business reviews and SMG representation on joint venture boards. Partners who are involved in direct patient care can also access clinical information through a secure electronic portal.

BEST PRACTICE GOVERNANCE   PVHS has a systematic process for identifying and deploying best practices across the organization. The elements of best practice sharing include:

- **Initiation.** Best practices may be identified by SMG or a director; Plan, Do, Check, and Act (PDCA) teams; or oversight committees such as performance excellence teams. The BSC is intentionally designed to highlight departments where internal best practices are occurring. Additional internal best practice identification comes through Learn and Lead programs, systems operations meetings, and the annual Quality Festival. PVHS also devotes significant resources to identifying external best practices inside and outside the health care industry. PVHS leaders and staff attend national conferences and build relationships with world-class organizations. A medical library containing more than

3,000 textbooks and 200 journal titles; special collections covering ethics, leadership development, quality improvement, and diversity awareness; and satellite broadcasts from CDC, VHA, and others provides additional sources for external knowledge. A medical cybrary page in VIC provides easy access to subscription-based online resources, such as MD Consult, CINAHL, MicroMedex, and online medical journals.

- **Policy.** For implementation of the best practice, the initiator prepares a draft policy or policy revision, seeks approval from the appropriate oversight committee, and presents it to the systemwide, multidisciplinary policy committee.
- **Education.** The initiator of a best practice is charged with developing an implementation plan, including identification of education and training needs.
- **Monitoring.** The appropriate oversight committee monitors implementation of best practices through mechanisms, including audits and Level III and IV Kirkpatrick evaluation. PVHS representatives also learn and shape best practices across the health care industry through organizations such as Magnet, VHA, and Institute for Healthcare Improvement (IHI). PVHS assembles and transfers organizational knowledge for use in cooperation, communication, and skill sharing.

PVHS fosters an organizational culture conducive to high performance and a motivated, engaged workforce. In addition to communication mechanisms described in the first section of this case, PVHS ensures cooperation, effective communication, and skill sharing within and across health care professions, work units, and locations:

- Interdisciplinary, strategic objective (SO) driven teams are at the core of PVHS work management and organization. From development of new services to provision of bedside care, PVHS engages teams to meet patient needs.
- Team members throughout the organization—including representation from staff, physicians, and volunteers—work together to provide the best possible care, participate in strategy development, monitor quality indicators, and coordinate improvement efforts. PVHS uses Situation, Background, Assessment, and Recommendation methodology, a technique that provides a framework for communication between members of the health care team about a patient's condition to ensure consistent and effective communication between nurses and physicians.
- The Learn and Lead program brings together managers from all PVHS departments for offsite training and holds attendees accountable for cascading learning to their staffs.

- The Reward and Recognition program rewards staff that cooperate across department lines.
- Formal education and training programs foster or require skill sharing within and across disciplines, departments, and locations. For instance, MCR leaders and the majority of MCR staff began their jobs at PVHS, working alongside their Poudre Valley Health System (PVHS) counterparts.
- To ensure the flow of accurate, real-time information, PVHS has established a secure, user-friendly electronic network and processes for transferring nonelectronic information and knowledge.

WORKFORCE AND LEADER DEVELOPMENT   The PVHS Workforce Development System (see Exhibit 8.5) balances organizational, department, and individual needs to support and engage the workforce in achieving the vision, mission, and values (VMV). Identification of learning and development needs is annual and ongoing, driven by processes and factors such as strategy development and deployment (SDD), regulatory requirements, retention data, and VOC for the organization; new policies and evidence-based practices for departments; and performance reviews for individuals. After systematic needs analysis and prioritization, a workforce development team designs and delivers appropriate instruction. Educators partner with learners and managers to assess instruction effectiveness (e.g., Kirkpatrick analysis) and drive improvements in instruction and learning/development

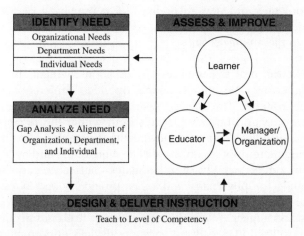

EXHIBIT 8.5 Workforce Development System
Courtesy of Poudre Valley Health System.

Education and training are essential to maintaining and strengthening core competencies, addressing strategic challenges, and achieving the strategic plan.

Performance Improvement, Technological Change, and Innovation   PVHS incorporates innovation into the organization in several ways:

- PVHS performance improvement methodology where leaders receive training on the PDCA process, which identifies education necessary to implement and maintain performance improvements.
- PVHS financially supports staff members to be active Corporate Performance Excellence (CPEx) and Baldrige examiners with the goal of understanding performance improvement and identifying external best practices to drive innovation at PVHS. PVHS currently has numerous Baldrige and CPEx examiners on staff. The quarterly performance excellence meetings provide education on the Baldrige framework.
- PVHS has become the national benchmark for deploying the Thomas Concept. More than half the organization has received training through this program, which helps PVHS build balanced, diverse teams that foster new ideas and, thus, drive innovation.
- The process used by the multidisciplinary product and equipment standardization and evaluation committee identifies training needs related to new technology.
- PVHS sends members of the workforce to seminars, conferences, and classes on numerous topics, including performance improvement methodologies and new technology. The primary goal with external educational opportunities is bringing back best practices to drive innovation in the organization.

Breadth of Development Opportunities   In addition to traditional classroom settings, classes may be offered online, by video conference, or through self-learning packets. The mentor program matches staff members with a willing mentor, and coaching occurs both within the organization and through contracted consultants. A new mentoring program was launched in 2010, offering more opportunity for staff wishing to expand their leadership skills and/or career path. PVHS coordinates conferences and semiannual Grand Rounds for physicians and other providers, and physicians may request one-on-one proctoring to learn new procedures/technology, such as robotic-assisted surgery. Telehealth transmits on-site classes to other facilities and rural sites. The PVHS team culture supports daily opportunities for informal training. PVHS offers tuition reimbursement and collaborates with area colleges on accelerated programs for nursing, radiology, and other health care professions.

Knowledge Transfer A comprehensive system of policies, procedures, and protocols documents the organization's knowledge base so critical information does not reside solely with one person. Also, department level cross training transfers knowledge using tools such as job rotation, secondary job codes, and interim job coverage. The goal with any employee departure is to hire a replacement to overlap with the departing individual. For instance, with almost 300 employees transferring from PVH to MCR when the new hospital opened, detailed staffing plans focused on backfilling vacated PVH positions in time for knowledge transfer to occur. Committees and teams use similar approaches to facilitate knowledge transfer associated with departing team members.

Knowledge Reinforcement Reinforcement of new knowledge and skills occurs through mechanisms including (1) new employee orientation training checklists of critical skills and follow-up skill tests; (2) Preceptor program, which pairs new nurses with seasoned staff; (3) Level 3 Kirkpatrick analysis with retraining if needed; and (4) recertification for licensed staff. In planning for MCR, human resources researched pitfalls of newly opened hospitals and extended the hiring timeline to allow key new staff to work side-by-side with current staff at PVH. This successfully reinforced knowledge and job skills and oriented new hires to the PVHS culture. Volunteers also have service descriptions that include competencies required for their assignment, and they have signed competency sheets. Following orientation, volunteers shadow experienced volunteers. Human resources plans and coordinates learning and development opportunities for leaders.

Personal Leadership Attributes The PVHS Leadership Competencies drive learning and development opportunities related to personal leadership attributes:

- The Learn and Grow series offers classes on team building, listening, coaching for performance, disciplinary dilemmas, confidentiality, service recovery, and numerous other topics that directly support leaders in living the Leadership Competencies.
- Regular leadership development opportunities—including monthly leadership meetings and semiannual retreats—focus on helping leaders understand and live the Leadership Competencies.
- Building Blocks of Leadership—the newest improvement cycle—is an intensive, cohort-based program with a standardized curriculum based on the Leadership Competencies. For physicians in new leadership roles, an orientation manual augments training provided by medical staff services and the three medical staff officers at each hospital. MEC members

receive training based on a nationally recognized methodology for medical staff governance, and medical staff officers attend annual training conferences. MEC members also attend a four-day training related to medical staff governance, which includes topics such as disciplining and leading committees. For the medical staff quality committee, new members receive training from the Quality Resources departments and conferences on physician peer review.

CORE AND INNOVATIVE BEST PRACTICES   PVHS exercises the core best practices identified earlier and has advanced knowledge in this area with new, innovative best practices.

Principle 5: Manage and Leverage Knowledge

- **Develop KM processes.** Establish and leverage best practice identification, gathering and sharing processes and technology solutions.
- **Leverage technology.** Partner with the information technology function to launch and maintain KMS and a very robust information technology infrastructure for organizational learning.
- **Develop expert locator systems.** Design and use expert locator systems to capture systems employee skills inventory within the enterprise to accelerate problem solving in Principle 4 and to optimize human capital.
- **Link KM with improved process performance.** Link best practice or KM processes with Principle 4, improve processes to capture solutions and innovations.
- **Share best practices.** Share best practices with strategic planning processes to better understand core competencies and possible strategic advantages.
- **Maintain a virtual KM Network.** Establish and maintain virtual network of KM experts throughout the enterprise to optimize results.
- **Innovative Best Practice.** PVHS links its knowledge, best practice sharing to its competency, leadership, and development models.
- **Innovative Best Practice.** PVHS department-level cross training transfers knowledge using tools such as job rotation, secondary job codes, and interim job coverage.
- **Innovative Best Practice.** PVHS focused its education and training on maintaining and strengthening core competencies for addressing strategic challenges and achieving the strategic plan.

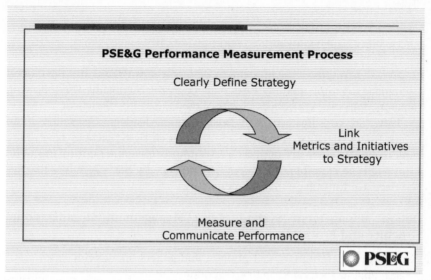

EXHIBIT 8.6 Embed Benchmarking and Best Practice Implementation
Courtesy of Public Service Electric & Gas.

Public Service Electric & Gas: Best Practice Case

PSE&G has developed several approaches to leverage and manage its knowledge principally in the form of (1) expert manuals and desktop guides and (2) best practices. For instance, PSE&G has developed a robust BSC desktop guide to support initial rollout and ongoing use of the BSC for employees.

The Performance Measurement Group (PMG) coordinates the benchmarking studies noted previously, and the participation in outside benchmarking studies, which yield both data sets and best practices. The BSC performance measurements linked to company strategy noted earlier provides a direct link to related best practices as depicted in Exhibit 8.6.

BEST PRACTICE SHARING FORUMS   PSE&G regularly hosts best practice sharing conferences with benchmark participants on a series of topics of mutual interest. The Gas and Electric Peer Review Panel, for instance, has a database of best practices related to the following topics:

- Store preparedness
- Poorest performing circuit identification and mitigation
- Workforce development

- Workforce effectiveness
- New service installations
- Facilities damage awareness and prevention

In order to effectively implement best practices PSE&G has developed a template for implementing best practices, which contains the following elements: Purpose, Objectives, Scope, Criteria, and Best Practice.

PMG, in coordination with business unit leaders, determine if an improvement initiative is warranted. Dozens of best practices have been implemented to bring about measureable improvement in performance. The following is an example of a recent best practice by BSC objectives that are now in place for outage management.

Outage Management System, Asset Management Organizational Structure and Processes

- Mobile data terminals, cell phones, and pagers on all vehicles.
- Have all techs trained as first responders.
- Develop scripted call center application.
- Educate fire and police personnel.
- Install automated routing application.
- Utilize home-based reporting.
- Mock exercises/mobile command center.

CORE AND INNOVATIVE BEST PRACTICES PSE&G exercises the core best practices identified earlier and has advanced knowledge in this area with new, innovative best practices.

Principle 5: Manage and Leverage Knowledge

- **Develop KM processes.** Establish and leverage best practice identification, gathering and sharing processes and technology solutions.
- **Leverage technology.** Partner with the information technology function to launch and maintain KMS.
- **Develop expert locator systems.** Design and use expert locator systems to capture systems employee skills inventory within the enterprise to accelerate problem solving in Principle 4 and to optimize human capital.

- **Link KM with improve process performance.** Link best practice or KM processes with Principle 4 processes to capture solutions and innovations.
- **Share best practices.** Share best practices with strategic planning processes to better understand core competencies and possible strategic advantages.
- **Maintain a virtual KM Network.** Establish and maintain virtual network of KM experts throughout the enterprise to optimize results.
- **Innovative Best Practice.** PSE&G pioneered best practice sharing among over 20 gas and 20 electric companies.
- **Innovative Best Practice.** PSE&G has innovated best practice sharing and developed standards for sharing across companies. For instance, a template for implementing best practices which contains the following elements: Purpose, Objectives, Scope, Criteria, and Best Practice.

Sharp HealthCare: Best Practice Case

Sharp HealthCare provides KM on several levels. Sharp sponsors the Nursing Leadership Academy for nursing leadership education, physician, and staff continuing education offerings, and an annual $1,000 educational fund per employee for external education. The system's annual Patient Safety Symposium is designed to share best practices and foster learning of quality improvement tools. The continuing medical education department sponsors educational activities for physician partners, vendor partners, and all professional staff. Finally, employee-led action teams present tested solutions at executive steering meetings, LDS, and employee forums (held regularly at each entity for all staff). These teams share different approaches to achieve Pillar goals with Trailblazer of Excellence presentations. Action teams deploy monthly behavior standard tool kits to facilitate teaching and learning among staff and tackle PI initiatives. Sharp and its senior leaders actively participate with focused learning organizations, such as The Advisory Board, Premier Supply Chain Breakthrough Series, the Scottsdale Institute, CHMR, and SG2 to spark innovation. Sharp's IRB supports and manages more than 320 research studies through which physicians and clinicians advance patient care. Additionally, Sharp leaders personally participate in succession planning through system and entity steering committees.

ORGANIZATIONAL KNOWLEDGE MANAGEMENT Sharp has identified key workforce knowledge management processes aligned with the Pillars (see Exhibit 8.7).

EXHIBIT 8.7 Workforce Knowledge Management Process

Pillar	Knowledge Regarding
Quality	Patient information processes (*e.g., Information systems*) How care is delivered (*e.g., P&Ps, Standard Orders*) How we are doing (*e.g., Clinical Outcomes*)
Service	How we treat customers (*e.g., AIDET, ACTT, Patient Satisfaction Surveys*)
People	How I do my job, lead, and grow (*e.g., Performance Evaluation System, LDS, Training, EOS*)
Finance	How operations run (*e.g., P&Ps, Financial Outcomes*)
Growth	How are we progressing (*e.g., market knowledge*)
Community	How are we are improving community health (*e.g., Listening and Learning Tools*)

Courtesy of Sharp HealthCare.

Senior leaders inspire a culture of inquiry, innovation, and knowledge sharing through the Customer Knowledge system and design knowledge transfer processes using SIPOC/COPIS noted in Chapter 7, and systematically evaluate the effectiveness of processes in meeting customer requirements via listening and learning tools, and feedback from leaders, employees, suppliers, partners, and collaborators.

Sharp's information system provide the infrastructure for the successful transfer of relevant knowledge from and to patients and other customers, suppliers, partners, and collaborators. Listening and learning methods are conducted to understand what the relevant and appropriate knowledge requirements are based on role responsibilities, privacy standards, and contractual agreements. Then processes are designed, implemented, and evaluated for effectiveness. Specific details and examples of knowledge management processes including customers, outputs, subprocesses, inputs, and suppliers are available onsite. Sharp systematically promotes the rapid identification, sharing, and implementation of best practices, promising practices, and lessons learned throughout the system.

Each senior vice president owns the process of best practice sharing, and there are several methods to identify, verify, and share the practice or lesson learned. The method of sharing depends on the target audience and the sense of urgency to spread the practice. Projects charted with spreading best practices across the system are tracked and opportunities are continuously identified and monitored. In order to systematically scan for best practice sharing opportunities, the 12th step of DMAIC (define, measure, analyze, improve, control) is spreading the solution through the verification of a best or promising practice and then using the Change Acceleration Program or CAP to translate the improvement strategy. Sharp has a systematic process for collecting and transferring all relevant knowledge to use in the strategic planning process. Each organization performs an entity-specific market assessment and SWOT analysis, which becomes the basis for the organization's strategies and action plans. Sharp manages organizational knowledge to accomplish transfer of relevant knowledge for use in the strategic planning process via reviews of internal results.

WORKFORCE AND LEADERSHIP DEVELOPMENT Educational curriculum and training tools are developed and implemented as shown in Exhibit 8.8.

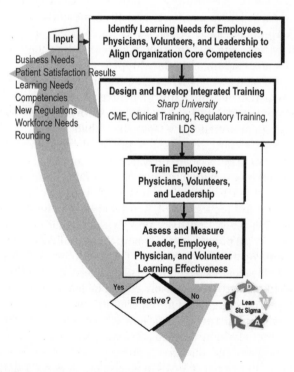

EXHIBIT 8.8 Workforce and Leadership Development
Courtesy of Sharp HealthCare.

Assessment and measurement are completed using such mechanisms as formal assessment competencies, system performance measures, and patient satisfaction. Sharp's workforce development and learning system addresses needs and desires for learning and development identified by the workforce by providing a process to collect and aggregate learning needs annually or as needed. Identifying staff licensure and recredentialing requirements, and the skills/competencies needed to meet strategic challenges, accomplish action plans, and implement system process improvements and new technologies are also part of the overall annual educational evaluation process. Sharp's organizational learning system consists of clinical education and The Sharp University.

Staffs have opportunities for coaching, mentoring, and work-related experiences, which are reinforced through skill-based competency assessments, evaluations, and return demonstrations. Education around the core competency of the Sharp Experience is provided through the tools. In clinical areas, all units have a specialist or educator responsible for competency-based education, coaching staff, mentoring, and providing opportunities to learn new skills. To ensure the transfer of knowledge from departing workers, each department uses formalized methods, including defined protocols, well-documented policies and procedures, operating manuals, information systems, intranet/Internet, communications tools, meeting minutes, EMR documentation, and trained replacement staff. To reinforce new knowledge and skills, competency assessment begins at new hire orientation and is conducted regularly thereafter by educators to teach new procedures, equipment, and technology. Employees attest to their proficiency through demonstrations, written tests, chart audits, and competency evaluations. Staff clinical education is provided by internal and external resources/material experts. Sharp educators offer multiple classes for all classifications of employees with hundreds of continuing education units (CEU) credits for clinical practice to ensure that employees stay abreast of clinical, regulatory, licensure, technological, and business changes through continual learning. The Sharp University provides curriculum for organizational learning, systemwide process improvement training aligned with Pillar goals, and formal training for Sharp leaders. The LDS track includes innovative coursework for leaders to develop personal leadership attributes, increase organizational knowledge, and ensure ethical health care and business practices. Key learning is integrated throughout the system using accountability grids. Leaders are equipped with a tool kit to deliver the information to staff in a consistent fashion. At each session, Sharp's CEO presents a system update, covering strategic direction, priority projects, system financials, and progress toward performance goals in the system Report Card. Key learning is summarized for managers to take back to staff and apply to work-related experiences.

The effectiveness of workforce and leadership development learning systems is assessed through evaluations, clinical data, outcomes, statistical analysis, and financial results. Final results are rolled up by entity and system to evaluate efficacy of the educational strategy. Posttests are used to demonstrate skills and outcome/variance data is analyzed to determine progress on action plans and goal achievement.

To manage effective career progression for the entire workforce, Sharp uses a three-tiered approach providing (1) advancement and growth opportunities, (2) training and education for certification and licensure, and (3) educational assistance and professional development. Entity and system leaders regularly identify growth opportunities and give priority to current employees for assignments and advancements. Employees are supported with educational reimbursement and promotional opportunities on completion of training/education programs. Both technical and leadership career paths exist in all clinical areas. Preceptor programs offer preceptor candidates experience in performing clinical competency evaluation. Managers assist employees in identifying projects for needed experience and creating professional development plans as part of the annual performance and competency evaluation process. Succession planning for management, administrative, occupational and health care leadership positions is accomplished through formal and informal methods at the system and entity level to ensure present and the future leaders. The board has defined succession plans for the system CEO and a system steering committee comprised of senior leaders develops overall succession planning strategies. At the system and entity levels, key positions and potential candidates are identified through applicant sourcing. Once candidates are identified, career development plans, growth opportunities, and key assignments are established. An example is the nursing leadership professional development and preceptor program that provides opportunities for mentoring, overseeing, and evaluating nurse competency, and career progression.

CORE AND INNOVATIVE BEST PRACTICES Sharp exercises the core best practices identified earlier; it has advanced knowledge in this area with new, innovative best practices.

Principle 5: Manage and Leverage Knowledge

- **Develop KM processes.** Establish and leverage best practice identification, gathering and sharing processes and technology solutions.

(Continued)

- **Leverage technology.** Partner with the information technology function to launch and maintain KMS.
- **Develop expert locator systems.** Design and use expert locator systems to capture systems employee skills inventory within the enterprise to accelerate problem solving in Principle 4 and to optimize human capital.
- **Link KM with improved process performance.** Link best practice or KM processes with Principle 4 processes to capture solutions and innovations.
- **Share best practices.** Share best practices with strategic planning processes to better understand core competencies and possible strategic advantages.
- **Maintain a virtual KM Network.** Establish and maintain virtual network of KM experts throughout the enterprise to optimize results.
- **Innovative Best Practice.** Sharp has identified key Workforce Knowledge Management Processes aligned with each of its Pillars; this goes further, to integrate strategic pillars and targeted workforce knowledge sets, than a more general KM system.
- **Innovative Best Practice.** At Sharp, in a more sophisticated link between process and KM, senior leaders inspire a culture of inquiry, innovation, and knowledge sharing through the Customer Knowledge System and design knowledge transfer processes using SIPOC/COPIS, and systematically evaluate the effectiveness of processes in meeting customer requirements via listening and learning tools, and feedback from leaders, employees, suppliers, partners, and collaborators.
- **Innovative Best Practice.** The scope of Sharp's KM Sharp's information system surpasses that of many award-winning enterprises; it provides the infrastructure for the successful transfer of relevant knowledge from and to patients and other customers, suppliers, partners, and collaborators.
- **Innovative Best Practice.** Sharp workforce and leadership development and Sharp University have required skills development including mandatory review of best practices.

Five Key Principles: Self-Diagnostic and Corporate Performance Management Roadmap

Pleasure in the job puts perfection in the work.

—Aristotle

By now you may be wondering, where do I start? How do I assist my organization to build momentum for our Five Key Principles journey? As a key first step, this chapter provides you with two diagnostic tools to conduct a self-assessment and baseline where you are in your corporate performance management (CPM) process and best practice journey. These two diagnostics are based on the award-winning case organizations.

CPM Core Process Blueprint (Diagnostic 1)

Careful research of the cases in this book reveals they follow a discernible set of core CPM processes organized within the Five Key Principles. These CPM processes were shown in Exhibit 3.1 to provide strategic context and a working framework to assist you in your organization.

How do you get started? A client, with the pseudonym *New Co,* is shown next. The pre-engagement scores are shown in the first column using a simple five-point scale with 1 being a low rating and 5 a best practice rating for Principle 1. This company just adopted the Five Key Principles as their management framework and has started to focus on building out their CPM office (Principle 1). The following sections outline their self-assessment.

- **Executive Sponsorship Process.** The CEO is very supportive and is sponsoring this newly formed function, so we have rated it a 5 on the five-point scale. The CEO has committed to build out this capability over the next two years, so we rate the next four quarters as 5 out of 5.
- **Recruit, Train, and Manage Enterprise CPM Expert Process.** We recognize that the CPM office team will have to be recruited and developed, so we scored this a 1 with gradual improvements each quarter over the next four quarters to build an expert team.
- **CPM Principles 2 to 5 Management Processes.** Since the team is being formed, their corresponding processes are viewed as relatively immature and were scored 1. However, the expectation is to select individuals with expert competencies in each of the four remaining principles and thus forecast gradual improvements each quarter.
- **Manage CPM Centers of Excellence Process.** Since the team and processes were both immature at this stage, we started with a score of 1. However, given the foregoing discussion on building the team and their core processes, the CPM office would accumulate expertise and build out the Center of Excellence over the next four quarters, again to arrive at an expert model by Q4.

By now, you can see they have adopted a continuous improvement approach of targeted gradual improvements in process maturity over the

EXHIBIT 9.1 CPM Process Self-Scoring Diagnostic

CPM Core Process Blueprint New Co—Self Scoring Diagnostic #1										
CPM Principles 1–5 Processes Blueprint	Scor	Year 1 Score				Year 2 Score			
		Q1	Q2	Q3	Q4	Q1	Q2	Q3	Q4
Principle 1: Establish & Deploy CPM Office									
• Executive Sponsorship and Trusted Advisor process	5	5	5	5	5				
• Recruit, Train, and Manage Enterprise CPM Expert process	1	2	3	4	5				
• CPM Principles 2–5 Management process	1	1	2	3	4				
• Manage CPM Centers of Excellence process	1	1	2	3	4				

next four quarters (see Exhibit 9.1). Let's turn our attention to the assessment of best practices.

CPM Core Best Practices Blueprint (Diagnostic 2)

Exhibit 9.2 presents the best practices for Principle 1, Establish a CPM Office and Officer Role at *New Co*. In column 1 note the self-assessment scores on a five-point scale with 1 being a low rating and 5 a best practice rating. For example, focus on Principle 1, Best Practice 1.1, executive sponsorship, and

EXHIBIT 9.2 CPM Best Practice Self-Scoring Diagnostic

New Co - Self Scoring Diagnostic #2									
CPM Principles 1-5 Best Practices	Score	Year 1 Score				Year 2 Score			
		Q1	Q2	Q3	Q4	Q1	Q2	Q3	Q4
Principle 1: Establish & Deploy CPM Office	1								
Core Best Practices									
• Executive Sponsorship	5								
• Organizational Level and Reporting Relationship	5								
• CPM Office Staff Size	2								
• Leadership and Ability to Influence	2								
• Ownership of CPM Processes and Methods	1								
• CPM, Industry, and Company Knowledge	1								
• Collaborative Maturity	1								
• Ability to Learn	1								
Innovative Best Practices									
• Network, Virtual Model	1								
• See cases for more innovative best practices									

score your achievement of this best practice. Since your CPM officer reports to the CEO, your score would be a 5. Using the same logic as the CPM process diagnostic you would in turn score all best practices and forecast your improvement targets (left blank below) over the next four quarters, and beyond.

Develop and Deploy Your Action Plan to Close the Gaps

Once you have scored all CPM processes and all CPM best practices, you are in a position to prioritize the highest-order opportunities or gaps as described in the prior step. Bear in mind that Hall of Fame, Baldrige, and APQC award winners did not achieve their stunning results overnight. Rather, I encourage appropriate thoughtfulness and a prudent time-phased plan for closing your gaps. At Crown, the CPM program bore early fruit; however, it was the concerted and cumulative effects of these efforts over time that created sustainable achievement. My CPM firm provides diagnostic and implementation planning services to assist in the exciting journey.

Develop CPM Expertise with CPM "Step-by-Step" Masters Classes

Research into over 100 companies, including the companies that became case study organizations in this book, provides a rich source of information to accelerate CPM results and attain similar awards.

A Model for Rolling out Integrated CPM Masters Executive Education Curriculums–
12 Two-Day Hands on Classes Cascaded ThroughYour Organization
"Implementing for Results"

Principle, Course No., Name	New Co - Integrated CPM Executive Education Plan by Month																	
	1	2	3	4	5	6	7	8	9	10	11	12	13	14	15	16	17	18
1.1 Establish CPM Office	■												■					
2.1 Formulate Strategy		■												■				
2.2 Prepare Strategic Plan			■												■			
3.1 Build Strategy Map and BSC				■												■		
3.2 Align and Motive with BSC						■			■									■
3.3 Manage Using BSC								■			■	■						■
4.2 Improve Using Six Sigma #1										■	■					■		
4.2 Improve Using Six Sigma #2											■	■				■		
4.3 Improve using 10 Step #1											■	■				■		
4.4 Improve Using 10 Step #2												■	■			■		
4.5 Improve Customer Focus											■	■						■
5.1 Leverage Knowledge												■	■					

EXHIBIT 9.3 CPM Executive Education Journey

EXHIBIT 9.4 CPM Office Course Modules

Principle 1: Establish CPM Office and Officer (2 day course)

- Course 1.1: Establish CPM Office and Officer

    - Key concepts in team building and facilitation (step-by-step exercise)
    - Understand change management key concepts (step-by-step exercise)
    - Review Five Key Principles Best Practices and prototype organizational structures
    - Principle 1: Establish CPM Office and Officer, Design your CPM Office (exercise)
    - Understand competencies required of CPM Office to achieve award winning results
    - Principle 2 competencies-overview of Strategy Formulation courses and examples
    - Principle 3 competencies-overview of Balanced Scorecard courses and examples
    - Principle 4 competencies-overview of Six Sigma courses and examples
    - Principle 4 competencies-overview of Process Improvement courses and examples
    - Principle 4 competencies-overview of Customer Survey course and examples
    - Principle 5 competencies-overview of Knowledge Management course and examples
    - Prepare CPM Office implementation plan (step-by-step exercise)

In addition to reviewing and emulating the experiences from the case companies, the Five Keys have been translated into a dozen two-day "Step-by-Step" CPM training seminars, conducted publicly and onsite, using award-winning case materials. The structure of the classes follows adult learning techniques including hands-on breakout sessions to develop the deliverables for your own organization. Exhibit 9.3 for *New Co* features a managed rollout of CPM classes to build out CPM capabilities in a new company. The classes also parallel the *New Co* ratings provided in the two prior self-scoring diagnostics.

For example, continuing our example of *New Co*, we began their journey with the two-day onsite class to form the CPM office, course 1.1 from our roadmap. Notice the curriculum in Exhibit 9.4 is designed with "Step-by-Step" exercises for participants to apply best practices.

The remaining CPM Masters Courses follow a similar "Step-by-Step" approach to enhance learning and deployment of the Five Key Principles of CPM in your organization. Best wishes as you leverage the generous insights provided by collaborative authors who unselfishly shared their cases, the CPM Process Blueprint, and the dozens of best practices.

The empires of the future are the empires of the mind.

—Sir Winston Churchill

Index

Action plans, 349, 398
Annual business planning (ABP)
    process, 96–102
  action plan development, 100
  action plan modifications, 101
  addressing strategic challenges and
      advantages, 99
  capital planning process (CPP),
      100–101
  early indicators of major shifts, 98
  evaluate the ability to execute
      strategic plan, 99
  expert panel process (EPP), 99
  key action plans (examples),
      101–102
  key performance measures and
      indicators, 102
  prioritizing and ensuring adequate
      resources, 100
  steps for, 97
  strategic SWOT analysis/
      environmental scans, 98
Arp, Phillip, 68

Balanced scorecard (BSC) system:
  Delta Dental of Kansas, Inc., 112,
      201–205
  Lockheed Martin IS&GS, 209–211
  M7 Aerospace, 216–218, 219

Mueller, Inc., 223–224
Omaha Public Power District,
      231–232
Poudre Valley Health System,
      234–238, 240–241
Public Service Electric and Gas
      (PSE&G), 242–246
software for, 208, 214–215, 227, 233
Behavior zones, 367–368
Benchmarking:
  City of Coral Springs, 197–198,
      283
  Delta Dental of Kansas, Inc., 207,
      292
  Lockheed Martin IS&GS, 214, 296
  M7 Aerospace, 220–221
  Mueller, Inc., 225, 305–306
  NSTAR, 310–312
  Omaha Public Power District, 233
  Public Service Electric and Gas
      (PSE&G), 247–248, 333–334
Best practice governance, 381–383
Best practice sharing, 349, 350, 362,
      387–388
Boosalis, Dean, 74
Brock, Pam, 79
Business performance review,
      188–189, 190
Business planning/funding, 109–110

Capability Maturity Model (CMM),
123–124
Cargill Corn Milling (CCM), 9
annual business planning (ABP)
process, 96–102
awards and honors, 11
best practice case, 50–53, 93–104,
185–193, 261–277, 348–352
best practice model (BPM) for
process improvement,
270–275
best practice sharing, 349, 350
best practices, Principle 1, 52–53
best practices, Principle 2, 40–41,
103–104
best practices, Principle 3, 42–43,
191–192
best practices, Principle 4, 44–45,
275–277
best practices, Principle 5, 46,
351–352
business performance review,
188–189, 190
communication strategy, 102–103
comparative data selection,
187–188
customer and market knowledge,
262–266
customer complaint process,
267–268
customer follow-up, 269
customer relationship building,
266–267, 268
customer satisfaction/loyalty,
268–270
development plan process (DPP),
187
executive views on CPM, 51

highlights, notable performance
results, 11–12
ideas to innovation (i2i) process,
274–275, 350–351
key access mechanisms, 267–269
knowledge sharing/transfer,
348–349
leadership system levels, 186–187
leadership system model, 95
learning and innovation practices,
274–275
measurement, analysis, and
knowledge management,
186–187
meeting management, 188
organization leadership, 51–52
performance management process
(PMP), 187
process development groups, 274
process management and core
competencies, 270
rewards/recognition, 189–191
risk integration in strategic
planning and management,
102
root cause analysis process, 275
strategic context, 94–95
strategic planning/formulation,
95–102
strategy review (SR) process,
95–96
vision of, 94
Carlson, Cherie, 74
Change acceleration process, 338
Change gap, 6–7
City of Coral Springs, 9
awards and honors, 12–14
benchmarking, 197–198, 283

best practice case, 53–55, 104–112, 193–201, 277–287, 352–353

best practices, Principle 1, 41, 55, 353

best practices, Principle 2, 111–112

best practices, Principle 3, 200–201

best practices, Principle 4, 45, 286–287

best practices, Principle 5, 46, 353

business plan funding and initiatives and department budgets, 109–110

communication strategy, 110–111

comparative analytics, 197–198

composite index, 193

core processes, 54

corporate balanced scorecard, 194–196

culture of process improvement, 285–286

customer complaint process, 281

customer input and strategic planning, 108–109

customer listening methods, 277–280

customer relationship building, 280–281

customer segmentation, 277

executive team, 54–55

executive views on CPM, 54

financial trend monitoring system, 193

highlights, notable performance results, 14–16

knowledge sharing/transfer, 352–353

meeting management and business analytics, 194

new process development, 285

performance improvement system, 106

performance management data types and integration, 196–197

performance management model, 194–196

performance reviews, 198–199

process improvement system, 281–283

process innovation and best practices, 284–285

purpose, vision, and core values, 104–105

rewards/recognition, 199–200

seven strategic priorities, 194, 195–196

strategic planning process, 105–107

time-phased strategy development, 107–108

visioning summit, 105

work system design, 283–284

Communication strategy, 102–103, 110–111

Comparative analytics, 197–198

Comparative data selection, 187–188

Competency development, 367–369

Competitive advantage, 118–119, 124

Competitive intelligence, 269–270, 315

Composite index, 193

Core and adjacency analysis, 131

Core Best Practices Blueprint (Diagnostic 2), 397–398

Core competencies, 270, 349–350

Core Process Blueprint (Diagnostic 1), 395–397

Core process key roles, 37, 48–49, 92, 184, 260, 347

Core process learning model, 38–46

CPM Core Best Practices Blueprint (Diagnostic 2), 397–398

CPM Core Process Blueprint (Diagnostic 1), 395–397

CPM Masters courses, 398–400

CPM office/officers. *See* Principle 1: Establish and Deploy a CPM Office and Officer

Crown Castle International, 2–3

Customer access mechanisms, 322–324

Customer and market knowledge, 262–266

Customer relationship building:
  Cargill Corn Milling (CCM), 266–267, 268
  City of Coral Springs, 280–281
  Poudre Valley Health System, 320–322
  Sharp HealthCare, 337–338

Customer sales management, 298–300

Customer satisfaction index, 315

Customer surveys, 308, 315–316, 330–331

Customer/constituent segmentation:
  Cargill Corn Milling (CCM), 262
  City of Coral Springs, 277
  Delta Dental of Kansas, Inc., 287–289
  Lockheed Martin IS&GS, 293–294
  Poudre Valley Health System, 319–320

Customers:
  complaint process, 267–268, 281
  follow-up, 269

  listening methods, 262–266, 277–280, 319–320 (*see also* Listening/learning methods)
  satisfaction/loyalty, 268–270

Data reliability, 205, 245

Davenport, Bryan, 68

Delta Dental of Kansas, Inc., 9
  awards and honors, 16
  balanced scorecard (BSC) system, 112, 201–205
  best practice case, 55–57, 112–120, 201–208, 287–293, 354–361
  best practice sharing forums, 354–355
  best practices, Principle 1, 57
  best practices, Principle 2, 41, 119–120
  best practices, Principle 3, 208
  best practices, Principle 4, 293
  best practices, Principle 5, 46, 359–361
  communication strategy, 119
  competitive advantage, 118–119
  constituent listening methods, 289–291
  constituent segmentation, 287–289
  CPM organization, 56–57
  data reliability, 205
  executive views on CPM, 55–57
  highlights, notable performance results, 16–17
  KMS article development process, 360
  knowledge management system, 355–358
  knowledge sharing/transfer, 354–355
  leadership team, 113–114

long-range planning (LRP) process,
115
meeting management and business
analytics, 205–206
people development and
intellectual property, 358–359
process improvement and
inititiative prioritization,
291–292
purpose, vision, and core values,
113
rewards/recognition, 206–207
strategic initiatives and budgeting,
118
strategic planning process, 114–118
strategy map, 119, 203–205
succession planning, 355, 356
target setting and benchmarking,
207
Departmental performance measures,
197
Direct sales contact, 265
DMAIC process, 338, 342

Early indicators of major shifts, 98
Ellison, Amy, 56–57
Employee development. *See*
Workforce development
Employee knowledge, 348
Environmental scans, 98
Ethics, 176–177
Event measures, 197
Expert panel process (EPP), 99

Financial trend monitoring system,
193
Five Forces analysis. *See* Porter Five
Forces analysis

Five Key Principles Model, 3–4
*Five Key Principles of Corporate
Performance Management*
(Palladino), 1–2
Full spectrum leadership (FSL),
122

Goals, strategic corporate, 146–147

Human resource planning, 176.
See also Succession planning

Ideas to innovation (i2i) process,
274–275, 350–351
Information and knowledge
management systems, 355–358,
362–363, 372–373
Information networks/portals,
379–380
Initiative alignment, 142
Initiative prioritization, 291–292,
295–296, 332–333
Innovation. *See also* Ideas to
innovation (i2i) process
historical highlights, 5
increases in, 3–5
learning and innovation practices,
274–275
Innovation encouragement, 199–200
In-process measures, 197
Intellectual property, 358–359
Izzo, Ralph, 242

J.D. Power survey, 315–316

Key community support, 177
Key intended outcomes (KIOs),
194–197

Key principles (5) of CPM, core
    processes, 36
Knowledge management (KM). *See
    also* Principle 5: Manage and
    Leverage Knowledge
  core best practices, 45–46, 347
  core process key roles, 346–347
  innovative best practices examples,
    46
  Knowledge workers, 364–365
Knowledge management (KM)
    process embedding, 45
Knowledge management (KM)
    systems, 355–358, 362–363
Knowledge reinforcement, 385
Knowledge sharing/transfer:
  Cargill Corn Milling (CCM),
    348–349
  City of Coral Springs, 352–353
  Delta Dental of Kansas, Inc.,
    354–355
  Poudre Valley Health System,
    380–381, 385
Knowledge workers, 364–365

Lack, Mark, 68
LaRossa, Ralph, 245
Leader development, 383–386,
    391–393
Lean principles approach,
    316–317. *See also* Six Sigma
    process improvement program
Lean Six Sigma process improvement
    program. *See* Six Sigma process
    improvement program
Listening/learning methods:
  Cargill Corn Milling (CCM),
    262–265

City of Coral Springs, 277–280
Delta Dental of Kansas, Inc.,
    289–291
Omaha Public Power District, 315
Sharp HealthCare, 335–337
Lockheed Martin IS&GS, 10
  awards and honors, 17–18
  benchmarking, 214, 296
  best practice case, 57–62, 120–128,
    209–216, 293–297, 361–366
  best practice sharing forums,
    362
  best practices, Principle 1, 40,
    61–62
  best practices, Principle 2, 128
  best practices, Principle 3, 215–216
  best practices, Principle 4, 296–297
  best practices, Principle 5, 365–366
  and Capability Maturity Model
    (CMM), 123–124
  communication strategy, 126–128
  competitive advantage, 124
  CPM organization, 60–61
  customer/constituent segmentation,
    293–294
  executive team, 61
  executive views on CPM, 59–60
  full spectrum leadership (FSL), 122
  highlights, notable performance
    results, 18
  information and knowledge
    management systems, 362–363
  initiative prioritization and ongoing
    management, 295–296
  meeting management and business
    analytics, 211–213
  mentoring, 364
  people development, 364–365

performance advocate (PA) role,
120–121
process improvement, 295
purpose, vision, and core values,
121
rewards/recognition, 213–214
strategic initiatives and budgeting,
122–124
strategic planning process, 121–122
strategy map, 124–126
succession planning, 363
target setting, 214

M7 Aerospace, 10
awards and honors, 19
balanced scorecard (BSC) system,
216–218, 219
behavior zones, 367–368
benchmarking, 220–221
best practice case, 62–66, 129–136,
216–222, 297–305, 366–370
best practices, Principle 1, 65–66
best practices, Principle 2, 42,
135–136
best practices, Principle 3, 221–222
best practices, Principle 4, 304–305
best practices, Principle 5, 369–370
budgeting, 133–134
communication strategy, 135
competency development, 367–369
core and adjacency analysis, 131
CPM organization, 64
customer sales management
process, 298–300
executive team, 64–65
executive views on CPM, 63
highlights, notable performance
results, 20–21

Lean Six Sigma process
improvement program,
301–304
meeting management and business
analytics, 218–220
planning and budgeting
integration, 134
priority action matrix, 300
purpose, vision, and core values,
129
quad chart, 300
rewards/recognition, 220
strategic initiatives and budgeting,
133–134
strategic planning process, 129–132
strategy formulation and
deployment process, 217
strategy formulation/evaluation,
133
strategy map, 134–135
succession planning,
367–369
SWOT analysis, 132
target setting, 220–221
Malcolm Baldridge Quality Award, 86
Market knowledge, 262–266
Martucci, Joe, 83
Medical Center of the Rockies (MCR),
327
Meeting management:
Cargill Corn Milling (CCM), 188
City of Coral Springs, 194
Delta Dental of Kansas, Inc.,
205–206
Lockheed Martin IS&GS, 211–213
M7 Aerospace, 218
Mueller, Inc., 225–226
NSTAR, 230

Meeting management (*Continued*)
Omaha Public Power District, 232
Public Service Electric and Gas
(PSE&G), 245
Mentoring, 364, 375–376
Metrics. *See* balanced scorecard (BSC)
system; performance
management data types
Miller, Ted B., 62
Minks, Adrian, 74
Mueller, Inc., 10
awards and honors, 21
balanced scorecard (BSC) system,
223–224
benchmarking, 225, 305–306
best practice case, 66–69, 136–144,
223–228, 305–308, 370–372
best practices, Principle 1, 68–69
best practices, Principle 2, 144
best practices, Principle 3, 227–228
best practices, Principle 4, 307–308
best practices, Principle 5,
372
branch target system, 224
budgeting, 143
communication strategy, 143–144
corporate strategy map, 141
CPM organization, 67–68
executive views on CPM, 66–67
highlights, notable performance
results, 21–22
initiative alignment, 142
integration of strategic planning
and budgeting, 142–143
meeting management and business
analytics, 225–226
performance analysis and review,
225–226

performance-driven culture (PDC)
maturity model, 137–140
rewards/recognition, 226
strategic initiatives and budgeting,
143
strategic innovations, 140–141
strategic links to ongoing process
improvement, 306–307
strategic objectives, 141–142
strategic scenario planning, 143
strategy development, 140
target setting, 225
workforce development, 370–371

NSTAR, 10
awards and honors, 22
benchmarking, 310–312
best practice case, 69–73, 145–170,
228–231, 308–314, 372–374
best practices, Principle 1, 72–73
best practices, Principle 2, 147–148
best practices, Principle 3, 231
best practices, Principle 4, 314
best practices, Principle 5,
374
business model, 70
CPM organization, 71–72
CPM tools, software, and
monitoring, 229
customer surveys, 308
executive team, 72
executive views on CPM, 70–71
future focus, 70
highlights, notable performance
results, 22, 23
information and knowledge
management systems, 372–373
key events, 69–70

meeting management and business
analytics, 230
organizational planning and
prioritization, 312–313
priority initiatives, 309
process improvement, 309, 313–314
project management and process
improvement methodology,
313–314
rewards/recognition, 230–231
strategic corporate goals,
146–147
strategic initiatives and budgeting,
146–147
strategic planning process, 145–146
strategy communication, 147
succession planning, 373–374
target setting, 228–229

Omaha Public Power District, 10
awards and honors, 22–24
balanced scorecard (BSC) system,
231–232
benchmarking, 233
best practice case, 73–77, 148–156,
231–234, 314–319, 375–379
best practices, Principle 1, 76–77
best practices, Principle 2, 155, 156
best practices, Principle 3, 233–234
best practices, Principle 4, 318–319
best practices, Principle 5, 378–379
business analytics, 232–233
CPM organization and key
processes, 74–76
customer listening methods,
315
customer surveys, 315–316
executive team, 76

executive views on CPM, 73–74
highlights, notable performance
results, 24–26
meeting management, 232
mentoring, 375–376
people development, 376–378
process management and
improvement, 316–318
purpose, vision, and core values,
148–149
rewards/recognition, 233
strategic communications, 154,
155
strategic planning process, 149–152
strategy map, 152, 153
succession planning, 376, 377
target setting, 233
Organizational knowledge standards,
380–381

PASSPORT, 363
Patents, 4–5
People development, 358–359,
364–365, 376–378
Performance improvement, 43–45.
See also Principle 4: Improve
Performance
core best practices, 44, 261
core process key roles,
260–261
innovative best practices examples,
44–45
Performance management data types,
196–197
Performance management models,
194–196
Performance reviews, 198–199,
225–226

Performance-driven culture (PDC)
    maturity model:
  chaos reigns stage, 137–138
  departmental optimization stage,
    138
  performance-driven
    culture-emerging stage,
    138–139
  performance-driven
    culture-realization stage,
    139–140
Personal leadership attributes,
    385–386
PESTEL, 121–122
Planning and budget integration,
    174–176
Porter Five Forces analysis, 121,
    131–132
Poudre Valley Health System, 10
  awards and honors, 26–29
  balanced scorecard (BSC) system,
    234–238, 240–241
  best practice case, 77–81, 157–165,
    234–242, 319–330, 379–386
  best practice governance, 381–383
  best practices, Principle 1, 80–81
  best practices, Principle 2, 164–165
  best practices, Principle 3, 241–242
  best practices, Principle 4, 45,
    329–330
  best practices, Principle 5, 46, 386
  comparative data sets, 236–237
  customer listening methods,
    319–320
  customer segments and voice of
    the customer, 319–320
  executive views on performance
    improvement, 78–79

  Global Path to Success, 158
  highlights, notable performance
    results, 29–31
  individual goal setting, 238–240
  information networks/portals,
    379–380
  innovative service excellence,
    321–322
  key access mechanisms and service
    recovery, 322–325
  knowledge sharing/transfer,
    380–381
  marketing and strategic planning
    function, 79–80
  organizational knowledge
    standards, 380–381
  patient/customer relationship
    building, 320–322
  performanc excellence cycle,
    326
  performance improvement,
    384
  process management and
    improvement, 325–329
  rewards/recognition, 238–240
  six steps for process design and
    innovation, 325–327
  strategic context, 157–158
  strategic objectives, 162–163
  strategic planning integration with
    community objectives, 161,
    164
  strategy communication, 164
  strategy development and
    deployment (SDD) process,
    158–161
  workforce and leader
    development, 383–386

Principle 1: Establish and Deploy a
    CPM Office and Officer, 38–40
Cargill Corn Milling (CCM), 50–53
City of Coral Springs, 53–55
core best practices, 38–40, 49
core process key roles, 48–49
Delta Dental of Kansas, Inc., 55–57
innovative best practice examples,
    40
Lockheed Martin IS&GS, 57–62
NSTAR, 69–73
Omaha Public Power District,
    73–77
Poudre Valley Health System, 77–81
Public Service Electric and Gas
    (PSE&G), 81–84
Sharp HealthCare, 85–89
Principle 2: Refresh and
    Communicate Strategy, 40–42
best practices, 103–104, 111–112
Cargill Corn Milling (CCM), 93–104
City of Coral Springs, 104–112
core best practices, 41, 93
core process key roles, 92–93
Delta Dental of Kansas, Inc.,
    112–120
innovative best practice examples,
    41–42
Lockheed Martin IS&GS, 120–128
M7 Aerospace, 129–136
Mueller, Inc., 136–144
NSTAR, 145–170
Omaha Public Power District,
    148–156
Poudre Valley Health System,
    157–165
Public Service Electric and Gas
    (PSE&G), 165–170

Sharp HealthCare, 170–181
Principle 3: Cascade and Manage
    Strategy, 42–43
Cargill Corn Milling (CCM),
    185–193
City of Coral Springs, 193–201
core best practices, 42–43, 185
core process key roles, 184–185
Delta Dental of Kansas, Inc.,
    201–208
innovative best practice examples,
    43
Lockheed Martin IS&GS,
    209–216
M7 Aerospace, 216–222
Mueller, Inc., 223–228
NSTAR, 228–231
Omaha Public Power District,
    231–234
Poudre Valley Health System,
    234–242
Public Service Electric and Gas
    (PSE&G), 242–249
Principle 4: Improve Performance,
    43–45
City of Coral Springs, 277–287
core best practices, 44, 261
core process key roles, 260–261
Delta Dental of Kansas, Inc.,
    287–293
innovative best practices examples,
    44–45
Lockheed Martin IS&GS, 293–297
M7 Aerospace, 297–305
Mueller, Inc., 305–308
NSTAR, 308–314
Omaha Public Power District,
    314–319

Principle 4: Improve (*Continued*)
  Poudre Valley Health System,
    319–330
  Public Service Electric and Gas
    (PSE&G), 330–334
  Sharp HealthCare, 335–344
Principle 5: Manage and Leverage
    Knowledge, 45–46
  Cargill Corn Milling (CCM),
    348–352
  City of Coral Springs, 352–353
  core best practices, 45–46, 347
  core process key roles, 346–347
  Delta Dental of Kansas, Inc.,
    354–361
  innovative best practices examples,
    46
  Lockheed Martin IS&GS, 361–366
  M7 Aerospace, 366–370
  Mueller, Inc., 370–372
  Omaha Public Power District,
    375–379
  Poudre Valley Health System,
    379–386
  Sharp HealthCare, 389–394
Process design and management
    SIPOC, 342
Process development groups, 274
Process facilitator, 37, 48–49, 92, 184,
    260
Process improvement:
  Cargill Corn Milling (CCM),
    270–275
  City of Coral Springs, 281–283
  city of Coral Springs, 285–286
  Delta Dental of Kansas, Inc.,
    291–292
  Lockheed Martin IS&GS, 294

Mueller, Inc., 306–307
NSTAR, 309, 313–314
Omaha Public Power District,
    316–318
Public Service Electric and Gas
    (PSE&G), 331–332
Sharp HealthCare, 339
Process innovation, 284–285, 325–327
Process management, 270, 316,
    325–329
Process measures, 197
Process owner, 37, 48, 92, 184, 260
Process participant, 37, 49, 92–93,
    184–185, 261
Process sponsor, 35, 48, 92, 184, 260
Project management, 313–314
Public Service Electric and Gas
    (PSE&G), 10
  awards and honors, 31
  balanced scorecard (BSC) system,
    242–246
  benchmarking, 247–248, 333–334
  best practice case, 81–84, 165–170,
    242–249, 330–334, 387–389
  best practice sharing forums,
    387–388
  best practices, Principle 1, 40, 84
  best practices, Principle 2, 42,
    169–170
  best practices, Principle 3, 248–249
  best practices, Principle 4, 45,
    334
  best practices, Principle 5, 46,
    388–389
  budgeting, 166–167
  CPM organization, 83
  customer surveys, 330–331
  data reliability, 245

executive team, 83–84
executive views on CPM, 82
highlights, notable performance
results, 31
initiative prioritization and ongoing
management, 332–333
meeting management and business
analytics, 245–246
metric recovery plan, 332
process improvement, 331–332
purpose, vision, and core values,
165–166
rewards/recognition, 247
strategic initiatives and budgeting,
166–167
strategic planning process,
166
strategy communication, 169
strategy map, 167–169
target setting, 247–248

Research and development contact,
266
Rewards/recognition:
Cargill Corn Milling (CCM),
189–191
City of Coral Springs, 199–200
Delta Dental of Kansas, Inc.,
206–207
Lockheed Martin IS&GS, 213–214
M7 Aerospace, 220
Mueller, Inc., 226
NSTAR, 230–231
Omaha Public Power District, 233
Poudre Valley Health System,
238–240
Public Service Electric and Gas
(PSE&G), 247

Risk, integrating into strategic
planning, 176–177
Root cause analysis process, 275

S-curve analysis, 117
Sharp HealthCare, 10
awards and honors, 32
best practice case, 85–89, 170–181,
249–258, 335–344, 389–394
best practices, Principle 1, 40,
88–89
best practices, Principle 2, 180–181
best practices, Principle 3, 257–258
best practices, Principle 4, 344
best practices, Principle 5, 393–394
clinical effectiveness organization,
86–87
ethics and risk integration in
strategic planning, 176–177
executive leadership, 87–88
executive views on performance
improvement, 86
highlights, notable performance
results, 32–33
human resource planning, 176
key business and support practices,
339–343
key community support, 177
listening/learning methods, 335–337
Malcolm Baldridge Quality Award
criteria, 86
mission/vision statements, 171–172
organizational knowledge
management, 389–391
patient and customer satisfaction,
337–338
patient and market knowledge,
335–337

Sharp HealthCare (*Continued*)
  planning and budgeting
      integration, 174–176
  process quality improvement
      methods, 338–343
  seven critical success factors, 171
  Sharp University, 393
  Six Pillars of Excellence, 172, 174
  Six Sigma process improvement
      program, 338–343
  strategic communication plan,
      178–179
  strategic objectives, 177
  strategic planning process, 171–174
  strategy communication, 177–180
  workforce and leader
      development, 391–393
Shifts, early indicators of major, 98–99
Six Sigma process improvement
      program, 301–304, 338–339
Strategic challenges, 349
Strategic communications, 154, 155
Strategic corporate goals, 146–147
Strategic initiatives and budgeting:
  Delta Dental of Kansas, Inc., 118
  Lockheed Martin IS&GS, 122–124
  M7 Aerospace, 133–134
  Mueller, Inc., 143
  NSTAR, 146–147
  Public Service Electric and Gas
      (PSE&G), 166–167
Strategic innovations, 140–141
Strategic input documents (SIDs), 129
Strategic objectives, 141–142, 177
Strategic plan SWOT
      analysis/environmental scans, 98
Strategic planning/formulation,
      145–146

annual business planning (ABP)
      process, 96–102
  budgeting integration, 142–143
  city of Coral Springs, 105–108
  customer input and, 108–109
  Delta Dental of Kansas, Inc.,
      114–118
  ethics and risk integration, 176–177
  external analysis, 149–151
  gaps and external threats, 151
  goals, measures, targets and
      strategic initiatives, 151–152
  integration with community
      objectives, 161, 164
  internal analysis, 149
  M7 Aerospace, 129–132
  Omaha Public Power District,
      149–152
  Public Service Electric and Gas
      (PSE&G), 166
  risk integration, 102
  Sharp HealthCare, 171–174
  strategy review (SR) process, 95–96
  time-phased strategy development,
      107–108
Strategic scenario planning, 143
Strategy communication, 40–42.
      See also Principle 2: Refresh and
      Communicate Strategy
  best practices, 103–104, 111–112
  core best practices, 41, 93
  core process key roles, 92–93
  Delta Dental of Kansas, Inc., 119
  innovative best practice examples,
      41–42
  Lockheed Martin IS&GS, 126–128
  M7 Aerospace, 135
  Mueller, Inc., 143–144

NSTAR, 147
Poudre Valley Health System, 164
Public Service Electric and Gas (PSE&G), 169
Sharp HealthCare, 177–180
Strategy development:
Mueller, Inc., 140
Poudre Valley Health System, 158–161
Strategy formulation/evaluation, 133, 217
Strategy management:
core best practices, 42–43, 185
core process key roles, 184–185
innovative best practice examples, 43
(*see also* Principle 3: Cascade and Manage Strategy)
Strategy maps, 124–126
Delta Dental of Kansas, Inc., 119, 203–205
M7 Aerospace, 134–135
Mueller, Inc., 141
Omaha Public Power District, 152, 153
Public Service Electric and Gas (PSE&G), 167–169
Strategy review (SR) process, 95–96
Succession planning:

Delta Dental of Kansas, Inc., 355, 356
Lockheed Martin IS&GS, 363
M7 Aerospace, 367–369
NSTAR, 373–374
Omaha Public Power District, 376, 377
SWOT analysis, 98, 121, 132

Target setting:
Delta Dental of Kansas, Inc., 207
Lockheed Martin IS&GS, 214
M7 Aerospace, 220–221
Mueller, Inc., 225
NSTAR, 228–229
Omaha Public Power District, 233
Public Service Electric and Gas (PSE&G), 247–248
Technical service contact, 266
Transaction measures, 197

Unity, 363

Voice of the customer, 319–320

Work system design, 283–284
Workforce development, 367–369, 370–371, 383–386, 391–393
See also Succession planning
Work-Out method, 338